# Traitors Among Us

# Traitors Among Us

## Inside the Spy Catcher's World

*Stuart A. Herrington*

PRESIDIO

Published by Presidio Press
505 B San Marin Drive, Suite 300
Novato, CA 94945-1340

**Library of Congress Cataloging-in-Publication Data**
Herrington, Stuart A., 1941–
    Traitors among us : inside the spy catcher's world / Stuart A. Herrington.
        p.    cm.
    ISBN 0-89141-677-3
    1. Intelligence service—United States—History—20th century.
    2. Spies—Communist countries—History—20th century.
    3. Herrington, Stuart A., 1941–    . I. Title.
    UB271.U5H47    1999
    327.12171'70171'3—dc21                    99-13408
                                                CIP

All photos from the author's collection

Printed in the United States of America

# Contents

*Dedicated to the intelligence professionals of the United States Army Foreign Counterintelligence Activity, the CIA, and the FBI*
*and*
*To our comrades in Germany in the Bundeskriminalamt, the Bundesamt fur Verfassungschutz, and the Generalbundesanwalt*
*as well as to these heroes of the Silent War:*
*Robert L. Bell*
*Lt. Gen. William E. Odom (Ret.)*
*Thomas Duhadway*
*Dr. Peter Frisch*
*and Gardner R. (Gus) Hathaway*

# Preface

This is a story of teamwork and cooperation between counterintelligence agents of the United States Army, the Central Intelligence Agency, and the Federal Bureau of Investigation. It is also the hitherto untold story of how, even as the curtain descended on the long, Cold War, American counterspies collaborated closely with German, Swedish, Austrian, and Italian security officials to unmask traitors among us who were selling top secret plans for the defense of Europe. These cases were run by my organization, the United States Army Foreign Counterintelligense Activity. The spies we ultimately netted had sold thousands of our most highly classified documents to the Soviet Union and her Warsaw Pact surrogates from 1972 to 1988. Taken together, the haul of secrets was so voluminous, so sensitive, and so strategically advantageous to Moscow that, had war broken out in Central Europe, America and her NATO allies would have been forced to choose between capitulation or the desperate use of nuclear weapons on German soil.

Although this recounting of the closing engagements of the Silent War is true, it is not complete. Missing from these pages are certain dimensions of the cases described that must remain classified. Some secrets must still be kept. The secrets omitted from this account are relatively few, and their absence does not preclude an accurate, meaningful telling of the story. In some few instances, for varying reasons, I have changed the names of the players.

One motivation for writing this account of the espionage wars was to salute the dedicated counterintelligence special agents who toiled tirelessly for their country in an underappreciated specialty known for yielding more criticism than kudos. The process of selecting cases and dramatis personae to showcase was not easy. For every special agent mentioned or featured in this account, there are hundreds of others whose achievements merit equal recognition. Unfortunately, the realities of the publishing business preclude a full account of their great work. I regret that I could not honor them all.

A number of friends assisted in ensuring that this account is as complete and accurate as possible; too many to mention here. However, I would like to thank Walt Mueller, former U.S. Army, Europe, liaison officer to the U.S. embassy in Bonn for his assistance during our investigations and for his recent help in communicating with officials of the German security services whose work made the Canasta Player case a success. Thanks also to Volkhard Wache, Manfred Rutkowski, and Dr. Rainer Mueller for answering my transatlantic appeals for help. I would also like to acknowledge the good will and support provided to my special agents and me during our time of need by Dr. Peter Frisch, president of the German Federal Office for the Protection of the Constitution.

Thanks must also go to many professionals of the Central Intelligence Agency, active and retired, for their encouragement and assistance, as well as to special agents from both army counterintelligence and the Federal Bureau of Investigation. I wrote this book in the wake of their persistent words of encouragement, usually after I had delivered one of my marathon lectures on spy catching. "This story needs to be told" was their refrain.

Although this book focuses on the agents in the trenches of the espionage wars, among whom I count myself, the reader will understand that the events related in these pages could not have happened without enlightened senior leadership in Washington. In the army, this consisted of Secretary of the Army John O. Marsh, Lt. Gen. (ret.) Sidney T. Weinstein, Lt. Gen. (ret.) Ed Soyster, Lt. Gen. (ret.) Ira "Chuck" Owens, Lt. Gen. (ret.) Charles Eichelberger, Maj. Gen. (ret.) Stan Hyman, Maj. Gen. (ret.) Charles Scanlon, Brig. Gen. (ret.) Larry Runyon, Brig. Gen. (ret.) Michael Schneider, Col. (ret.) Charles Cleveland, Col. (ret.) Jim Linnon, and Mr. Tom Taylor. No commander charged with the challenges and responsibilities that I and the agents of FCA faced could have hoped for better bosses and advisers. A particular debt of gratitude is owed to General Runyon and to Lt. Col. (ret.) Dave Owen, who together made things happen in the headquarters of the Intelligence and Security Command during some pretty tough times.

Finally, I would like to thank copyeditor Barbara Feller-Roth and my editor at Presidio Press, E. J. McCarthy, whose encouragement and acute editorial instincts made this work what it is.

# Introduction

For thirty years, I was privileged to serve as an army intelligence officer. Working with the finest corps of intelligence professionals to serve any army, and often supported by our German allies, U.S. Army counterintelligence waged an unrelenting war against our opposition, the intelligence services of the Soviet Union, her allies, and surrogates. Today, highly visible and often spectacular technological means dominate much of the intelligence craft. Our war was different. My colleagues and I were Huminters, human intelligence operatives, skilled in espionage and counterespionage. Ours was a traditional, low-tech business, often called the world's second oldest profession. Betrayal was the coin of the realm: turning our adversary's citizens into traitors, and preventing them from doing the same to our people. The stakes were high for both winner and loser.

This volume is a memoir of our war, once aptly called "the Silent War" by President Ronald Reagan. Waged in the shadows of the Cold War, its battles were one of the sole points of direct confrontation between the United States and the Soviet Union. The campaign's objective, drilled into us at places such as Fort Holabird, Maryland, Fort Huachuca, Arizona, and Camp Perry, Virginia, was the "hostile threat" to U.S. national security. Seismic events such as the crushing of the 1968 Prague Spring under Soviet tank treads convinced us that communism was a permanent feature of the international landscape. Persuaded beyond any doubt of the inherent evil of our adversary, we toiled in the netherworld of human intelligence that one observer has labeled a "wilderness of mirrors." Our mission was spy versus counterspy, an intrigue-laden, real-life board game to which many of the contestants became addicted.

Our superiors charged us with the mission of being the nation's eyes and ears in the enemy's camp, while denying him the same access to our secrets. We became the masters of worst-case analysis and planning, usually taking our adversary's strength for granted while probing relentlessly for any weakness that might gain an advantage for the United States in its contest with the specter of Soviet communism.

Engaged as we were in the trenches of this struggle, most of us would have to admit with some embarrassment that we somehow failed to note the approach of the mind-numbing events that rocked the world from 1989 to 1991. When the Berlin Wall came down and Boris Yeltsin triumphed in Moscow, we were as surprised as anyone. A world without Soviet communism was something that most of us never thought we would see. The feeling was one of both exhilaration and anxiety. Some harbored suspicions that it was all a gigantic ruse. After all, they pointed out, had not Lenin warned that one day the communists would mount a great "peace offensive" and lure the gullible West to its doom?

Now we were forced to accept that the milieu we had known was suddenly gone. In its place, a new, more complex world had emerged. We would have to change. When Soviet foreign minister Shevardnadze announced with a puckish grin in 1988, "We are going to do something that will really hurt you; we are going to remove 'the threat,'" his words contained greater wisdom than he could have known. When the Soviets went away, many in the West simply did not know how to cope with new realities. Change has never been our strong suit, in or out of military intelligence.

My journey came to an end in 1994, sparing me from many of the painful adjustments that the next generation now confronts. No longer "operational," I shunned staff duty, electing instead to serve out my remaining years in the idyllic surroundings of the United States Army War College. After twenty-six years of virtually unending adventure, I craved the time and perspective to reflect on that journey. It had been a long odyssey—from the shadow of the Berlin Wall to the rice paddies of Vietnam, from Heidelberg to Hanoi, from the invasion of Manuel Noriega's Panama to the showdown in the Iraqi desert.

Ultimately, the end of the Cold War bequeathed to me and a handpicked team one final mission. In 1992, I was charged with establishing a special task force to mount a quest into the graveyard of the former Soviet Union. The mission? Search for information on our missing comrades, prisoners of war who Russian president Boris

Yeltsin indicated might have been incarcerated in the Soviet gulag during the long Cold War.

It was during this quest that I sat next to former KGB Colonel Vyacheslav Mazurov on a memorable flight from Moscow to Vladivostok. As we winged our way into the Siberian night, Mazurov, emboldened by prodigious amounts of vodka, shared with me the KGB view of Operation Lake Terrace, recounted in this book. It was a rare opportunity to compare notes with a former adversary.

Most of what army counterintelligence agents did during the Cold War was shrouded in secrecy, as it had to be. For almost a half century, silence was one of our major weapons. That was the nature of the business. At considerable expense, we excluded our wives and loved ones from our daily triumphs and setbacks, denying ourselves the support and comfort that form the backbone of most normal families. If an operation went bad, headlines often trumpeted the news. When we won, our triumphs were almost always veiled by layers of security caveats.

The men and women of the United States Army's Military Intelligence Corps with whom I served bore that burden with the maturity and class that one would expect from America's finest. They were, as their coat of arms advertises, "Always Out Front," making history. Their sacrifices and achievements during the closing years of the Cold War have left a legacy that deserves to be documented. Although the memories are mine, the story is theirs.

## The Zoltan Szabo/Clyde Conrad Espionage Organization
## Four Generations of Spies

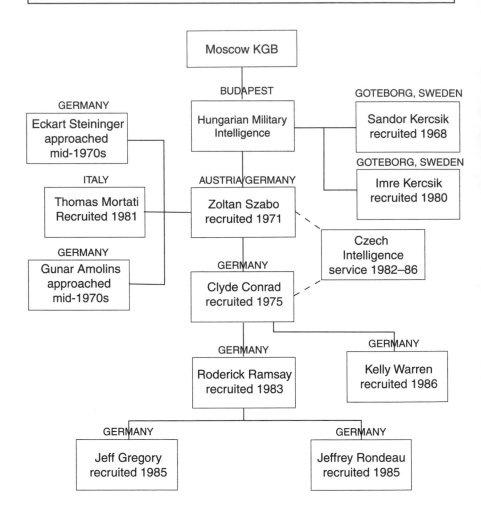

# Part I
## Cold War Berlin

# 1: Operation Lake Terrace

## East Berlin: Summer 1985

The operations officer of the KGB's Karlshorst Detachment tossed the message into a classified waste bin and scowled. Twice in one week his superiors at the Moscow Center had laid down the law. Karlshorst's failure to place a new agent inside the American signals intelligence site in West Berlin was unacceptable.

The colonel knew that he and his men were paying the price for success. For almost three years, fate had smiled on the men of the KGB's Third Chief Directorate, whose job it was to penetrate American intelligence units on the other side of the antifascist wall. In 1982, a brash American sergeant had literally appeared on the Soviet doorstep and volunteered to serve as Moscow's man in Field Station Berlin, the high-tech electronic eavesdropping post that was the KGB's top-priority target. From their bases in West Berlin, the colonel knew, the Americans and their allies were carrying out an unrelenting intelligence collection campaign against Soviet and Warsaw Pact forces. The field station was the enemy's most dangerous unit, but the colonel and his Karlshorst team had it well covered—at least until recently.

For three years, the American sergeant had plundered the sensitive facility, exchanging thousands of pages of highly classified documents for a great motivator—stacks of hundred-dollar bills. The man, code-named Paul, was arrogant—his ego required constant stroking—but he was bold. The operation was a KGB officer's dream. With each pickup of top-secret documents, the Karlshorst Detachment was able to provide the Moscow Center with a clearer picture of the remarkable capabilities that the Americans and their technology wizards had packed into the mountaintop installation.

All had benefited from the operation. The colonel and several of his case officers had received promotions and decorations. The Center was well pleased, and it directed its petulant carping at some other unfortunate operational element. Technicians in the KGB's supersecret Sixteenth Directorate pored over the stolen documents provided by Paul and busily pondered ways to counter the Americans' electronic warfare systems.

Then the good life came to an abrupt halt. The Americans transferred the valuable agent to a new assignment in the United States—New Jersey, the colonel seemed to recall. There the greedy sergeant would be controlled by KGB colleagues working under cover at the United Nations. The transfer of their agent was traumatic for Karlshorst. With its top-producing source gone, the detachment's production plummeted. Soon the Center began its incessant badgering. Moscow analysts had become spoiled by the steady flow of secrets that had flowed from East Berlin.

"Where is the man's replacement?" Moscow demanded. "That field station is your highest priority. It must be covered. Failure is out of the question."

The colonel summoned his secretary, the dumpy Ukrainian wife of one of his case officers. East Germans could not be trusted. "Tell Kiryukhin to see me as soon as he gets in," the colonel growled.

For several months, case officer Valery Mikhailovich Kiryukhin had been touting his latest lead as a worthy successor to the departed American sergeant. Tall, good looking, and given to wearing American jeans acquired during a tour at the Soviet Mission to the United Nations, Kiryukhin could be unnervingly arrogant and overbearing. "Telephone intercepts confirm that the guy is in financial trouble," the English-speaking Kiryukhin reported. After several preliminary meetings with the American, Kiryukhin was supremely confident. Like the departed Paul, his new recruit was a sergeant, and he had already crossed the bridge by delivering some secret documents. The cocky Kiryukhin boasted to anyone who would listen that his new man would develop into a fine agent.

In Moscow, the Center was pleased at the prospect of renewed coverage of the Teufelsberg Field Station—pleased, that is, until Kiryukhin was forced to admit that his gold-plated new recruit had broken contact. No one knew why the American had failed to deliver the latest batch of secrets he had promised. Kiryukhin was sure that the sergeant was still in Berlin. Perhaps the indebted soldier had lost his nerve, he suggested.

The colonel cursed silently as he thought to himself: The only way to get Moscow off our backs is for Kiryukhin to force the issue with the timid sergeant. If Valery Mikhailovich had to shower the American with hundred-dollar bills, then he must do so.

## West Berlin: November 1985

The narrow break in the window blinds permitted only a limited view of the dimly lit street. Passersby ambled along the sidewalk, their muffled voices barely audible through the window. Berliners were engaged in their favorite pastime—walking along the lakeshore. Since before dusk, we had maintained our vigil at the window, straining to spot a familiar figure on the street. I fidgeted and glanced at my watch, its dial barely visible in the blacked-out room.

It was well past 7:30 P.M., the appointed time of the meeting. A wave of pessimism swept over the occupants of our hidden observation post. Where was he? Had something unforeseen derailed the operation? The possibility that we might be outwitted again by our cunning adversaries was almost too painful to bear. Six months of work for nothing.

A gentle nudge cut short these self-doubts. Something was happening. Barely visible in the darkness, the unmistakable figure of a man on crutches lurched past the window in the direction of a nearby lakeside restaurant—exactly as instructed. I let loose a sigh of relief and gave the thumbs-up signal to my three companions. The figure on crutches—our man—was quickly out of sight. Within minutes, he would enter the Restaurant Seeterrassen. Once inside, the carefully coached double agent would sit facing the door as instructed and await his dinner partner, an English-speaking officer of the Soviet KGB. The trap was set.

On that November evening in 1985, we were operating in the heart of the French sector of West Berlin. Within three hundred yards of our concealed command post, dozens of undercover American and French counterintelligence agents prepared to carry out their assignments. With luck, the plan would come together. If it did, officers in the KGB's aggressive *residenz* in East Berlin would be forced to spend the night dispatching frantic cables to the Moscow Center explaining why their highly touted penetration of American intelligence had suddenly blown up in their faces.

More than forty years after V-E Day, Berlin remained an occupied city, in some ways as bitterly contested as it had been during the war. But in 1985 the contest was not between Hitler's war-weary legions and advancing Allied armies. This was the Cold War. The arena was divided Berlin, and the gladiators were the intelligence services of the western powers and the Soviet-dominated Warsaw Pact.

Situated more than a hundred miles inside communist East Germany, Berlin was surrounded by a Soviet occupation force of some 300,000 Red Army soldiers. Bequeathed to us by the politicians who drew up the postwar map even as battles still raged, the western half of the historic city had risen Phoenix-like from its own rubble and ashes. As the Cold War raged, the free half of the former Nazi capital had become an insular observation post deep in our Soviet adversary's rear. Allied forces in West Berlin sat directly astride the supply lines that Moscow's armies would depend upon in the event of a war with the North Atlantic Treaty Organization (NATO). As a consequence, the three western allies had packed their West Berlin garrisons with a formidable array of intelligence units, all of which spied on the Soviets around the clock by every conceivable means, technical and human.

Among intelligence professionals, Berlin was deservedly known as the world's undisputed capital of espionage. Of some five thousand American civilian and military personnel stationed in the city, almost two thousand were directly engaged in intelligence and counterintelligence duties, and they were joined by both British and French intelligence contingents. Viewed through Moscow's strategic prisms, western intelligence agencies in Berlin loomed as a serious threat. In the event of war, our efforts would guarantee an advantage to NATO by providing early warning of Warsaw Pact preparations. And our Soviet adversaries could not be comfortable with the behind-the-lines mischief that we would most certainly launch from our West Berlin bases if war were to erupt.

But this game could be played by both sides. Allied sensitive units in West Berlin also posed a tempting intelligence collection opportunity for the opposition. By deploying a full array of sophisticated military and civilian intelligence collection activities in the surrounded city, Washington, London, and Paris served up thousands of targets for possible recruitment by Soviet and Warsaw Pact spymasters. To make matters worse (or better, if one were Soviet), because the Soviets were one of the four powers responsible for the continuing occupation of the entire city, Moscow's operatives enjoyed unrestricted access to West Berlin, a freedom that they exploited to the maximum. Stark evidence of this was the presence of thousands of Soviet and Warsaw Pact intelligence agents on both sides of the Berlin Wall, all jousting for position in their unrelenting efforts to penetrate American, British, and French security. For intelligence professionals of both sides, Cold War Berlin was the place to be— an espionage Mecca where the shadowy game of spy versus counterspy was daily fare.

On this particular evening in November 1985, the drama was being played out between agents of my unit, the 766th Military Intelligence Detachment, and the Karlshorst Detachment of the Soviet KGB's Third Chief Directorate. Earlier in the year, the KGB had made what they believed to be a bold and successful recruitment of an American sergeant. For months, the East Berlin–based Soviets had met the young noncom and plied him with cash in exchange for classified documents, unaware that their promising new recruit was a loyal soldier who had been under the control of American counterintelligence from the beginning. Now it was time to end the operation on our terms. If all went well on this chilly November evening, army counterintelligence would deliver a strong counterstroke to the Soviet operation.

As agents in Berlin prepared to spring their carefully orchestrated trap, counterintelligence staff officers in Munich, Heidelberg, and Washington awaited the jubilant signal that would flash from the streets of Berlin if the 766th's plan succeeded in besting our Soviet adversaries. The stakes of the operation were high, not the least important of which was the professional reputation of our counterintelligence unit. Some in our Munich headquarters had scoffed at the plan, believing that it was not possible to put so many agents in this small lakeside promenade undetected by the KGB's vaunted countersurveillance personnel. We were determined to prove them wrong.

Our command post this evening was the darkened front room of a nineteenth-century red brick building belonging to the West Berlin Water Works. Gazing intently through the narrow opening in the blinds, adrenaline pumping, I had no time to mourn the obvious—that our chilly vigil was not high on the list of activities one might choose for a Friday night, particularly in a city famous for its nightlife. To complicate matters, my parents were visiting from their Florida retirement retreat. This was supposed to be a night on the town, an excursion to Berlin's famous Kurfurstendamm and dinner at one of the elegant city's five thousand restaurants.

Earlier that day, all of us involved in the operation had made polite but obscure excuses to our families. Business would keep us out late, possibly past midnight. We couldn't tell our loved ones that "business" was a euphemism for the Soviet KGB.

Beside me in our clammy observation post pressing a radio to his ear was unit operations officer Bob Thayer. The thirty-eight-year-old Thayer was the brains behind this six-month, high-stakes sting of the KGB. If events unfolded as planned, Vasily, an English-speaking Soviet operative, was destined to have a bad night. Crouched beside Thayer were Maj. Bill Wetzel, a U.S. Army military police officer, and Alain Bianchi, an agent of the French Surete. Together, we constituted the control element of a forty-person dragnet of American and French special agents deployed in the surrounding streets and restaurants. If Vasily took the bait and paid our agent for the secret documents he was carrying, American and French special agents would take the Russian into custody and swiftly cordon off the area to trap his confederates.

We had gone to ground in the dank observation post in midafternoon, aided by a cooperating official of the West Berlin Water Works who smuggled us in a closed van into the ancient pumping station. When the German employees went home, their darkened office became our command post.

By 1985, Bob Thayer had been operating against the KGB for fifteen years. A native of Sioux City, Iowa, the popular operations officer of the 766th Military Intelligence Detachment had inaugurated his career in 1970 as an enlisted special agent before converting to civilian status. With service in the United States, Korea, and Panama, Thayer knew the enemy better than any of us. Patient, methodical, and demanding, the veteran investigator had the right stuff for duty in West Berlin, where not a week passed without some challenge involving our communist adversaries.

Years of experience had taught Thayer that Soviet countersurveillance agents would cautiously check out the neighborhood several hours prior to the scheduled meeting with their agent. The KGB men, trained to sniff out a trap, would be looking for signs of unusual activity that might indicate trouble. Outwitting the Soviets would not be easy. Somehow, the neighborhood would have to be saturated with special agents without leaving any telltale signs that American counterspies were in the area. Any hint of unusual activity would be detected by the KGB men, who would alert Vasily to abort the meeting with the American source.

Several days earlier, agents of the 766th had cased the lakeside site and reported that the streets would be far from empty in the early evening. Late vacationers from all over Germany were still enjoying the resort atmosphere. This news inspired Bob Thayer. Why not rent recreational vehicles with German license plates and park them in the neighborhood? The RVs would blend in perfectly with the resort atmosphere and provide ideal hiding places for teams of special agents. Linked by radio communications to the command post, agents could spring from the vehicles on command, and the RVs could be used as roadblocks. Any Soviets trapped in the tight circle would have no choice but to surrender.

Thayer also knew that our trained KGB adversaries' suspicions would be alerted if they detected too many males, particularly in pairs, in the area of the planned meeting. This was a problem for the 766th, which had few female agents in its ranks. The seasoned operations officer overcame this problem by a variety of measures. He concealed many of our male agents in the RVs. Agents assigned to the streets and in the restaurants were a disarming mix of men and women. Any KGB snoops looking for danger signs would see

couples strolling on the waterfront and families with children re-
laxing in the restaurants and coffee shops of the neighborhood.
There would be no trace of grim-faced spooks lying in ambush.

To accomplish this ruse, Thayer had drafted virtually all of the
women in the unit—translators, secretaries, archivists, even the supply clerk—and put them on the streets with the men. Then, to guarantee eyes on the target, he boldly posted two 766th agents in the
restaurant where the KGB man had told his American spy to meet
him. One was a female, the other a veteran German American who
was dining with the borrowed wife and children of a colleague, enabling him to blend unthreateningly into the restaurant's family
clientele. When Vasily entered the quaint Restaurant Seeterrassen,
the KGB man would have no way of knowing that the silver-haired
fellow with the attractive wife and two children in a nearby booth was
wired for communications. Special agent Hilmar Kullek's mission
was critical. The moment he saw our agent pass an envelope to the
Russian, Kullek would sound the alert and the trap would be sprung.

Thus the stage was set for what would become known in the annals of the Silent War as Operation Lake Terrace. If all went according to Bob Thayer's plan, the arrest and humiliation of Vasily
and his colleagues would send a clear signal to Moscow that American soldiers were not for sale, contrary to the teachings as taught in
the KGB's training institute. At the same time, photos of the apprehended Soviets would provide convincing proof that the hostile intelligence threat to U.S. forces in Berlin was alive and well.

In Moscow, Mikhail Gorbachev had just taken the first steps down
the road of glasnost that would lead to the end of the Cold War. But
on the streets of West Berlin, the battle of wits between American
and Soviet intelligence services continued unabated.

# 2: The Road to Berlin

This was my second tour as a military intelligence (MI) officer in West Berlin. In 1968, as a captain assigned under cover to a human intelligence (HUMINT) unit, I was part of a team of intelligence officers whose mission was to recruit Soviet and Warsaw Pact citizens to betray their countries' secrets. Because West Berlin was a crossroads for citizens of Eastern European countries, hunting was always good for the 430th Military Intelligence Battalion. Couriers, low-level observation agents, even an occasional principal agent, who might recruit others to the cause, were our stock-in-trade. In the days before sophisticated satellites, an agent who could ride a bus past a Soviet garrison and count the tanks in the parking areas was worth the time, risk, and effort to recruit.

That initial tour in Berlin had been a moving experience. Young, idealistic, and in search of a career that measured up to the ideals of my liberal arts education, I felt that duty in Berlin resonated from the beginning. Like most Americans who made pilgrimages to the historic city, I was shaken deeply by its stark isolation and hated wall. But I couldn't avoid being seduced by West Berlin's beauty and friendly, pro-American population. Orchestrating espionage against the communists was heady stuff, and our cause was just. One needed only to glance across the wall or read the newspapers to see the drab fate that communism offered.

Not only was the cause just, the duty was exciting. In August 1968, Red Army tank units garrisoned around Berlin had suddenly disappeared from their installations—mobilized for "exercises," according to our Russian counterparts. As American and allied intelligence units frantically employed all available agents and technical capabilities to locate the missing Russians, Soviet and Warsaw Pact forces stormed across the Czech frontier.

I was the Berlin Command's staff duty officer that night. When the alert was sounded from our Heidelberg headquarters, I notified the command group, then watched in awe as grim-faced generals and colonels assembled in the command's subterranean operations

center. Other than a symbolic alert of our small garrison (one reinforced tank company—thirty tanks—and three infantry battalions),
there was little anyone could do other than watch helplessly as
Moscow's forces wrote the final bloody chapter to Alexander
Dubcek's Prague Spring.

At one point, an alarming report hit the wire. A Soviet armored
unit was heading for the inter-German border. Everyone held his
breath. Were the leaders in the Kremlin crazy enough to start World
War III under the cover of the Prague operation? The report was
quickly discredited, but the lesson was not lost. We lived in an exposed, dangerous environment, and the Russians were playing for
keeps. As Moscow's legions ruthlessly mopped up resistance in
Prague, we monitored the piteous, unanswered appeals for help that
the beleaguered Czechs broadcast on clandestine radio transmitters.
("This is Free Prague. They are killing us. Please help.")

But there was no help. The hapless Czechs learned the hard way—
as had their Hungarian neighbors twelve years earlier—that all the
hoopla in the West about rolling back communism was just that:
cheap talk and political posturing. Refugees from the Soviet crack-
down streamed into Austria and Germany.

With the flood of displaced Czechs came bountiful operational
opportunities for the Berlin intelligence community. In the months
following the August invasion, we busied ourselves with countless
refugee debriefings of those Czechs fortunate enough to escape the
Soviet blitzkrieg, always on the alert for someone who knew someone. Did the retired Czech engineer sitting across the table perhaps
have a son who had remained behind in Prague? Might the young
man be of draft age and likely to be inducted into the disaffected
Czech army? And had the gentleman worked out ways to communicate with his son? Moscow's heavy-handed treatment of its ally had
offered up a treasure trove of operational leads for us—thousands
of angry, dispossessed men and women who might lead us to someone with "placement and access" (our jargon) to key military targets
behind the Iron Curtain.

Shortly after the subduing of the Czechs, the army sent me to the
Bavarian village of Oberammergau to study the German language,
for which I had some affinity. Eventually, I learned German well. By

the time my tour in Berlin ended in December 1969, I had become a card-carrying Germanophile. More importantly, although I initially didn't realize it, was the fact that I was hooked on a career in military intelligence. At age twenty-eight, I had adapted effortlessly to the intelligence business, and the army had plans for me. Vietnam was beckoning.

By 1969, the American people were all but unanimous in their rejection of the Vietnam War. The surprise attacks during Tet of 1968 and the resulting bloodletting portended an eventual stalemate, if not defeat. President Johnson, worn down and demoralized, had already retired to his Texas ranch. His successor, Richard Nixon, promised the electorate that he would end U.S. involvement in the unpopular war. Disinclined to volunteer for what seemed to be a lost cause, I departed Berlin and separated from active duty at the end of 1969. My boss and mentor, Maj. Tom Dillon, strove in vain to change my mind, bluntly telling me that I would not find anything in civilian life that could compare to a career in military intelligence.

Dillon was correct. Within seven months, I was back in uniform, having volunteered for duty in Vietnam as the price of readmission into the ranks of military intelligence. Private industry could not compete with the excitement and sense of purpose of a military career. I had found my calling.

The Vietnam phase of my career lasted the better part of four years. Two of those years were spent in a remote Vietnamese province near the Cambodian border ferreting out the communist agents who made up the Vietcong's shadow government. (This story is recounted in *Stalking the Vietcong: Inside Operation Phoenix,* Presidio Press, 1997.)

Vietnam was my first inside look at the netherworld of counterintelligence, where the intrigue of stalking Vietcong agents was almost addictive. Unmasking and neutralizing enemy operatives was more satisfying than recruiting spies, although it was clear that a grasp of recruitment techniques and espionage tradecraft made one a far more effective spy catcher. This truism would determine the path I would follow for the next twenty-five years.

For me, and all of us who answered the call and served in Vietnam, the war had an unhappy ending. In my case, almost four years spent in the cause of our hapless Vietnamese ally ended when I departed the roof of the U.S. embassy in a Marine Corps evacuation helicopter on April 30, 1975, at 5:30 A.M., scant hours before the North Vietnamese Army entered Saigon and renamed it Ho Chi Minh City. (This is related in *Peace with Honor? An American Reports on Vietnam, 1973–1975,* Presidio Press, 1983.)

Eight years transpired between the fall of Saigon and my spy-catching assignment in West Berlin. As a German linguist with operational experience in both Berlin and Vietnam, I was qualified for the sensitive post in spite of my lack of formal counterintelligence schooling. Not that there was much serious competition from my fellow officers. Spy catching was widely regarded as a career dead end. Few MI careerists were willing to risk the lower promotion rates associated with the Silent War.

This all mattered little to me. Command of the 766th Military Intelligence Detachment meant an opportunity to return to Berlin, where I had friends in the intelligence community and which held nothing but fond memories of the halcyon days of the 1960s. But most importantly, for anyone who thirsted for the chance to practice the craft of intelligence in a challenging and difficult operational environment, literally surrounded by the opposition, Berlin was the place to be.

# 3: The KGB Strikes

By the time we set up our 1985 stakeout in the French sector, I had been in command of the 766th Military Intelligence Detachment for more than two years. The detachment traced its lineage to the army's Counterintelligence Corps (CIC) in the victorious summer of 1945. For almost fifty years, until its deactivation at the end of the Cold War, the 766th's principal mission had remained constant: Detect and foil the attempts of our communist adversaries to turn American soldiers into traitors.

Ours was a war waged in the shadows. The agents of the 766th were key players in a game known irreverently as "the world's second oldest profession." But regardless of what one chose to call it, espionage and counterespionage was a fascinating business. The stakes were high, the mission a worthy one, and all of us loved its thrills.

These were fast-paced years, packed with a daily regime of intrigue as we jousted with the Soviet intelligence services (the KGB and the GRU—Soviet military intelligence), the East German State Security Service (MfS, or Stasi), the Czech STB, and the Polish SB. In the early years after V-E Day, assassinations and kidnappings by Soviet agents were not unusual. By the waning days of the Cold War, the rules were more civilized but the game was the same: Penetrate the enemy's units by recruiting his most vulnerable soldiers. Operation Lake Terrace was but one example of our stock-in-trade, recounted here in detail because it was, in many ways, a microcosm of what we faced in Berlin's contested environment.

The events that led to our vigil in the West Berlin Water Works that chilly November evening in 1985 had begun six months earlier. The KGB moved the first pawn.

A young American soldier, SSgt. Lowry Wilcox, had received several phone calls from an auto finance company in the United States. The sergeant's car payment was overdue, a polite voice reminded him. Naturally, the finance company did not want to involve his commander. Was there a problem, or could he send the payment promptly? Wilcox assured his creditors that he had experienced a temporary problem but he would pay up soon. It was the kind of conversation that happened almost daily to underpaid GIs stationed around the world.

But this conversation was different. Crouched at a console on the communist side of the Berlin Wall, a Soviet KGB signals intelligence technician was listening.

The American sergeant was serving in West Berlin in one of the command's most sensitive communications sites, Field Station Berlin. Perched on the peak of the Teufelsberg, a small mountain formed from the rubble of the bombed-out city in 1945, the field station was the highest point in West Berlin. Festooned with antenna arrays and domes, Wilcox's unit was one of the Soviet intelligence service's priority targets. When one of the field station's soldiers had a conversation with a creditor, the KGB paid attention.

Every day, thousands of long-distance telephone calls from the United States and Europe were beamed through the airwaves to recipients in West Berlin. Sophisticated computer consoles in East Berlin, many of them embargoed American and Japanese technology purchased for the Soviets and East Germans by front companies, intercepted each call. To accomplish this, agents of the KGB's Signals Directorate programmed phone numbers of interest into their consoles. When a targeted phone rang in the home of a soldier assigned to a sensitive job in Berlin, Soviet ears were alert for any clues that the American might be in trouble.

Each day, the Soviet signals intelligence unit could cull these targeted conversations from the daily harvest of intercepts and pass them on to KGB translators. Intercepts revealing well-placed Americans with personal problems were fed to KGB case officers (human intelligence recruiters).

The rest was simple. English-speaking KGB officers would assess the target's problem, which was often financial, then contact the needy soldier with an attractive "business proposition." In Staff Sergeant Wilcox's case, this entire process took less than a week. Years of practice had forged a close supporting relationship between Soviet signals intelligence units and the KGB's aggressive recruiters.

Within days of receiving the finance company's final warning, Sergeant Wilcox's home phone rang once again. The caller, speaking accented English, identified himself cryptically as Mr. Fisher, a "friend of a friend" of Wilcox's family. Fisher was direct. He understood that the sergeant was a talented fellow who might be interested in a lucrative business opportunity. Could the two of them get together the following evening to discuss the venture? Wilcox, whose alertness exceeded his financial management skills, was instantly suspicious. Nonetheless, he played along. By the end of the conversation, the two men had agreed to meet the following evening at a hotel near Berlin's fashionable Kurfurstendamm in the British sector. Before hanging up, Fisher cautioned Wilcox to keep their business confidential, a telltale feature of Soviet intelligence modus operandi.

As it happened, one of Wilcox's neighbors was a special agent in the 766th Military Intelligence Detachment. The staff sergeant recalled the security briefing that he had received upon arrival in Berlin and promptly sought out his neighbor. Wilcox's description of Fisher's cryptic offer, the man's accent, his insistence on secrecy, and the recent phone call about an overdue car payment all added up to a classic Soviet approach. It was all there: Soldier assigned to a sensitive unit; financial troubles aired on the phone; and a generous stranger offering a tempting and timely opportunity to rake in some quick cash.

To the seasoned Bob Thayer, the Wilcox encounter was a category 1 case, meaning that it was almost surely the real thing: a contact initiated by an agent of a hostile intelligence service. Thankfully, other than our agent, the sergeant had told no one about his encounter. Secrecy had been maintained, making Fisher's phone call a viable opportunity to mount a secret operation to turn the tables on our Soviet adversaries.

To do this, the staff sergeant would have to agree to be a double agent. If willing, Wilcox would be coached by army counterintelligence to play along with Fisher. The goal would be to draw the Russian into relationship that Thayer and his agents would control, to set the stage for a headline-making apprehension of Fisher. To outfox the KGB, Wilcox would have to be carefully coached. Although he would have to appear to Fisher and his superiors as a greedy, dis-

loyal American, he dare not appear too anxious. Nor could the debt-
ridden sergeant display a lack of the normal human fears and inhi-
bitions of someone involved in the betrayal of his country. The penalties for espionage were severe.

This was dicey business, and our KGB opponents were trained to
detect such ruses. For the operation to succeed, the American agent
would have to be bold and quick witted. Thayer's case agent discreetly checked out Wilcox. Was the young sergeant the sort of man
who could be mentored successfully to play this role? Feedback obtained by the case agent was positive. Wilcox was a solid citizen with
above-average smarts and a clean military record. Had the assessment
been negative, or had Wilcox shown little inclination to volunteer
for the planned sting, he would have been instructed to sever all contact with Fisher. But the sergeant had impressed our case agent as a
quick-thinking noncom who could follow instructions. Equally important, he was ready, though not eager, to participate.

Agents prepared the nervous young sergeant for what might occur when he met Fisher. The caller would almost certainly abandon
his flimsy cover and announce himself to be a Soviet. This would be
a "cold pitch." As such, we warned our volunteer, he could expect
to be put under immediate pressure at this initial meeting. The man
would probably attempt to lure Wilcox to East Berlin, either in a Soviet diplomatic vehicle or via the subway. Even though the KGB
worked with impunity in West Berlin, Moscow's operatives were more
comfortable on their side of the Berlin Wall. Agents also warned
Wilcox that the Russian might urge him to go immediately to Teufelsberg and steal some classified documents. If this happened, the Soviet would probably argue that it was necessary as "a show of good
faith—so I can convince my boss that you are for real."

The 766th agents advised their new man that he could expect
quick money to be waved in his face, which he was authorized to accept. But under no circumstances, agents warned, was he to travel
to East Berlin, nor was he to agree to visit his unit for a nocturnal
theft of sensitive documents. To ease his fears, Wilcox's case officer
provided the sergeant with plausible reasons he could give for refusal.

All of these preparations took place within twenty-four hours of
Fisher's phone call. Meanwhile, Bob Thayer overcame the army's

primitive secure communications and coaxed permission for the operation from our headquarters—often a greater challenge than dealing with the Soviets. With but a few hours until the appointed meeting, the courageous but nervous sergeant was dispatched to meet the furtive Mr. Fisher.

Our hastily trained recruit would be on his own. Certain that Fisher's Soviet comrades would be out in force on a countersurveillance effort, Thayer had elected not to shadow Wilcox. The 766th was blessed with talented agents who regularly practiced the difficult art of discreet physical surveillance under Bob Thayer's tutelage, but a spontaneous surveillance of this all-important first meeting would be risky. Better to let the sergeant attend the meeting "clean" as a way of convincing the Soviets that he had not reported Fisher's phone call to the authorities. As a consequence, agents would have to rely on Wilcox to report on his encounter with Fisher.

Trust played a major role in such operations. If the Soviets managed to intimidate our man and spirit him into East Berlin, he might be interrogated by a trained Soviet communications specialist about the field station. If that happened, the operation would be an instant success for Moscow. Worse yet, the inexperienced Wilcox might lose his nerve and comply with a Soviet demand that he go to Teufelsberg and steal a stack of top-secret documents to prove that he was a genuine traitor. In either case, I chided Bob Thayer, he and I could open a used car lot in Paducah, Kentucky, because our careers in military intelligence would be over.

Several hours after the scheduled meeting, Wilcox called from a neighbor's apartment. In Berlin, it was not unheard of for the KGB to follow their man after such a meeting, looking for some sign that he might actually be under American control. Soviet surveillance personnel would likely be watching the sergeant's every move on the homeward trip to the American sector. Had he stopped to make a call from a phone booth (a sure sign of control) or, worse, if he had gone directly to the headquarters compound, where numerous American intelligence units were located, the KGB would terminate the operation.

"Everything is okay," Wilcox assured his case agent in a voice quavering with unconcealed excitement. "But you were right—he was a Russian, and he tried to get me to go through the wall."

Later, at his debriefing, Wilcox related the details of his first encounter with the KGB. He had shown up at the hotel, taken a seat on the outdoor terrace, and ordered a beer. Within minutes, a tall, dark-haired man dressed casually in jeans and a Members Only jacket approached and inquired if he was "Sergeant Wilcox." Wilcox nodded, and the man strode off, indicating that Wilcox should accompany him. The pair walked a short distance to one of Berlin's many small plazas and sat down on a park bench.

"My name is Vasily," the tall stranger began, "and I am a Soviet officer." Wilcox's throat was dry. Before he said a word, Vasily continued. "I have a car nearby, and I want you to go with me to East Berlin where we can speak freely."

The sergeant shook his head in unfeigned fear. "I'm afraid to go over there," he told the Russian. "If I get caught, my career will be ruined and I'll go to jail."

Vasily pushed. "No, it's not like you think. We won't go through Checkpoint Charlie. We'll go through a checkpoint where there are no MPs. I'll give you a wig, so no one will recognize you. Believe me, we'll be safer over there than on this side."

Wilcox remembered his instructions and shook his head. The Soviet relented, then fired off a barrage of questions about the noncom's unit—nothing extremely sensitive but sufficient to confirm that he had the right man, someone with the required placement and access to secrets who would make a good recruit. What was the classification of the documents in the sergeant's office? Could he manage to smuggle some of them out the door? How much longer did the sergeant have in Berlin? The conversation was short and hurried, the classic "cold pitch." No gentle lead-in, no lengthy assessment, just a blunt invitation: "You have something we need, and we have something you need," as if the discussion concerned the purchase of a pair of slacks. "This is business, nothing more. What do you think?"

That was it. Our agent nodded his agreement, stammered something about how careful they would have to be, and promised to "get something" from his workplace. Vasily assured his new recruit that security would be uppermost, then insisted one final time that his superiors were expecting the two in East Berlin. Wilcox again demurred. It was too dangerous.

The tall KGB officer accepted the sergeant's refusal without further argument and passed him an envelope—"from my bosses, as a show of good faith." The envelope contained a thin stack of crisp hundred-dollar bills, more than enough to cover Wilcox's delinquent car payment. The officer sternly cautioned the sergeant not to tell his wife or anyone else about their business, then provided his new recruit with the time and place of their next meeting, two weeks in the future. In the meantime, he reminded Wilcox sternly, "You know what we want."

The stunned sergeant related this story to his case agent with some amazement, almost as if it had happened to someone else. He couldn't get over the fact that virtually everything that his 766th contact forecast had transpired, almost as if American counterintelligence had written the script for the Soviet, right down to the clumsy gambit to get him into East Berlin.

The fact that Wilcox had not been caught off-guard gave him confidence in his American case agent. This would pay great dividends, for the two men would see a lot of each other in the coming months. If the case conformed to the KGB's modus operandi, Vasily would continue to meet his new recruit in the West but would press the sergeant to accompany him into East Berlin. Not only that, the Russians would expect impressive production from their spy—stacks of highly classified documents from the field station. Because we could not permit this, the sting would have a relatively brief life span. A genuine spy would agree to the East Berlin trip and provide his Soviet masters stacks of classified documents. If our man was a good actor, we might fool Vasily for a few months, but no longer.

Experience also taught that the operation would take an increasing share of Wilcox's free time, although the dedicated sergeant would not be permitted to keep the money he earned from his Soviet contacts. We could thus expect problems as the months passed, not the least of which would be a troubled wife's discomfort over whatever it was that her husband was doing at night, and the need for the sergeant to obtain time off from work to lead his double life. All were common problems that cropped up during such operations. Fortunately for the 766th, Lowry Wilcox was a level-headed soldier who adopted a positive, uncomplaining attitude throughout. His wife, whom we eventually took into our confidence, was supportive, as was his commander at Teufelsberg.

The operation dragged on through the early summer of 1985. Vasily pursued Wilcox aggressively, coaxing and urging the nervous sergeant to steal more and better classified documents from his workplace. Additional envelopes of hundred-dollar bills materialized as an incentive for production. At one point, Vasily admonished his new agent that the documents he was providing weren't worth the money Moscow was paying. The Soviets were acting in character.

Then the KGB threw a curveball. In a departure from the usual script, the Soviet urged Wilcox to steal "the good stuff," put it in an envelope, and deposit it in the slightly open window of a Soviet-built Lada sedan. Vasily provided the noncommissioned officer with a map of the exact location where the car would be parked, in the British sector near the Funkturm.

"Drop off the documents and keep walking," Vasily instructed. "We'll pay you later, after my superiors have evaluated the documents."

This was an unwelcome development. From the beginning, the objective of the operation had been to apprehend Vasily in the act of accepting classified documents from his American recruit. By introducing the Lada vehicle, the cautious Russian had just removed himself from the equation. If the KGB officer was no longer going to accept stolen secrets during face-to-face meetings, how could we arrest him? Morale sank among those of us in the detachment who knew of the highly compartmented operation. This hitherto unseen Soviet ploy had all the earmarks of a KGB effort to avoid a trap, despite our best efforts to convince Moscow that Wilcox was a genuine traitor.

On the other hand, why shouldn't Vasily smell a trap? Our sergeant could not be permitted to steal wholesale quantities of highly classified documents from his workplace. We were thus confined to a stalling tactic, doling out barely classified documents to keep the Russian on the hook while we busied ourselves choreographing the arrest scene and obtaining approvals for each move from higher headquarters. It was a delicate balancing act that Thayer could not sustain for long. Vasily knew that Lowry Wilcox's mountaintop workplace was awash with top-secret documents, and that the field station's security was lax. Sooner or later, the seasoned KGB officer or his superiors would realize that the man's failure to deliver "the good stuff" could mean only one thing: The sergeant was under the control of American counterintelligence.

Twice in the past nine years, Soviet KGB operatives had been successfully mousetrapped in Berlin under circumstances strikingly similar to those of the Wilcox case. In both instances, Moscow had approached American soldiers from intelligence units and offered dollars for documents. Each man had agreed to spy for Moscow while covertly cooperating with agents of the 766th. Both operations ended with humiliating apprehensions of Soviet officers on the streets—caught red-handed, as it were, in the act of meeting their "spy" to exchange documents for money. One had to wonder: With such a history, why would the KGB bite again?

In truth, the Russians had little to lose. By relentlessly approaching soldiers with access to secrets and promising them stacks of hundred-dollar bills to commit espionage, the law of averages was Moscow's ally. Some soldiers were bound to bite. Of those who took the bait, many might report the approach and come under American control, but others would be genuine traitors. If the KGB's cost of doing business was an occasional bad headline and a few embarrassed agents, wasn't this well worth the results? After all, the "take" in stolen secrets provided insights into the inner workings of the American intelligence community. Because KGB officers carried cover documents that identified them as diplomatically immune Soviet embassy personnel, the worst that could happen was a brief detention (measured in hours, not days). True, the professional incentives to avoid this humiliation were strong. In the paranoid ranks of the KGB, detention by the Americans, however brief, could cast a permanent shadow over an officer's reliability. Nonetheless, the Moscow Center considered its operations to penetrate our intelligence community as well worth the risk.

Soviet defectors had told their interrogators what KGB trainers taught about Americans. New KGB officers were imbued with the credo that virtually any American noncommissioned officer (NCO) could be bought if you offered him three times his annual salary. Officers, too, could be won over, the KGB assured its trainees, but with far more difficulty. Officers were better educated and better paid and came from the reactionary circles of American society. Underpaid sergeants with daily access to secrets were the best targets, KGB trainers preached—and they were correct.

One former KGB operative told his American debriefers that KGB trainers taught the acronym MICE in classes on recruitment approaches to Americans; MICE stood for money, ideology, corruption, coercion, and ego. "We were told that if an American professed a belief in our ideology, we should reject him as a likely provocateur [double agent]," the defector explained. "We did not expect the capitalist Americans to accept our ideology. Our trainers emphasized that money was the proven path to obtain the loyalty of most Americans."

The 766th operations officer Bob Thayer was hoping that Vasily saw the incarnation of this principle in Lowry Wilcox. The cash-strapped staff sergeant had dutifully provided classified material in exchange for money and expressed his willingness to go for "the big score" at work. Until Vasily's introduction of the car trick, the operation had been on track. We struggled in vain to come up with a way to outsmart the Russian on this one, but without results. Neither I nor Thayer could think of a way to put us back on track—defined as a resumption of face-to-face meetings between our bogus traitor and Vasily. If Wilcox put classified documents into that Lada, we were marching to the beat of Moscow's music.

Perhaps Don, our Central Intelligence Agency (CIA) counterpart, could offer advice. I strolled the short distance to the rear of the Berlin headquarters compound and entered the heavily secured building that housed the agency's Berlin base. Seated on the couch in Don's well-appointed office, surrounded by stereo music to foil electronic eavesdropping, I described our dilemma and reviewed the options. Impatient for a successful climax to the case, I favored a heavy-handed approach. Why not instruct Wilcox to comply with Vasily's instructions and drop the documents in the car—then apprehend whoever showed up to drive it away? Any Soviet would do.

Don shook his head. "They'll claim it was a provocation, and all you'll get is egg on your face, because there will be those out there who will believe it," he counseled. "You need to stick to your original objective, even if it means passing on this event."

The CIA officer's counsel was unwelcome. We had set our sights on an arrest, and nothing less would do, even if the best we could do was the arrest of a Soviet driver. At least the Russian would be apprehended in the act of conveying stolen secrets.

Don disagreed. "Be patient. They're not going to let loose of your man if he fails to dump the stuff in that car," he advised. "They'll come sniffing back, and then you can have it your way."

Don's arguments were persuasive, but putting the whole operation on hold and risking the loss of the opportunity to outwit the Soviets was distasteful. As an operation progressed, it was common to see the various moves and countermoves as a game. Unless great self-discipline could be maintained, pride and ego could cloud judgment and spell defeat. I was falling into that trap, propelled by an overpowering desire to post Vasily's name in the unit trophy case beside the names of KGB officers who had been apprehended in the past.

Bob Thayer sided with Don on this one, and Thayer was an operations officer whom a commander ignored at his peril. Not only was he more experienced than I, he was usually right. Not without misgivings, I relented. At their next meeting, Thayer's case agent instructed the plucky Sergeant Wilcox not to follow Vasily's instructions. We would not permit the KGB to control the operation. The next move was thus up to Vasily. If he wanted his newly recruited spy to hand over additional secrets, he would have to meet him in person.

Disappointed, I privately concluded that we had seen the last of Vasily, and got on with other business.

# 4: Business as Usual

Like detective work, counterintelligence is often embellished by outsiders who write about it. In novels and movies, the life of a counterspy is most often depicted as glamorous and risky—a derring-do existence replete with intrigue, violence, and high drama. Real counterintelligence agents, like their law enforcement counterparts, know better. Much of the daily fare of the average agent revolves around the routine and the mundane. Surveillance operations, furtive contacts with agents, and dramatic arrest scenes are the exception; records checks, interviews, and endless report writing are the norm. Legions of counterintelligence agents served during the Cold War. Most never caught a single spy, and only a small number ever directly confronted our communist adversaries. Of those fortunate enough to do so, many did it in West Berlin.

Counterintelligence duty in West Berlin approached the overdrawn characterizations of the novelist. There was no shortage of business in the city's intrigue-laden environment. Each day in the 766th MI Detachment brought with it a menu of opportunities and choices, any one of which could quickly transform itself into an operational triumph or mushroom into an embarrassing catastrophe. Thanks largely to the efforts of a smart operations officer and his enthusiastic agents, between 1983 and 1986 triumphs outnumbered catastrophes. But in the latter category, the case of special agent B. J. Conlin stands out.

Sergeant First Class Conlin arrived in West Berlin in September 1983. Fresh from a delicate assignment in Washington, D.C., the thirty-year-old NCO showed up unexpectedly on our unit doorstep. This was somewhat unusual, but the new noncom had come from an undercover assignment where his move to Germany could have been handled outside of normal personnel channels. Conlin produced movement orders assigning him to Berlin, and everyone knew that the personnel system was far from perfect. Pleased at our good fortune to obtain the services of a relatively senior agent, we

notified our Munich headquarters of Conlin's somewhat unorthodox arrival and put him to work.

Almost immediately, disquieting things began to happen. A loner
with a Barry Manilow hairstyle, Conlin elected to rent a bachelor
apartment in a German neighborhood. The 766th's agents were a
tight group during their off-duty hours, but B. J. kept to himself.
Soon Bob Thayer began to receive disturbing reports. Special agent
Conlin was spending far too many hours perched on a bar stool in
Berlin's Checkpoint Noncommissioned Officers' Club. Thayer
sought me out and reminded me of his initial reaction to B. J. Within
days of the man's arrival, Bob had screwed his face into a distasteful
smirk and delivered his first take on the new guy from Washington:
"Sir, I don't know about B. J.," he warned. "There's something there
I just can't put my finger on, but I'm not comfortable with him."
From that day on, Thayer had kept close tabs on B. J. Conlin.

Bob's instincts were borne out. Within a month, B. J. passed out
as he departed the NCO club bar. Confronted in my office the
following day, Conlin denied that he had an alcohol problem
but "volunteered" on my urging to seek assistance. Going by the
book, we sent him to a high-speed, army-run detox course in Bad
Canstadt, Germany. The 766th's mission included the scrutiny of
American soldiers to determine if they could be trusted with secrets. The unit could not afford to harbor an unreformed alcoholic in its ranks.

B. J. was gone for more than a month. An important part of the
man's therapy, counselors informed me, was an assurance from me
that he would be returned to duty upon graduation. I was willing to
do my part, although giving an alcoholic a sensitive job in a unit such
as ours didn't make a lot of sense, then or now. Nonetheless, when
B. J. returned to Berlin, a job was waiting for him. I hedged our bets
by one cautious measure. B. J.'s new supervisor would be special
agent Al Thornton, a veteran chief warrant officer who happened
to be a Mormon. If B. J. were to relapse, Chief Thornton would easily sniff out the problem. Should this occur, it was our responsibility
to muster B. J. out of the army as a rehabilitative failure.

Within a few weeks, Thornton was camped on my desk with a look
on his face as if he'd just smelled dog manure. "Sir," he reported,

"B. J.'s drinking again. He's coming to work late, and I can smell the alcohol on his breath."

Confronted with his supervisor's suspicions, B. J. emphatically denied taking a drink. "I've still got my marbles, sir," he insisted, proudly displaying a pair of marbles given him upon graduation from the detox school. (Counselors had instructed each graduate to carry the marbles as a reminder that one drink constituted "losing one's marbles.")

I instructed Chief Thornton to await the next occasion when B. J. arrived late to work with an obvious hangover, at which time we would order the first sergeant to escort him to the hospital for an immediate blood-alcohol test. If the results were positive for alcohol, SFC B. J. Conlin would be put on the fast track to civilian life. It was a sound plan, and would have worked.

Trouble struck before we could execute the plan. In December 1983, German authorities notified the MPs that an American had been found unconscious on the street at dawn. The man's name was Conlin, and he had apparently passed out sometime in the middle of the night after a drinking binge.

We learned of the problem on a Saturday. Conlin, the MPs told our duty agent, had been taken to the Martin Luther Clinic. After alerting Bob Thayer, I drove the few short blocks from my home to the clinic.

B. J. was lying on a gurney in the emergency room, his chin and hands bleeding from a three-point landing. A somber German policeman and a grinning MP corporal leered at the prostrate figure on the gurney as I introduced myself as the man's commander.

Conlin was clad in jeans, under which he had donned a pair of smoke gray lady's panty hose. Setting off his outfit was a pink shirt, unbuttoned to midtorso, and a black motorcycle jacket with silver studs. To complete his getup, B. J. had affixed exaggerated false fingernails—painted shocking purple—on both hands. The sergeant's skin was deathly pale, beads of sweat shone on his forehead, and he was staring at the ceiling in a near comalike state. The stench of sweat and alcohol emanating from him was sickening.

"Some kind of special operation, sir?" the MP grinned, barely able to keep his composure. Unamused, I threatened the corporal with dire consequences if he told anyone at the provost marshal's office what he had seen—knowing that he couldn't wait to spread the word about the kinky spook on the gurney (which is just what he did). I reached inside B. J.'s jacket. Sure enough, he was carrying his special agent's badge and credentials, a serious offense when off-duty.

Disgusted, I called Bob Thayer, arranged for the man's transport to our military hospital, and contacted the army lawyer who supported our detachment. I wanted a blood-alcohol test done immediately on B. J. and permission to search his apartment. Everything about the strange creature on that gurney cried out for immediate scrutiny of his loner lifestyle. If the sergeant's idea of fun was to cruise around Berlin on a Friday night in drag in an alcoholic haze, God only knew what we might find in his quarters. To make matters worse, agents who recovered B. J.'s black Trans Am from a downtown parking lot discovered a folder containing a classified document on the front seat.

Within an hour, Bob Thayer and I, accompanied by a Berlin police officer, entered the apartment in Zehlendorf that B. J. called home. The search proved to be a mind-numbing expedition into Conlin's weird world. As we uncovered item after item that bespoke of B. J.'s kinky off-duty lifestyle, Thayer and I shook our heads. The man was a sergeant first class in the U.S. Army and a special agent in army counterintelligence, yet he had somehow detected and exploited every fault in the system that existed to keep people like him out of our ranks.

Paperwork recovered in the apartment established that B. J. was a career drunk whose alcohol problem had been tolerated in prior assignments. Conlin had obviously removed the documents from his medical records while in transit to Berlin. Later, we learned that while assigned in Washington, B. J. had wrecked a government sedan after a heavy drinking bout. The event was swept under the rug, and he was able to retain his top-secret security clearance.

B. J. was an espionage freak. His apartment contained a disturbing collection of James Bond memorabilia, including an entire album of Sean Connery photos that he had taken in darkened theaters. Confiscated audiotapes led to the discovery that B. J. had installed a clandestine taping system in his Trans Am and had secretly taped conversations with his passengers.

B. J. was the universal man. His wide-ranging interests included an eclectic collection of magazines depicting transvestite sex, sado-masochistic sex, kinky sex, animal sex, and everyday, garden-variety sex. Had there been such a thing as vegetable sex or mineral sex, B. J. probably would have had magazines on those subjects as well. The twisted sergeant's collection of panty hose, cosmetics, and girdles was second to none among our male agents. Carefully secreted in a locked attaché case were two loaded, unregistered weapons. B. J. rounded out his all-American profile with a German girlfriend, Ingrid, who came complete with leftist ties and a criminal record.

Bob Thayer discovered a cigar box that portended real trouble. In it was a bewildering and illegal collection of cover documentation—dozens of military and civilian ID cards, many already laminated, adorned with his picture and a fictitious name. Conlin could be a full colonel, a captain, a senior civilian, or whatever merely by reaching into his magic cigar box. Credit cards and driver's licenses supported each identity. Cover documentation of this sort was supposed to be tightly controlled by the unit that B. J. had just departed.

Bob Thayer thumbed through the documents. "B. J. was a busy boy in Washington, sir," he quipped with a sardonic grin. Later, we learned that Conlin had created the computer program in Washington that was used to keep track of all cover documentation.

B. J.'s uniforms and other military equipment were concealed in a locked cupboard. His landlord and German girlfriend later confirmed that he had told them he worked in the American consulate. In the German neighborhood, the American with the modish hairstyle was known as "the diplomat." No one knew that he was a sergeant in the U.S. Army.

Conlin's apartment yielded other telling and disturbing documents. Among them was a bar bill. Within hours of his release from the alcohol detox course, B. J. had celebrated his graduation with five martinis at the nearby Holiday Inn bar.

Other papers advertised B. J.'s imaginative approach to managing his military career. One document testified that he had reenlisted in the army prior to his Berlin assignment and collected several thousand dollars in reenlistment bonus money. Additional papers made it clear that the wily sergeant had then doctored his finance records and managed to delete all references to the reenlistment and the bonus, thus clearing the way for his prompt separation from active duty, money and all.

But most disquieting of all was an ominous cache of papers and rubber stamps. B. J. had collected stamps that would enable him to mark documents as confidential, secret, or top secret. He also had amassed a sizeable stockpile of security cover sheets that were routinely attached to classified documents, as well as a diverse library of letterhead stationery. These materials were a forger's dream. With them, B. J. could create bogus classified documents not only from the Department of the Army but also from other services, and even the U.S. Congress.

Together with a small amount of genuine classified documents, these finds escalated the strange sergeant's breaches of conduct into a more serious matter. Because he was on the verge of leaving the army, it appeared likely that, at a minimum, the kinky agent was planning to establish a "paper mill"—espionage slang for someone who creates bogus classified documents and sells them to the highest bidder for profit. In West Berlin, where B. J. planned to remain upon discharge, willing buyers were plentiful.

Major General James Boatner, the U.S. commander in Berlin, was displeased. Fixing me with a stern gaze, Boatner vented. How could the 766th have harbored such a weirdo? Were we not the guardians—counterintelligence special agents whose sole purpose was to prevent such things?

I gamely (and lamely) tried to persuade the general that we actually deserved credit for unmasking the weird agent. After all, Conlin had come to us from Washington, where he had lived out his fantasies and carried on unscathed and undiscovered. In fact, hidden papers found in his apartment told it all: The devious sergeant had so smoothly snookered his superiors in Washington that he had managed to promote himself and forge orders assigning him to his unit of choice in Berlin. That explained the unexpected arrival that had so perplexed us.

After consulting with army lawyers, we decided to court-martial B. J. At the hospital, we shackled him to his bed and posted an armed agent outside his door. The wall and East Berlin were but ten minutes away, and there was no doubt that the man was a flight risk. Within a week, the lawyers compiled so many charges against the strange noncom that it took me thirty minutes to read them to him in his jail cell. Shocked, B. J. adopted a new defensive tactic, feigning insanity and claiming that he was hearing voices in his molars.

This novel twist led to a medical evacuation to Walter Reed Army Medical Center—in custody—followed by a pathetic, months-long war of attrition waged by B. J. against the unfortunate shrinks. Every time therapists would declare him recovered and prepare to ship him back to Berlin to face his court-martial, the shrewd NCO would recoil in horror. Within hours, a chorus of voices in his molars would be again tormenting him. After several months of this sham, the slippery agent outlasted the Walter Reed staff and was mustered out of the army (with a temporary medical disability). Meanwhile, back in Berlin, we were left to pick up the pieces of our unit's reputation for excellence.

To this day, when the saga of B. J. Conlin comes up, Bob Thayer grins and reminds all present that he was the first to suspect that something was not quite right.

While I was mired in the muck spawned by the B. J. problem, Bob Thayer fielded many of the daily operational balls that typified life in the 766th. Many of these challenges appeared at the Clay Kaserne front gate. Hence the name *walk-ins*. A walk-in was anyone who showed up and requested the gate guard to put him in touch with an American intelligence service. The petitioner might ask to see the CIA or some other specific unit, but no matter. Regardless of whom a walk-in wished to see, standard operating procedure in the Berlin intelligence community dictated that debriefers from the 766th MI Detachment would handle the initial contact. Counterintelligence agents would then differentiate between intelligence nuisances (strange types who would pop out of the woodwork with some bizarre story; B. J. would have qualified), provocateurs (or "dangles")—people dispatched by the Soviets or another opposition services to confuse or otherwise occupy us, and genuine operational opportunities, such as a defector. On any given day, one never knew who might walk in.

One of the more legendary walk-ins showed up in the late 1960s; he was a furtive, graying man who urgently needed to speak to the *Amerikanischen Geheimdeinst* (American Secret Service). Speaking in conspiratorial tones and clutching a sealed pouch to his breast, the visitor assured the duty agent that he had obtained highly classified material of great interest. The material was *streng geheim* (top secret) he insisted, and could be shown only to the "highest authority." The 766th duty agent nodded understandingly and summoned his line supervisor.

Satisfied, the visitor unwrapped the pouch while his debriefers held their breath in anticipation of some stunning intelligence coup (Soviet war plans would have sufficed). With a flourish, the walk-in proudly produced his crown jewels—a dozen eight-by-ten glossy photographs of Adolf Hitler and other Nazi Party luminaries. Like many walk-ins, the visitor was over the edge. Agents politely accepted the proffered photos, thanked him for his vigilance, and added his name to the growing "intelligence nuisance list" that we kept in common with our British and French allies.

But it was not always this way. On yet another day, a young and extremely nervous Czech, accompanied by his wife and infant child, approached the guard and insisted that he had to meet with the American CIA. Within minutes the visitor was seated in our debriefing room.

His name was Alexander, the visitor informed the interviewing agent. "You should remember me," he continued. "I visited you once before and you sent me away."

A quick check of our central records confirmed Alexander's story. Many months earlier, when he was a student in Prague, the young Czech had indeed walked in and requested asylum in the United States. Annotated on the file card prepared at the time by our agent was the cryptic note that Alexander had seemed sincere but naive. He had been politely told that admission to the United States could not be obtained merely for the asking. Resettlement in the United States would be possible only if he were to possess some significant intelligence information that would tempt the American authorities.

Reminded of this, the young Czech beamed triumphantly. "Indeed," he confirmed, "that is what you told me. And I have taken your advice. I now have brought you significant intelligence." He was, he announced dramatically, an officer in the STB, the Czechoslovakian State Security Service. Having just served a tour in Warsaw, Poland, he was now on orders to an assignment in his country's embassy in a faraway Asian capital.

Alexander repeated his plea for asylum. He hated the communists and wished to defect. "You told me to come back when I had something significant," he repeated, "so here I am." His decision to defect was irrevocable, Alexander argued emotionally, which was why he had brought his wife and child with him. To establish his credentials, the young officer clutched an attaché case stuffed with classified documents. This time around, he insisted, we could not turn him away.

A quick glance at the contents of the case confirmed that the visitor was either the real thing or a well-planned provocation. Alexander's collection of sensitive documents included multiple passports in different names, his Czech State Security Service identity card, and Aeroflot tickets to Moscow. In Moscow, he explained, he was scheduled to pay a liaison visit to the KGB "friends" before resuming his journey to Asia.

Alexander's pilgrimage to our front door coincided with a period of great turmoil in Poland, which was threatened with a Soviet invasion. The Polish communists had declared martial law and were ruthlessly suppressing all dissident elements. A Polish Catholic priest had recently been murdered by Polish security agents, and the Solidarity Union was in the middle of its epic struggle with the communists. Amid these tensions and events, Alexander's recent service in Warsaw with his Polish comrades could constitute an intelligence windfall. We copied his documents and turned him over to our CIA colleagues. They would check his story, scrutinize his bona fides, and process his request for asylum if he withstood their rigorous vetting.

Weeks later, we learned that Alexander had passed muster. He had brought a wealth of information with him on the situation in Poland and Czechoslovakia. This timely contribution earned him his longstanding goal: resettlement in the United States. Alexander's case was a classic example of why all walk-ins had to be taken seriously until proven otherwise. In his case, our efforts had yielded a genuine defector.

Another walk-in case began in much the same way but led to a dramatically different outcome. The affair began with the interview of a lanky Austrian construction worker, Ernst Fessl. Like the others, Fessl showed up at the gate of the Berlin headquarters compound and asked to speak to a representative of the American security service. During an interview with one of our senior agents who had handled hundreds of walk-ins, the twenty-nine-year-old Austrian confided that he was in trouble and needed advice.

As Fessl told it, while he was working for an Austrian construction firm in East Berlin, an officer of the Soviet KGB attempted to recruit him as a spy. The Russian, Fessl insisted, had been extremely persistent, badgering him until he finally accepted recruitment.

The unsophisticated Austrian elaborated. The KGB had pursued him because he was a citizen of a neutral country who could travel to the West without arousing suspicion. Fessl apologetically admitted that he had performed various low-level casing missions in West Berlin for his KGB masters—test missions, he called them. But, the Austrian added, he was fed up with the shabby treatment that he was receiving from Alexei, his Soviet case officer. Denouncing Alexei as abusive, arrogant, and cheap, Fessl vowed that he wanted no more to do with the Russian.

Then came an offer. Fessl expressed a sincere desire to atone for his past, assuring the interviewing agent that he would tell us anything we wanted to know about his KGB affiliations, after which he merely wished to move on with his life. Then, almost as an afterthought, the Austrian dropped a tantalizing fact. Within a few days, he told his interviewer, he was supposed to meet Alexei in East Berlin. But, Fessl declared, his jaw set, he had no intention of keeping the appointment with the "KGB swine."

At first glance, it looked like a fine opportunity to get into the KGB's knickers. Fessl was already on Moscow's payroll and made no secret of his disaffection with Alexei. Because he had already accomplished low-level missions in West Berlin, who knew what tasks the KGB might entrust him with in the future? With luck, the Soviets might use Fessl to meet American spies or pay him to service dead letter drops—hiding places for the clandestine passage of documents from an agent to his handler. If we could recruit the Austrian and convince him to continue meeting Alexei, great benefits might flow from the arrangement, not the least of which could be a tip-off to a disloyal American. Recruit a spy to catch a spy was the name of the game. This was spy versus counterspy at its best. Or was it?

It all looked quite tempting, but the experienced agent who was dealing with Fessl had a bad feeling about the Austrian: nothing specific that he could identify, just a vague sense that this one looked almost too textbook perfect to be true. Not out of generosity, we provided Fessl a comfortable place to stay and a companion while we reassessed his statements and summoned a polygrapher. At a minimum, the Austrian had already admitted to spying for the KGB against the Berlin allies. If he was genuine, of course, this could be forgiven. But if he failed screening, he was subject to arrest for espionage. The polygraph was essential in such a case. Under no circumstances would we attempt to recruit Fessl and dispatch him to meet the KGB without first assuring ourselves that he was not a dangle, approaching us on orders from the Soviets.

Later that week, Ernst Fessl's world collapsed. When the polygrapher asked the Austrian if anyone had coached him to approach U.S. intelligence with his "I hate the Russians" story, the needle on the lie detector registered jumps that looked like an eight on the Richter scale. Shortly thereafter, the tearful, would-be double agent confessed. He had not been completely honest with us, Fessl moaned. It was true, he confided, that he had performed low-level missions for Alexei. However, the despondent Austrian added, slumping in his chair, the KGB officer had concocted the rest of the story.

At a safe house in the Karlshorst section of East Berlin, the KGB had primed Fessl for his mission. After rehearsing him in his lines, Alexei instructed the naive Austrian to contact the Americans in their Clayallee headquarters and tell them of his disenchantment with the KGB. The Soviet had exuded confidence. Once he had told his story, Alexei cooed, the Americans would take the bait and recruit him. Fessl was told to accept recruitment and report back to East Berlin.

"Pay close attention to details," Alexei had directed. "We will want to know who talked to you, what they looked like, what they said, and what instructions they gave you."

The hapless Fessl recalled bitterly that Alexei had not warned him about the polygraph, or the kinds of tough questions the Americans might ask. According to the Russian, Fessl whined, it was all supposed to have been so easy.

This was a cheap, low-risk operation for the KGB. The young bumpkin from a neutral country was expendable. If he performed well and the Americans recruited him, Alexei would have a window into the American counterintelligence unit. Through their new agent, the KGB could also manipulate us by providing bogus information to shape our perceptions and lead us down false, time-consuming investigative paths.

Late that evening, we turned over a tearful Ernst Fessl to the West Berlin police. The Austrian was convicted of violating Allied Kommandantura Law and served a short sentence in a West Berlin jail. Thanks to an alert veteran agent and a skilled polygrapher, a Soviet dangle operation had failed.

Some of the 766th's missions were mundane and unappealing to enthusiastic young agents who had signed up for counterintelligence duties with visions of stealthy investigations and exciting double agent operations. At the head of this list was the conduct of routine background investigations. The 766th had an entire section devoted to personnel security investigations (PSI), standard background checks that were carried out to either grant or renew the security clearances of American military personnel. Occasionally, a background investigation would uncover derogatory information on a soldier that might result in the suspension or revocation of a security clearance. But more often than not, these background checks—as important as they were—were dull and routine.

In one memorable background investigation in 1982, special agent Ron Sidwell encountered a not-uncommon problem. The subject of the investigation was a twenty-five-year-old sergeant assigned to Field Station Berlin. Sidwell ran the standard checks in the local command and uncovered a problem. The sergeant, one James Hall, had recently bounced a few checks—unacceptable conduct for any soldier, especially those with top-secret security clearances.

Sidwell was a promising buck sergeant who displayed the right stuff to become a fine agent. The conservative son of an equally conservative Ohio coal miner, he exhibited tenacity, on the basketball court and in the conduct of his duties. In 1984, Sidwell competed for the honor of being named the 66th Military Intelligence Group's "Soldier of the Year." He finished a close second in the grueling competition. Miffed at being beaten out, Sidwell told the group sergeant major that he would return. The following year, after working long hours in boning up for the rigorous competition, he did just that— and bagged the title. Sidwell would have made a superlative infantryman. When he set his sights on a goal, he charged.

Sidwell interviewed Sergeant Hall, a slightly rotund, cocky New Yorker, who explained that he had experienced temporary financial problems as the result of a recent marriage and the birth of a child. Hall assured his interviewer that the problem was under control, now that his parents were helping him out with expenses. It was a common difficulty. Sidwell reported that Hall had been cooperative and provided a persuasive, positive explanation, neatly tied to a solution. The sergeant with the sensitive position in the field station would be granted five additional years of top-secret access. On the surface, this was a routine, normal day's work for our background investigators. But in this case, army counterintelligence and Ron Sidwell had not heard the last of James Hall.

Another memorable and humbling experience was the case of "the dirty Kurd." Concerned that one of our most sensitive American units with a vital counterterrorism mission had been penetrated by the Soviets, we received exceptional authority to recruit a member of the unit to spy on his colleagues, virtually all of whom were non-Americans. The concept was simple. We would select a member of the targeted unit and sensitize him to the profile of a spy. Our new recruit would passively observe his office colleagues, looking for signs of undue affluence, unusual travel patterns, excessive curiosity, or other modes of behavior that might indicate hostile intelligence control. Such operations were controversial and unpopular.

Commanders of American units deeply resented the notion that MI might recruit an agent to spy on their soldiers. But in West Berlin, where spying by all sides was rampant, our higher headquarters had ruled that the recruitment of a passive source to protect this unit was a necessary evil.

By early 1983, a candidate named Ali had been selected, recruited, and trained. The new recruit happened to be an Iranian Kurd, whose selection for employment had been partially dictated by his unique language abilities. As part of the normal vetting process, Ali had passed a polygraph examination to determine if he was under the control of a hostile intelligence service.

At first, all went well. Ed Simper, Ali's case officer, met his source regularly to provide guidance and to receive any reports that might indicate a security problem in the man's unit. But in the summer of 1983, shortly after I assumed command, trouble struck.

It happened during a routine meeting. Simper departed our headquarters and traveled around the American sector to "clean" himself (slang for detecting or shaking any possible surveillance). Traveling at a discreet distance from Simper was special agent Gary Pepper, a young Floridian, in one of his first street assignments to perform countersurveillance duties. Recently graduated from counterintelligence and German language training, Pepper was to determine if Ed Simper or the Kurd were under surveillance by the opposition.

The plan called for case officer Simper to meet the Kurd on the street near the American hospital. Initially, all went well. Ed spotted the Kurd, made eye contact, and ambled in the direction of the Altenstciner Krug restaurant. Ali followed.

But as the two men walked along the tree-shaded street, trouble reared its head. Observing the pair from a discreet distance, Gary Pepper noticed something odd. A tall blond male was walking behind Simper, but the man had a newspaper open and seemed to be reading it. Pepper did a double take. No one walks on a busy sidewalk while reading a newspaper. When Ed crossed the street, so did the blond stranger. Pepper momentarily lost sight of the man but knew that Simper and his agent had entered the restaurant. The man with the newspaper was nowhere in sight.

Pepper remembered his training. Entering the restaurant, he took the only unoccupied seat at the bar. Seated directly on his right was the guy who read the newspaper while walking.

As Pepper later recounted, the man nodded a cordial greeting, then turned his attention to a napkin on the bar, on which he seemed to be doodling. Pepper surveyed the interior of the small neighborhood restaurant. Case officer Simper and his agent sat at a table in the rear of the crowded room deeply engaged in conversation.

Pepper stole a glance at his neighbor's napkin and caught his breath. Something was seriously wrong. The stranger's doodling consisted of a hasty sketch of the dining room, with small circles representing each table. On the circle representing Ed Simper's table, the man had marked an X. Clearly the operation had been compromised and the meeting was under surveillance.

Suspending disbelief, Pepper moved quickly to the men's room, which took him past his colleague's table. A danger signal had been agreed upon before the operation. If Pepper detected surveillance of the meeting, he was to approach Simper and make eye contact. As the young agent passed Simper, he stared straight into the older man's eyes. The veteran agent scowled but reacted immediately, paying the bill and departing. Agent Ali left separately, followed by the mysterious doodler. As Pepper made his way back to headquarters, he felt sick, certain that Simper would be furious at the interruption by a novice agent who was seeing things.

But this was not a case of a green agent with a vivid imagination. There was simply no innocent explanation for Pepper's insistence that the man at the bar had sketched the meeting site and highlighted case agent Simper's table. The episode in the Altensteiner Krug restaurant triggered an intense investigation to determine which intelligence agency had attached itself to the operation. Could the curious stranger have been an agent of the Soviets or the East Germans? Was Ali a double agent in the employ of Moscow or East Berlin? Or was the Kurd clean, and a hostile agent had attached himself to Simper when he departed his Clayallee office? Standard tradecraft procedures required 766th agents to "dry clean" themselves en route to meetings by following circuitous routes and employing a variety of proven countersurveillance measures. Nonetheless, a determined Soviet could have defeated Simper's efforts to shake any possible tails.

The resulting investigation culminated in a new polygraph examination of our Kurdish source; he failed miserably. Ali, who had been recruited to sniff out possible hostile agents in his unit, was himself an agent. The Kurd tearfully confessed after failing his second lic detector test, explaining that he had approached the Israeli embassy in Bonn some weeks prior to his employment in West Berlin to request assistance in obtaining West German asylum for a fellow Kurd. The opportunistic Israelis responded by offering a bargain. If Ali would provide any information he might pick up among his Middle Eastern friends that portended a threat to Israeli property or citizens, the Israelis would weigh in with the Germans on behalf of his friend.

Weeks later, Ali accepted employment with the Americans. When he informed his Israeli case officer that he was now working for the Americans and had been granted access to secret information, the Israeli declared their formal relationship at an end, explaining that his country was an ally of Washington. Tel Aviv's man added one proviso. If Ali encountered information that portended terrorist attacks against Israeli interests, he should feel free to report it. The Kurd consented and returned to his American office. The 766th had unknowingly recruited an Israeli agent.

The whole affair was not only embarrassing, but it showed a major weakness. Because Ali was asked on his preemployment polygraph examination if he was in the employ of a hostile intelligence agency, he was able to reply in the negative and fly through the examination. After all, the Israelis were not hostile to the United States. Had the Kurd originally been asked if he was in the employ of any other intelligence service (as he was after the restaurant incident), his deception would have been detected.

The case of the "dirty Kurd" caused us to rethink our security screening procedures. A time-consuming damage assessment had to be done to determine what information he might have passed to his Israeli case officer, and the hapless and repentant Ali had to be released from his position. As for the Israelis, they had fallen into the operation by chance, and with anti-Israeli terrorism in Europe rampant in the early 1980s, Tel Aviv could be excused for expressing interest in any information that might warn of a terrorist attack against their citizens. Someone at echelons above Berlin might have told the Mossad that their efforts were not appreciated, but for us the case was just another reminder that counterintelligence in West Berlin was the real thing. We had been lucky on this one, thanks to Gary Pepper's alertness.

A stark reminder of what was at stake in West Berlin occurred on March 24, 1985. In the East German town of Ludwigslust, some seventy miles northwest of Berlin, a Russian sentry shot and killed a U.S. Army intelligence officer as he attempted to photograph Soviet tanks in their sheds. The officer, thirty-seven-year-old Maj. Arthur D. "Nick" Nicholson, was assigned to the United States Military Liaison Mission (USMLM), which had its headquarters in West Berlin.

Called "the Mission" by those of us in the intelligence community, the USMLM had the charter under a 1947 agreement between the victorious Allies to travel around East Germany, ostensibly conducting "liaison" with the Soviets. Actually, like its Soviet counterpart organization in West Germany, the Mission conducted low-level, eyes-on-the-target collection against Soviet and East German armed forces. Cruising around East Germany in specially equipped, high-powered vehicles was often risky and hair-raising business for the Mission's determined tour officers and their gutsy NCO drivers. A typical tour involved carefully planned routes that would enable the observer to check on the status of key Soviet and East German military units. If a tempting collection opportunity were encountered, such as the chance to photograph or "requisition" a key piece of Soviet military equipment, so much the better. During the Cold War, the ability of the Mission's officers to prowl about East Germany had developed into an important part of NATO's early warning capability. If Soviet units were out of their garrisons and it was not the usual time for an exercise, Indications and Warning analysts in Heidelberg needed to know what they were up to. Year after year, the best answers to these questions came from the Mission.

In late December 1984, tour officer Nick Nicholson had pulled off one of the Mission's more spectacular intelligence coups, the details of which were later uncovered and printed by the *New York Times*. Taking advantage of lax security on New Year's Eve, Nicholson boldly entered an unguarded Soviet tank warehouse in Ludwigslust and clambered into a first-line T-72 tank. When the gutsy major returned to West Berlin, he brought with him a series of valuable photographs that laid bare some of the new tank's secrets.

On a quiet Sunday afternoon several months later, when Nicholson attempted to repeat the feat, Soviet security was not as lax. A sentry, apparently unseen by Nicholson's driver-lookout, burst out of a nearby tree line and killed the major.

When the news broke of the March 24 shooting, I received a phone call from my Munich headquarters, directing me to link up with Col. Roland Lajoie, Major Nicholson's commander. My mission was to conduct a debriefing of Sgt. Jesse Schatz, Nicholson's driver, who had been detained by the Soviets for several hours after the incident. "Find out what happened," Col. Bob Wheeler directed, "and get your report on the wire as soon as possible." The report was to be sent to the 66th Military Intelligence Group in Munich; to the army's European headquarters in Heidelberg; to Lt. Gen. William Odom, the army's senior intelligence officer in the Pentagon; and to the White House Situation Room.

Sergeant Schatz was a deeply shaken young man, struggling to keep from choking up as he described the tragedy. The shooting had taken place at around 3:30 Sunday afternoon, he reported. Major Nicholson had felt that security at the Ludwigslust facility would be lax. It would be a good time to check out the warehouses. The major had climbed out of their four-wheel-drive vehicle and left Schatz at the wheel as a lookout. Following standard collection procedures, Schatz opened the vehicle's sunroof and stood up to get a better view of the nearby tree line.

As Major Nicholson approached the doors of the tank warehouse, camera in hand, a Red Army sentry emerged from the trees, shouted, and opened fire—all within seconds. Schatz yelled a warning to Nicholson, then dropped down and jammed the vehicle into reverse to close the distance between the two. Nicholson sprinted a few paces toward the approaching vehicle, but the Soviet soldier's aim was good. A bullet from the AK-47 rifle entered the major's chest—a mortal wound. Schatz grabbed a first-aid kit and moved to help his fallen officer, but the excited sentry waved him off at gunpoint. Forced back into the vehicle, the frightened and distraught NCO watched helplessly as other soldiers arrived on the scene. Even though one Soviet soldier carried a first-aid kit, no one examined the stricken major until more than two hours after the shots were fired.

Schatz, Colonel Lajoie, and Nicholson's comrades in the USMLM were devastated by the tragedy, as was the entire Berlin garrison. Mission tour officers knew their area of operations well, including which Soviet installations had tight or lax security. Ludwigslust was a safe bet to be a soft target on a Sunday. To encounter a Soviet sentry there on a Sunday afternoon who had shoot-to-kill orders somehow didn't track. Either the unfortunate officer was the victim of abysmal bad luck, or someone had ordered the Soviet commander to tighten up his security.

I dispatched my report to Washington and grieved with the rest of the Berlin garrison at a memorial service for the popular officer, unaware that almost five years later my agents and I would stumble onto the missing link that explained the Nicholson tragedy.

# 5: Springing the Trap

As the summer of 1985 raced past, it appeared that the KGB had indeed given up their pursuit of Sgt. Lowry Wilcox. By late July, there was still no sign of Vasily. I bemoaned our bad luck to Thayer. We should have instructed Wilcox to dump some classified documents in the Soviet car and put the *habeas grabus* on the driver, I groused. We would not hear from Vasily again. Opportunity had beckoned, and we had blinked.

But Moscow had big plans for Lowry Wilcox. As Berlin's idyllic summer came to an end, Vasily suddenly called the noncom at his home and set up a meeting, acting as if nothing had happened. Don, the CIA base chief, and Bob Thayer had been correct. The operation was back on track. We threw ourselves into the task of steering it toward our desired endgame—a dramatic arrest of KGB operatives.

The KGB would take but one more bite at the apple. This time around, Thayer was certain that Vasily would expect Wilcox to deliver highly classified documents—material that was simply too sensitive to consider giving away, even in support of an operation such as ours.

Therein resided our dilemma. Any KGB officer with half a brain would look at the material the young sergeant was peddling and know that the man was not genuine. A real spy assigned to Field Station Berlin would be able to harvest a cornucopia of classified secrets.

We instructed our man to play up his need for cash and renew his pledge to Vasily. He would go for the big score at work and deliver it at their next meeting.

The two met in a small park in the British sector. Vasily was chummy, revealing that he had even roamed the grounds of the recent German American Volksfest in hopes of bumping into Wilcox. The KGB man complained about the sergeant's no-show earlier in the year and once again reminded him that he must deliver material of greater value. Moscow would not dispense hundred-dollar bills for low-level classified documents.

The well-coached NCO replied with an Academy Award–caliber performance. The break in the operation had given him time to think, he told Vasily, and he was now determined to go for the gold. Pleased, Vasily suggested that the two meet in early November at the Lake Terrace restaurant, a popular locale located on the lakefront in the French sector. Wilcox was to smuggle a large quantity of highly classified documents out of the field station and bring them to the meeting.

Our KGB adversaries had done their homework well. By choosing the French sector for the meeting, they greatly complicated the role of American counterintelligence, which normally avoided that part of West Berlin. The long-anticipated arrest operation would have to be coordinated with the French. Fortunately, our detachment enjoyed a close social and professional relationship with the French military counterintelligence service and public safety officials. Nine years earlier, during Operation Beau Geste, 766th agents and their French counterparts had apprehended four Soviet officers in the act of meeting an American double agent. History was repeating itself.

Nonetheless, Vasily's choice of a restaurant in our ally's territory was unwelcome news. Not that we didn't trust the French; we did— to a point. But we didn't fully trust anybody in West Berlin, a mentality that is common to counterintelligence professionals. The 766th routinely compartmented our operations from the French, Germans, British, and other American units. Even within our own detachment, only a selected few were aware of the Wilcox case. That was the nature of the business. One indiscreet word, a single leak to the Soviets or the East Germans, and our laboriously orchestrated operation would fail.

To optimize security, Bob Thayer recommended that we invite the French public safety officer, Alain Bianchi, to our unit and request his cooperation in the sting. Experience taught that Bianchi's superior, the French commandant, would probably have to consult Paris. Veteran agents recalled that Soviet officers arrested during the 1976 Beau Geste operation had immediately demanded to speak with a French officer. It was essential to have French security agents on the streets with us when Vasily was grabbed.

At this critical juncture, I departed Berlin for a long-planned vacation to Switzerland, a timely absence that would spare Bob Thayer the agony of my compulsive second-guessing as he wrestled with the details and coordination of the plan. It also provided a fortuitous opportunity for us to deceive the Soviets. Prior to departing the city for Switzerland, I called our headquarters in Munich and Heidelberg on an open phone line and announced that all was quiet in the city. My parents were in town, I explained, and I was on my way to Switzerland for a week and would return on November 7 (which was one day prior to the planned apprehension). These calls, we felt certain, would be intercepted, translated, and provided to Vasily. Hopefully, they would reassure the KGB that the 766th MI Detachment was blissfully unaware of their recruitment of Sergeant Wilcox.

During my absence, Thayer encountered yet another obstacle. Whether deliberately or by accident, Vasily had chosen a date to meet Wilcox that coincided with the visit of French president Mitterrand to West Berlin. Security measures for the president would fully engage all French security forces as well as a large part of the German police in the French sector, all of which might reduce Vasily's risks. But the really bad news was conveyed apologetically by Bianchi. The French garrison commander would not sanction an apprehension of any Soviets in his sector while President Mitterrand was in town.

The French decision posed a problem that could derail the entire plan. Our case agent would now have to instruct Sergeant Wilcox to skip the planned Wednesday night meeting and attend instead the prearranged alternate meeting two days later. (Vasily had followed standard espionage modus operandi and set up a primary and an alternate meeting time with Wilcox. The primary meeting time was Wednesday evening. If, for any reason, the sergeant was unable to make this meeting, the KGB man instructed him to show up at the same place at the same time, forty-eight hours later.)

Not that we couldn't adjust our plan—we could—but it was a second-best way to go. Wilcox had already been a no-show earlier in the year when he had failed to drop documents in the Soviet sedan. If the American agent was a no-show for the second time, would the KGB reappear two nights later or would the Moscow Center write off the operation as a bad bet? And if our man succeeded in meet-

ing Vasily at the alternate time, what convincing excuse could he offer to explain his failure to appear at the primary meeting?

While I basked in the autumn sun in Gstaad, Switzerland, Bob
crossed this and other bridges too numerous to mention in this account. To add to his already formidable challenge, Thayer labored
under continuous second-guessing from a cheeky headquarters type
in Munich—a lieutenant who suffered from delusions that he was a
qualified operations officer. Thayer overcame these and other obstacles, but the novice lieutenant's persistent coaching was distracting.

By the time I returned to Berlin, Thayer's nicotine intake had doubled, but a viable plan was in place. All necessary approvals to apprehend Vasily and his KGB colleagues had been obtained. But for
one sticky question, Operation Lake Terrace was ready to execute.

The challenge was how to defuse any blowback caused by the need
for our agent to skip the primary meeting. Vasily would certainly be
uneasy about this and predictably unhappy at having hovered
around the meeting site for an agent who failed to show. To allay the
Russian's suspicions, we needed to dream up a credible explanation
for Sergeant Wilcox's failure to show up on Wednesday evening.

Bob Thayer had a suggestion. What if our man were to suffer a
"sports accident" and appear at the alternate meeting with his ankle
in a cast? Would not Vasily's countersurveillance comrades observe
him arriving on crutches and deduce the reason for his Wednesday
no-show? Bob thought so. If Wilcox arrived on crutches, any suspicions that Vasily might harbor about the reason for his no-show at
the primary meeting time would be allayed. The bulky Wilcox with
his dark mustache looked more like a pizza chef than an olympic ath-
lete, but Thayer considered the plan a plausible gambit.

I thought it more than merely plausible; it was a stroke of genius.
Even a pizza chef could get injured at a picnic. Not only that, because
we had excellent contacts in the Berlin Army Hospital, the ruse was
easily achievable. A discreet contact with one of the doctors and
everything was arranged. The physician placed a cast on Lowry
Wilcox's left ankle and issued him a pair of crutches. Staff Sergeant
Wilcox would hobble to the meeting on crutches, pass his Soviet contact a stack of secret documents, and accept another wad of hundred-

dollar bills. As the pair consummated the deal, Thayer's men would spring the trap.

I glanced at my watch. It was almost 8:00 P.M., more than thirty minutes since Wilcox had lurched past on his way to the restaurant. Bob clutched the radio expectantly, listening for the alert signal that our agent in the restaurant would broadcast to trigger the arrest. All agents were operating on strict radio silence since deploying to the neighborhood earlier in the afternoon. The detachment's low-tech army radios were not secure, and Soviet countersurveillance measures sometimes included a search of the bands for radio chatter that might portend danger. Only when Vasily and our man had exchanged documents for money would the radios be used to coordinate the resulting dragnet.

Specially organized teams would cordon off the area, block access to the subway, and commence a 100 percent ID check of everyone within the target area. Only by these tactics could we ferret out Vasily's lookouts and apprehend them. If the exchange took place in the restaurant, the Soviet would be apprehended as soon as he stepped out the door, thereby sparing diners a disruptive scene. Should the KGB man steer our agent outdoors to conduct business, agents sitting in window seats in nearby coffeehouses would be able to observe and report on the two men's direction of movement.

Bob Thayer again peered nervously through the opening in the curtain. We'd thought of everything, it seemed, but something had obviously gone wrong. No one fitting Vasily's description (six foot three, clean shaven, and uncommonly handsome for a Russian) had passed by our vantage point, and the silence from the restaurant was ominous. Gradually, we succumbed to pessimism. The KGB men must have sniffed out something that alarmed them, despite all our efforts.

Sitting in our dismal pumping station command post, we wallowed in a sense of helplessness, frustration, and disappointment. In hushed tones, Thayer and I discussed our options, determined to wait at least one hour beyond the meeting time. If by then Vasily had not made his move, the 766th contingent would depart the area quietly in small groups, just in case the Soviets had aborted the meeting but lingered in the neighborhood to see if they could spot something that might confirm their suspicions.

We did just that. When 9:00 P.M. came and went with no signs of Vasily, we wrote off the operation. Thayer, Major Wetzel, Bianchi, and I slipped out of the water works building and headed home.

Cruising down Berlin's Avus Autobahn in the direction of the American sector, I reviewed our preparations for the evening, particularly the operational security measures built into the plan to avoid tipping off the Soviets. I couldn't think of a place where we had erred, but I knew that the odds against success of such operations in Berlin were relatively high. Had someone made a single indiscreet comment on the telephone? Was there a penetrator in the French sector, perhaps in Alain's office? Or could there be a low-level observation agent in any of the several places in the American headquarters where we had been directed to coordinate the operation? Or the unthinkable: Did we have a mole in the 766th MI Detachment itself?

Bob Thayer also drove home in a deep funk, cursing our bad luck and dreading the thought of facing the second-guessers in our Munich headquarters.

But the evening was young. As Thayer and I licked our wounds, stunning events were occurring on the ground. Their operations officer and commander may have written off the operation, but the agents of the 766th MI Detachment did not give up so easily. The Soviet KGB was indeed in the area.

Apparently Vasily had shown up for the meeting but taken a route to the restaurant that did not pass by our pumping station command post. Then the cautious Soviet officer decided not to enter the restaurant. This was not uncommon for the KGB. A case officer would often tell his agent to meet him at a specific location, with no intention of actually meeting there. Instead, the KGB man would intercept the agent as he approached the planned meeting site and spirit him to some other location. Business would be transacted as quickly as possible. The KGB knew that the time of greatest risk was when agent and case officer were face-to-face.

Vasily sat patiently and unnoticed on an outdoor park bench that offered a view of the restaurant's exit. Our restaurant lookout never spotted the Russian. From his vantage point, as from ours in the water works, Vasily was a no-show. Eventually, some time after Bob Thayer and I departed the neighborhood, Wilcox tired of waiting and began to lumber on his crutches in the direction of the nearby parking lot. As the sergeant approached his car, Vasily overtook him. The KGB officer had decided to conduct a hasty exchange of documents and money right there in the parking lot.

This situation had all the makings of a disaster. Vasily was about to exchange envelopes with Wilcox and slip out of the area unmolested. If the Soviet KGB were to obtain the documents carried by the sergeant, we were all in trouble, for the secrets Wilcox carried that night were genuine and sensitive. We had been given permission to use the documents only as props in an apprehension situation, with the clear understanding that they would be recovered within seconds of being passed to the KGB. Headquarters had been adamant. The Soviets could not be permitted to leave the scene with these documents.

Thayer had arranged to use genuine classified documents because there was a slight chance that the operation might bag a Soviet who did not have diplomatic immunity. In such a case, the spy could be tried in a Berlin court for espionage. To ensure successful prosecution, attorneys advised, it was important that the secrets purchased by the Soviet agent be genuine and damaging.

Enter Lady Luck, in the form of special agent Jodene Thayer (Bob's wife) and her partner, Rick Shelton. By sheer happenstance, the two agents were moving from their posts along the waterfront promenade and approaching the parking lot. Special agent Thayer looked up and spotted something strange. Standing in the unlighted parking lot engaged in conversation were two men—a tall stranger and a shorter man on crutches.

Thayer did a double take. "Rick," she exclaimed, "look at that. It's our man, and that must be Vasily. The thing's going down right in front of us." The two agents broke into a sprint, heading straight for the parking lot, while Shelton broadcast the alert on his radio. In seconds, the pair confronted Wilcox and the startled Russian, who had just passed an envelope of cash to the American. Vasily turned and made a move to escape.

"Stop," Thayer called out. "You're our prisoner." Rick Shelton moved around the Russian to block his departure. Vasily shoved the stocky agent and snarled, "Get out of my way." Jodene Thayer, a diminutive five-footer, grabbed the huge Russian by the right wrist and commanded, "You stop that. You're under apprehension." The surly KGB officer growled, then attempted to discreetly drop the envelope containing the incriminating documents into the dirt. Thayer observed his ploy.

"That won't work," she barked. Then, with her hand still clamped on the Russian's wrist, Thayer bent down to retrieve the envelope, forcing the tall Russian to bend at the waist. It was, her partner later related, a ludicrous sight. The ninety-eight-pound Thayer maintained her death grip on the strapping Russian's wrist, refusing to let him go until reinforcements arrived. Vasily, nonplussed by this humiliating development, made no further effort to flee.

As this memorable scene unfolded, detachment personnel reacted to the radio alert, regrouped, and executed their assigned tasks. Within minutes they had cordoned off the area, blocked access to the subway station, and established checkpoints. This done, French and American counterspies began to screen the identity documents of several hundred people caught in their net. A curious German police officer happened on the scene and offered his assistance.

Within an hour, the search teams had netted two more Soviet officers. The first was spotted hurrying out of the area in the direction of the subway. At the command, *"Ausweiss Bitte,"* he produced a document asserting that he was a "second secretary" in the embassy of the USSR in East Berlin. The Russian submitted without bluster and was politely detained. Certain that there had to be at least one other KGB man, agents searched the neighborhood methodically.

Special agent Garland Marks, a college-educated North Carolinian, noticed a stocky male sitting quietly on a park bench. The man was calmly reading a German newspaper. To Marks, there was something incongruous about his calm disinterest in all the excitement. When Marks politely requested the bystander's identity documents, the "German" smirked and produced Soviet diplomatic papers. Agents now had bagged three Russians. Members of the search team located a Russian-built Lada sedan parked nearby and obtained the keys from one of Vasily's comrades. Then, triumphant, the group placed their prisoners in separate vehicles and convoyed to the American sector, with an American agent behind the wheel of the tinny Russian car.

My home phone rang at almost 11:00 P.M. It was Bob Thayer. "Sir, you're not going to believe it," he crowed. "They got Vasily and at least one other. It went down after we left, and they're on their way to the Clay compound."

At the Clayallee headquarters, the count was up to three Russians in custody and one Lada sedan captured in action. The three sullen Russians were escorted into separate rooms and left to contemplate their situation. Triumphant agents described the events by the lakeside. The documents were safe—that was welcome news—and the envelope that Vasily had passed to Sergeant Wilcox contained a mere two hundred dollars. Later, in the Russian's wallet, we discovered three hundred dollars in additional U.S. currency, all in the KGB's preferred form of payment—hundred-dollar bills. Vasily appeared to be playing an old trick. Having given two hundred dollars to Wilcox, he could report to his superiors that he had paid the agent five hundred dollars, and pocket the difference.

The KGB man's diplomatic documents identified him as Valery Mikhailovich Kiryukhin, a forty-four-year-old officer who held the rank of second secretary in the USSR embassy in East Berlin. One of Kiryukhin's lookouts was identified as Anatoly Viktorovich Agafonov, thirty-six. Agafonov's documents proclaimed him to be an attaché in the East Berlin embassy. The third KGB prisoner produced documents advertising himself as Vyacheslav Londovich Latyshev, a forty-seven-year-old officer also assigned as a second secretary in Moscow's East Berlin embassy.

In the trunk of the Lada sedan, searchers discovered several bags of new clothing and other items purchased earlier that day at West Berlin's Kaufhof department store. The KGB men had taken advantage of their travel privileges to buy western goods for their wives. Subway tickets made it clear that two of the men had crossed into West Berlin on the S-Bahn, while the third had driven the Lada through a checkpoint and linked up with his comrades. The times recorded on the subway tickets and store receipts told us that the KGB men had probably visited the lakeside meeting site by midafternoon to check it out.

Vasily was surly and carefully programmed, demanding to see an officer of the USSR embassy and loudly protesting "this illegal and improper interference with his right as a Soviet citizen to freedom of movement in all of Berlin." This was all in Russian, not the fluent English he had displayed to Staff Sergeant Wilcox.

Long-established procedures existed for orchestrating such detentions. A foreign–service officer of the U.S. Mission would call the Soviet embassy in East Berlin and inform his Russian counterpart that we had three of their officers in custody who had engaged in misconduct. Would the Russians please send someone to pick up the truant officers?

As a State Department officer made the required call, we conducted some final business.

The detachment photographer took a picture of all three detainees for posterity—over their protests. Then the three KGB officers were each privately interviewed. After being reminded that the evening's events did not bode well for their career advancement, all were offered the chance to throw in their lot with the West.

Moscow's men had three options: Accept the offer and defect on the spot, accept the offer but return to East Berlin and work clandestinely for the U.S. government, or decline.

Had Kiryukhin, Agafonov, and Latyshev known what was going to happen to Soviet communism and the KGB within five years, they might have responded differently. However, no one, least of all this trio, could have foreseen the total collapse of the Soviet Union and the disgrace of the KGB.

All three Russians declined the offer to defect. One agonized over the decision. Under different circumstances, he explained, he would like to live in America and take his children to Disney World, but he couldn't bear to leave his family. Vasily was arrogant and blunt. "Get fucked," he told his interrogator in well-enunciated English.

More than an hour after notification, a grim-faced Soviet consular officer arrived to accept release of the erstwhile spies. Kiryukhin managed a touch of bravado as he strolled to the Lada, grinning and calling back to our small group, "Bye, guys."

That was Operation Lake Terrace. Six months of tough, satisfying work had yielded six hours of drama, excitement, and a small victory over the opposition that would barely merit a footnote in the history of the Cold War. Our proud agents would be deeply disappointed by the press guidance from the U.S. embassy in Bonn, which instructed the Berlin Command to play down our victory over the Soviet KGB. President Reagan was soon to have a summit conference with Mikhail Gorbachev, and the Department of State deemed it unseemly for us to gloat over the Russians' embarrassment at such a time. The following day, a cryptic story appeared in *The Stars and Stripes*, briefly relating that several Soviets had been detained as they attempted to meet a soldier assigned to Field Station Berlin. That was it.

Ultimately, SSgt. Lowry Wilcox and the agents involved in the operation received medals for their efforts. Each citation was carefully written to avoid the usual enigmatic prose that told the reader nothing about what had actually happened. Veterans of Operation Lake Terrace each have a citation lauding them for personally participating in the apprehension of three Soviet KGB agents on the streets of West Berlin—something that their parents, spouses, children, and grandchildren can read years later and understand what their loved ones had actually done.

Records checks revealed KGB agent Valery Kiryukhin (Vasily) to be an officer who had served in the KGB's First Chief Directorate. This was the elite of the KGB, manned by talented, language-trained recruiters who served in Soviet embassies throughout the world. Kiryukhin, we determined, had once served a tour in the Soviet Mission to the United Nations in New York City, which accounted for his mastery of colloquial English. The intelligence windfall that a recruitment of Sergeant Wilcox would yield had prompted the Soviets to bring in a high-powered English speaker to run the operation. Normally, our KGB adversaries in West Berlin were from the KGB's Third Chief Directorate, men whose mission was to protect Soviet forces in East Berlin and East Germany from American intelligence collection efforts. Third Chief Directorate agents were generally less sophisticated and experienced in dealing with Americans than their colleagues in the First Directorate.

Later that month, Alain Bianchi and the team of French agents who had joined us on the streets arrived at the headquarters of the 766th MI Detachment. With some ceremony, I produced a wood box containing a two-liter bottle of fine French Armagnac. Presented to our unit in 1976 by the French after the Operation Beau Geste arrests, the bottle came with a set of instructions affixed to its box. Written by the colonel who had commanded the 766th at that time, the letter charged future American commanders to preserve it until the next successful U.S.-French operation against the Soviets. At that time, the author directed, "Open the bottle, consume it in good fellowship with our French comrades, and notify the undersigned that 'the bottle is empty.' This will tell me that we got the bastards one more time." Ever mindful of the importance of tradition, we accomplished that final mission, pronouncing toast after toast to French American amity, to Sergeant Wilcox, and to the street agents who had saved the day by their alertness.

Glowing with a sense of accomplishment and victory on that cheerful day in November 1985, none of us would have been so upbeat had we known that in foiling one attempt to penetrate the secrets of the field station, we had missed another. It would be three years before we would realize this, when a case erupted whose significance would dwarf Operation Lake Terrace.

# 6: Berlin's Own Meister

Love, greed, jealousy, and sex played roles in many of our cases. But in no case were all of these ingredients more present than the case of Huseyin Yildirim, "the Meister." And in no case were the consequences so protracted and damaging.

The case commenced in 1982 with an ominous tip from the West Berlin Staatschutz, or security police. A jailed former American soldier named Jackson was leveling serious charges against two other persons. An agent from the 766th Military Intelligence Detachment responded and interviewed the man in jail. Jackson, an African American in his late twenties, was serving time for burglary. Invoking patriotism as his motive, he told our agent a sinister story.

A woman named Ella Pettway, Jackson related, had betrayed some of the secrets of Field Station Berlin to the East Germans. Pettway, he elaborated, was his ex-girlfriend and a former field station soldier who had separated from the army and remained in Berlin. According to Jackson, Ella Pettway had been taken across the Berlin Wall to meet the East Germans by a Turk who worked as a mechanic-instructor in the American command's auto craft shop. The mechanic, Jackson declared, was actually a communist agent on the payroll of the East German State Security Service. The Turk had delivered Pettway to the East Germans for an interrogation about her sensitive duties in the field station. Pettway, Jackson insisted, had been kicked out of the army and was shacked up with the Turk. Jackson knew the Turk only by his nickname, "the Meister." The Meister, he alleged, would do anything for money.

If true, Jackson's allegations were grave, further evidence of the unabating attack of the opposition against the secrets of the mountaintop field station, the same unit to which Sergeant Wilcox was assigned.

Despite Jackson's patriotic protestations, agents had to question his motives for denouncing Ella Pettway and the Turk to army counterintelligence investigators. In a convoluted series of events, Jack-

son, Pettway, the Turk, and several other characters had been involved in a series of shenanigans, including smuggling and black
marketing of artifacts and gems from Africa, and an underground
pipeline of pornography to Turkey. Apart from that, the Turk appeared to have stolen Jackson's girlfriend.

Investigators quickly divined that the Meister was one Huseyin
Yildirim, the popular head instructor at the army's auto craft shop,
where members of the military could service their own cars with the
advantage of army-provided tools and expert advice. The craft shop
was situated on Andrews Barracks, where soldiers assigned to Field
Station Berlin were billeted. It was an ideal location for the East Germans to place an agent.

Yildirim, a preliminary investigation revealed, was a hardworking,
cheerful fellow who was known for his uncanny mechanical abilities
and who displayed a penchant for off-duty wheeling and dealing. He
had been working at the craft shop since 1979.

The agents who conducted the investigation discovered that although Yildirim was married to a Turkish woman, he had indeed carried on an extramarital affair with Ella Pettway. In fact, investigators
confirmed, Pettway had been living with the jailed Jackson until they
had a falling out, at least partially due to a budding relationship between her and Yildirim. Inquiries revealed that Ella Pettway had been
assigned to the field station. As a single parent with a wild teenaged
daughter and a prodigious alcohol problem, Ella had been mustered
out of the army for unsuitability before taking up with Yildirim. After breaking up with Jackson, Pettway accused him of stealing her
stereo, which was how the man came to be in a German jail. To the
investigating agents, these circumstances cast doubt on Jackson's
credibility.

As an American civilian living overseas, Ella was technically not
within the jurisdiction of army counterintelligence to investigate,
even though she was a recent veteran. Yildirim, however, worked for
the U.S. command and was fair game. Agents summoned the fifty-
two-year-old Turk for an interview.

The Meister showed up eager to cooperate. His debriefers got to
the point. Did Yildirim know Ella Pettway? Had he taken her to East
Berlin, and what did he have to say about Jackson's allegations? The

affable Turk reacted with what appeared to be genuine outrage and hurt at the idea that he would commit such a disloyal act. He loved America, the Turk declared. He would never betray her.

Yildirim openly discussed his relationship with Ella, admitting with a roguish grin that he was married but that the Pettway affair was just that—an affair. He passionately denied ever having taken Ella, or anyone else, to meet anyone in East Germany. The Turk insisted that he was a fervent anticommunist. Jackson, he accused, was slandering him out of jealousy. The man was no more than a common thief who wanted to get even with Ella for having him thrown in jail. Hand clutched over his heart, in a voice quaking with emotion, Yildirim repeated his vow that he loved America and could never do such a thing. He reminded the agents that he been working for the American command since 1979, and his record was excellent. Without hesitation, he agreed to submit to a polygraph examination to prove his truthfulness.

With the exception of several ill-fated smuggling ventures, Yildirim's record was clean. Still, these were petty offenses, and such peccadilloes were not uncommon among Berlin's large Turkish community. Petty smuggling was one thing; espionage was something quite different.

With Jackson's motives thus impugned and Yildirim falling all over himself to cooperate in a polygraph exam, the case was quietly closed by Bob Thayer's predecessor. Yildirim was not polygraphed, and agents never spoke with his alleged coconspirator, Pettway. Had they, agents reasoned, Ella would have certainly denied Jackson's allegations, and then what? The case looked like a dog, in the vernacular of the detachment's Munich headquarters, and it was closed. We would have cause to explain this decision in the future.

Months later, I undertook the restoration of a Volkswagen in the auto craft shop in my spare time. As I wrestled with a particularly stubborn bolt, one of the shop's instructors intervened. "Watch me," he counseled, then sharply rapped the top of the bolt with a hammer. "Now you try again; it be okay," he said with a grin. I applied the wrench and twisted; the bolt turned. "You see," he said, laughing, "very easy; just must think." I thanked the fellow, who I learned from the sergeant in the next bay was the Meister, a craft shop institution who could accomplish anything with tools.

For the next three months, with the Meister's help, I completed a total restoration of the car, working four and five nights a week. If there was a problem, the cheerful Meister was always available to assist. He was a colorful fellow with a genuine talent for anything mechanical. At one point, he proudly showed me his scrapbook, which contained an article about him that had appeared in the *Berlin Observer,* the command newspaper. "Berlin's own Meister," the article touted, had once been an artillery officer in the Turkish army. Well liked by all, Huseyin Yildirim was a registered auto mechanic with a Meister's certification, trained by the Mercedes-Benz firm. Also included in the scrapbook were a number of letters from officers and NCOs of the command, testifying about the Meister's good deeds to all. "Maybe some day you write one for me?" the Turk suggested with his winning grin.

On another occasion, the Meister approached me in an ebullient mood. "I got great chance to make money, much money," he announced. "You look." Unfolding a thick towel, the Turk displayed a pair of primitive iron heads that had the look of African artifacts. "Very valuable, from museum, worth lots of money," he assured me, as if extending an oblique invitation for me to either buy them or assist in their disposal.

"Meister, where did you get these things?" I asked.

The Turk flashed a mischievous grin, signaling that I didn't want to hear the answer.

"Meister, I don't ever want to see these things again. You're going to get yourself in trouble," I admonished. Undaunted, the Turk rolled up the ugly items and stashed them in the trunk of his rusting Mercedes.

At work that week, I mentioned the Meister to several of the agents. One told me, "Hey, sir, you know we once had a case on him, don't you?" Surprised, I raised an eyebrow and shook my head. Later, I called for the case file and scanned it, nodding knowingly at the accounts of the Meister's wheeling and dealing. Noting only that the case was closed after Jackson's allegations were discredited, I sent the dossier back to the repository and thought no more about it.

Each time I visited the auto craft shop, the Meister was attentive and eager to assist. From the other mechanics, I learned that some hard feelings existed over the Turk's self-promoting ways, in particular his habit of soliciting letters of praise from officers whom he had assisted. So, when the Meister revived his request for a testimonial letter, I wrote instead a letter to the craft shop's supervisor naming not only Yildirim but also his coworkers who had assisted me. The Meister was disappointed, but I told him that the letter was fair and that it did not put him in a compromising position with his fellow workers.

Later that week, the doorbell rang at my home. It was the Meister, dropping by to present me with a small block of lucite in which a single dollar bill was encased. A little gift, he said with a grin. "Just want say, thank you."

Several months passed before I again encountered the Meister. The little man bounced up to me with good news, his ill-fitting toupee askew. He had a girlfriend, a "very rich lady from Florida," and had recently traveled to Clearwater to meet her. The Meister had always proclaimed that his life's dream was to go to America. I could see what was going through his mind and told him so.

The Turk grinned. "No, she love me too much. Maybe I go Florida for good." The Meister flashed his characteristic grin.

"If you do," I replied, "with your skills, you can get rich fixing Mercedes cars over there."

"She verrrry rich," he intoned. "Her husband die."

I knew what this one was all about. The Meister's new girlfriend most certainly looked good on her blue American passport. The incorrigible Turk's dream—a ticket to America.

Several weeks later, I again encountered the Meister working in the craft shop on a small car with a German license plate. This was odd because only GIs' cars were supposed to be worked on in the facility. A dumpy woman who appeared to be in her sixties hovered near the car. The Meister looked up and waved, beckoning me to come over.

"This Peggy, my friend," he explained cheerfully. "She live near Clearwater, in Florida." I greeted the woman politely, marveling to myself at the sacrifices the Meister was willing to make for a ticket to the United States. The matronly Peggy Bie, widow of a retired U.S. Air Force officer, seemed to be somewhat befuddled but cordial enough. She was apparently studying music in Berlin. The Meister had indeed found a live one.

Some weeks later, as the holidays approached, our doorbell rang. It was almost nine o'clock in the evening, and we were not expecting guests. While my wife escaped to put on a robe, I opened the door. It was the Meister, Peggy, and a nice-looking young man in his twenties. Peggy's son was in town, and the couple had just dropped by to introduce him. I invited them in, somewhat taken aback by their late appearance at the door but determined to be cordial. Within a few minutes, my wife joined us. Peggy's son was impressive, a graduate of Yale University. I offered refreshments, we made small talk, and the Meister presented us with a small gift, nicely wrapped, "for holiday." Peggy waxed enthusiastically about a planned trip to Florida, and I repeated to her the advice I had given the Meister— that a man of his talent could make a fortune in the Sunshine State by opening his own Mercedes repair business.

Clearly mesmerized by the Turk, Peggy Bie nestled up to him on the couch, casting occasional admiring glances in his direction, which the Meister sheepishly returned. It was difficult to keep a straight face, the way the Turk was playing the gullible woman and grinning at me, telegraphing the message that this was his trophy. As for their untimely visit, this was the second time the Meister had popped in uninvited. He's a Turk, I explained to my wife later, and hasn't mastered our social graces.

That was the last time I saw Yildirim in Berlin. Within a month or two, in my visit to the craft shop, the mechanics told me that the Meister had resigned, abandoned his Turkish family, and gone to Florida with Peggy. I chuckled at the thought of the crafty Turk with a Florida tan, charming Florida's Mercedes-driving senior citizens and raking in piles of cash. I did not expect to see him again.

# Part II
## The Clyde Conrad Investigation

# 7: FCA

By the summer of 1986, I had spent eight years in Germany, five of them in the shadow of the Berlin Wall. The expectations of excitement and intrigue at the helm of army counterintelligence that had lured me back to the famous city had been generously fulfilled. In the wake of Operation Lake Terrace and other operational achievements, the 766th Military Intelligence Detachment was widely regarded as the best counterintelligence outfit in Europe. Don, our loyal CIA base chief, took the unusual step of recommending to the army that the unit be cited for its unprecedented string of successes. Among the many American and allied intelligence agencies in the city, the detachment was regarded as a competent, reliable team player, a notable achievement in a profession where parochial turf wars are not unknown. We were proud that our unit had juggled many sensitive balls since 1983 without dropping any, at least that we knew of at the time.

Operation Lake Terrace had taught us that there was no substitute for smart, well-trained agents when locking horns with the KGB. The after action assessment of the operation told the tale. The KGB agent Vasily and his two comrades were lieutenant colonels in their midforties who had worked the streets for an average of more than fifteen years. The special agents who bested them were kids by comparison. Many were in their early twenties, fresh from training and serving in their first operational assignments. True, they had one of the best mentors in the business in Bob Thayer, but Bob himself was but thirty-eight at the time.

Yet that's the way it was for the duration of the Cold War. Our Soviet adversary routinely overmatched us in resources—human and material. A host of seasoned KGB and GRU field-grade officers operated against our small band of youthful special agents, many of whom wore the three stripes of a buck sergeant on those rare occasions when they donned their uniforms. These were unfavorable odds for a small band of spy catchers responsible for the defense of a critical, heavily targeted bastion such as West Berlin. It was an imbalance that led to serious consequences for national security—consequences that would surface in a pair of stunning cases recounted later in this book.

Washington bestowed the Department of the Army's Superior Unit Award on the detachment, the first military intelligence unit to be so honored. In July 1986, I departed West Berlin with the satisfaction that comes from having been the captain of a winning team and a conviction that I had found my calling in the counterintelligence field.

Command of another counterintelligence unit beckoned. To lock in the assignment, I declined consideration for battalion-level command, a critical career milestone all but essential to ensure promotion to full colonel. Conventional wisdom held this decision to be career suicide. But as one of the few intelligence officers of my rank to cling to a field that was widely regarded as a career dead end, I had set the stage for almost ten years in command of counterintelligence units at what turned out to be the vortex of the most exciting and explosive counterespionage operations of the Cold War.

## Fort Meade, Maryland: July 1986

Compared to stalking the KGB on the darkened streets of Berlin, counterintelligence duty at Fort Meade was tame. I served in the famed 902d Military Intelligence Group (the Deuce), which had a proud tradition of its own. My new command was one of the 902d's subordinate units, the Operations Security Support Detachment, known simply as OSD. Commanding this little-known but highly specialized unit demanded an entirely different mind-set and array of skills than did Berlin's vaunted 766th MID.

The OSD mission was relatively mundane. During the Cold War, the army research and development community had spawned a host of special access programs. Called SAPS, or black programs, these were typically sophisticated weapons development projects on the cutting edge of technology. Black programs were funded with monies that were not a part of the unclassified ("white") defense budget and were generally regarded as the army's most sensitive projects. Knowledge of them was tightly limited.

Counterintelligence (CI) agents in OSD ensured that each program manager in the so-called "black world" established and followed stringent security requirements. In Berlin, CI agents were spy catchers; in the 902d, the sixty members of OSD were known as Opsecers, an acronym fashioned from operations security.

Their job was often frustrating. As the army's security watchdogs, OSD agents had to goad their industry and government clients into elaborate security measures that were costly in both time and money—unwelcome in a highly competitive research and development world where the most visible litmus test of a program's success was staying on schedule and within budget.

To further complicate matters, our mission, called Opsec Support, was widely denigrated by the mainstream counterintelligence community, to whom counterespionage (spy catching) was the only real CI work. Still worse, although one might think that the enemy would have been the Soviets and other foreign intelligence services, it soon became apparent that the greatest threat to the secrets of the black world was not agents of the nefarious KGB but the enterprising American media. During the eighteen months I commanded OSD, we had more than a few bad days because some aggressive investigative reporter at the *New York Times* or the *Philadelphia Inquirer* had stumbled onto one of our programs and exposed it in print.

The media regarded the Pentagon's secret programs as fair game in their righteous quest to expose fraud, waste, and abuse. But to the Cold Warriors of OSD, a reporter who blew a sensitive program in the Sunday edition was an unpatriotic nuisance who thought nothing of serving up his nation's secrets to the Soviets—all for a byline.

Because of the sensitivity of black programs, we were directly responsible to the vice chief of staff of the army. If one of our sensitive programs (I was "read on"—granted access—to thirty-five) made it into print, we would have to respond to a four-star general. At the time, the "vice" was the brilliant, ascerbic, and feared Maxwell Thurman, unaffectionately nicknamed Mad Max. An Orville Redenbacher look-alike, General Thurman was probably the smartest officer of any rank on active duty in the army. He was also a fire-breathing workaholic, legendary for his demanding nature and intolerance of mistakes. As a result, life as commander of the Opsec

Support Detachment could be characterized much as one pundit once described life in combat—long periods of boredom punctuated by brief moments of stark terror (usually when something went wrong that could not be kept from General Thurman). Still, as in Berlin, the detachment was blessed with a stable of quality agents, military and civilian. I survived initial entry shock and settled into a professionally satisfying eighteen-month command tour.

Although a sojourn into the world of black programs was a broadening experience, it lacked the intrigue and magnetism of spy catching. In counterespionage, the thrill of the hunt dominated. Success could be easily measured by the unit's box score against the opposition. The hardworking agents in the Opsec Support Detachment were engaged in a mission that was the equivalent of preventive medicine. If they were successful in pushing their prescription of enhanced security defenses, it would be far more difficult for our adversaries to place a human agent into one of the army's black programs.

It was a vital mission, but I had been spoiled by duty in West Berlin. Outwitting Vasily and his comrades was far more exciting than serving as the black world's security watchdog. Spy catching was the surgery of counterintelligence. When preventive medicine failed, the foreign agents who infected our units had to be identified and removed like the tumors they were. A single disloyal soldier with access to sensitive secrets could cost our government billions of dollars in damages and raise the cost of victory in the event of a conflict. Recalling Operation Lake Terrace, it was not lost on any of us what the consequences would have been had not Sergeant Wilcox reported the KGB's approach. The sergeant's unit, Field Station Berlin, represented an investment of hundreds of millions of dollars in state-of-the-art technology. Soviet penetration of its secrets would have been a disaster for national security.

In August 1987, I was selected for promotion to colonel in spite of my narrow specialization in counterintelligence. The impending promotion required that I relinquish command of the Opsec Support Detachment and find a job that required a full colonel. The question was, where? Most positions for a bird colonel in my field were staff billets at major headquarters, duty for which I lacked the patience. With silver eagles on my shoulders, there was only one truly operational job—commander of the army's elite Foreign Counterintelligence Activity, known in the business as FCA.

Headquartered conveniently on Fort Meade, FCA was a secretive outfit whose members cultivated and relished the unit's elite image. Established in the early 1970s as the Special Operations Detachment (SOD), the unit was renowned for its counterespionage successes and known as a protective organization that almost never admitted outsiders into its ranks. What little I knew about FCA came to me via Bob Thayer, who had been an FCA investigator prior to his tour in Berlin. The unit's commander, Col. Bob Lunt, was a respected veteran with almost thirty years of experience in human intelligence and counterintelligence. Lunt, it was rumored, was contemplating retirement.

The FCA operations officer was a controversial, entrenched lieutenant colonel named Noel Jones. Jones had served an unheard-of fourteen consecutive years in the organization, acquiring along the way a reputation for brilliance and heavy handed leadership. Obsessed with compartmentation and elitism, Jones tolerated no one who was not absolutely loyal to him. He was wily, aggressive, and endowed with formidable operational instincts; even the man's numerous detractors admitted that his talent and hard work had played a major role in making the Foreign Counterintelligence Activity the best unit of its kind in the Department of Defense.

But Jones had been permitted to homestead in his powerful position too long. Never a team player, he had come to consider himself as omniscient and infallible, a mind-set reinforced by the hardcore group of sycophantic supporters with whom he surrounded himself. Worse, he trusted no one, saw hostile intelligence penetrations everywhere, and had come to regard his own higher headquarters, his sister units, and other civilian intelligence agencies with arrogance, distrust, and disdain. It was not an uncommon profile; the CIA had endured the same problem during the long reign of its brilliant but paranoid counterintelligence czar James Jesus Angleton.

The civilian deputy commander of FCA in late 1987 was a hulking six-foot-four-inch, 250-pound Pennsylvania Dutchman from Harrisburg, Bob Bell. Like me, Bell was a member of the "Berlin Mafia," those of us who had cut our teeth in the Divided City in the 1960s and returned there for repeated tours of duty. The outspoken Bell had departed Berlin a year sooner than I and been assigned directly to FCA, where he had promptly locked horns with its imperious operations officer. As I discreetly sniffed out the chances of landing the FCA position, Bob offered little encouragement. Noel Jones, he advised, would oppose any candidate for the plum job who was an outsider. With fourteen years in place, Bob warned, the cagey operations officer had cemented powerful contacts in high places and accumulated markers that he could redeem if threatened. Jones was a survivor, a powerful force deemed by most observers to be all but untouchable. Everyone knew that the hard-nosed officer had more than once defeated those who had tried over the years to dislodge him from his throne at FCA. Under these circumstances, I harbored no illusions that I might be selected to replace Bob Lunt, whose retirement was imminent.

But there were other powerful forces at work. The Intelligence and Security Command's commanding general, Maj. Gen. Ed Soyster, and his deputy, Brig. Gen. Chuck Owens, had become disenchanted with the growing arrogance and elitism that had overtaken FCA. Operationally, the unit was the army's counterintelligence flagship. The generals were determined to turn it around.

Within a month, General Owens took me aside at a change-of-command ceremony with good news. General Soyster had named me as the new commander of FCA. I was to report to the unit in January (1988).

By selecting me for the coveted command, the generals were sending a signal. Outsiders are usually brought in to clean house. Rumors proliferated that I was under orders to solve the problem of the homesteading operations officer. They were accurate. As one with a reputation for collegiality, I had my orders: "Bring FCA back into the army" while not hurting operations.

The commander of the Foreign Counterintelligence Activity controlled counterintelligence operations and investigations throughout the world, with operational teams deployed around the world.

Counterespionage cases handled by the unit were the most sensitive in the army. At any one time, there might be several hundred army investigations under way in the world. Only a handful—those with the greatest sensitivity—were conducted by the Foreign Counterintelligence Activity.

A comprehensive account of FCA successes would be a highly classified book in itself, even today, long after the denouement of the Cold War. In its brief history, the secretive unit had a record of achievements against foreign intelligence services that is unequalled in the annals of military intelligence history.

Most of the exploits of the Foreign Counterintelligence Activity occurred in the quiet shadows of the Cold War. An exception was a case known as Landlord Paper, which made a rare media splash. The drama occurred in 1982, when FCA agents and their FBI partners orchestrated the arrest in Augusta, Georgia, of Otto Attila Gilbert, an agent of the Hungarian Military Intelligence Service. Gilbert, a courier for the Hungarians, was caught in the act of purchasing military secrets from a U.S. Army warrant officer whom Budapest believed to be a traitor. Actually, the man was a double agent recruited years earlier by FCA. Newspaper coverage of the arrest depicted it as another example of the vigilant FBI at work, which it was—to an extent. Behind the headlines, however, was the signature of the Foreign Counterintelligence Activity, which had set the stage for the arrest.

The case began in the mid-1970s when army chief warrant officer Janos Smolka, a Hungarian American stationed in Germany, traveled to Budapest to visit his mother. During the visit, the Hungarian Military Intelligence Service approached Smolka with a tempting offer. If he would agree to provide U.S. and NATO secrets, the Budapest government would pay good money and ensure VIP treatment for his aging mother. The approach was consistent with the modus operandi of the Hungarians, who were known in American counterintelligence circles to favor recruitment of their own nationals.

The conscientious Smolka was a military police investigator. He promptly reported the incident to his local army counterintelligence field office. Army regulations made it mandatory to report any contact with a national of a communist bloc country, even if no approach to commit espionage was tendered. In this case, there was no ambiguity. Smolka had been "cold-pitched."

Budapest's blatant approach posed an operational opportunity. Foreign Counterintelligence Activity agents assessed Smolka and liked what they saw. From that point on, after careful vetting, Janos Smolka served as a double agent, accepting recruitment and providing classified information in exchange for money, all under the watchful tutelage of seasoned FCA case officers. By the early 1980s, his case officer was special agent Norman Runk.

Himself a chief warrant officer, Runk was one of FCA's shrewdest operators. With his family roots in Germany, Runk was born in Baltimore in early 1945. The son of a skilled die-setter, Runk graduated from high school and joined the army, just in time for Lyndon Johnson's buildup of American forces in Vietnam.

By the time he met Smolka in 1980, Runk was a veteran of fifteen years' service—fifteen years into which he had crammed a lifetime of adventure. By his thirtieth birthday, the street-smart agent had risen through the ranks and been appointed a warrant officer. He had conducted investigations in the United States, spooked around Thailand for more than a year, recruited spies in Germany, and tutored double agents on four continents. Along the way, Runk also served a wartime tour in Vietnam with the 5th Special Forces Group, during which he ran agents into Cambodia to surveil the Ho Chi Minh trail.

Foreign Counterintelligence Activity case officers ran Smolka much like the 766th ran SSgt. Lowry Wilcox in West Berlin during Operation Lake Terrace. While assigned in Europe, Smolka delivered sixteen rolls of film to the Hungarians, for which he received $3,000. Then Budapest offered him $100,000 to provide cryptographic materials and classified information on certain weapons systems. Smolka played along.

By 1981, Smolka was stationed at the army's Criminal Investigation Laboratory on Fort Gordon, in Georgia. There he continued to communicate with his Hungarian spymasters by mailing coded postcards to cutout addresses in Austria. The orchestrated treason continued, although the case was now run jointly by Norman Runk and an FBI opposite number. In April 1982, Runk and the FBI decided to use Smolka to lure a Hungarian courier to the United States. To do this, Smolka would have to persuade his Hungarian handlers that he had obtained a load of secrets but could not get away from his new job to travel to Hungary.

Budapest took the bait and dispatched a courier. The meeting spot would be at the base of the Confederate War Memorial in downtown Augusta, Georgia. The unfortunate courier was Otto Gilbert. Gilbert, a native Hungarian, was a naturalized U.S. citizen who normally drove a cab in New York City.

Runk's instincts told him that the impending visit of a Hungarian courier posed yet another opportunity. In his view, FCA should permit the courier to make the pickup, then shadow him from Augusta to wherever he might go in the United States, thus possibly identifying other agents. It was the classic stuff of the double-agent game: Orchestrate a controlled espionage drama in order to smoke out how our adversaries recruited and ran American traitors, then use this valuable information to identify other spies.

But Runk was overruled. As the meeting approached, he learned that Noel Jones and the FBI had decided to arrest the Hungarian courier as soon as he accepted the documents. Runk protested. Not only did this course of action forfeit the opportunity to learn more about the courier's contacts, but it would have devastating impact on the faithful Smolka, who would never be allowed to visit his mother in Budapest once the Hungarians awoke to the news of the arrest. Runk was told that he didn't know the whole story, that there was a higher priority. Apparently, there was a supersecret investigation under way in Europe that had the highest national priority. In support of this case, it was vital to capture a Hungarian and interrogate him. Runk was tersely informed that he had no need to know about the mystery investigation.

Otto Attila Gilbert, unaware of the great debate over his fate, arrived in Augusta and met Janos Smolka at the Civil War memorial as planned. As soon as he exchanged an envelope containing $4,000 for a package of classified documents, the FBI pounced. For his espionage, Gilbert was sentenced to fifteen years in prison. Attempts to interrogate him for clues to unlock the secret investigation failed. Norman Runk could not have known it at the time, but the investigation so cryptically described by his superiors would one day change his life.

With Otto Gilbert behind bars, Runk and the FCA, quiet professionals, slipped into the shadows while the FBI accepted well-earned public kudos for the joint operation. That was vintage FCA. Within the counterintelligence community and the senior army leadership, where it counted, everyone knew that the elite unit had performed with its usual brilliance.

In the fall of 1983, FCA agents got their man under bizarre and unorthodox circumstances.

The case revolved around the mysterious disappearance and apparent death of a soldier assigned to Field Station Sinop in Turkey, a sister unit of Field Station Berlin. Duty at the isolated mountain-top site could be lonesome and nerve wracking. Combating stress and boredom was always a major leadership challenge for whomever commanded at Sinop.

In late September 1983, Sgt. Dennis Bray approached his superiors. "I can't take it here anymore," the distressed noncom complained. "This place is driving me crazy." Efforts to placate the rattled NCO were unsuccessful. Bray was inconsolable and threatened to go AWOL—a serious matter for soldiers whose duties made them privy to sensitive secrets. The colonel who commanded the unit granted the stressed-out soldier a special morale and welfare leave to recharge his batteries.

Bray signed out on leave for a vacation in the United States and did not return. This made the missing sergeant a KAWOL, army-speak for knowledgeable AWOL, a missing soldier with secrets in his head. The alert went out, and it was soon determined that Bray had gone fishing on Little Cayman Island in the Caribbean.

Officials in the British West Indies reported that a man fitting Bray's description had rented a boat, gone fishing, and failed to return. The United States Coast Guard discovered Bray's rubber boat floating inside the coral reef that surrounds Little Cayman Island. Its occupant, the Coast Guard concluded, had fallen overboard and no doubt been eaten by sharks that infested the warm waters. What the sharks hadn't eaten, Coast Guard and Island officials speculated, was probably at the bottom of the two-thousand-foot-deep Yucatán trench, on the far side of the reef.

When news of the mysterious disappearance reached Washington, the generals summoned the FCA commander. There was something fishy about the whole affair, senior officers believed. The Foreign Counterintelligence Activity must "get someone down there and take a look."

Special agent Dave Guethlein drew the unusual mission. The thirty-year old Guethlein was a Cincinnati German who had been a counterintelligence agent since his 1972 enlistment. The six-foot-three warrant officer was an excellent choice for the unorthodox challenge. After a decade of duty in Japan, Germany, and the United States, Guethlein was a no-nonsense, methodical investigator known for his thorough, persistent approach. He and his partner, special agent Stan Nemitz, were not averse to tackling a challenge in the Caribbean. Within hours, the selfless pair had booked a flight to Jamaica.

In Jamaica, Guethlein and Nemitz were astounded at the frantic activity on an island known to be a sleepy resort. At the U.S. embassy, the defense attaché—a colonel—was unenthusiastic about the two spooks' mission. The United States had just invaded the island of Grenada, and American troops were in a fierce battle with armed Cubans at an airfield they had been building for Grenada's neo-Marxist government.

"I'd advise you to postpone your mission and hole up in a hotel here," the colonel warned. "We've got a report that the Cubans have offered a hundred-thousand-dollar reward for anyone who can make a hit on an American in the Caribbean."

Guethlein and Nemitz were not intimidated. The pair had orders to proceed to the Grand Caymans. Taking a sabbatical in Jamaica on the way was not part of the deal, war or no war. The following day, the partners boarded an interisland puddle jumper and flew to Little Cayman Island.

The pair checked in with the local constabulary, where officials reaffirmed the assessment of the Coast Guard. They had recovered the boat and fishing tackle. The missing sergeant was almost surely in Davy Jones's locker.

Guethlein and Nemitz were unpersuaded. Armed with the ritual suspicious nature of all successful counterintelligence agents, the FCA men knew that Bray fit the profile of someone who might stage his own demise. Reluctant to return to Washington empty-handed, the two agents lingered on the tropical island, which was, after all, not bad duty. Frequenting bars and restaurants where Bray might have been seen (counterintelligence people make such sacrifices regularly), they cast their investigative net widely in search of clues to the missing soldier's fate.

Yet Guethlein was also plagued by doubts. If the man was so beset by personal problems that he had staged his own death to escape them, was it not likely that he had already fled the island to begin a new life in the United States? After seven days on the lush island, the two agents reluctantly decided that it was time to return to Fort Meade.

Hope springs eternal. The dirt road that led to the island's small airstrip passed by the beachfront where the missing sergeant had last been seen. Guethlein and Nemitz drove slowly, eyes peeled in one last attempt to locate the missing man.

The rest became the stuff of legend in the corridors of FCA. As the two agents rounded a curve on the narrow beach road, a thin, bearded man emerged from the foliage and darted across their path.

Both agents had studied file photos of Bray. Guethlein recalls the encounter as if it happened yesterday. "He was dressed in a tattered shirt and ragged shorts—looking for all the world like a refugee from Gilligan's Island. I said to Stan, 'Son of a bitch, that looks like him.'"

Nemitz shouted at the man. "Hey, you! Bray!"

"The guy responded to his name," Guethlein recalls with a grin. "Then he fed us a line. He claimed to be Captain Dennis, leader of a Special Forces A Team, and insisted excitedly that he and his team had landed on the island, but all of his men had been wiped out."

The two FCA men displayed their army intelligence identity documents. The game was over, they told the bearded deserter. It was time to come home. Their man surrendered meekly, then launched into unconvincing attempts to persuade his captors that he was suffering from amnesia.

Guethlein and Nemitz spirited their captive back to the United States—no small achievement, because Bray had no passport or other identity documents. Guethlein and his partner flashed their special agent badges and mobilized all of their persuasive powers to convince the authorities that the man was an American soldier in their custody.

Blind luck and persistence had paid off, adding in the process yet another chapter to the growing FCA mystique.

Bray was housed in the psychiatric ward of Walter Reed Army Medical Center, where he played cat and mouse with the hospital staff for weeks, not unlike the infamous B. J. Conlin. Doctors declared him mentally competent but recommended his release from the army.

With each success, FCA added to its reputation for excellence, and the finest agents in army counterintelligence lined up for admission to its ranks. If Berlin's 766th MID was the best place in Europe to lock horns with the Soviets, FCA was the unrivaled premier posting from which one could engage our historic adversaries globally.

Bob Lunt had served more than four years at the unit's helm. Because of FCA's unique, specialized mission, the customary two-year limit for commanders did not apply. I was facing four or more years in one of army intelligence's most coveted positions.

FCA's homesteading operations officer recognized the handwriting on the wall and announced his retirement shortly after I assumed command. The generals concurred with my recommendation that Noel Jones should be honored with the Legion of Merit. By so doing, the army would acknowledge the departing officer's many genuine accomplishments while deemphasizing his problems of recent years. It was not lost on anyone that the brilliant officer had become entrenched and controversial because the army had permitted him to homestead in FCA for fourteen years.

# 8: Canasta Player

They called it Canasta Player. Several weeks before I assumed command of FCA, Bob Lunt referred cryptically to the tightly compartmented investigation. It was, he assured me in conspiratorial tones, the most sensitive case in the history of army counterintelligence, "a bombshell waiting to explode."

General Owens echoed Lunt's words. I was to clear the decks and "get ahold" of the Canasta Player case as soon as possible. The case had grave national security implications. It required my personal attention—full time, if necessary—even at the expense of other duties.

Though not yet formally briefed on the closely held case, I knew that it was related to the urgent orders we had received in West Berlin from our Munich headquarters three years earlier. The 766th MID had been directed to give up two of its best agents to a "sensitive project." Bob Thayer and I were told that we had no need to know further details. Scuttlebutt had it that the agents would serve on a special investigative team searching for a spy who was selling war plans to the Soviets.

I also knew that one of the agents we had dispatched from Berlin, Gary Pepper, had been continually laboring away on the investigation since 1985 from a secret base somewhere in Germany.

As I would soon learn, Canasta Player was the most sensitive secret in the U.S. Army. Not only that, but the case was about to take a dramatic turn that would propel the agents of the Foreign Counterintelligence Activity, the FBI, the CIA, and West German security officials on a journey that would shake up NATO, dominate the network news, and make the cover of *Newsweek* magazine.

The case we called Canasta Player traces its roots to the October 1956 Hungarian Revolution. At the time, I was an impressionable teenager in Pittsburgh, Pennsylvania, watching sympathetically as the people of Hungary made their vain bid to shake off Soviet domination. When surprised Red Army commanders were forced by the Freedom Fighters to retreat from the city amid a shower of Molotov cocktails, we applauded the Hungarians' bravery. Then came the Soviet betrayal and counterattack, followed by poignant images of frightened and forlorn Hungarians fleeing over the famous Bridge at Andau into neutral Austria and lonely exile.

Among the refugees who reached sanctuary in Austria were Louis and Clair Szabo and their eighteen-year-old son, Zoltan. By the spring of 1957, the Szabos, like many displaced Hungarians, had migrated to the United States. The family settled near Plainfield, New Jersey. There, while the homesick senior Szabos dreamed of returning to their beloved Hungary, son Zoltan learned English with commendable speed.

But in 1959, twenty-year-old Zoltan ran afoul of the law. The transgression was not major. The inventive Hungarian had embraced capitalism and was caught fabricating and selling near-perfect cardboard counterfeits of New Jersey license plates. This brush with the authorities propelled the teenager into a new life as a soldier in the U.S. Army.

The talented emigré adapted well to the army, which shipped him to Germany. Comfortable in his native Europe, Zoltan Szabo perfected his command of German and English. During his off-duty hours, the handsome soldier soon linked up with a twenty-two-year-old refugee from East Germany, Renate Jaschke, who had settled in Landshut, Bavaria. Daughter Andrea was born in the fall of 1960, and the couple married the following spring. In late 1961, a son was born.

Zoltan Szabo was assigned to a subordinate unit of the army's 8th Infantry Division. The alert noncom showed such promise that he was recommended for commissioning. By now a U.S. citizen, Staff Sergeant Szabo attended officer candidate school and was commissioned a second lieutenant in the armor branch in 1967.

The war in Vietnam was raging. The young tanker rose with wartime speed to the rank of captain and served a combat tour in Vietnam. Decorated with a silver star for bravery under fire, Captain Szabo returned to duty in Germany. With combat experience and a silver star on his chest, his career seemed to be on track.

Then came a humiliating setback. Like thousands of other Vietnam-era officers who lacked a college education, the decorated captain was caught up in an army-wide, post-Vietnam reduction in force (RIF). Ordered in 1973 to separate from active duty, Szabo complied. Because of his enlisted service, he was permitted to reenter active duty and serve as a noncommissioned officer. The diligent soldier, once again a staff sergeant, returned to duty in the 8th Infantry Division, where he was assigned to the G-3 staff section. In 1979, Zoltan Szabo retired after twenty years of active duty. By then divorced from Renate, he settled in Austria, close to his parents, who had moved from New Jersey to a corner of Austria near their beloved homeland.

Ironically, the soldier who had entered the army under a legal cloud ended his career the same way. By retirement time, Staff Sergeant Szabo had come to the attention of the army's Criminal Investigation Division for the black marketing of GI gasoline ration coupons. Perhaps out of respect for his Vietnam heroism, the army gave Szabo a break. After spending his final two years of active duty in the post housing office, and with a service record clouded by no fewer than three Article 15 disciplinary actions for various petty offenses, Zoltan Szabo was permitted to retire honorably and draw the pension of his officer rank. He had spent most of his twenty-year career in Germany.

Career patterns such as Szabo's were not uncommon during the Cold War, particularly for soldiers with German wives. The U.S. Army had more than 200,000 troops in Germany, many of whom adjusted readily to the beer and hospitality, not to mention the sheer enjoyment of life in historic old Europe—a life lived at bargain basement prices, thanks to army housing and a strong American dollar. The Hungarian American's proclivity to homestead in Germany thus failed to arouse the suspicions of his superiors.

But Zoltan Szabo had a secret. The seemingly passionate anticommunist Hungarian American was actually a recruited and trained agent of the MNVK/2, the Hungarian Military Intelligence Service. Since 1972, he had been delivering classified documents to his Hungarian masters. Sometimes Szabo would make his deliveries through a courier who would meet him in Germany to exchange documents for money; on other occasions he would make a quick drive to the Austrian cities of Innsbruck, Salzburg, or Vienna to meet with his communist agent handlers. Periodically, Szabo would travel discreetly to Hungary to meet with officers of the Center. Hungarian Tokay wines, fine cuisine, and a stunningly beautiful woman became a part of Zoltan's secret life, as did the use of a villa on picturesque Lake Balaton, courtesy of Budapest's privileged intelligence service.

The bold and quick-thinking Zoltan was good at what he did. The cascade of documents he was looting from the G-3 of the 8th Infantry Division made a strong impression on his Hungarian superiors, who shared with Moscow all secrets provided by the star agent. Soviet KGB officers were impressed. Clearly, the Hungarians had landed a big fish who enjoyed access to the crown jewels—U.S. and NATO war plans. Soon, Szabo was selected and trained to serve as one of Budapest's principal agents. His new job was to spot, assess, and recruit other disaffected or greedy U.S. and NATO military personnel. Urbane, wily, and perceptive, Zoltan Szabo was a perfect choice to troll for soldiers who had access to military secrets and would bend the rules to generate extra cash.

Szabo's double life commenced in late 1971, during what was intended to be a carefree vacation. When the young armor officer took his German wife and young children on a trip to Lake Balaton in his native Hungary, agents of the Hungarian Military Intelligence Service accosted him and accused him of being an agent of the American CIA. Szabo hotly denied the allegation. The Hungarian interviewer shifted gears. Over a bottle of wine, he reminded Szabo of his duty to his homeland and gauged the captain's reactions. The assessment was positive. Officers of the MNVK/2 decided that he was an excellent candidate for espionage who should be courted.

Within a few weeks, Zoltan's parents informed him that a former Hungarian schoolmate wished to meet him in Austria. When Zoltan arrived at the meeting, he found himself face-to-face with Budapest's agents once again. This time the Hungarians made Szabo an attractive offer. In exchange for his agreement to provide classified documents, the Hungarians would shower the young officer with more money than he had ever seen. At the same time, Hungarian spymasters would arrange for preferential treatment for his homesick parents, who were contemplating repatriation to their native country.

Budapest's cold pitch to Zoltan Szabo was a classic example of the espionage art. Spot a target with access to the enemy's secrets, then uncover and exploit a motivation that would incline the person to

accept recruitment. Money and loyalty to his parents would motivate
Szabo initially. Later, after the humiliating loss of his officer rank,
ego and revenge would play a role.

Zoltan Szabo performed brilliantly for his Hungarian masters for
sixteen years. Until his retirement in 1979, he personally delivered
thousands of pages of classified documents stolen from under the
noses of his trusting superiors, a record that one Hungarian intelligence officer described as unequalled. But more importantly, the inventive and resourceful operative developed into a skilled principal
agent, aggressively spotting and recruiting fellow soldiers for membership in Budapest's growing stable of disloyal Americans. The enterprising teenager from New Jersey eventually spawned an espionage ring that penetrated the innermost military secrets of the
United States and her NATO allies, a ring that ultimately grew to four
generations. Zoltan Szabo's espionage empire operated with impunity from 1972 to 1988, and its full dimensions are not known to
this day. It was these fruits of Szabo's labor that Gary Pepper and
eventually the entire Foreign Counterintelligence Activity would
seek to identify and neutralize in the case known as Canasta Player.

Another teenager caught up in the 1956 exodus from Hungary
was Sandor Kercsik. Sixteen-year-old Sandor, an intense and serious
fellow, fled the bloody chaos without his parents and younger
brother, Imre, who remained in Hungary. Sandor's path to freedom
ended in Sweden. There the hardworking, bright emigré was able
to obtain Swedish citizenship and pursue his ambition of becoming
a physician. To continue his medical education, the newly minted
Swedish citizen elected to study in his native Budapest.

By 1967, the Hungarian Military Intelligence Service turned its attention to Sandor. As a citizen of a neutral country in a Europe divided by the passions of the Cold War, the aspiring young doctor was
a perfect candidate for recruitment as a legal traveler, someone who
could flash a neutral passport and move freely between NATO and
Warsaw Pact countries.

Today, Kercsik insists that he declined the Hungarian service's first
recruitment approach. Then the Hungarians played the family card.
If he would agree to spy for his native country, his mother, who was

in ill health, would receive preferential medical treatment. Sandor accepted the offer but insisted that he never be tasked to operate against his adopted country of Sweden.

The new recruit served initially as a clandestine courier, a link between agents who were stealing NATO secrets in Germany and their Hungarian controllers in Budapest. If a Hungarian mole in the U.S. Army had a stash of stolen secret documents for delivery, Sandor (code name Alex) would receive an encoded message from Budapest on his shortwave radio. The physician would meet the agent and deliver the booty to the Hungarians, often serving as Budapest's paymaster.

Like Zoltan Szabo, whom he would ultimately meet in 1971, Sandor Kercsik performed yeoman duty for the Hungarians. From 1967 to 1988, the Swedish Hungarian physician made hundreds of trips as Budapest's bagman, giving him access to many of the Hungarian service's most successful penetrations of NATO. Money, privileges, and recognition as a hero of the socialist cause were his. But most importantly, Sandor's dedicated service to his native country made life tolerable for his family under Hungary's austere, Soviet-dominated system.

One of Sandor's most tangible rewards for his double life came when the Hungarian intelligence service supported the emigration to Sweden of his younger brother, Imre. Like Sandor, Imre learned that favors from the Budapest government had a price. By the early 1980s, having followed in his older sibling's footsteps and attended medical school in Budapest, the young physician had also obtained Swedish citizenship. In late 1980, Imre Kerscik was recruited by the MNVK/2 to serve as a support agent. The Center provided him the code name Viktor.

Both brothers married and settled in Goteborg, Sweden, where they practiced internal medicine at a local clinic and became respected members of the community. Imre embraced his adopted country, even joining the Swedish army as a reservist. But during their off-duty hours, the two decrypted coded instructions received by radio from Budapest and regularly shuttled between Sweden, Germany, and Austria—key links in a ring that was engaged in an unprecedented looting of NATO secrets.

In the spring of 1987, none of this was known to the U.S. government. Sandor Kercsik was in his twentieth year as one of Budapest's agents, brother Imre had served almost seven years, and Zoltan Szabo had been betraying secrets since 1972. By following time-tested rules of espionage tradecraft and exploiting weaknesses in the American army's security practices, the operatives of the MNVK/2 had covered their tracks well.

Had it not been for our colleagues in the Central Intelligence Agency, it is likely that the Hungarian Military Intelligence Service's landmark penetration of NATO would never have been unmasked. Understanding how the CIA stumbled onto the trail of betrayal in Central Europe and provided army counterintelligence the tip that led to the Canasta Player investigation requires a journey back to the year 1978.

The latter half of the 1970s was a bad time for the United States and its allies. The Cold War raged unabated. Soviet advisers and their Cuban surrogates were deeply involved in penetrating the African subcontinent, and the paranoid Kremlin leadership was about to make a fateful decision to invade neighboring Afghanistan. At home, the American people remained in a depressed, wound-licking mode in the wake of our humiliation in Vietnam. Morale in America's "hollow army" was at an all-time low as the Department of Defense struggled with its historic but faltering conversion to an all-volunteer force. Soon, the shah of Iran would be swept aside, our embassy staff in Teheran taken hostage, and America's weaknesses further exposed by a bungled hostage rescue attempt in the Iranian desert.

It was against this backdrop that CIA sources behind the Iron Curtain provided their American agent handlers some alarming news. Your military in Europe is penetrated, the agency's sources warned, possibly at a very high level. The spy in your ranks, agents confided to their CIA masters, is someone who has access to top-secret war plans and other documents. Your most sensitive military secrets are being delivered regularly to the Hungarian Military Intelligence Service.

Due to strict compartmentation, the CIA's sources did not have access to the American traitor's identity, but they were able to provide tidbits of information that might assist in unmasking the spy. Budapest's agent, they explained, was delivering large quantities of war plans, measured by the kilogram. The Hungarian service was in turn sharing the take with their Soviet ally. In fact, one source confided, the stolen documents are so impressive that the Soviet air force attaché in Budapest—a GRU officer—was flying each haul directly to Moscow for evaluation. Another source pointed out that the operation had been going on for many years. Yet another source revealed a particularly disturbing morsel: On one occasion, allegedly in the spring of 1978, the spy had been paid an unprecedented $50,000 for a single document, thought to have been the plan for a war in Central Europe. In Moscow, the CIA sources advised ominously, the Hungarian penetration was regarded as the most lucrative espionage success in Europe since the end of World War II.

Senior agency officials realized the importance of their agents' warnings and brought the grave news to the Department of Defense in 1978, cautiously withholding any information that could endanger their well-placed sources. The agency tip led to what would ultimately become the longest-running, most sensitive, most tightly compartmented, and costliest counterespionage investigation in history. If the agency's spies were correct, NATO's ability to defend Western Europe against the Soviets and their Warsaw Pact allies was in jeopardy.

Outgunned by armor-heavy Soviet formations in Central Europe, allied forces were committed to a defensive strategy. To prevail, it was essential that NATO dominate the key terrain, receive timely intelligence to identify the attacker's main effort, and be able to quickly shift U.S. and NATO units to repel the onslaught. Successful execution of this strategy would be dangerously undermined if the Soviet commander had read the NATO plans before the first shot was fired.

The agency's warnings portended catastrophe. Armed with such information and convinced that they might prevail, the Soviets might be tempted to attack in Central Europe. From the highest levels of the Department of Defense, the order was given: Unmask the alleged spy and put him out of business.

Army counterintelligence established a special investigating team in Europe to uncover the mole. Because it was by no means certain that the spy was a soldier, agents of the air force's Office of Special Investigations (OSI) opened their own case.

Even though the CIA's sources had warned of a possible high-level penetration, investigators knew that the traitor could be someone in the ranks. Whoever the spy was, he or she had regular access to large quantities of sensitive documents and had apparently managed to serve continuously in Europe for years. In the American military, this sketchy profile was inconsistent with a high-ranking officer. Officers are under considerable career pressure to accept new assignments every three years. Noncommissioned officers remain on station longer and perform much of the hands-on work, including the securing and handling of classified documents.

The investigation was initially given the code name Canfield Score. For several years, frustrated agents in Europe struggled in a fruitless needle-in-a-haystack hunt. In any investigation where the subject or target is unknown (CI agents call such cases "unsubs"), success requires great patience. Profiling is utilized, whereby investigators seek to identify a set of facts or assumptions (a profile) about the target in order to whittle down the list of possible suspects.

In the Canfield Score investigation, agents were cursed with the worst possible set of circumstances. Facts about their target were few: a penetrator in Europe who was giving the Hungarians large quantities of sensitive documents during the 1970s in exchange for big money. Such a profile was too thin and fit too many possible candidates to yield success. The small cell of agents who wrestled with the frustrating investigation were further hamstrung by the need to keep the very existence of the investigation a closely guarded secret. Protection of the CIA sources was of paramount importance. Under such constraints, the Canfield Score case went nowhere. The possibles who could have fit the sketchy profile numbered in the tens of thousands, overwhelming the few investigators allocated to the case. By the early 1980s, even as Cold War tensions escalated, the hunt for the elusive Hungarian mole was relegated to the "too tough" box.

# 9: The CIA Comes Through

The Canfield Score case file would surely have lain forgotten in a safe in Germany were it not for the actions of two men in the tight circle of those who were aware of its existence. One of them was a career CIA intelligence officer, Gardner R. "Gus" Hathaway. A native Virginian, Hathaway was no stranger to the U.S. military. After enlisting in the army immediately after his 1943 high school graduation, he had fought with the 14th Armored Division in southern France and received a battlefield commission. When the unit was demobilized in 1946, he entered the University of Virginia, graduating in 1950 with a major in history. Along the way, Hathaway spent one summer studying French at the University of Geneva, where he demonstrated a formidable capability to master foreign languages. Over the years, he would study and master German, Russian, Polish, Spanish, and Portuguese.

Hathaway recalls that his original ambition was to become an attorney, to which end he enrolled in the University of Virginia's prestigious law school. But when the Korean War broke out, the twenty-five-year-old veteran heard the call of public service. Dropping out of law school, he applied for career service in the CIA and the FBI. The CIA saw great potential in a former combat arms officer with overseas experience and a flair for languages. By October 1951, the agency hired Gus Hathaway as a paramilitary officer and sent him to paratrooper training.

During the next thirty-five years, Hathaway made a career out of working the Soviet target, not as a paramilitary but as a career case officer and operations officer. Serving ten years in Germany, nine years in Latin America, and four years in the Soviet Union, he established a reputation for excellence that placed him at the top of a highly competitive peer group. His overseas postings ultimately included two of the most coveted Cold War outposts: chief of station (COS) Bonn and COS Moscow.

At CIA headquarters in Langley, Virginia, Hathaway made his name in the agency's power base, the Directorate of Operations, serving as a branch chief in the Latin America Division, as operations officer of the SE (Soviet/East Europe) Division, and finally, in what some regarded as the most influential job in the Operations Directorate, chief of the powerful Soviet/East Europe Division.

Gus Hathaway was also one of a small number of senior agency officials whose appreciation of counterintelligence had survived the demoralizing witch hunts of the infamous James Jesus Angleton, the brilliant but paranoid CIA counterintelligence chief who had all but torn the agency apart in his quest to uncover a high-level mole he believed the Soviets had placed in Langley. In January 1985, when Hathaway returned from Bonn, the veteran sixty-year-old operator was asked by CIA director William Casey to assume responsibility for the agency's counterintelligence staff.

Hathaway knew that counterintelligence was seen as a career-killing, backwater discipline. In the CIA, recruitments were the coin of the realm. Spy catching did not lead to a seventh-floor office. Nonetheless, ever the soldier, he accepted the new challenge and took over the agency's counterintelligence staff in March 1985. During his five-year tenure, he would be promoted to associate director of operations for counterintelligence, establish a Counterintelligence Center, and inaugurate the long-overdue and painful rebirth of counterintelligence in the CIA.

Hathaway's low-powered counterintelligence staff was in shambles. Counterintelligence staffers had been excluded from sensitive cases being run in the Directorate of Operations by the Soviet/East Europe Division. Within the SE empire, no fewer than three sources were feeding their CIA case officers information on the Hungarian penetration in Europe. Having served in Moscow and Bonn, and as SE Division chief himself, Hathaway was struck by one thing: Fearful of endangering their sources, cautious CIA operators were reticent to share everything they were learning about the penetration with army counterintelligence investigators.

Armed with his long operational experience and a fraternal approach to dealing with the military counterintelligence community, Hathaway breathed life into the stalled investigation. The leads, he argued forcefully to agency officers in the closemouthed SE Division, were not a cleverly contrived Soviet provocation. They came from more than one source and had the ring of truth. Worst of all, they indicated that the disloyal American had been operating for more than a decade. The spy, Hathaway urged, could be identified only if the agency fully shared its information with army counterintelligence investigators.

Although Hathaway was certain that this could be done without endangering the agency's sources, he met resistance from officers in the SE Division. Wielding the powers of his associate director's position, he refused to back down. If the CIA doled out bits and pieces of the lead information, he declared, the army would never identify the traitor.

Fortunately, the determined insider had the necessary credentials to silence his critics. At a meeting with Col. Bob Lunt shortly after assuming leadership of the agency's CI staff, Hathaway made a promise. He would personally ensure that all relevant information in the hands of the CIA would be shared with FCA so that Lunt's investigators could identify the penetrator.

As his initial contribution to this goal, Hathaway caused a thorough review of all information bearing on the alleged spy that could be gleaned from CIA contact reports. If any information that could assist military investigators to profile and ultimately identify the spy was being held back by the CIA, he wanted to know about it.

As Gus Hathaway was reviving interest in the investigation in the corridors of the CIA, across the Potomac River in his Pentagon E-Ring office, Lt. Gen. William E. Odom, the army's senior intelligence officer, was doing the same thing. Odom was a brilliant officer. Like Gus Hathaway, he had made a career of studying the Soviets. By the time he became the army's assistant chief of staff for intelligence in 1981, Odom had an impressive service record, including tours in Germany and the Soviet Union as well as a four-year stint in the White House as military assistant to the president's assistant for National Security Affairs, Zbigniew Brzezinski. The West Point graduate's impressive resume also touted a Columbia University PhD, mastery of the Russian language, and a list of publications that was the envy of many self-respecting political scientists. By any measure, the gifted three-star general was one of the U.S. government's premier strategists and Kremlinologists.

When he took the job, Odom asked a time-honored Pentagon question: "What could blow up on my watch?" Surveying his staff, he made an assessment not unlike that of Gus Hathaway. The counterintelligence section, Odom remembers, "resembled a geriatric ward." When staffers informed him that the CIA had locked onto a hemorrhage of war plans in Europe that army counterintelligence had been unable to stop, the three star recalls that he "went up in smoke."

"I knew things were bad in Germany," he remembers, "but not that bad. I was determined to get it fixed before apprising Army Chief of Staff John Wickham, but the CI folks kept giving me pessimistic assessments emphasizing how tough the case was to crack."

After being told at least twice that the search for the elusive spy was next to impossible, Odom decided that he had no choice but to ratchet up the pressure on the counterintelligence community. He began by warning Army Chief of Staff Wickham that the war plans in Europe were being betrayed. Wickham reacted with predictable displeasure: The situation was unthinkable; fix it.

"I had to introduce some theater," Odom explains, "to get the message across to the counterintelligence people that I wanted the case tackled with reckless abandon. This was not something that could be approached as routine business; this was about our war plans and the lives of American soldiers."

On January 7, 1985, General Odom summoned Col. Bob Lunt to his spacious office. If there was a spy selling our war plans in Germany, the general intoned gravely, it was unconscionable that the case was not the top priority of army counterintelligence. If the CI people in Europe had written off the investigation as too tough, then the Foreign Counterintelligence Activity must resurrect it and pursue the leads until the traitor had been exposed and put out of business. There could be no question of a shortage of resources, the impatient Odom continued. The Foreign Counterintelligence Activity and its parent headquarters, the Intelligence and Security Command, must conduct the investigation on a priority basis, throwing all necessary resources at it. If Lunt encountered any problems, he should make them known to Odom personally.

Odom's theater had the desired impact. Bob Lunt left the demanding general's office infused with a sense of urgency. By now the spy had been providing war plans to the Hungarians for a decade or longer. The treachery simply had to be stopped. Failure to do so would entail great risk should a war ever break out in Central Europe.

Odom's marching orders to Bob Lunt coincided with Gus Hathaway's similar efforts in the CIA. With this strong backing, the case was reborn, with the Foreign Counterintelligence Activity at the helm. The search for the Hungarian mole was given a new name, Canasta Player.

Lunt promptly formed a dedicated investigative team at FCA's Fort Meade, Maryland, headquarters. Special agent Al Eways, a charter member of the Canasta Player team, recalls the day.

"Lunt sent the word down that several of us should wrap up whatever we were doing and get ready for a new challenge. We trooped up to the director's office, where we were briefed on the CIA leads. Then Colonel Lunt charged us with a single mission: 'Identify the spy in Europe or come back and tell me you can't do it.'"

The FCA men reviewed all that had been done by their unsuccessful predecessors. Lunt knew that his agents would operate with one distinct advantage over the European-based agents who had initially tackled the case. With FCA on the hook to solve the case, close liaison between the CIA, the senior army leadership, and the FCA commander would ensure the kind of emphasis and resources that were needed. The Foreign Counterintelligence Activity was the only unit in army counterintelligence with worldwide capabilities, seasoned agents who could execute a case that would require a long-haul approach, and access to a bushel of the taxpayers' money.

In 1985, the stalled case began to move. At CIA, Gus Hathaway drafted two talented and experienced officers, Martha Graves and John Whiteley, and charged them to roll up their sleeves and assist army investigators. Graves and Whiteley had both enjoyed exciting careers during the Cold War. The top-priority counterintelligence case would be their final challenge before retirement, and the two tackled it with a passion. If FCA investigators required assistance—in Germany or elsewhere—Graves and Whiteley would do whatever was required to make it happen. Working long hours, Whiteley, Graves, and Hathaway identified additional facts from agency sources that they believed would be helpful to the FCA investigators. These included recently obtained lists of documents that the CIA sources had identified as being part of the betrayed material. The lists might enable military investigators to deduce the unit or headquarters from which the documents had been stolen.

Hathaway overruled the persistent arguments of some agency officers that the investigation could jeopardize the lives of their sources and passed the important lists and other information to FCA investigators. One of the new clues was a sobering but potentially useful tidbit: One agency source had confided in his CIA contact that the original American spy had been at his work for so long that he was "on ice." Army investigators interpreted this to mean that the original spy might have retired and recruited his successor. Agents could be looking for a pair of traitors.

Foreign Counterintelligence Activity investigators were dismayed at the lists of betrayed documents, at least six of which were secret and top-secret war plans. One entry jarred everyone who saw it: "U.S. Army Europe Operations Plan 4102, with Annexes." Oplan 4102 in this form was a top-secret road map for the transition from peace to war by the U.S. Army in Europe. It described in microdetail how the European-stationed army would react, almost hourly, to a Warsaw Pact attack across the inter-German border, to include detailed plans for bringing in reinforcements from the United States, equipping them, and putting them under NATO command. During my 1980–81 service as a war plans officer in the army's Heidelberg headquarters, copies of this document were numbered and kept in a vault.

These revelations confirmed everyone's worst fears: The spy or spies had access to the crown jewels and had no compunctions about marketing them to Budapest. Armed with this kind of information, Warsaw Pact commanders could anticipate and counter NATO's transition to a war-fighting posture. Bob Lunt's small team of investigators realized more than ever that they were playing a high-stakes game.

In Washington, the list of betrayed documents was shown only to the small circle of senior army officials who were aware of the existence of the closely held Canasta Player investigation. Inevitably, pressure began to mount on Bob Lunt to identify the traitor. General Glenn T. Otis, the commander of all U.S. Army forces in Europe, was briefed in his Heidelberg office by Bob Lunt, at the direction of the secretary of the army. It was Otis and his NATO allies who would have to fight disadvantaged in the event that war broke out.

Otis, a popular officer known for his unflappable nature, reacted with cool professionalism when told that his war plans were being passed regularly to the Soviets. He would cooperate fully with the investigation, he pledged, although he was not personally familiar with the methodology and difficulties in ferreting out such a mole. However, the laid-back four-star general also told Bob Lunt that he expected a maximum effort to put an end to the hemorrhage of classified documents—the sooner, the better.

At Fort Meade, the Canasta Player team reviewed the new lists of betrayed documents and redoubled its efforts to refine and narrow the profile of the unidentified traitor.

The spy, the team members decided, was most likely a noncommissioned officer. If he had indeed pocketed a stunning $50,000 in 1978 for a single document, the target could also be someone whose personal finances might reflect sudden wealth.

Based upon the betrayed documents on the CIA-provided lists, the culprit was probably in the army and most likely assigned to a division or higher-level headquarters in Europe, where he enjoyed access to war plans. The list of compromised documents was still too short and random to provide a clue concerning the traitor's actual duty location.

Still, the list did suggest yet another possible element of the profile: the spy's duty position within his organization. Because some of the compromised documents were winding up in Moscow within one to two months of their publication, it was clear that the mole enjoyed ready and unrestricted access to war plans. This suggested to investigators that their target might well be serving on a G-3 (Operations and Plans) staff, a G-2 (Intelligence) staff, or some similar position in a major headquarters.

To flesh out the new profile, FCA investigators drew on their considerable institutional knowledge of the Hungarian intelligence service—extensive data accumulated since the 1950s that described how the Hungarians actually conducted espionage operations to penetrate the U.S. Army. The data in question had been painstakingly accumulated from counterintelligence operations targeted against the Hungarians (such as the Gilbert case, described earlier) as well as from debriefings of captured spies and defectors.

The evidence suggested that the Hungarian service's modus operandi was somewhat rigid. Budapest favored the recruitment of ethnic Hungarians. Once a recruitment was made, Hungarian agent handlers preferred to meet their agent in neutral Austria. Contacts with sources stationed in Germany would be conducted via radio or through a courier. Two possible elements of the new profile could thus be Hungarian ethnicity and travel to Austria.

By 1985, the FCA team was looking for a Hungarian American NCO who was currently serving on active duty on the war planning staff of high-level headquarters. Their man would have more money than his salary would normally provide, and he would have served continuously in Europe since the early to mid-1970s. Weekends would find him traveling often to neutral Austria.

Lunt's investigators, who by now included Eways, special agent Dave Groff, and special agent Al Puromaki, knew that any or all of the elements of their profile could be false, but at least the profile provided a starting point. Still, even with this detailed profile, investigators faced a daunting challenge. Since the early 1970s, some twenty-five to thirty thousand soldiers—thousands of whom were NCOs—had served in Germany in duty positions with access to such documents. Determining who these people were, where they might be in 1985, and whether or not they met other elements of the profile was formidable in the days before the proliferation of automated systems.

Even a task as seemingly simple as determining possible Hungarian ethnic background was easier said than done. If a soldier was born in Hungary, that fact would appear at a certain place in his records. But if the soldier was not born in Hungary but his father was Hungarian, investigators were reduced to the crude and unreliable method of searching for Hungarian-looking names. Worse yet, if a soldier's mother was Hungarian and his father's name was, say, O'Brien, FCA investigators had no easy way of detecting the Hungarian background on his maternal side. Clearly, Hungarian ethnicity was not a promising road to identify the traitor.

Month after tedious month, the persistent FCA agents worked long hours exploring every possible avenue that might lead to their man. By late 1985, the Fort Meade office was supplemented by an office in Germany, where much of the data required for the manhunt was available. It was to this cell that Bob Thayer and I had dispatched special agent Gary Pepper from the 766th in Berlin.

Twenty-six-year-old Sgt. Gary Pepper was serving his first tour as a special agent but had already demonstrated uncommon alertness. It had been Pepper who spotted the Israeli surveillance of the meeting with the "dirty Kurd" in Berlin—an alert performance that led to the unmasking of a penetration of one of Berlin's most sensitive units. Pepper, a graduate of Florida State University, had been a criminology major who enlisted in the army because he wanted to catch spies. The son of a career infantryman who had fought in Korea before himself becoming a counterintelligence agent, the promising investigator was a handsome six-footer with a thick mane of brown hair and a mustache. Before arriving in West Berlin, the native of Winter Park, Florida, had attended the Defense Language Institute in California for an intensive course in German. Had Bob Thayer and I known in 1985 when we dispatched Pepper from West Berlin that he was destined to play a central role in a history-making investigation for the next thirteen years—with startling results—it would have made his loss from West Berlin more palatable.

In FCA's new German office, Pepper and his colleagues were forced to carry out every investigative step behind a cloak of secrecy. Only a handful of senior officers in Europe knew about the existence of the case. And the FCA team could not count upon help from our West German allies, who knew nothing about the CIA-inspired case. Consequently, many nominally simple tasks, such as checks of personnel records or license plates, had to be carried out in a piecemeal, discreet manner that would not attract attention.

More than one dry hole was tapped by investigators. Because it was possible that the spy had recruited his replacement, agents postulated that he might have attempted to recruit a loyal soldier who could have reported the approach. Exhaustive analysis was done of hundreds of reports of suspicious contacts that had been rendered over the years by security-conscious soldiers, in hopes that the spy had slipped up at some point in time. The reports revealed nothing. Whoever the spy was, he had apparently not made a mismove.

These same files were also examined for any evidence that someone might have noticed and reported a fellow soldier who was displaying sudden undue affluence. This, too, led nowhere.

Persistent FCA investigators tried yet another approach. They retrieved all known information dealing with each espionage case in which the Hungarians were involved since the early 1970s and searched for clues to the spy's location. Theoretically, they reasoned, it might be possible to deduce the spy's unit of assignment by examining the kinds of questions and taskings that Budapest had levied on other agents. It would have been significant, for example, if Hungarian agent handlers expressed no interest in Heidelberg, even though logic would argue that the home of the Headquarters, U.S. Army, Europe, should have been a priority target. Lack of interest in an otherwise lucrative target could be an indicator that Budapest or Moscow already had a productive agent there. This approach, too, yielded the frustrated sleuths nothing.

Undaunted, the Canasta Player team went back to the tedious, largely manual task of screening hundreds of unit rosters and reconstructing rosters of those who had served in positions where they would have had access to the kinds of documents that CIA sources identified. If the profile was valid and the spy was a sergeant who had homesteaded for years in a sensitive position, this tack was most likely to produce results.

At Fort Meade, Col. Bob Lunt could report to his superiors only that his agents were deep into the tedious, step-by-step methodology that was the nature of unknown-subject investigations. The veteran colonel, who had spent his entire career in the human intelligence business, was confident that patience and hard work would eventually pay off. But by the end of 1985, the bottom line of his progress reports was negative. Lots of time, money, and effort expended, but no spy.

At CIA headquarters, Gus Hathaway kept Canasta Player from dropping off the radar screen. Throughout 1984 and continuing into 1985, CIA sources behind the Iron Curtain began to respond to taskings from their American masters. Additional facts surrounding the elusive American traitor began to trickle in.

Newer, more comprehensive lists of stolen documents surfaced, lists that became the Rosetta stone that would eventually enable investigators to unlock the Canasta Player mystery. Once again the lists evoked a collective gasp from the small circle of knowledgeable senior officials in Washington. The dates of the betrayed documents confirmed everyone's worst fears: The espionage had commenced in the early 1970s and was continuing in the mid-1980s. Analysis of the new lists revealed another alarming fact. In some cases, each time a war plan was revised, copies of the changes were being promptly passed to the Hungarians, who were reading them at the same time as U.S. field commanders (and passing them to Moscow). Still worse, the spy—or his replacement, if he had indeed recruited his replacement—continued to enjoy apparently unrestricted access to virtually the entire family of secret and top-secret war plans. Most alarming was the revelation that the betrayed documents included a number of highly sensitive and current plans that laid out the wartime general defense plans (GDPs) of many of the army's European-based combat units. For example, the CIA lists made it clear that the 1982 GDP for V Corps (Oplan 33001) and its 1984 rewrite were already on file in Moscow.

The documents that outlined the GDPs of each army unit in Europe were distinctively labeled as the 33001 series. These plans were indeed the crown jewels; they contained nothing less than precise descriptions of where each unit would go upon the outbreak of war and how individual combat units would use the hills and valleys of the rugged West German terrain to conduct the defense in depth of their respective sectors.

The realization that the spy had compromised the wartime defensive plans of the U.S. Army corps responsible for the NATO defense against a Warsaw Pact thrust through the famed Fulda Gap caused FCA investigators to shake their heads. What kind of a soldier would sell the enemy a document that revealed the very spot on the map where he himself would be located in the event of war?

Once our CIA colleagues began to recover lists of betrayed documents in earnest, the overworked and frustrated FCA investigators in Germany and Fort Meade began to make headway in their quest. It appeared all but certain that the spy was assigned somewhere in the U.S. Army's V Corps, which had its headquarters in Frankfurt. Directly south of the V Corps area of operations, with its headquarters in Stuttgart, was VII Corps, which was assigned responsibility for defending against a Warsaw Pact attack that might be mounted out of southern East Germany and neighboring Czechoslovakia. Although some of the betrayed war plans dealt with U.S. units in VII Corps, most could be traced to V Corps and its two subordinate divisions, the 3d Armored Division and the twenty-thousand-man 8th Infantry Division, headquartered west of Frankfurt in the town of Bad Kreuznach.

Eways, Groff, Puromaki, and Pepper further refined their profile. The date on at least one of the compromised war plans told investigators that the betrayals were continuing into 1985. Agents pored over unit rosters and personnel records looking for an NCO, assigned somewhere in V Corps, possibly in the 3d Armored Division, the 8th Infantry Division, or one of a number of corps support units. Their man would probably be assigned to a headquarters staff element where he would have access to top-secret war plans. His personnel file would no doubt reflect a pattern of repeated assignments in Germany, and it would not be a surprise if he were to have an ethnic Hungarian background. The hunt was narrowing.

# 10: I'll Bet This Is Our Man

Special agent Al Puromaki had worked on the Canasta Player investigation for what seemed to him like his whole life. A senior warrant officer with almost twenty years in the army, Puromaki had been with the team through its darker days as it sifted through thousands of pages of unit rosters and personnel files in a vain attempt to identify a spy who team members were not even certain at the time was still actively engaged in espionage. A serious, conscientious agent of Finnish ancestry, Puromaki usually kept to himself, frequently working long nighttime and weekend hours on what had become almost an obsession to him. More than anyone on the Canasta Player team, the dedicated officer put himself under considerable pressure to achieve a breakthrough on the case. Like his teammates, the soft-spoken agent knew the stakes for which they were playing. The case had been under way in one form or another for almost eight years at a cost of God knew how much. Their target was certainly one of the most damaging traitors of the Cold War, and careers were tied up in the quest to bring him to justice.

Under such circumstances, it was little wonder that Puromaki and his colleagues were skittish. All knew that one poorly thought out move or a single careless breach of security could tip off their man, who would surely flee to the safety of Budapest, leaving FCA and army counterintelligence with egg on their collective faces. Such a disaster had recently befallen the FBI in its investigation of CIA traitor Edward Lee Howard, who had managed to slip the noose of an FBI surveillance and flee to Moscow. The lesson of this embarrassment haunted everyone involved in the Canasta Player investigation.

By January 1986, Puromaki, Gary Pepper, and two other agents in their Wiesbaden office had been systematically plugging away for months on the profiling approach. Having determined which units in Europe would have maintained copies of all known betrayed documents, the FCA men had laboriously accumulated rosters of all soldiers who had served in those units during the time frame of the most recent security hemorrhages—from 1982 to 1984. The result-

ing lists were then further refined and reduced by eliminating soldiers who had not served in staff sections where they would have had
unlimited access to war plans. Persons remaining on the list were designated priority-one candidates. All such candidates were then subjected to detailed scrutiny, beginning with a careful screening of their
military records. This tedious approach was a calculated, logical, and
methodical process that took Puromaki and the men in Wiesbaden
six months to pursue.

The effort paid off. Late one evening, as Al Puromaki reviewed
the personnel files of soldiers assigned in the mid-1980s to the Bad
Kreuznach headquarters of the 8th Infantry Division, the veteran
agent thumbed through the records file of an NCO. Puromaki
scanned the sergeant's assignment history and paused. No doubt
about it, the taciturn agent mused, this guy has been a regular in Germany. Puromaki reread the sergeant's record of assignments, then
nodded his head slowly. "I'll bet this is our man," he announced triumphantly to his office mates. His words marked the end of an eight-
year hunt.

The NCO whose record Puromaki held was SFC Clyde Lee Conrad. When Conrad's name "popped" and agents put their new suspect under the microscope, things began to fall quickly into place.
Conrad was born in 1947 in Bergholz, Ohio, and had entered the
army in 1965, shortly before his eighteenth birthday. A file photo
showed a handsome, pleasant-looking man with a round face,
topped by a close-cropped mane of salt and pepper hair. Thumbing
through the file, Puromaki was surprised. Judging by his record,
Conrad was a "water walker," a top-notch NCO. Clyde Conrad had
established a reputation as a talented noncommissioned officer who
was clearly blessed with strong leadership qualities, an efficient work
ethic, and other traits that guaranteed success in the structured environment of the U.S. Army.

Puromaki also noted that Conrad, an infantryman, had served
twenty years of active duty, including a tour in Vietnam, and risen to
the rank of sergeant first class before retiring just four months earlier, in August 1985, at the age of thirty-eight. The retired NCO's
records also revealed that his GT score, the army equivalent of the
IQ test, was in the high 120s. Clyde Conrad was one smart fellow.

But it was Conrad's assignment record that caused Puromaki's pulse to pound. After completing basic training in the United States, Conrad had spent almost his entire career in Germany, and most of that in the 8th Infantry Division. His final assignment prior to retirement had been as the noncommissioned officer in charge (NCOIC) of the division's G-3 War Plans section. In fact, Puromaki noted, Conrad had served almost sixteen years of his twenty-year career in Germany, most of it in the 8th Infantry Division, where he had become an institution in the unit's Bad Kreuznach headquarters. Not only that, from the late 1970s to his 1985 retirement, the sergeant had served in duty positions where he had direct access to the war plans that appeared on the CIA lists.

There was more. Conrad had been assigned to stateside units three times since 1967—at Fort Bragg in North Carolina; Fort Carson in Colorado; and Fort Ord in California, where he had attended German language school in Monterey. In each case, the record revealed, Conrad had cut short his tour and returned to duty in Germany, each time to the 8th Infantry Division and its stock of sensitive war plans.

Clearly, the Ohioan fit several elements of the profile: an NCO; someone who had homesteaded in Germany; a person who had occupied a headquarters staff assignment within V Corps; and someone who had served in a position with access to the kind of secrets that were showing up in Budapest.

Additional, thorough records checks and other standard counterintelligence investigative measures were now warranted, to include discreet interviews with persons who might shed light on the retired sergeant's activities. If Conrad was the long-sought-after spy, an intensive look at his finances, travel, personal associations, and activities would probably unmask him. Because such investigative techniques were intrusive in nature, the Wiesbaden team and FCA headquarters submitted detailed justifications to show probable cause and obtain permission to probe deeply into their new suspect's activities and lifestyle. Armed with the go-ahead, FCA agents in Germany and the United States began to circle their target, taking great care to do nothing that might alert Conrad and cause him to flee.

Until his August 1985 retirement, Conrad had been a key player in the Bad Kreuznach headquarters. Hardworking and well liked, the popular NCO had earned the nickname "Mr. Plans" out of respect for his unequalled knowledge of the unit's war plans. Trusted and respected, Sergeant First Class Conrad was a mentor to the younger soldiers in the headquarters, an NCO who had made himself so indispensable to his superiors that they more than once intervened to shield him from the usual rotations to the United States. When the division deployed to the field for war games, the German-speaking Conrad could be counted upon to make *gasthaus* reservations for the staff. If an officer forgot to bring an item to the field, no problem; Sergeant First Class Conrad could be counted on to have a private stock of essentials. When the unit was in garrison, soldiers noted, Clyde was a dedicated, hardworking NCO, almost to the point of being a workaholic. One officer told agents that he had repeatedly admired Conrad's work ethic.

"Clyde was always in the office, day and night, typing, copying, and doing all of the paperwork that makes a plans shop tick," the man told agents.

Clyde Conrad had made himself the institutional memory of the War Plans section. In most U.S. Army divisions, captains and majors authored the war plans. But in Bad Kreuznach, with Conrad's unmatched knowledge of the division's mission and its area of operations, he often wrote the plans.

"SFC Conrad was principally responsible for the preparation of a significant change of the Division's wartime defensive plan," wrote one officer in Conrad's glowing annual efficiency report.

Another rating officer trumpeted Conrad's virtues in an efficiency report that was destined to be read one day in a court of law: "An absolutely outstanding NCO . . . An administrative genius . . . possesses outstanding leadership qualities; leads by example; inspires his subordinates and successfully trains them." A major enthused, "During a shortage of officers, Conrad took over all responsibilities of the Assistant G-3 Plans Officer and handled this job for more than four months in an outstanding manner."

And in August 1983, a lieutenant colonel passed this judgment on the FCA suspect:

SFC Conrad's performance of duty was outstanding. His knowledge of operations planning, document procedures, and the creation of plans and orders is the best that I have seen. In the entire corps, he is recognized as the expert for the General Defense plans as well as for the plans of higher, subordinate, and neighboring units. SFC Conrad regularly carries out demanding and independent work, his best successes being in the carrying out of complex staff deployments that demand initiative, judgment, and an understanding of human nature. His knowledge of division-level operations and his fluent German language have been of inestimable value in the cooperation with our German allies.

As the War Plans NCOIC, investigators learned, Conrad had served as the G-3 top-secret-document custodian continuously from March 1978 until his 1985 retirement. Scanning Conrad's efficiency reports, Puromaki and his men noted an entry in the duty description section of a 1983 report: "SFC Conrad controls and is responsible for approximately 1000 top secret, secret, and confidential documents of the G-3 section." Investigators marveled when they uncovered an entry revealing that Conrad was also assigned as the "Document Reproduction Control NCO." This was almost too much. Not only was the veteran NCO the watchdog of his duty section's classified documents, he was also the person who was supposed to guard against unauthorized copying. Puromaki and his coworkers shook their collective heads. If Clyde Lee Conrad was indeed the long-sought-after traitor, the man had been the proverbial fox in the chicken coop.

Conrad's personal life also raised eyebrows. A bachelor until age twenty-two, in 1969 he married Annja Brennan, a German woman who was on the rebound from marriage to another American. Seven years older than Clyde, Annja had two daughters, Heidi and Sonja. Almost overnight, Clyde Conrad the carefree bachelor was responsible for a family of four. In 1975, the family grew to five with the birth of the couple's son, Andre.

Because of Clyde's continuous assignments in Bad Kreuznach, the Conrad family enjoyed a measure of stability denied to most army families. Both daughters graduated from the Department of Defense high school in Bad Kreuznach. Initially, Conrad and his instant family lived in an army-provided stairwell apartment. Money was tight, and the hardworking Annja took on demeaning work scrubbing stairwells to supplement the family income. More than one person recalled that "poor Clyde" never seemed to have any money. On more than one occasion, Conrad's superiors had to counsel the young sergeant about letters of indebtedness mailed by his creditors to his commander. Sometimes, one soldier related, the affable NCO's friends would spot him a few bucks so he could attend periodic headquarters social gatherings.

But in the mid-1970s, several observers remarked, the Conrad family seemed to suddenly prosper. One woman who had attended high school with the Conrad girls recalled the envy she had felt for Heidi and Sonja. The two Conrad girls always seemed to wear the best and most fashionable clothes. After the birth of son Andre in 1975, Annja no longer did the backbreaking *putzfrau* chores. Clyde, once so strapped for cash that he couldn't buy a round at the bar, became an enthusiastic coin collector. Agents located witnesses who revealed more than one occasion after 1975 when Conrad proudly showed off an impressive collection of gold Krugerrands, touting it to one man as "the best in Europe." Others reported that, at one point in the late 1970s, the family appeared to have tapped into a source of elegant oil paintings in the Netherlands. By 1980, Conrad and his family had rented one of the nicer homes in the quaint, wine-producing village of Bosenheim, just outside of Bad Kreuznach. There, village women buzzed about Annja's costly collection of Hummel figurines and her impressive gold jewelry. The Bosenheim rumor mill had it that Annja had somehow gotten a lot of money from her millionaire ex–father-in-law. More than one source described the Conrad's new furnishings and decorations as "lavish."

Checks of Conrad's finances were revealing. Between December 1985 and February 1986, the recently retired sergeant had deposited $24,000 in cash to his local bank account, carefully dividing the sum into three deposits, each in an amount less than $10,000. Splitting up the sum ensured that the bank did not report the deposits to the Internal Revenue Service, often a dead giveaway of illegal income.

Investigators noted that the retired sergeant's monthly take-home pension was $764, hardly sufficient to live well on the expensive German economy. Yet since his retirement in late summer 1985, Clyde had not taken on another job and Annja remained unemployed. Despite this, the family paid $400 monthly rent on the Bosenheim house. Parked in the driveway were two cars—Clyde's new Audi sedan and a Volkswagen for Annja with her initials in gold on the doors. Even more intriguing, FCA agents learned, in early 1986 an administrative error occurred in the office that dispenses military pension checks. For several months, Clyde Conrad's monthly retirement checks were not sent to his bank. Most military retirees would have complained promptly, but not Conrad, who apparently did not notice the problem for months. Clearly, the Conrads were not living from paycheck to paycheck and were able to maintain a comfortable lifestyle in spite of the sharp drop in income that went along with retirement.

Conrad's travels also proved to be a fruitful avenue of inquiry. Noting from his leave records that he rarely traveled to his hometown of Sebring, Ohio, agents keyed on a trip he had taken in mid-1978 to attend a class reunion. Recalling the CIA source's tip that the mystery spy had been paid $50,000 for a single document in early 1978, FCA investigators spent countless hours screening the contents of dusty cartons of U.S. Customs Service landing cards stored in a basement room in New York's World Trade Center building. Landing cards are filled out by all arriving international passengers upon landing in the United States. In 1978, all travelers were required to declare whether or not they were bringing in sizeable amounts of cash or other negotiable instruments. If Conrad had suddenly hit it big in Germany, perhaps he had carried some of his booty to the States.

Shuffling through the thousands of cards from the time of the suspect's 1978 leave, the persistent Al Eways finally hit paydirt. On a card filled out by Conrad, the man who had recently been so down and out that his wife had resorted to scrubbing floors declared that he was bringing "$10,000 cash" into the United States.

This discovery, combined with the piecemeal bank deposits, was as close to a financial smoking gun as Eways and his FCA colleagues could uncover. Even though Conrad was taking precautions to conceal his income, an unexplained $34,000 made it all but certain that, beginning in 1975, their suspect had another source of income. Whether the supplemental income was legal (an inheritance, for example) or was from the Hungarian intelligence service or some other illegal activity required further investigation.

Another dimension of the FCA profile—the Hungarian connection—initially seemed not to fit Conrad. Delving into the man's family background, investigators determined that the recently retired sergeant had ancestors who came to the United States from Czechoslovakia. There were no family ties to Hungary that would have made him a priority target of Budapest's Military Intelligence Service.

Then, while scanning Conrad's efficiency reports, agents noticed that his supervisor in Bad Kreuznach during 1975 and 1976 had been a senior NCO named Zoltan Szabo. The name Szabo, Hungarian for tailor, is common in Hungary. This connection between Clyde Conrad and ethnic Hungarian Zoltan Szabo unlocked yet another key piece of the Canasta Player puzzle.

Zoltan Szabo was no stranger to Puromaki and his men. As a former Hungarian American soldier whose security dossier contained an unsubstantiated allegation that he was a Hungarian agent, Szabo, long since retired, had not made the FCA list of priority-one suspects because it seemed clear that he could not be the spy who was peddling secrets in the 1980s. Yet Zoltan Szabo, like Clyde Conrad, had homesteaded for years in the 8th Infantry Division, initially as an officer, then later, after the post-Vietnam cutbacks, as an NCO. Equally intriguing was the discovery that Szabo had worked in the G-3 staff section, where, like Conrad, he had enjoyed access to sensitive war plans. According to his service record, Zoltan Szabo had retired from active duty in 1979, six years before Conrad.

Puromaki and Pepper dug deeper. The more they probed, the clearer it became that Zoltan Szabo fit elements of the profile of the original spy derived from the CIA's 1978 tip. This realization begged two questions. Was it possible that the retired Szabo was the original traitor, the spy who CIA sources had said was "on ice"? And could Szabo have recruited his subordinate, Conrad, to serve as his replacement?

Agents discovered yet another tantalizing fact. Since his 1979 retirement after twenty years of active duty, Zoltan Szabo had lived exclusively in neutral Austria, far from the reach of American law enforcement authorities. Equally interesting to FCA investigators was
the discovery that Zoltan Szabo was living with his second wife in the
small Austrian village of Weiden am See, a few kilometers from the
Hungarian border. His bride, Ilona, was a dark-tressed, strikingly
beautiful Hungarian folk opera singer who it was said he had met in
Budapest. These revelations catapulted Szabo into instant celebrity
status among the army investigators, who now had a second strong
suspect. Years of hard work were finally paying off.

# 11: David

Colonel Bob Lunt and Gus Hathaway had developed close ties as Lunt's investigators pursued clues provided by the CIA. From 1985 on, the FCA director's weekly routine included a visit to Hathaway at his Langley office, where he made sure that the CIA official was kept current on the progress of the investigation. Soon after Al Puromaki's identification of Clyde Conrad, Lunt apprised Hathaway that the sergeant at the 8th Infantry Division was a good candidate for the long-sought traitor. Nonetheless, the FCA director added, considerable investigative spadework now faced his agents in Germany. Making the case for espionage was no simple feat.

Unbeknownst to Lunt, as his investigators focused on suspects Conrad and Szabo, the CIA was engaged in a bold and delicate operation in Europe. If it succeeded, the agency might well be able to break the Canasta Player case wide open with a single stroke. The agency's operation was a gamble, but with NATO's war plans being funneled to the Soviets, this was a time for risk.

The operation, code-named David, began in April 1986 when an envelope addressed to the CIA arrived in the mail at the U.S. embassy in Vienna. This was not an uncommon occurrence. People with various agendas were always writing to the CIA or appearing at the gates of American embassies with urgent information to impart. Some letters were bona fide, others were dispatched by scamsters and crazies, but all reached the desk of a professional intelligence officer whose job it was to sort them out.

The contents of this particular envelope captured the attention of agency officers. A brief letter, written in Hungarian by a man who signed his name David, contained an offer of cooperation. David explained that he was an officer in the Hungarian intelligence service who was willing to do business with the CIA. David claimed to have a friend, also a Hungarian intelligence officer, who was interested in resettling in the West. In exchange for money and a guarantee of eventual resettlement in the West, David and his unnamed friend would provide information to the Americans concerning a penetration agent in Europe being run by the Hungarian intelligence service. As proof of this claim, David enclosed extracts from some classified documents that Budapest was collecting from their American agent. Check them out, David advised, and if you are interested in doing business, place a "lost dog" ad in the *Frankfurter Allgemeine Zeitung*. The ad should be in the name of Alfred Martin, David instructed, and contain a phone number that he could call to arrange a meeting with agency officers.

Hungarian-speaking CIA agents examined the letter and declared it to be written by a native Hungarian. At the agency's Langley headquarters, officers in the Soviet/East Europe Division were divided in their opinions about the validity of the overture. At its worst, David's offer could be a scam or a Hungarian-orchestrated provocation. It could also be a solid-gold opportunity to unmask the target of the Canasta Player investigation. Colonel Bob Lunt's army investigators were making progress in the elusive case, but the prospects of a bold breakthrough were tempting.

David had enclosed cryptic extracts from nine secret documents in his offer of cooperation. Agency officers decided to ask the army to evaluate them. Without revealing their source, CIA officers passed the extracts to FCA with an agency request for assistance in determining their origin and validity. If the nine items were genuine and sensitive, this could mean that the David overture posed the possibility of a CIA recruitment of a high-level officer of the Hungarian service. In such cases, strict rules of compartmentation governed. Army investigators had no need to know how the CIA had acquired the nine pieces of information.

The Canasta Player team in Europe quickly determined that four of the CIA-provided items had originated in the G-3 of the 8th Infantry Division, probably from the Emergency Action Console (EAC), the division's operational nerve center. The EAC was a restricted-access vault within the G-3 that handled the division's most sensitive communications, including those related to nuclear-release procedures. To agents Gary Pepper and Al Puromaki, the fact that such items had recently fallen into the hands of the CIA reinforced their conviction that the 8th Infantry Division was penetrated. Unaware of the details surrounding the David operation, the FCA investigators reported their findings to the CIA. The secret documents were genuine, recent, and highly sensitive, and stemmed in part from the 8th Infantry Division headquarters.

One of the documents provided by David bore a 1986 date. Clyde Conrad had retired in 1985. Agency officers realized that if David's alleged penetrator was the long-sought Canasta Player target, and if Conrad was a spy, this could mean that before he retired, Mr. Plans had recruited an operative in the division G-3 who could assist him in looting the division's secrets. Keeping the possibility of penetrating the Hungarian service through David strictly compartmented, CIA officers did not share this possibility with FCA investigators.

In Langley, the army feedback was decisive. Agency officers in Europe were given authorization to contact David. An ad was placed in the newspaper, which resulted in telephone contact between a Hungarian-speaking CIA officer and David. At the outset, David made it clear that he and his friend needed money as a sign of the CIA's sincerity and willingness to pay for their risks. A meeting in Zurich, Switzerland, was arranged for mid-May 1986. David instructed the CIA to dispatch an officer to a spot in a city park. The officer, David insisted, must be unaccompanied. David described a specific location in the park where a red bicycle would be found. At a precisely dictated hour, David instructed, the CIA man should drop a parcel containing cash beside the bicycle and depart the area. No face-to-face meeting would occur.

At this meeting, a CIA officer appeared at the Swiss meeting site, located the red bicycle, and delivered an envelope containing 100,000 German marks—at the time approximately $45,000. In Bonn and Vienna, agency officers, anticipating a possible meeting with David and his friend, awaited a call. Days passed with no word from the mysterious Hungarian.

In Langley, a highly charged debate ensued. It was one thing to take risks to unmask the Hungarian penetration, Gus Hathaway argued, but to hand over large amounts of cash to someone who wouldn't even let his agency contact see him was ludicrous. Hathaway's CI staff was not running the David operation. That was the job of SE Division. Nonetheless, the veteran operator opposed the degree of risk being taken with large amounts of cash. There was nothing wrong with going for a possible high-level recruitment, he argued, but it was essential that officers remain skeptical and avoid foolish actions. To Gus Hathaway, whose commitment to Canasta Player was total, handing over cash to a red bicycle failed these tests.

Between May and November 1986, David regularly communicated with CIA officers in Europe by telephone and mail. In every communication, the elusive Hungarian dangled the possibility that his colleague might accept CIA recruitment and assist in unmasking a dangerous American spy. Ultimately, in their efforts to orchestrate a face-to-face meeting with David's alleged friend, frustrated CIA officers made a total of five meetings in Switzerland with David, during three of which no one laid eyes on the Hungarian's face. In July, agency officers deposited a cash-filled pouch behind a stone wall in Lucerne, but they failed to meet David. Six weeks later, at a surrealistic meeting on a bridge in Zurich, a CIA officer was approached from the rear and instructed to gaze over the water and not turn around. More money was passed to David, once again without seeing him.

In October, in an underground shopping area in Zurich, the CIA once again met David. This time the brief meeting was face-to-face, and David was told that the CIA was not satisfied with the progress of the operation. Patience in headquarters was wearing thin. David was informed that it was essential that he arrange a personal meeting with his friend, during which he and CIA officers could discuss his future. By November 1986, after one additional brief meeting next to a bank in Lucerne, the CIA had passed a total of 210,000 deutsche marks to the mysterious Hungarian, more than $100,000. At the Lucerne meeting, David's CIA contact made a final appeal. David would have to arrange a meeting with his friend soon. Otherwise, it would no longer be possible to continue the contact.

David was never heard from again. Agency officers placed additional lost dog ads in the newspaper from Alfred Martin, but David did not rise to the bait. The smooth-talking Hungarian had simply disappeared, taking more than $100,000 with him. In Bonn and in Langley, the failed operation generated heated disagreement. Either David was a phony who had neatly swindled the CIA, or the Hungarian's overtures to the Americans had been detected by his service, in which case he and his unnamed friend were in mortal peril. Either way, the agency's high-stakes gamble to recruit a Hungarian intelligence officer who might crack the Canasta Player investigation had failed. In Washington and in Germany, FCA personnel were not told of the ill-fated operation. Army investigators would ultimately learn about the caper, but their information would come from an unlikely source.

During 1986, while CIA officers were attempting to meet David's disaffected friend, Al Puromaki's hunch about the retired sergeant named Conrad was panning out. Agents noted that Conrad had elected to retire and settle in Germany, a not uncommon choice at the time for a German-speaking NCO with a German wife. By itself, Conrad's marathon homesteading in Germany was hardly unprecedented among the NCO corps and could be innocently explained.

Yet there were alternative, more sinister explanations for Conrad's affinity for Germany and his failure to seek out a civilian job with the U.S. Army in nearby Bad Kreuznach. Perhaps Clyde had not sought a postretirement job because he already had one, as an agent of Budapest. Furthermore, if he was a Hungarian agent, a preference for duty in Germany could be interpreted as a business decision. Like Willi Sutton, who quipped that he had robbed banks because "that's where the money is," Conrad's affinity for the 8th Infantry Division could signify that he was crouched on a soft espionage target. The 8th Infantry Division War Plans office in Bad Kreuznach's Rose Barracks was "where the secrets are."

Not only that, by settling in Germany, severing all ties to the U.S. military, and avoiding travel to the United States, Conrad was placing himself safely out of reach of American civilian and military law enforcement authorities. As an American private citizen living in Germany with no ties to the military, he was subject to German law, which since World War II had been notoriously lenient on persons convicted of espionage. True, there was an extradition treaty between the United States and Germany, but the treaty specifically exempted political crimes. At the top of the list of such crimes was espionage. If Conrad had spied, he had made safe choices in retirement. (It was not lost on investigators that Conrad's friend Zoltan Szabo, comfortably ensconced in neutral Austria, was also safe from American law enforcement authorities.)

No one questioned FCA's authority to investigate Conrad. But if the investigation proved he had committed espionage, Conrad could not be arrested by army counterintelligence as long as he was on German soil. Ultimately, this dilemma would become one of the most hotly contested issues of the Canasta Player investigation.

# 12: The Chameleon

Al Puromaki's identification of Conrad in early 1986 moved the Canasta Player investigation into a new phase. In Washington, the electrifying news quickly translated into one key question: How soon can we take him down? Shortly after Conrad was identified as the top suspect, Col. Bob Lunt summoned Puromaki, Al Eways, and Dave Groff into his office. Eways recalls Lunt's words:

"My first order was to find the spy or tell me you can't do it," Lunt reminded the three men. "Now I'll give you your second order. I agree that Conrad is our man, but you must prove it."

At the point in any investigation when the question of proof surfaces, a true counterintelligence professional knows that it's time to get the lawyers involved. Once investigators have their man in the crosshairs, and every instinct says that the suspect is "dirty," the real investigation has just begun. Intuitive knowledge that a person is engaged in espionage simply does not suffice when the objective is a military or civilian courtroom. To bring a case such as Canasta Player to a successful conclusion, hard, irrefutable evidence is required. Such evidence consists not merely of suspicious circumstances that point to espionage but of facts that prove the elements of the crime; for example, did the suspect knowingly betray classified defense information to agents of a foreign power for personal gain with the knowledge that this would harm the United States of America or benefit the foreign power?

Now that the target had been isolated, it was time for Bob Lunt's men to develop the case along these lines. When and where had Conrad given classified information to an agent of a foreign power for personal gain, in the knowledge that this act was harmful to the national security of the United States? What specific material had he betrayed? To which foreign power? And where was the money he had gained from his actions? Collecting sufficient facts to establish a case for espionage that would survive in a court of law was a tall order.

To complicate matters, Bob Lunt and his agents faced a difficult operational problem. Was the suspect operating alone, or did he have confederates? Failure to ask this question and pay attention to the answer could result in a premature move to arrest Conrad, only to learn that he was part of a network that a measure of patience and guile could have exposed. At a minimum, agents suspected, there were actually two suspects—Conrad and Szabo—although Szabo was out of reach in demilitarized, neutral Austria. In Germany, where hundreds of thousands of Americans were stationed, FCA investigators could sleuth about discreetly behind the backs of our German allies. In Austria, American agents would stand out unacceptably, and each investigative action would constitute a violation of Austria's neutrality.

It took considerable leadership on the part of Bob Lunt and his FCA team to ensure that no rush to judgment on the case took place. Heeding the advice of military attorneys, Lunt recognized that the next challenge was to cautiously circle the target and collect information that would make the case for espionage. It was a delicate balancing act. All future investigative measures had to be carefully planned to avoid alerting Conrad, yet it was necessary that investigators move closer to their suspect to uncover the required information, all the while without apprising our German allies.

Lunt also quickly learned that advice was not to be scarce from this point on. The dramatic identification of Conrad after so many years of frustrating searching had catapulted the case into prominence, even though it remained the most compartmented investigation under way in the army. *Prominence* is the correct word; the small circle of knowledgeable officials included the secretary of the army, the chief of staff of the army (four stars), the army's deputy chief of staff for intelligence (three stars), the judge advocate general of the army (two stars), the commander in chief, U.S. Army, Europe (four stars), and the commanding general, V Corps, in Frankfurt (a three-star general named Colin Powell). Regular progress reports on the sensitive case to the senior leadership became mandatory, usually provided face-to-face. Foreign Counterintelligence Activity agents were told that Secretary of Defense Richard Cheney had made President Bush aware of their investigation.

Meanwhile, FCA investigators around the world began to discreetly interview persons who the records reflected had served with Conrad. It was a dicey but necessary approach, given the fact that no one had a clue at the time whether Conrad had managed to recruit some of his coworkers. During these interviews, agents concentrated on reconstructing Conrad's activities prior to his retirement. With whom did he seem to be close in the division headquarters? Did he travel on weekends? Did he appear to have any non-American friends? What about his financial situation?

Foreign Counterintelligence Activity investigators operated with the burden that one bad decision or a single unlucky break could blow the case. The worst nightmare was that one of the interviewees might be in league with Conrad. Should that occur, agents knew, Conrad would get a phone call telling him that the spooks were asking questions about him. Within hours of such a call, the retired sergeant could be out of reach in Austria or Hungary.

But luck seemed to be with Bob Lunt and his men. Around the world, investigators conducted dozens of interviews with veterans of duty in the 8th Infantry Division's Bad Kreuznach headquarters. Interviewing agents did their best to obscure their focus by avoiding up-front, blunt inquiries concerning Conrad himself. These efforts gradually permitted FCA investigators to bring the retired sergeant into focus. Above all, one question haunted agents. How could a soldier whose personnel records portrayed him as a "water walker" possibly be responsible for the worst treachery against the army since World War II? Something simply did not add up, at least on the surface.

But the more agents delved into Conrad's career through the eyes of his fellow soldiers, the more they realized that the talented noncommissioned officer had lived a double life. Sergeant First Class Conrad might have appeared to his superiors as the model NCO, but the face that "Old Clyde" put on for his fellow soldiers was quite different. Conrad, agents learned, was a skilled and charismatic chameleon.

Interviewed in Arizona, MSgt. Danny Wilson recalled an encounter with Conrad in the mid-1970s. Wilson was assigned at the time to the 8th Infantry Division, where he had come to admire and respect Clyde Conrad. He and Conrad were participating in a field training exercise, Wilson recalled, when the two had taken a break under a tree.

Conrad had raised an inquisitive eyebrow and asked, "Danny, are you an honest man?"

The soldier hesitated momentarily, then nodded.

Conrad's voice betrayed disappointment. "Oh," he said simply, followed by an uncomfortable silence.

Wilson was curious. "What would you have said if I had answered differently?" he queried Conrad.

"Well," Conrad replied, "I would have offered you a way to make some easy money, a thousand or so a month." To earn this princely sum, Conrad added, all his friend would have to do was transport money to various European cities and service bank accounts.

The young soldier thought for a moment, then asked if the activity was legal.

Conrad demurred. "There are ways to make money, and then there are other ways," he replied cryptically, clearly implying that the offer involved something illegal.

Danny Wilson was a religious family man for whom the notion of jeopardizing his career for easy money was out of the question, even if the offer came from someone whom he regarded as a friend and role model.

"I just figured that Old Clyde had something going, like almost everyone else at that time in the army," the sergeant recalled sheepishly to investigators as he admitted that he had not reported Conrad's approach to anyone in his chain of command.

Master Sergeant Danny Wilson was not the only soldier who recalled being tempted by Conrad with an offer to make easy money in some unspecified enterprise. Several others described similar experiences. Sometime in the mid- to late 1970s, soldiers reported, Conrad had enticed them with a "business opportunity," usually having something to do with unspecified, travel-related tasks involving some sort of "deliveries." None of the soldiers reported Conrad's overtures, but all insisted that they had declined the offer. One soldier opined that he believed that Conrad was smuggling East Germans into West Germany for profit. Another stated that she believed that Conrad was involved in either black marketing or narcotics. A third soldier said that he recalled Clyde boasting about some sort of "organization" that he had going, in which good money could be

made. All of the interviewees insisted that Clyde had never mentioned espionage.

Several soldiers recalled that Conrad's mentor and close friend
during the 1970s had been a sergeant named Zoltan Szabo, who had
retired and departed Bad Kreuznach some years back. Sources also
named a number of younger soldiers who seemed to hang around
with Conrad. Most were lower ranking enlisted people who were
known to work for Conrad in the G-3 or who socialized with the popular sergeant. Some soldiers told investigators that the self-confident
Conrad had played a father-figure role for a tight circle of young enlisted protégés. Their names were added to the growing list of soldiers and former soldiers who would have to be carefully looked at
as possible coconspirators.

The allegations that Conrad was actively seeking recruits for some
sort of lucrative enterprise were significant. Having identified several
soldiers who had rejected Conrad's overtures, overburdened FCA investigators had to assume that Conrad had probably been successful with an unknown number of others. On everyone's lips were two
questions: How many did Conrad approach, and how many had succumbed to his tempting offers of big money? Common sense suggested that the answers to these questions would not be good. The
army of the 1970s was a hollow, dispirited force in which drug use
was common. Recruits for illegal activities that promised quick cash
would not be difficult to locate. If Zoltan Szabo was the progenitor
of the espionage ring, and Clyde Lee Conrad his protégé, it was likely
that the ring had entered its third generation.

It all made sense. Particularly by 1985, Conrad would have seen
the urgency of recruiting a confederate—an insider—because after
his planned August retirement he would no longer enjoy direct access to classified documents. If the veteran sergeant had succeeded
in recruiting one or more of the young soldiers who had worked with
him, the espionage within the division headquarters might be continuing. This meant that investigators would have to target the 8th
Infantry Division's Bad Kreuznach headquarters as well as Conrad
himself. The only safe assumption was that Clyde, like Szabo before
him, had recruited his replacement (if indeed Szabo was involved,
which at this point in the case was sheer speculation, however much
it seemed to make sense).

With the identification of Clyde Conrad as the principal suspect, the director of the Foreign Counterintelligence Activity was drawn more and more to the center of a major interagency effort. The once low-profile investigation was about to mushroom into a complex endeavor that would demand close coordination with the FBI, the CIA, the Pentagon, and the Department of Justice, not to mention FCA's parent headquarters, the Intelligence and Security Command. At the same time, careful guidance and direction had to be developed and provided to FCA investigators in their Wiesbaden offices. From this point on, the center of gravity of the investigation would be in Germany as the circle around Conrad was tightened.

Bob Lunt had his work cut out for him. Running an investigation in Germany from his Fort Meade headquarters was a tall order, but the veteran colonel had broad shoulders.

In Wiesbaden, leadership of the FCA team rotated between agents Puromaki, Eways, and Groff in two-month intervals, an awkward arrangement that was not conducive to continuity but permitted each agent a break from hotel living. Life in a Wiesbaden hotel was particularly hard on Al Puromaki, whose dedication to the case was total but who deeply missed quality time with his young son in Maryland. Nonetheless, Puromaki and his colleagues set about the risky and difficult business of stalking their target, a task rendered more complex by the fact that the team was operating on foreign soil, without the knowledge or permission of our West German ally.

Ever since the end of World War II and the division of Germany, American intelligence and counterintelligence agencies had operated under the assumption that the West German government was deeply penetrated by the Soviet-trained and -supported East German intelligence service—the Ministry of State Security (MfS). Bilateral intelligence relationships with our German counterparts existed but were always clouded by security concerns on our part. Periodically, embarrassing spy cases at the highest levels of the Bonn government would make the headlines, reminding us that our West German allies had their own special problem. Operationally, this meant that it was not prudent to share major secrets with the Germans. The Canasta Player case was thus pursued unilaterally, without the assistance that the German Federal Office for the Protection of the Constitution (called the BfV) or the Federal Criminal Office (the BKA) could have provided. To have told the West Germans about the case when the original tips came to the CIA in the late 1970s would have endangered the case and the agency's well-placed sources.

But for FCA special agents, this restriction meant that many of the investigative arrows that would normally be in their quiver were missing. If Conrad lived in the United States, a judge's permission could have been obtained to tap his telephone, and the postal service could have provided information on his correspondence. In Germany, such measures were impossible without German cooperation. Deprived of a full range of investigative capabilities, the Wiesbaden team was forced to settle on less intrusive measures.

The FCA team mounted a discreet, intermittent surveillance of Conrad's home in Bosenheim. Random drive-bys of the house might develop useful information on their suspect's comings and goings. Additionally, by keeping track of the license tag numbers of cars parked at the Conrad home, Gary Pepper and his teammates were able to develop a list of the retired sergeant's visitors.

Risks were taken. Conrad was well known and popular in the Bad Kreuznach area, but agents nonetheless selectively interviewed local people. Care was taken to put "smoke" around the real target of such interviews, which meant that inquiries had to be cautiously structured. When conducting records checks, an investigator might request access to twenty personnel records when in fact only one of the twenty files was of interest.

Gradually, the real Clyde Conrad was coming into focus. Skilled at his job and well liked, Clyde was also a heavy beer drinker with a strong competitive drive and was known to be fond of pool, poker, and fast driving. Since retirement, he had maintained ties with senior NCOs in the division headquarters, primarily through an informal poker club that convened periodically for an evening of male bonding. These revelations made Lunt's men even more skittish, certain that Conrad had eyes and ears everywhere in Bad Kreuznach.

To establish who on the division staff might still be close to their chief suspect—and who therefore might be in league with him— an attempt was made to penetrate the headquarters with an undercover agent. Hoping that a trained agent might be able to spot suspicious activity in the division G-3 offices, the Wiesbaden team arranged for a man to be assigned there. With luck, they speculated, they might even hook into the ring of traitors if their man could get himself recruited by Conrad or one of his confederates. Clyde, agents had noted, displayed a predilection to bond with younger soldiers. In an understandable but lamentable error, a junior agent was selected for the delicate role. He was assigned as a clerk-typist in the division G-3 office.

The plan backfired badly. At that time, clerk-typists were in particularly short supply, yet the new man had dropped out of the sky when there was no opening for him in the G-3. By itself, this was cause for suspicion. Further complicating matters was the fact that the agent himself had a maturity problem. Given to heavy drinking, he unwisely hinted to his new coworkers that he was working under cover. Labeled as a snitch from the beginning by enlisted soldiers on the division staff, the man could not accomplish his mission. In an inauspicious start to the new phase of the investigation, the hapless agent was pulled out of the headquarters after he fell from a truck (some continue to speculate that he was pushed) and injured his leg.

# 13: Mr. Plans

Clyde Conrad popped open another beer and took a long swallow. At age thirty-nine, he had been retired less than a year. His Swiss bank accounts were bulging with cash, a new car sat in the driveway, and his collection of gold coins was stashed in a safe place. In spite of this, Clyde couldn't shake a sense of depression and foreboding. Every day, it seemed, his sagging morale plummeted in an unarrested free fall.

Part of the problem was the adjustment to retired life. For years he had been the respected boss of the division's War Plans shop. Officers came and went, but Clyde Conrad was the constant. Noncommissioned officers really did run the army, Conrad believed, among other things because they were willing to work hard—and, in his case, because he was smarter than the parade of mediocre officers who trooped in and out of the division G-3 office, lingering just long enough to punch their tickets before skating away to another, ill-deserved promotion. No doubt about it, Conrad mused, he had been the real power in the G-3 shop. After all, had not more than one gullible colonel or general intervened with Washington over the years to keep the indispensable Mr. Plans in Bad Kreuznach?

Now, as he approached the first anniversary of his retirement, Conrad reflected sadly on his dull life, a humdrum existence devoid of the excitement and prestige that came from being the top dog in the headquarters and the secret superstar of Budapest's stable of spies.

To make matters worse, Clyde recalled bitterly, his carefully laid plan for an exciting, lucrative retirement had been derailed. The enterprise that he had envisioned would keep him in the fast lane after retirement had gone sour. First there was that fool Rod, who got himself caught up in the drug screening. All the hard work invested to mold the brilliant young soldier into a first-class espionage recruit had turned to instant shit. Now his talented protégé was useless, a civilian living somewhere in Florida, probably frying his brain with drugs and doing flunky work for slave wages. Dumb shit.

Conrad grimaced, thinking of all the chips he had cashed in to get Rod accepted for duty in the War Plans shop at the army's European headquarters in Heidelberg. It had been the perfect arrangement. Rod could have done the actual collection while Clyde the superstar managed relations with Budapest. In Heidelberg, a well-trained spy would be like a kid in a candy store. With Rod in the G-3 vault, Clyde's prospects for earning big money from the Hungarians were even greater than in Bad Kreuznach. Now, with Rod out of the army and several other promising prospects gone on to duty in the States, Clyde was in a deep funk, wallowing in self-pity. Even an idiot knows that a spy without access to classified documents is useless, he bemoaned. Maybe it had been a big mistake to retire.

Conrad tossed the empty beer bottle into the trash and popped open another. A year ago, things had looked so good. Rod had brought a retirement gift to the small flat in Bad Kreuznach that Conrad rented for the business. The apartment served as a convenient safe site for the storage and processing of stolen documents. Clyde smiled as he recalled the young soldier's gesture. The cocky sergeant had sauntered into the apartment sweating so hard that his granny glasses were fogged. Slung over his back was an entire duffel bag full of stolen documents—"the mother lode," Rod had called it with a broad grin. Conrad chuckled. The thing must have weighed a hundred pounds. It took balls for Rod to heist that much stuff in broad daylight and lug it out of the headquarters all by himself. The bag's stash of secrets could be parceled out for years to Clyde's Hungarian case officer, Miklos. Nothing to it, Clyde laughed to himself. Just tell the gullible Hunky that I've got a comrade on the inside, then palm the stuff off piecemeal, changing the dates on selected documents to convince Budapest that it was the latest stuff. Budapest would have paid good money for Rod's mother lode, Conrad sighed, which was why he had laboriously squirreled away an entire five-drawer filing cabinet of such material before retiring, even before Rod produced the duffel bag of stolen secrets.

But now, even that backup plan was in jeopardy. Ominous things were occurring, Conrad sensed—dangerous things—and the thought of what might happen frightened and depressed him. It started with the alert from the wife of one of his poker buddies. The woman, who lived around the corner in Bosenheim, worked at the local military banking facility. A few months ago, she came home from work and told Conrad's wife, Annja, that some investigator type had come in to do finance checks on a list of soldiers. This was not unusual, the neighbor pointed out. Records checks were a routine event at the bank, and she would have thought nothing of it had she not noticed that Clyde's name was on the list. From experience, Annja's friend knew that such checks were done on active-duty soldiers only when the army was conducting a routine background investigation or when someone was in trouble. So why was her retired friend on the list? the woman wondered. Had Clyde gotten tired of hanging around the house and applied for a civilian job? she asked Annja over coffee.

Conrad swore silently to himself and swilled down a huge mouthful of beer. One of the reasons he had decided to retire was to avoid just such scrutiny. His decade-long relationship with Miklos and the Center in Budapest had been exciting and lucrative, but everything had its limits. It was time to retire, step back, and adopt a new, safer approach to "the business." Inserting a mole in Heidelberg had been a stroke of genius. The real risks of the business were taken by the guy who had to smuggle documents out of his workplace. With good training, Rod would have been a natural for this role. All Clyde would have had to do was keep Miklos happy and rake in the payments. Conrad grimaced. If Rod hadn't screwed up, he reminded himself for the twentieth time, little Clyde Conrad from Sebring, Ohio, would have already been well on the way to making his second million.

Now the tip from Annja's friend at the bank had plunged him into depression. As the weeks passed, he could almost see his rugged, salt-and-pepper hair turn snow white. Every unexpected visitor caused him to catch his breath, certain that it was only a matter of time before a knock on the door would signal the end of his exciting double life.

And exciting it had been. Conrad had to keep from laughing out loud every time he had walked into a roomful of people at work, knowing that he was something special, that he had a secret life that would astonish everyone if they knew. There was something unique and invigorating about having such a secret, having power and control over your life while lesser men who lacked boldness and vision still limped along from paycheck to paycheck.

Since 1975, Clyde had basked in this intoxicating knowledge. His status as Budapest's superstar reminded him every day that he was smarter than his college-educated superiors, and it provided the continuous, satisfying awareness that he was living a profitable double life right under everyone's nose.

Then came a second shock. Annja's ex-husband, that drunk Brennan, called his daughter Sonja in California and told the poor girl that the feds were after her stepfather. Two guys in civilian clothes had flashed official-looking ID and asked twenty questions, some of them about Clyde. Alarmed and confused, Sonja immediately called her mother in Bad Kreuznach and relayed her father's drunken ramblings. Annja managed to soothe Sonja's fears before hanging up, but she trembled as she shared the disturbing news with her husband. Clyde kept his cool, outwardly. It was probably the IRS, he told Annja. Don't panic.

But privately, Clyde knew that this was serious. Had something gone wrong to tip off the authorities? Maybe Szabo has thrown me to the wolves, Conrad thought, recalling their many business differences that had eventually led to a cooling of the long friendship. Clyde still thought that Szabo was too cautious. The older man could be counted on to shrink from Conrad's bold schemes, brainstorms that usually involved outwitting the Americans and Budapest to increase profits. No, Conrad thought, Szabo was safe. The greedy Hungarian is so deep into the business that he's not going to talk to anyone. The guy's got money, vacation houses, a beautiful wife, and VIP privileges in Hungary, all from the business. On top of that, Conrad thought with a laugh, just like me he's collecting military retirement pay from Uncle Sam. No, Clyde reassured himself, no reason to worry about Szabo; he's got too much to lose.

But the more Clyde thought about it, the more he couldn't shake a haunting feeling that something was wrong—very wrong. Perhaps Rod had slipped up and was in trouble with the law. Drugs again? Could he be trusted to keep his mouth shut? Swilling down yet another beer, Clyde decided that important precautions were in order. What would happen to him if agents raided his house in Bosenheim?

In the basement, searchers would easily locate the small room that contained his stash of classified war plans, an array of expensive photo equipment, and other espionage paraphernalia accumulated over the years. Still worse, there would be no way to explain the short-wave radio, not to mention the cipher keys stashed elsewhere in the house. Then there was the computer with dozens of floppy discs loaded with electronic images of all the goodies that had gone to Budapest for the past ten years. Conrad groaned. Then they'd home in on the money, the financial statements from five Swiss banks, the gold coin collection, and more.

Fortified by another beer, Clyde carefully and methodically began to clear the decks for any contingency. Should the worst occur, it was vital that the house be clean and that arrangements exist so that Annja and eleven-year-old Andre would not have to worry about money. Clyde rebuked himself. Don't overreact; these are merely precautions. The Americans can't touch me here in Germany, and if the Germans should knock at the door, the worst I might get from them is an eighteen-month sentence, a mere tap on the wrist.

Still, just to be on the safe side, Clyde decided to make some prudent adjustments. The Bosenheim house had to be clean. Better safe than sorry.

# 14: Stalking the Target

In Wiesbaden, FCA agents struggled throughout 1986 to close the ring around Conrad. After the aborted attempt to place a source in the division headquarters, no one seemed to have a good idea of how to get close to their target. True, the dozens of interviews conducted around the world had filled in many gaps concerning Conrad's character and personal associations, above all with the shadowy Zoltan Szabo. Most importantly, agents had amassed persuasive information about the retired NCO's aggressive attempts over the years to recruit soldiers as workers in some kind of business that yielded good profits. But in spite of this, headquarters in Fort Meade reminded Al Puromaki and his Wiesbaden agents that they had uncovered few hard facts that could be converted to evidence in a court of law that would persuade a jury that Clyde Lee Conrad was a spy for the Hungarian Military Intelligence Service. If he was, lawyers asked, where were the Hungarians? Where was the money? Who could stand up and testify to the treason? Everything in Puromaki's bones told him that Conrad was their man, but how to prove it?

Phase one of the Canasta Player investigation had consisted of identifying a suspect. Because of the needle-in-a-haystack character of the dragnet, no one in the Pentagon had crouched on FCA's back to produce instant results. Now phase two, stalking the target, had commenced, and officials in Washington were becoming less forgiving. Pressure mounted to show progress toward neutralization of Conrad while FCA investigators wrestled with their dilemma. Everyone wanted to close in on Conrad, but the bold action that the situation seemed to demand was fraught with the danger that a mismove could alert Clyde and propel him into sanctuary behind the Iron Curtain.

Foreign Counterintelligence Activity investigators in Wiesbaden continued their cautious approach to the case. In April 1986, their patient stalking paid off. During a routine Saturday afternoon drive-by of Conrad's Bosenheim home, Gary Pepper circled the corner lot on Elfelderstrasse. Conrad's driveway was directly across from the village swimming pool. The silver Audi was in its usual place, but beside it was an unfamiliar car with a Munich license plate. Clyde had company—either someone from Munich or someone with a rental car, many of which were registered in Munich. The young agent made a second pass by the property, his heart pounding. Perhaps the car belonged to Zoltan Szabo, he thought. Ever since the identification of Conrad, Pepper and his colleagues had speculated that a conspiracy might exist involving Conrad and Szabo, but no one had been able to establish that the two men had been in touch since Szabo's 1979 retirement. The car was a white Opel, and Pepper was able to jot down its complete tag number. Later that night, a third pass on the house established that the visitor was still there. It appeared that Conrad's guest was staying the night.

No one had better contacts in Munich than Al Eways, who had worked for years as an intelligence liaison officer in Bavaria. Cashing in a chip with a former German colleague, Eways was able to inconspicuously trace the mystery car in a matter of days. As Pepper had suspected, the Opel was a rental car. It had been leased on Friday at the Munich airport. In a significant investigative coup, Eways had even managed to obtain a copy of the car's rental contract. The document contained a watershed clue. The Opel had been rented by Dr. Sandor Kercsik, who listed himself as having been born in 1940 in Budapest, Hungary, with a current address in Goteborg, Sweden. Between the time the car was rented on Friday until it was turned in two days later, it had been driven 1,500 kilometers. Had the white Opel been rented by Zoltan Szabo, Pepper and his teammates would have been ecstatic. But a Hungarian physician from Sweden was even better. Gary Pepper recalled the reaction in Wiesbaden: "The revelations from the rental contract obtained by Al Eways screamed 'courier' to all of us."

Agents homed in on the new lead. Cautious inquiries by CIA colleagues in Sweden revealed that Sandor Kercsik was a Hungarian-born physician who practiced internal medicine in Goteborg, a port city west of Stockholm. A naturalized Swedish citizen, the forty-eight-year-old doctor had emigrated from Hungary in October 1956 in the wake of the abortive Hungarian Revolution. Agents were also able to determine that Sandor Kercsik had a younger brother, Imre, thirty-four, who was also a physician. He, too, lived and practiced medicine in Goteborg.

Records of the credit card used by Sandor Kercsik to rent the Opel established that the Kercsik brothers were frequent travelers, routinely flying in and out of Frankfurt and Munich and leasing vehicles upon their arrival. The itineraries of the brothers were revealing. Both regularly flew a circuit from Goteborg to Frankfurt or Munich, with frequent connecting flights to Vienna and Budapest. Veteran agents recognized this travel pattern as consistent with a clandestine courier, a support agent who could be the link between Clyde Conrad and his Hungarian masters. In status-conscious Europe, with the highly respected title of doctor on their neutral Swedish passports, the brothers would be able to travel between East and West without raising suspicions. If the Kercsiks were couriers, Budapest had chosen well.

Yet one perplexing detail bothered Al Eways. Sandor Kercsik had stayed overnight at the Conrad residence. Eways, a Palestinian American with more than twenty years of service in Germany, knew that all intelligence services followed strict operational practices designed to minimize security risks—collectively labeled "tradecraft." A central principle of intelligence tradecraft that ensured security was called compartmentation. To the maximum extent possible, members of an espionage conspiracy were kept in the dark about the organization in which they played a role. Couriers simply did not drive to an agent's home and spend the night, or at least they weren't supposed to. In Eways's book, Sandor Kercsik was a courier; of that he felt certain. As for the overnight visit, he thought with a grin, the guy's breaking the rules.

Like everything in the Canasta Player case, the breakthrough in Wiesbaden was shrouded in ambiguity. Still, everyone in Washington sensed that, somehow, Sandor Kercsik's Hungarian background could not be a coincidence, any more than Conrad's relationship with Zoltan Szabo was. Foreign Counterintelligence Activity investigators were certain that, like the enigmatic Zoltan Szabo, the Swedish Hungarian doctors were the sought-after Hungarian connection.

Bob Lunt decided to act. Recalling that his agents' interviews had uncovered a number of soldiers who had been approached by Conrad with an offer to make some extra money, Lunt reached into his extensive operational experience and produced a bold stroke. Why not select one of these soldiers, check him out carefully, then recruit him? The Foreign Counterintelligence Activity could then arrange for him to be transferred to Germany, with instructions to reestablish contact with his old friend and comrade, Clyde.

Lunt explained it this way. Conrad would approach a soldier with an illegal offer only after assessing his potential recruit and concluding that he was worth the risk. If his target declined recruitment but did not report the illegal approach, as required by regulations, Conrad's trust in the person would be reinforced. Clearly, Conrad would reason, here was a person who would wink at a rule.

With this in mind, Lunt counseled, could not Conrad be tempted to reapproach a soldier who had not taken the bait when originally pitched? Now retired and deprived of direct access to classified information, Conrad would need active-duty confederates to steal secrets for him. Why not put such a person in our suspect's path and see if he takes the bait?

Should the gambit succeed, Lunt reasoned, FCA would open a window through which Clyde Lee Conrad could be scrutinized from all angles—money, activities, travel, and associations. The idea was gutsy but fraught with risk. If Conrad saw through the ploy, he might promptly seek refuge in Hungary. Lunt told his investigators that they would have to minimize this risk by selecting the right man for the job. If investigators did their work well and Conrad fell into the trap, he might even recruit the FCA source. If this happened, Wiesbaden investigators would be calling the shots, well positioned to provide answers to the legion of questions that demanding Department of Justice attorneys insisted were a precondition to arrest and prosecution.

Lunt's idea made a lot of sense, particularly because no one had a better idea. The case was stalled, and patience in some quarters was wearing thin. Inside the Beltway, it was being said that FCA seemed unable to figure out how to wrap up the investigation.

Agents chose MSgt. Danny Wilson to play the key role. In the ten years since Conrad had asked him if he was an honest man, Wilson, now in his early forties, had seen his career blossom. When Bob

Lunt's investigators located him, the senior NCO was stationed at Fort Huachuca in Arizona, where he was serving on the faculty at the army's Intelligence Center and School. Since the 1970s, Wilson had maintained occasional contact with Conrad, for whom he retained considerable admiration.

After departing Bad Kreuznach, the bright, smooth-talking Texan had been retrained as a counterintelligence special agent. His memories of Conrad were positive. Like many of the young soldiers in the division headquarters at the time, Danny Wilson had developed a respect bordering on reverence for Mr. Plans. Clyde, Wilson told FCA agents, had all but run the G-3 shop and was a revered role model for the younger soldiers.

Agents contacted Wilson and interviewed him once again about his associations with Conrad. The master sergeant proved to be quick witted and intelligent, with an aura of self-confidence that bordered on cockiness. But cocky or not, Danny Wilson was a man of deep principles who displayed an impressive talent for thinking on his feet. Based on this preliminary assessment, investigators arranged to have the master sergeant take a polygraph examination. The sole purpose was to reassure agents that their candidate for recruitment was providing a faithful account of Conrad's approach in the mid-1970s. It was essential to confirm that Wilson had been entirely truthful when he stated that Conrad had not mentioned espionage, and that he had rejected Clyde's offer. If the master sergeant was to be used as bait in a trap to snare his former friend, he had to be squeaky clean. After being told only that he was being considered for participation in a special project, the NCO willingly took and passed the polygraph exam.

Things now moved quickly. Wilson was told that his friend Clyde Conrad was suspected of espionage and that he had been selected to prove or disprove these suspicions. The master sergeant was incredulous.

"No way, not Clyde," he insisted vehemently. The deeply principled career sergeant simply could not believe that his former buddy and role model was capable of such betrayal. Wilson was adamant, telling FCA agents Eways and Puromaki that Clyde Conrad was not the kind of person who would do such a thing.

Puromaki and Eways reassured Wilson that Conrad was only a suspect, telling the master sergeant that his cooperation could be critical to clearing his friend. Their message to Danny Wilson was persuasive. "If you're correct and Conrad is clean, the best way to prove it is for you to assist us."

Danny Wilson signed up for the mission, which was purely voluntary, clearly convinced that this was exactly what would happen. Now a recruited source of U.S. intelligence, he was given the code name Controlled Source 170 (CS 170). Henceforth, in all operational and investigative reports, his name would not appear.

In volunteering to work with FCA, the veteran master sergeant signed up for an onerous mission. First, he and his family would have to agree to move from the United States to Germany. Once he had succeeded in reestablishing contact with Clyde Conrad, the investigation could be expected to take on a life of its own. As the key man in the operation to expose or clear Conrad, Wilson would have to submit unquestioningly to his FCA case officer's instructions. If the plan worked and Conrad took the bait, the role of Controlled Source 170 would require the feisty master sergeant to lead a complex and demanding double life, always at the beck and call of Conrad and his FCA case officer. This was the reality of life as a so-called double agent, which is what Danny Wilson would become in the event that Conrad responded as hoped and recruited his old friend to join him as a spy for the Hungarians.

In its simplest form, a double agent works for two intelligence services at the same time, with only one of the services understanding this. If Danny Wilson, under the clandestine control of FCA, began to pass documents to the Hungarians through Clyde Conrad, he would qualify for this exotic appellation. But unlike the glamorous, exciting images in espionage fiction, the work of a double agent is tedious, demanding, and lonely. Risks are taken, it is true, but the double agent of the 1980s carried no Walther PPK. As for the bevy of beautiful women who grace the lives of James Bond, in Danny Wilson's world the femme fatale was his wife. Shut out from the secrets of her spouse's conspiratorial career, Shirley Wilson would sustain him as best she could.

As a counterintelligence agent himself, Wilson understood these sacrifices and accepted them. Still, the patriotic NCO could not have foreseen the magnitude of the demands and stresses that would be thrust upon him and his family, nor could he (or his FCA masters) have anticipated that he had embarked on a road that would dominate the next three years of his life. Wilson's double life would ultimately cost him countless nights and weekends away from home; he would put more than 20,000 hard miles on a new car in pursuit of the case; and he would still be responsible for performing his regular duties in his new unit. At the end of each month, there would not be an extra dollar in his paycheck for the countless hours of extra effort.

# 15: Playing to an Empty House

Bob Lunt's gamble paid off. The recruitment of Danny Wilson proved to be a decisive turning point in the Canasta Player investigation.

Foreign Counterintelligence Activity investigators arranged for their new recruit to be reassigned from Arizona to Stuttgart, Germany, in early 1987. There, the master sergeant was assigned to the 527th Military Intelligence Battalion, with duties at its Stuttgart office. From his home to Conrad's haunts in the Bad Kreuznach area was more than a two-hour drive.

The Canasta Player investigation remained the single most restricted case in the army. Particularly in Europe, where the homesteading Conrad seemed to have connections everywhere, even the fact that such an investigation was under way had to be closely held to ensure that neither Budapest nor suspect Conrad became aware of the FCA effort to put the ring out of business.

A certain amount of intelligence tradecraft training was necessary, although far less than would have been required if Danny Wilson had not already been a trained special agent. An important element of that training dealt with techniques for keeping his dual life a secret from superiors, fellow soldiers, and, most importantly, from Clyde Conrad.

Gary Pepper would serve as Danny Wilson's case officer. Pepper explained to the brash master sergeant that Conrad, if he were indeed an agent of the Hungarians, would have received considerable training himself in communications and surveillance detection. Extreme care would thus have to be taken to keep their relationship clandestine. Wilson would be schooled in basic countersurveillance measures. Meetings between Pepper and Wilson would be discreet and conducted during weekends or evenings. Long hours were in store for both men.

In April 1987, the FCA team in Wiesbaden orchestrated the long-awaited approach to reinsert Danny Wilson into Clyde Conrad's world. Taking a cue from Wilson, agents opted for a natural and direct approach. The gutsy master sergeant would drive to Bosenheim and pay a surprise visit on old friends Clyde and Annja. From there, Wilson was to let things take their course. A cover story was developed that Wilson could use to explain his sudden appearance in Germany. But most importantly, Pepper urged, Danny should be relaxed and natural. He shouldn't push it.

Wilson drove to Bosenheim and knocked on the door of Elfelderstrasse 16. Annja Conrad opened the door, greeted Danny with a hug, and called out, "Clyde, come see who's here."

When Conrad appeared, Danny stuck out his hand and called out, "Hi, Clyde, how you doin'?"

Conrad blanched. There was no backslapping greeting or hearty handshake for an old friend. Instead, he stared at Wilson for an instant before speaking in a tense voice.

"Are you here on your own, or did they send you?"

Now it was Wilson's turn to be taken aback. Unaware of the reason for his friend's lukewarm reception, the agile agent didn't miss a beat as he launched into his cover story.

"What do you mean, Clyde? Of course I'm here on my own. I've been sent over from the States on a three-month temporary assignment. Just thought I'd drop by and check in, that's all. You gonna invite me in for a beer or not?"

Conrad seemed to snap out of whatever was troubling him. He invited Wilson into the house and liberated two bottles of beer from the refrigerator. The two men relaxed in Annja's overdecorated living room.

Wilson explained his three-month assignment. He had been sent to Germany to assist the 527th Military Intelligence Battalion in a rewrite of its war plans. Conrad perked up. Before Wilson departed, Clyde made it clear that the two should keep in touch. Danny Wilson returned to Stuttgart with the sense that everything had gone well, still convinced that Clyde was no spy.

As time passed, Controlled Source 170 succeeded in ingratiating himself with Conrad, a process that went more quickly because of the two men's former association. The glib Wilson salted his conversation with cynical remarks about how tough things were at his duty station in Stuttgart, how dumb his officers were, and how fed up he was with the system—themes carefully calculated to appeal to Conrad.

Conrad apparently liked what he was hearing. Danny Wilson and he seemed to have a lot in common. Danny, Conrad sensed, had finally realized that the whole army thing was a big game, orchestrated and coached by egotistical officers and other lifers for their own gratification, all at the expense of the enlisted men. As the friendship matured, Conrad warmed up perceptibly. The more Danny bitched about the hassles of army life, the more Clyde realized that the reappearance of his former friend was a timely piece of good fortune.

This was the critical point in the Wilson gambit. Agents banked on Conrad taking the bait. After all, Danny was a stand-up guy, not a snitch.

Bob Lunt's agents also gambled on a phenomenon that is common to people who are willing to betray their country—what some call the "playing-to-an-empty-house syndrome." Spies almost always think they are something special. When someone such as Clyde Conrad looks in the mirror, he sees the world's cleverest, boldest, and most enterprising fellow. Entering a crowded room, the Clyde Conrads of the world gaze on the assembled masses with pity: These are the ordinary slobs who don't have a clue about how one makes it big in life. Only he, the spy who leads an adventure-laden, dual life, has overcome the odds and broken the code that leads to riches and fulfillment.

But the ego that breeds disloyal and conspiratorial behavior demands recognition. A spy who had amassed a fortune as a communist agent might be seized with an irresistible urge to share his big secret with someone. The frustration of playing to an empty house can be overwhelming, yet the spy realizes that the rules of the espionage game and the consequences of breaking those rules are serious business.

As luck would have it, when Danny Wilson appeared on Clyde Conrad's doorstep in 1987, his old friend was in the throes of this dilemma. In Clyde Lee Conrad's mind, his secret achievements were crying out for recognition and appreciation. Recently retired, deprived of direct access to the classified material that had become his financial mainstay, and haunted by fears that he was about to be arrested, Conrad was deserving of the nickname I eventually gave him—"the once and future spy." Torn between an almost paralyzing fear of arrest and a compulsive desire to resume his ego-gratifying status as the pride of Budapest's agent stable, Conrad needed a new friend and accomplice, someone in whom he could confide, someone who could reinforce his exalted self-image. The Foreign Counterintelligence Activity provided that friend by delivering Danny Wilson.

The two men's friendship reblossomed with astonishing speed. Soon Conrad was offering up cryptic comments about the great opportunities that were out there for a man with Wilson's smarts. Ten years earlier, when Conrad started down this road, Danny Wilson had turned him off. This time around, the Texan played along, nodding understandingly. Conrad caught the signals and began to talk guardedly about his money-making enterprise. Clyde chuckled as he described himself as a highly successful independent information broker. Each time the pair met, Clyde became more explicit, sometimes emboldened by the prodigious quantities of beer he regularly consumed.

Conrad bombarded Wilson with tutorials about his philosophy of life, insisting that he was "totally apolitical" when it came to the confrontation between the Free World and communism. Danny should remember that whatever sins Washington laid at the feet of the Kremlin were no worse than what our own country had done in Vietnam. Clyde solemnly told Wilson that he had taken his son, Andre, to West Berlin. As they stood on a platform gazing into East Berlin, Clyde asked the boy if he knew the difference between the people on each side of the wall. When Andre demurred, Clyde replied, "Nothing. Absolutely nothing," and urged the eleven year old to remember that all political systems were equally bad; none was any better or any worse than any other.

Like a broken record, Clyde drove home his message to Danny. There was a real opportunity for apolitical information brokers. Nothing was more valuable in the world than information—not gold, not diamonds, nothing. Besides, Clyde said with a grin, "They're gonna get it anyway, so why don't we take advantage of it?"

By early summer 1987, Danny Wilson could no longer avoid the truth. His buddy Clyde—his role model, Mr. Plans—was indeed a spy for the communists. Not only that, it appeared that Conrad, having confided in him, was on the verge of a recruitment pitch. The realization was a victory for the case but deeply depressing to the decent and disillusioned Wilson.

During one strange conversation, Conrad became maudlin and rambled on drunkenly. "You don't know how much it means to me that you came along when you did, Danny. You saved my life."

Wilson reported the cryptic remark. No one knew at the time exactly what Conrad was talking about, but if he was feeling indebted to the FCA double agent, so much the better. The plan was coming together.

Throughout the summer of 1987, Conrad spoke of his double life with astonishing candor, openly boasting that he had made a fortune selling secrets to the Hungarian Military Intelligence Service before his retirement. For years, Clyde mused, he had given the Hungarians "whatever they wanted" from the safes of the 8th Infantry Division. Budapest, he was certain, had passed the plundered documents to Moscow. Conrad added with unmistakable pride that until a recent spate of problems with Budapest, he was so highly regarded behind the Iron Curtain that his Hungarian case officer had been awarded a medal by the Soviets.

Retirement had been a difficult adjustment, Conrad observed. But now that Danny had reentered his life, he was determined to mend fences with Budapest and resume his career as an agent. Zoltan Szabo had gotten him started in the business in the mid-1970s before retiring from active duty four years later, he explained. The two friends, Conrad admitted, had eventually had a falling out over how to deal with the Hungarians. Szabo was Budapest's cautious, compliant servant, Clyde noted with disdain. Budapest, he groused, had its fair share of unimaginative, timid souls, men who sometimes failed to appreciate his bold, innovative approach to the business.

Conrad was proud of his achievements, telling Wilson that before his retirement he had been "the best in the business." Since then, he boasted, he had devoted considerable time to developing a vision for a computer-age spy ring. With Wilson on board, Clyde prattled on enthusiastically, there was nothing that they couldn't achieve. Big money was there for the taking. To underscore his point, Conrad confided that he had salted away more than two million marks of his espionage earnings (approximately $1.5 million) in safe-deposit boxes in various Swiss banks.

Clyde showed Danny a Casio pocket calculator. The device, he explained, could store information in an encrypted compartment that no one could access without the password. While demonstrating the Casio, he revealed its password, which the alert master sergeant memorized. (The password, which would one day be useful, was Damian, the middle name of Conrad's son, Andre.) Indicating a small hole in the calculator's case, Conrad said that in an emergency he could zero out the secret compartment by merely inserting the tip of a ballpoint pen. Wilson, Clyde instructed, should acquire a Casio exactly like his. Inside the Casio's encrypted vault, Clyde volunteered, was the phone number of his Hungarian case officer, Miklos, as well as phone numbers of the Center in Budapest.

Danny Wilson was blessed with a keen memory. After each marathon session with Clyde, he was able to provide Gary Pepper with an almost verbatim account of Conrad's revelations. Pepper, in turn, documented the unfolding story in a series of startling contact reports. In Washington, the small circle of people authorized access to the investigation were amazed. The objectives, which had seemed risky and ambitious at the outset, were being fulfilled at a remarkable pace. Conrad's bold recitation of his career as a spy for Budapest to an FCA agent was nothing less than astounding.

To some observers, it all made sense. By exploiting their understanding of the mind-set of the average spy, FCA investigators had brilliantly smoked out one of the worst traitors of the Cold War. But others scoffed at the fantastic stories that Wilson attributed to Conrad. If Conrad were such a successful secret agent, why would he take the risks involved with baring his soul to Danny Wilson? Some argued that the retired sergeant was making it all up to impress his protégé.

During one meeting, after consuming his usual beer ration in a Bad Kreuznach *gasthaus,* Conrad wrote several phone numbers on a coaster and passed it to Danny. The numbers, he confided, were those of the Hungarian and Czechoslovakian security services as well as the personal extension of a high-ranking Hungarian case officer. To further impress his recruit, Conrad opened yet another window on his secret life, confiding that he and Zoltan Szabo had sometimes doubled their return on stolen documents by peddling the same material to the Czech and Hungarian intelligence services. As Conrad made these startling admissions, a tape recorder concealed on Wilson's body preserved them.

Approvals to wire Wilson had been obtained in Washington. By the summer of 1987, sufficient probable cause pointing to Clyde Conrad's espionage existed to justify this investigative measure. Danny Wilson understood the risks of wearing the device but undertook them uncomplainingly. During the Bad Kreuznach meeting, the gambit almost blew the entire investigation. As Clyde and Danny ambled down a pedestrian-only shopping concourse, the cigarette pack–sized cassette recorder came untaped from Wilson's sweaty thigh and began to travel down his leg. The quick-thinking NCO didn't panic. Telling Clyde that he had to relieve himself, Wilson slipped into a nearby alley and hastily refastened the traitorous machine. The comical episode makes a good war story now, but for Wilson it was a near miss. What if the beer-swilling Conrad had decided that he, too, needed to take a leak? Wilson faithfully reported his close call and turned the beer coaster over to Gary, who gleefully added it to the growing list of items that would someday be used in a court of law against Conrad. When the telephone numbers were traced, they proved to be exactly what Conrad said they were.

The egotistical Conrad could not resist sharing yet another juicy fact with Wilson. Because he was Budapest's star agent, Clyde boasted, the Hungarians had recently set up an emergency escape plan. If he were in danger of compromise, the silver-haired spy elaborated in a low voice, he would be spirited to Hungary via an underground escape railroad that led through Denmark and Finland.

On another occasion, waxing sentimentally over a beer at one of his favorite watering holes, Conrad revealed an almost unbelievable episode. In 1986, his fertile mind had exploded with one of his most cunning brainstorms. Why not further multiply the earnings of the business by selling stolen secrets back to the Americans? Doing it had been easy, Clyde said with a grin. Last year, he and a Hungarian accomplice had contacted the CIA. His friend had posed as a disaffected Hungarian intelligence officer whose colleague was interested in defecting. The CIA had jumped at the chance for a recruitment, Clyde said. He and his friend had managed to string along the agency clowns for six months and take them for a small fortune before backing out undetected. Later, Conrad said with a frown, Zoltan Szabo had learned of the freelance operation and blown the whistle in Budapest, creating problems with the Center. It was typical Szabo, Conrad quipped: overly cautious and always looking out for himself.

Wilson dutifully shared Conrad's latest revelation with Gary Pepper, who reported it to FCA headquarters in Washington. When Bob Lunt passed the news to the CIA, the impact was explosive. The David affair, which the agency had embraced as a long-shot opportunity to identify the spy in Europe, had been a scam all along. The news was embarrassing, but the unmasking of the truth behind David's overture to the CIA went a long way to establish the credibility of FCA agent Wilson. After Wilson solved the David mystery, people in Washington paid closer attention to his accounts of Clyde Conrad's revelations.

By July 1987, Conrad openly urged Wilson to sign on to his envisioned high-tech spy venture. To join the team, Clyde told his friend, it would be necessary to impress Budapest. To do this, Conrad counseled, Wilson would have to do something that would show a commitment. In Clyde's lexicon, this meant that Wilson had to cross the espionage Rubicon by stealing classified documents from his office at the 527th Military Intelligence Battalion in Stuttgart.

Conrad had it all mapped out. Danny would steal some documents and Clyde would pass them to the Hungarians with the announcement that he had acquired a valuable new source. It would take some weeks for Budapest to evaluate the material, he explained, but if Danny provided good stuff, Budapest would bless the recruitment and welcome him on board. The key was the commitment.

In Wiesbaden and Washington, Wilson's successful manipulation of Conrad was vindication of the FCA approach to the case. When Wiesbaden agents reported that Conrad had finally abandoned all caution and asked CS 170 to steal classified documents, Washington authorized the FCA double agent to give Conrad a sheath of genuine secret documents. It was a time-proven principle in action: Give a little, get a lot. On August 1, 1987, three months after his appearance at Conrad's Elfelderstrasse home, Danny Wilson made his first delivery of stolen secrets. Over the coming year, the master sergeant was to make eleven such deliveries to his old friend, for which he would be paid almost $30,000.

Danny Wilson's first theft of secrets seemed therapeutic for Clyde Conrad, who was becoming increasingly obsessed with his vision of a high-tech espionage ring. The documents, he told Danny, would show his Hungarian case officer, Miklos, that Budapest's star had latched onto a new, lucrative source of secrets. Because payment from the Hungarians might take some time, Clyde opened his billfold and gave his new recruit 2,000 deutsche marks.

The money came with some sage advice from the veteran spy. "Get some new clothes, Danny. A good spy must dress well."

# 16: The Play Within a Play

Bob Lunt was right. Canasta Player was a ticking time bomb. When I pinned on silver eagles and assumed command of FCA in January 1988, the case was ready to blow. Zoltan Szabo had been located in neutral Austria and identified as the progenitor of the ring. Clyde Lee Conrad had been uncovered as the elusive spy with intellectual, but not legal, certitude. Danny Wilson, Controlled Source 170, had wormed his way into Conrad's confidence and accepted his mentor's recruitment overture to join him in an information-age spy ring. Already, Wilson had made four deliveries of secrets to Clyde for transmittal to the Hungarians.

Two years had already passed since special agent Al Puromaki pointed to Conrad's name on a roster and declared that the recently retired sergeant was the elusive spy. Almost ten years had elapsed since the original CIA warning to the Pentagon that an American traitor was peddling NATO's most sensitive war plans to the Hungarians.

In Wiesbaden, an exhausted Al Puromaki presided over a weary team of investigators and a small surveillance element. Frustrated by the difficulties of communicating with their headquarters in Fort Meade, and overworked and in constant fear of a compromising mismove, Puromaki, Gary Pepper, and their Wiesbaden teammates were understandably fatigued. Foreign Counterintelligence Activity's veteran deputy commander, Bob Bell, was deeply concerned about the situation in Germany. Now that we had the perpetrator in our sights, patience was growing thinner in Washington and Europe. How much longer could Conrad be permitted to walk the streets? Bob pointed out that some people had begun to cynically opine that "FCA folks are making a career out of this case."

I didn't doubt that Bob was on the mark, but when Al Eways and his partner, Chet Boleski, explained the case to me, it was clear that we faced a serious dilemma. Although everyone was certain that Conrad was the spy and that it was time to take him down, no one had any brilliant ideas about how to wrap up the case. Worse yet, it was not possible to review the standard investigative plan that underpins each counterintelligence case: There was none. Canasta Player was being run on the fly, with too many hands stirring the pot. There had been a clear goal when investigators recruited MSgt. Danny Wilson and reassigned him to Europe: Put an agent out there whom Conrad would trust and possibly recruit. But once that milestone had been achieved, no one seemed to know where to go next.

The FBI and the Department of Justice believed that the only way the army could collect the information needed to successfully prosecute Conrad was to request West German assistance in the case. In their view, a partnership with the Germans would enable us to tap Conrad's phone, surveil him full-time, and obtain answers to the many unanswered questions essential to obtaining an indictment and subsequent conviction in a U.S. court.

Seasoned attorneys from the Internal Security Section of the Department of Justice (DOJ) visited FCA's Fort Meade headquarters to plead their case soon after my assumption of command. The DOJ men were accompanied by FBI agents who were working the bureau's piece of the complex investigation—at the time a single spin-off case on an ex-soldier thought to have been recruited by Conrad during his service in Bad Kreuznach. The message of the FBI and Department of Justice attorneys was clear: It was all well and good to get Clyde Conrad to take the bait and recruit Danny Wilson as his agent, but this activity, the "FCA-orchestrated dance" between Conrad and Wilson, was not the big case. The real issue was Conrad and his unnamed accomplices and what they had done together from the 1970s to the present. Department of Justice agents were politely skeptical. The Conrad-Wilson relationship, they admonished, was a subplot, a play within a play that could distract us from our real objective—Conrad's espionage for the Hungarians. It was a compelling observation.

Department of Justice attorney John Dion put it well: "You don't want to arrest Conrad, who might be the worst Army spy since World War II, and prosecute him for this flimsy relationship with Danny Wilson. You want to get the guy on the bigger crime of giving away the war plans for the defense of Europe."

The FBI-DOJ visitors advocated the immediate establishment of a formal Canasta Player steering committee in Washington. Membership, they urged, should be limited to the army as the lead agency in the case; to the FBI, which would conduct all stateside spin-off cases dealing with former soldiers; and to the Department of Justice, whose advice was essential if we ever expected to see Clyde Lee Conrad in a federal courtroom. Once again, DOJ attorney John Dion's voice was the most persuasive: Ill-considered investigative measures could harm our chances for an eventual indictment and conviction.

"If you have a choice of two ways to achieve a given investigative objective," the Justice Department attorney elaborated, "one of those techniques might play well in a courtroom, while the other could be impeached by a smart defense attorney. We're not trying to run your case for you, but we are asking for the chance to make timely input that will make our job easier later on."

These were sound arguments. Who wanted to do a bush-league investigation that no self-respecting prosecutor would touch? After all, wasn't obtaining an indictment and conviction the desired endgame?

But there was a serious problem with this otherwise reasonable proposal. It lacked any mention of a role for our CIA colleagues, without whom there would have been no investigation. I had already visited Gus Hathaway and knew that the CIA was continuing to provide valuable advice and assistance to FCA on all sorts of important case-related matters. The CIA had continuing equities in the investigation, not the least of which was a valid interest in protecting their sources. Equally important to the investigation were the agency's well-placed contacts and other capabilities in Germany that the FBI and army intelligence lacked.

When I pointed this out, the DOJ and FBI visitors remonstrated strongly. Both agencies were uncomfortable with any CIA role in the proposed steering committee, something that will come as no surprise to anyone with Washington experience. Our Department of Justice colleagues placed a premium on openness and legality. Potentially, anything we did in the investigation, and anyone who played a role in the case, was subject to scrutiny at some future date in the unforgiving light of a U.S. courtroom. The CIA certainly did not advocate a rogue investigation, but its culture was of necessity secretive. Espionage, after all, was illegal in most nations of the world, even though all nations practice it. To the average CIA officer, a courtroom was a place to be avoided. Consequently, the Department of Justice viewed fooling around with the secretive CIA as anathema, just as our CIA friends felt that testifying in open court was hardly a career-enhancing endeavor for anyone whose profession depends upon anonymity. As for the FBI, its agents were not prone to demonstrate overflowing affection for the CIA in 1988.

A team player by nature, I was receiving a baptism in inside-the-Beltway politics. My preference was to avoid taking sides in an issue that was at least partially rooted in parochialism, but this was not possible. Having politely heard the arguments made by my visitors, I expressed the view that Canasta Player was a joint endeavor. A steering group made sense to improve communications and develop smart courses of action. But army counterintelligence insisted that the steering group include all agencies with an equity in the case—the U.S. Army, FBI, Department of Justice, and the CIA. It was not a popular ruling with my visitors.

Within a few weeks of assuming command, I traveled to Germany to visit the Wiesbaden team and to chair a full-dress meeting of all parties who were participating in any aspect of Canasta Player. Participants included Washington- and European-based representatives of the FBI, CIA, Department of Justice, FCA, and U.S. Army, Europe.

The strategy session convened in the U.S. embassy on the banks of the Rhine River in Bonn, Germany. Arrayed around the intimidating expanse of the embassy's conference table and in chairs lining the room's perimeter sat more than twenty attendees. Most of the meeting was devoted to a discussion of strategy and support-related issues, most of which were routine and uncontroversial.

The nadir of the conference occurred when the FBI and the Department of Justice tabled their proposal to bring the Germans into the close-hold investigation. To move the case along, they argued, German investigative assistance was essential. Unassisted by German investigative agencies, the army would never collect the information required for an indictment.

I had given this matter considerable thought since it surfaced in Washington several weeks earlier. The FBI and Justice Department officers were correct in one sense. German involvement would yield a tap on Conrad's telephone and access to investigative resources that would facilitate collection of the information required to wrap up the investigation. But the risks of sharing the case with our German allies far outweighed the possible gains.

Gus Hathaway and I had each spent years in Germany. Both of us shared a great deal of respect for our German colleagues. But reality was reality. The Germans were penetrated. We could not enlist them as partners in the case at this time unless we were willing to accept the very real possibility that the case's existence would become known to the East Germans, who would warn the Soviets or the Hungarians. Determined not to budge on this vital issue, I closed the discussion after fifteen minutes of animated but polarized exchange. Canasta Player would remain a unilateral, U.S.-only investigation for the foreseeable future. The time might come when confiding in the Bonn government would be necessary, but that time had not arrived. The ruling was not welcomed by our FBI and Department of Justice partners, but it was the correct decision, as events would later prove.

# 17: Legendary

Clyde Conrad was a dynamo of activity. Resurrected from depression and lethargy by the windfall appearance of a new recruit, the rejuvenated spy affixed himself to MSgt. Danny Wilson like a pilot fish. Once Wilson had crossed the line and coughed up secrets from his unit's safes, Conrad began to summon his protégé to frequent meetings, during which he would ramble nostalgically about past espionage glories and hold forth on his brainchild—the creation of a ring of high-tech agents. To surveil Conrad's increasingly frequent meetings with Wilson, FCA agents were reinforced with agents from Lt. Col. Jack Hammond's German-based 527th Military Intelligence Battalion.

On February 3, 1988, Danny Wilson met with Clyde Conrad and handed over a thick bundle of classified documents for passage to Budapest. Another dip into his unit's safe was vital, Clyde had told Danny, because Budapest was not yet convinced that the new recruit was for real. Wilson feigned anger over Budapest's vote of no-confidence. "What does a guy have to do to become accepted?" he complained. He had made his commitment more than six months ago, Danny reminded Clyde, yet Budapest was still waffling. Didn't they know the risks he was taking and the penalty if he were caught?

Wilson's angry words were intended to put Conrad under pressure. The deeper he could become embroiled in Conrad's conspiracy, the more he could learn, all of which would be reported to Gary Pepper. Impatience with Budapest's lukewarm reaction to his commitment was natural. Danny needed some sign of encouragement that his risks were appreciated.

Conrad was apologetic. Danny shouldn't worry. He was a member of the team, even if Budapest was slow to show its appreciation.

Clyde thumbed through the latest stack of secret documents and grinned.

"These look great," he enthused. "It's time for you to meet one of my friends." The friend was courier Imre Kercsik. Within minutes, with Wilson at his side, Conrad dialed Kercsik's number in Goteborg in a clear attempt to signal Danny that he was indeed a trusted member of the team.

A meeting was arranged. In ten days, Danny, Clyde, and Imre Kercsik would rendezvous in the Mainz Hilton Hotel. Wilson was finally going to have a glimpse into the business through the eyes of one of its Hungarian participants.

This significant development, which was flashed to headquarters in Fort Meade, generated a frantic reaction. The Department of Justice had repeatedly emphasized how important it was to the case to catch Conrad in the act of meeting with agents of a foreign power. A surveillance of the planned meeting in Mainz might accomplish this goal. To complete the task, it was essential to further reinforce the surveillance team in Wiesbaden.

Within twenty-four hours, twelve volunteers were identified at Fort Meade and dispatched to Germany, all equipped with surveillance radios and wearing European-manufactured clothing that would blend into the surroundings in the riverside German city. Pat Griffin, FCA's miracle-working budget officer, seemed to produce money from thin air for the high-cost deployment. During the next six months, Griffin would conjure up more than $850,000 of unprogrammed dollars to finance the finale of Canasta Player.

In Wiesbaden, Gary Pepper coached his agent as the day of the meeting approached. Foreign Counterintelligence Activity technical wizard Dick Bankston outfitted Wilson with a miniature microphone and a tiny, low-powered radio frequency (RF) transmitter. The microphone, concealed in Wilson's clothes, would pick up conversation and beam it a short distance to an agent carrying a tape recorder. As the time of the meeting approached, FCA surveillance personnel flooded the area around the modern hotel. Among them were agents bearing still and video cameras.

On February 13, 1988, Wilson showed up at the Hilton carrying secret documents that Conrad could pass to the Hungarian. With counterintelligence agents blanketing the area, Conrad and his new recruit entered the hotel's ground-floor cocktail lounge, The Bistro.

Clyde introduced Danny Wilson to a tall, slim, dark-haired man. A Buddy Holly doppelganger in horn-rimmed glasses, Imre Kercsik grinned and shook Wilson's hand.

For the next several hours, the trio sat at a table and chatted. A raucous Fasching celebration was under way in the lounge, which was packed with revelers, many in wild costumes, most of them drinking heavily. Imre and Conrad were clearly close friends, Wilson noted as the two spies consumed impressive quantities of wine and beer. The more Conrad and Kercsik drank, the bolder their reminiscences about life as secret agents of Budapest became. Obviously intent on impressing Wilson with their exciting and lucrative clandestine lives, Conrad and his sidekick from Sweden swapped stories of their espionage exploits. As the pair rambled on, the RF transmitter concealed on Danny Wilson beamed their words to a tape recorder carried by special agent Meg Reilly. Because of the short range of the device, Reilly had been directed to get as close as possible to the conspirators. This she did, finding a chair so close to Conrad that Clyde was later heard on the tape commenting about the good-looking woman at the next table.

Some of the two men's revelations were new; some Wilson had heard before. Zoltan Szabo, Conrad and Imre Kercsik revealed, held the rank of colonel in the Hungarian Military Intelligence Service. Szabo had indeed brought Conrad into the business in the 1970s and mentored him, but their relationship had cooled after Szabo had informed Budapest about Clyde's freelancing. Conrad had first met Sandor Kercsik at the time of his recruitment, when Budapest assigned the elder physician as his courier. Later, Imre followed in his brother's footsteps to become Conrad's courier. Imre boasted that his brother had been working for the Hungarians for the better part of two decades. Both men talked openly about Conrad's Hungarian case officer, Miklos.

But the high point of the meeting was when Conrad, in his cups, goaded Imre Kercsik: "Go on, Imre, tell Danny what they think of me in Budapest."

The Hungarian smiled. "Why, that's easy, Clyde. In Budapest, I hear what they say about you. You're the best since World War II—you're legendary."

Before the meeting ended, Conrad furtively slipped a parcel of classified documents into courier Imre Kercsik's shoulder bag. Danny had come through again.

• • •

It would be satisfying to gloat about how perfectly FCA surveillance agents captured the compromising Mainz rendezvous in living color, but this was reality, not Hollywood. In spite of the presence of agents with still and video cameras, none of the surveillance photography proved usable. Investigators obtained pictures of feet, legs, the ceiling, and neighboring customers, all of it useless. Fortunately, Danny Wilson's hidden transmitter had picked up key parts of Conrad and Imre Kercsik's espionage braggadocio, in spite of the Fasching blowout under way in the bar and Clyde Conrad's soft voice.

These audiotapes produced valuable information. The chummy bragging session between Clyde Conrad and Imre Kercsik reinforced the picture of the Szabo-Conrad conspiracy that Danny Wilson had been reporting since the summer of 1987—a significant contribution to the case. Nonetheless, I could not ignore the disappointing results of the technical surveillance of the Mainz meeting. If we were to document Conrad's espionage as the Washington lawyers were demanding, our agents urgently needed training in clandestine photography. Taking pictures with small cameras concealed in purses or attaché cases was a demanding skill that required trained agents with an aptitude for the techniques.

Weaknesses such as this could not be permitted to plague the investigation. We turned to our FBI partners for training support. Within days, special agent Joe Avigone, the FBI's premier expert in clandestine photography, arrived in Wiesbaden. Each day, the skilled agent patiently spent hours with the FCA surveillance team, which by now numbered more than two dozen people. After demonstrating the correct techniques, Avigone would turn his students loose on the streets of Wiesbaden to take practice rolls of film. Then the FBI expert selected those agents whose pictures demonstrated promise. Finalists received additional training and practice. In the future, they would be our dedicated photographers.

The challenge of mounting effective surveillance operations was significant. In 1987, FCA had established army counterintelligence's first permanent surveillance team and received valuable start-up training from the British Strategic Intelligence Wing in Ashford, England. Our skilled British cousins, with extensive experience in North-

ern Ireland, had provided valuable and realistic training in surveillance techniques in an urban environment. Nonetheless, conditions
in the more rural Bosenheim–Bad Kreuznach area made day-to-day
surveillance of Conrad difficult. To complicate the challenge, Conrad had been trained by the Hungarians in countersurveillance tactics, which he employed when on the move. Fearing compromise,
the agents assigned to tail Conrad had become wary, perhaps overly
so. No one wanted to be the goat.

# 18: I've Got a Guy in V Corps

Clyde Conrad was driving Danny Wilson crazy. Once Clyde had his claws sunk deeply into the master sergeant, his greed escalated. Each time the hapless Wilson received a cryptic phone call from his new mentor summoning him to yet another meeting, it meant long hours behind the wheel of a car. And, because the hard-pressed master sergeant was our man as well, each rendezvous with Conrad could become three meetings. Typically, Wilson would first meet with Gary to plan his actions for the Conrad meeting. Then he would meet with Conrad in long, tedious sessions during which Clyde the Glide would drink beer and talk incessantly in a soft voice. Afterward, there would be a debriefing with case officer Pepper. It was a man-killing pace that Pepper and Wilson were to maintain for almost eighteen months.

Shortly after the meeting in the Mainz Hilton, the phone in Danny Wilson's Stuttgart quarters rang. It was Clyde.

"Good news," Conrad announced cheerfully. "Meet me next Wednesday [February 26] at the Heidelberger Hauptbahnhof, the main railroad station in Heidelberg."

Foreign Counterintelligence Activity investigators in Wiesbaden reacted to Wilson's alert. Was Conrad about to introduce Wilson to his Hungarian case officer, Miklos? Once again, the cool Wilson arrived in Heidelberg wearing a microphone and tape recorder, while FCA surveillance agents hovered near the gray stone railroad station.

Conrad arrived in his silver Audi after another breathtaking run down the autobahn at almost 200 kilometers per hour (close to 125 miles per hour). The conspirators linked up in front of the railroad station and went to a nearby Chinese restaurant for lunch. No Hungarian joined the pair.

Clyde was upbeat. Sucking down his first beer, he grinned at Wilson. Someone in Budapest had finally made a decision. Danny was on board.

"Congratulations," he gushed. "They liked the stuff you provided. You're a member of the team now, with a starting salary of fifty thousand deutsche marks a year." A beaming Conrad slid a white envelope across the table. "Here's the first ten thousand on account."

Wilson pocketed the envelope as the silver-haired spy continued to speak.

"There are some things they want you to try and obtain," Clyde explained as he passed Wilson a piece of paper the size of a three-by-five card. It was a neatly printed wish list, beginning with two documents. One was the secret war plan (Oplan 33001) for Danny's unit, the 527th Military Intelligence Battalion; the other was a request for the battalion's classified document accountability record. The latter document amounted to a shopping list, a menu that would tell the Hungarians which sensitive documents were available for theft from Wilson's unit. Other entries on the list included "Battalion cooperation and collaboration with CIA, FBI, BND, MAD" (the latter two being West German intelligence and security organizations) and "Structure of the battalion, organization, strength." The final entry on the list was a request that Wilson reveal the targets of his unit's current counterintelligence investigations.

This tasking by Budapest was particularly noteworthy. Conrad and the Hungarians surely saw a major advantage in the recruitment of Danny Wilson. After all, what better place to have a source than in the local army counterintelligence unit? The new recruit could serve a valuable function by revealing which Americans were suspected of disloyalty—a perfect safety net to protect Warsaw Pact agent operations. Small wonder that once Conrad got over his initial fright at seeing Wilson on his doorstep, he decided that the reappearance in Germany of his former comrade was a godsend. Conrad the spy had recruited a spy catcher.

Conrad handed Wilson a second list.

"These are things that they want me to get. You can keep it in case you can pick one of them up."

Danny Wilson glanced at the list on the card and caught his breath. Included on the list of ten documents were secret and top-secret war plans that he recognized as some of the most sensitive secrets of the American military in Europe. Conrad took a large swallow of beer, lowered his voice, and dropped the bomb.

"I've got a guy in V Corps who is going to get me some of these in a couple of weeks."

Wilson, knowing immediately how critical this tidbit would be to Gary and his people, shot Clyde a wide grin. "I've really got to hand it to you, Clyde. You never cease to amaze me."

Conrad beamed and rewarded himself by ordering yet another beer.

Shortly after the Heidelberg meeting, a somber Danny Wilson turned over the two lists to Gary Pepper. They were sobering proof that his old friend Clyde was not only a spy but a serious threat to the entire defense of Europe. Wiesbaden agents copied the originals, prepared chain-of-custody documents, and bagged the incriminating lists for possible future use as evidence in a court of law. The originals were brought by courier to Washington. There, FBI laboratory experts quickly concluded that both documents were printed on water-soluble paper consistent with that used by the Soviets and other Warsaw Pact intelligence services. (The paper dissolves almost instantly in the mouth or when thrown in a toilet.) The fact that the wish lists were written on this type of paper, in a style consistent with that of a European drafter (December was abbreviated "Dez" instead of "Dec," for example), indicated that the lists were probably provided by Budapest, as Conrad had claimed. Had Conrad himself made up the lists to impress Wilson, it was unlikely that they would have shown this oddity.

There was jubilation in Wiesbaden and Washington. Foreign Counterintelligence Activity's controlled source had pulled it off. Danny Wilson was now a recruited agent of the Hungarian Military Intelligence Service. That was the good news. But the challenge was to cope with the bad news, and it was truly bad news. Conrad seemed to have succeeded in recruiting a well-placed confederate, possibly in the Frankfurt headquarters of V Corps. I would have to report this development to Gen. Glenn T. Otis, the four star who commanded the U.S. Army in Europe.

At my Fort Meade headquarters and in Wiesbaden, FCA investigators focused on developing an aggressive investigative game plan for General Otis's approval. If we were going to ask the general for time to unmask Conrad's source, I would have to have a plan with an envisioned endgame. It would be indefensible to ask for an open-ended continuation of the decade-long case.

# 19: Clyde

## Spring 1988

Clyde Conrad took a big swallow of beer, then resumed his attack on the keyboard of his Apple computer. The more he dwelled on the shabby treatment he was getting from Budapest, the more he was tempted to tell Miklos and his bosses to go to hell. Couldn't the fools see the opportunity that was staring them in the face? By now, his boy Danny had provided classified documents no fewer than five times. Conrad reflected bitterly on the fact that more than six months had elapsed since Danny Wilson made the big commitment. Six months, yet still no feedback or money was forthcoming from Budapest.

This is no way to run a business, Clyde grumbled to himself as he banged angrily on the keyboard. Why should I have to keep paying Danny out of my own pocket to keep him on the hook? The guy is perfect for a key role in the new network, a controller who can actually recruit new sources. Don't those idiots appreciate how hard it is to locate and cultivate someone with the smarts and nerve to function in that role? Clyde knew that his only recourse was to go over the stubborn Miklos's head, and that's what he was doing.

Someone in Budapest has to know what a break it was to latch onto Danny and how shitty he's being treated, Clyde muttered. Miklos has lost his nerve, and that's that. He sees MI double agents behind every door. Yeah, Danny's an MI guy, but that's the beauty of it. The boy is our ace in the hole, our safety net, a master sergeant sitting in a counterintelligence unit where he can provide early warning if something goes wrong. That clown Miklos just doesn't get it, Clyde moaned as he punished the Apple's keyboard. He ought to know that I'm too experienced to be taken in. Danny's for real, and with his gift of gab and access to the good stuff, he'll make us all rich.

Clyde put the finishing touches on an emotional letter to the Center. The text was blunt and uncompromising. Budapest needed to

have it laid out in spades, Conrad felt. The letter did just that, documenting in strong words the shameful lack of response to Wilson's
obvious contributions. He owed it to Danny to make his case to Miklos's superiors. Who could blame Danny for complaining? I asked
him to make a commitment, and he did, Clyde recalled. I'd be pissed
and ready to quit, too, if I were in his boots.

Conrad proofread his letter to Budapest, his eyes falling on the
key paragraph that described the problems he was having with Miklos as he attempted to keep the increasingly impatient Danny Wilson on the hook.

> The guidance that I gave to the individual was to provide
> something—anything, so long as it was classified. I told him this
> would show good intent and get things started. He would get
> a little money and we would have a basis for operating. He said
> no, this wasn't just a small shipment but also represented a com-
> mitment on his part and that he wanted to see a commitment
> on your part. I told him no problem, everything would be OK.
> This guidance was based on personal historical data. I know ex-
> actly what I received and what I provided the first time, which
> was nothing classified. Your representative's response was to say
> it wasn't worth anything and there was no payment and no com-
> mitment. THIS PASSIVE OPPOSITION SERVED NO PUR-
> POSE EXCEPT TO DAMAGE MY CREDIBILITY WITH THE
> SOURCE. Something I must maintain if I want to do business.

Conrad recalled nostalgically his start in the business. Szabo, who
at the time was his supervisor in the headquarters, had begun to
speak coyly of an opportunity to do some "good business." Conrad
chuckled, recalling how easily he had guessed what Zoltan was leading up to and how he had let the older man play his hand. Sure, he
told Szabo, he was amenable in principle to any proposition that involved a chance to earn some extra cash. In the late autumn of 1975,
Szabo suggested a meeting with an unidentified friend who could
provide more details about a lucrative second career. Conrad readily agreed.

Clyde could still picture the booth in a *gasthaus* in nearby Gau-
Bickelheim. There was Szabo, all business, with his usual thin smile,

introducing Clyde to Sandor Kercsik, code-named Alex. As the three men dined and drank, Szabo and Kercsik popped the question without great fanfare. Their business was providing classified information to the Hungarian Military Intelligence Service, and Clyde had been evaluated as a potential bright star who would do well in the enterprise. What did he think?

Conrad recalled how surprised the two men were at his unhesitating agreement to sign up for the enterprise. When Alex bluntly asked him what he was prepared to steal from his workplace, Conrad had replied simply, "everything." Clyde remembered his first operational test as if it had been last week. After lunch, Szabo and Kercsik informed him that Budapest desired an immediate demonstration of his sincerity and commitment. Within minutes, with Szabo at the wheel, the pair arrived at the Rose Barracks headquarters of the division. Clyde strode boldly into the G-3 Plans section and stole a pile of documents. It had been that simple. Sandor promptly transported the haul to Budapest, where the Center declared its satisfaction with the take.

That was it. Almost overnight, Clyde remembered with a smile, he had become a recruited source in the Hungarian stable. By January 1976, Sandor had escorted Clyde to Innsbruck, where he had met his first case officer, Lajos. The Hungarian had trained his new pupil in espionage tradecraft, including surveillance and countersurveillance measures, clandestine communications, and agent photography. Conrad excelled. Henceforth, Budapest instructed, the new recruit would be known by the cover name Charlie. For this successful recruitment, Budapest awarded the proud and satisfied Zoltan Szabo a 25,000 deutsche mark bonus.

And well he ought to have been rewarded, Conrad thought with a grin. As Budapest's newest recruit, he had gone on a collection frenzy. Those Hunkies in Budapest never knew what hit them. By 1980, the bold and diligent Charlie had stolen so many secret and top-secret documents from his office safes that delighted officers at the Budapest Center proudly informed Zoltan Szabo, "Conrad is the best agent that the entire East Bloc has recruited since the Second World War."

With that record, Conrad reflected angrily, how could they treat him with such disrespect on the eve of his greatest triumph? His brainchild, "the enterprise," the high-tech espionage ring he would build around himself and Wilson, would revolutionize spying for all time. It had been a lot of work, Conrad recalled with satisfaction, but the efforts had paid off. Even now, the plan for this history-making ring of spies—Operations Plan 001—was nearing completion. But if the timid bureaucrats in Budapest couldn't open their small minds, Conrad lamented bitterly, the opportunity of a lifetime would elude them all.

Clyde folded the completed appeal to Budapest with satisfaction and prepared it for dispatch. This was a desperation measure, he knew, but he had been patient for too long. After all, how can you run a streamlined, high-tech business if those backward jerks in Budapest can't do better than six months' turnaround on evaluation and payment? If Miklos's feelings are hurt, fuck him. I made the guy's career for him, he's had months to respond, and I'm still holding Danny's hand and paying him out of pocket. I deserve better than that.

West Berlin, 1986: Author and 766th MI Detachment operations officer Bob Thayer. Thayer orchestrated Operation Lake Terrace and the James Hall investigation.

Special agent Jodene Thayer, who captured KGB Lt. Col. Kiryukhin, receives a decoration from Brig. Gen. Thomas Griffin, commander, Berlin Brigade. Colonel Tony Lackey looks on.

"Vasily," KGB Lt. Col. Valery Kiryukhin, detained by 766 MI Detachment agents in November 1985.

KGB officer Vyacheslav Londovich Latyshev, detained in November 1985 while serving as a lookout for Kiryukhin.

KGB agent Anatoly Viktorovich Agafonov was also detained by the 766th MI Detachment during Operation Lake Terrace.

Courier Sandor Kercsik serviced Zoltan Szabo, Clyde Conrad, and others for twenty years.

Zoltan Szabo and Clyde Conrad in mid-1970s after Szabo recruited friend Clyde to sell war plans to the Hungarians.

Vienna, June 1988: FCA surveillance photo showing Conrad meeting with his case officer "Miklos," Hungarian intelligence agent Andras Berenyi, in the Gosser Beer Hall.

Ilona Szabo, the Hungarian folk opera singer wife of Zoltan Szabo.

Courier Imre Kercsik broke the rules and befriended Conrad.

Former paratrooper Thomas Mortati, recruited by Szabo and arrested by the Italians in 1989.

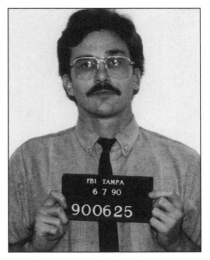

Former Sergeant Rod Ramsay, arrested by the FBI in June 1990.

Staff Sergeant Jeffrey Rondeau stole documents from the 8th infantry division; arrested by FBI and sentenced to 18 years.

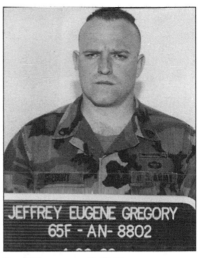

Staff Sergeant Jeff Gregory, arrested by FBI in April 1993; sentenced to 18 years.

Kelly Church Warren, arrested by FBI; sentenced to 25 years.

August 23 1988: Arrest! Clyde Conrad in mugshot taken by Germans.

"Miklos," Clyde Conrad's Hungarian case officer.

History is made. Clyde Conrad, minutes after receiving the first and only life sentence for treason in German history.

June 1990: in front of courthouse in Koblenz, Germany; Conrad is sentenced to life in prison. Author, Norman Runk, and Gary Pepper.

Volkhard Wache, GBA prosecutor who prosecuted Clyde Conrad.

BKA investigator Holger Klein, who took Conrad into custody.

Manfred Rutkowski captained the BKA investigative team.

GBA prosecutor Friederich Hecking.

Lieutenant General William E. Odom, without whom the Clyde Conrad ring would probably have escaped justice.

Canasta Player team in Weisbaden, Germany. Active agent on left blurred, Norman Runk, 2d from left; Joe Herda, 4th from left; Meg Reilly 6th from left, Dave Grof, 9th from left; Gary Pepper, top right; Dave Guethlein, 3d from right,back; Bob Gaiter, 4th from right, back; Mike McAdoo, 6th from right, back.

James Hall as he was led to a hearing on pretrial confinement at Fort Meade, Maryland, December 1988.

The Meister, Huseyin Yildirim, after his arrest by the FBI. Yildirim is serving life in prison.

The CIA team that helped break the Canasta Player case. Martha Graves, Gus Hathaway's secretary (who is still active and is blurred), Gus Hathaway, and John Whiteley.

FCA agent Nick Pokrovsky receives award from CIA director William J. Casey.

Spring 1989: CIA headquarters, Langley, Virginia. CIA director William Webster presents award to author and the FCA team for their triumphant work in the Conrad and Hall cases. From left, Dave Owen, Jim Whittle, Bob Thayer, Director Webster, Bob Watson, author, Norman Runk, Bob Bell, Al Puromaki, and Gary Pepper.

# 20: The Full-Court Press

Within days of Conrad's unsettling boast about his V Corps source, I prepared to depart for Germany, Heidelberg bound. The trip's immediate purpose was to provide the commander in chief (CINC), General Otis, a progress report on the investigation. My debut with the powerful four star did not promise to be pleasant. I could report progress on the investigation, but Conrad's boast that his "V Corps guy" was poised to deliver more war plans was a dark cloud that would surely eclipse our hard work. The colonel from Washington was not bearing good tidings.

The discovery by Danny Wilson that another betrayal of secrets was imminent threatened our efforts. My superiors were urging that we move the decade-long investigation to a rapid conclusion, but how could we comply with this guidance when a new investigative challenge now loomed in the form of a mole somewhere in V Corps?

How much latitude we might still have depended upon General Otis. As commander in chief of the U.S. Army in Europe (CINC-USAREUR), the four star was responsible for the lives of some 200,000 American soldiers in the event of war. If he were to declare the impending betrayal of his latest war plans unacceptable and demand an end to the investigation, who would argue with him? The stakes of my briefing were thus high. Somehow, I had to obtain a green light for one final phase of Canasta Player.

On the eve of my trip, a disquieting sense that the investigation was bogged down had taken hold in Washington. In Wiesbaden, Al Puromaki and his hard-pressed agents were gaining valuable insights into Clyde Conrad's state of mind, but events seemed to be controlling the investigation. Each time Conrad would summon Danny Wilson for a meeting, Puromaki's Wiesbaden agents would be in hot pursuit, always struggling to satisfy the sometimes shifting priorities relayed from their Fort Meade headquarters. This reactive posture and the embarrassing weaknesses in surveillance photography were not the only problems in the investigation. Other than Conrad's boasts to Danny Wilson, we had still failed to link the retired sergeant with a known agent of a foreign power. Imre Kercsik, our Department of Justice colleagues informed me, did not qualify. Miklos did. Imre Kerscik and brother, Sandor, were Hungarian emigrés who carried Swedish passports. Somehow, we needed to trigger a meeting between Conrad and a card-carrying line officer of the Hungarian Military Intelligence Service.

But most importantly, FCA investigators needed to take positive control of the investigation and direct events along lines that satisfied the case's objectives, which had now been expanded. We were to document Conrad's espionage to the satisfaction of the lawyers so that he could be arrested, tried, and convicted. Along the way, we had to uncover the mysterious V Corps mole. We needed a plan to do this, something that would sell in Washington and Heidelberg. If General Otis recommended an immediate end to the investigation, we were dead in the water.

At the top of the agenda had to be an escalation of the surveillance effort. In spite of the FBI training, overworked surveillance agents had struck out once again in Heidelberg with their clandestine cameras. The solution, FBI trainer Avigone emphasized, was simple: "Practice, practice, practice." It was essential to put an end to the embarrassing strikeouts and produce pictures of Conrad as he pursued his clandestine contacts.

The audiotapes from the Heidelberg restaurant meeting were better than those of the Mainz meeting, but they would have to be enhanced to filter out the distracting background noise. This was another service that the FBI would perform.

But there was another problem with the tapes, one that could not be fixed electronically. The difficulty was Danny Wilson, who had an irritating habit of talking when he should have been listening. Truly artful at getting Conrad to drop his guard and open up, the loquacious master sergeant also had a penchant for interrupting at key moments when it seemed that Conrad was about to reveal something critical. Case officer Gary Pepper needed to get on top of this one, because it was driving everyone crazy—above all, the lawyers. If Conrad was inclined to talk, we counseled Gary, tell Danny to let him ramble. Wilson should feel free to nudge the conversation into productive directions, but he must let Clyde do most of the talking. Hours of tapes dominated by Danny Wilson's voice were not the objective.

Pepper doggedly attempted to persuade Danny Wilson that silence could be a virtue. Let Clyde fill the voids, Pepper urged. You might be surprised at what he reveals. But the strong-willed Wilson resisted. "Clyde has known me for years," he retorted. "He knows how I am—how I tend to dominate the conversation—and it won't seem natural if I suddenly change." Pepper shrugged his shoulders. Truth be known, he thought to himself, if we make Danny change too much, he won't be comfortable with the new image, and he'll probably be less effective. Until the end of the case, Danny Wilson did it his way.

In Wiesbaden, FCA investigators prepared to escalate the investigation. The plan I would carry to General Otis called for a full-court press of Conrad in a risky attempt to smoke out any possible confederates. The new tactics would begin with a stepped-up, around-the-clock surveillance of Conrad and his residence in place of the sporadic, event-related surveillance we were currently conducting. All agents were briefed on the need to identify everyone whom Conrad contacted.

Apart from the heightened risk of detection, a surveillance of this magnitude is extremely manpower intensive. Fifty trained agents are required to maintain an around-the-clock surveillance for an extended period of time. From the ranks of the FCA and other army intelligence units, agents packed their bags and booked flights to Germany.

Foreign Counterintelligence Activity surveillance pilot Capt. Bill Burns deployed to Germany, bringing with him a package of technical gear and tricks that would permit close coordination with surveillance agents on the ground. Nicknamed Sky King by his comrades, Burns would rent a suitable aircraft upon his arrival and mount the electronics on it.

The aircraft was necessary because the village of Bosenheim was small and isolated and because Conrad was terrorizing FCA surveillance people with his reckless driving. Not only did he have an obsession with driving a hundred miles an hour, he was given to doubling back and employing other driving gambits that agents recognized as countersurveillance measures.

Sky King arrived in Germany and located a suitable light aircraft at the Darmstadt Air Club. Burns and FCA technical expert Dick

Bankston promptly festooned the rented plane with antennae and electronic tracking equipment. As Burns took the modified craft through its paces, Murphy's Law took over. When the plane landed, a metal antenna dragged along the runway and sent sparks flying. An elderly German woman on the small airfield had been watching the strangers tinkering with the plane and wondered what they were doing. When the sparks began to fly, she called the local police. Terrorists were operating out of the *flugplatz*.

German police responded to the call and confronted the hapless pilot. Burns explained that they were U.S. Army personnel engaged in testing new weather surveillance equipment. Mollified, the police backed off, but not before a report of the incident traveled to the army's Heidelberg headquarters, where it had to be defused by intelligence staff officers.

In one chilling episode, with an FCA surveillance vehicle in hot pursuit, Conrad had raced down a narrow country road and wheeled into a *gasthaus* parking lot. Clamoring out of the silver Audi, Clyde leaned against its rear fender, lit a cigarette, and stared down the road he had just traveled. Foreign Counterintelligence Activity agent Bob Gaiter, code-named Gator, was controlling the surveillance from a nearby hilltop. Observing Conrad's gambit through binoculars, the Gator keyed his radio. "Don't go down that road," he shouted at Conrad's tail. The warning was received with seconds to spare. The FCA vehicle stopped just before it would have rounded the corner and come face-to-face with the target.

The Gator and his team were also frustrated by the fact that it was impossible to inconspicuously park a surveillance vehicle within visual observation of Conrad's house. Bosenheim was a tiny village. Strangers in unfamiliar vehicles cruising the neighborhood would be noticed. To overcome this problem, agents had parked an empty car at a key village intersection, with an agent concealed in the trunk. Technicians had drilled a tiny observation hole in the car's rear fender, which enabled the entombed agent to observe Conrad's driveway. If Clyde climbed into the Audi, the FCA lookout would broadcast the alert to surveillance vehicles deployed on the outskirts of the tiny village. But hot or cold weather made this tactic uncomfortable, if not risky. The arrival of FCA aerial observers in Germany would solve this problem. With Sky King overhead, surveillance vehicles could lurk far from Conrad's neighborhood, awaiting an alert from the aircraft that their target was on the move.

Another technical feature of the full-court press was a homing beacon. To assist in tailing the wild-driving Conrad, we secured approval in Washington to employ an electronic tracking device. After renting an identical Audi and practicing repeatedly on it, Dick Bankston installed the beacon on the frame of Conrad's car. If Budapest's star commenced another death-defying run down the autobahn, the beeper would provide FCA aerial observers insurance against losing him.

As we hammered out the details of the planned full-court press, FCA deputy director Bob Bell made the perceptive observation that investigators actually knew little of what Conrad did when he was not meeting with our man Wilson. Who were Conrad's friends? Where did he go at night? Was he traveling to other cities? Above all, we were interested in nearby Frankfurt, which housed the V Corps headquarters. And most vital—other than Danny Wilson, who were Clyde's associates? The truth was, most of what we knew about our man was what investigators had learned from files and interviews, supplemented only by Danny Wilson's reporting. What the once and future spy was up to when he was not playing the mating game with Gary Pepper's source was anybody's guess. Perhaps a second source operation to supplement the enhanced surveillance would open revealing additional windows into Conrad's comings and goings.

Conrad had repeatedly told Wilson that he was in search of new sources. "I'm out there thrusting," he assured his protégé. Now he had unveiled his "V Corps guy." Agents in Wiesbaden believed that Clyde would direct his recruitment efforts to the unit in V Corps that he was most familiar with, the 8th Infantry Division War Plans office in Bad Kreuznach's Rose Barracks. This was Conrad's turf. It was convenient to Bosenheim, and no one knew better than Clyde the secrets that were available in the division's safes. Al Puromaki and Gary Pepper believed that because the 8th Infantry Division was a subordinate unit of V Corps, Conrad's "V Corps guy" could be working in Rose Barracks. Of one thing agents were certain. If Clyde Conrad had indeed recruited someone in V Corps headquarters, surveillance operations indicated that he was not meeting the mole in Frankfurt. Based upon this logic, the Wiesbaden team stepped up its efforts to recruit a source in Conrad's former office. If the retired sergeant was feeding at the 8th Infantry Division's trough of secrets, an agent inside the headquarters might detect this.

Danny Wilson noted that Conrad's behavior was sometimes bizarre and unpredictable. Wilson told Pepper that Conrad, usually after a few beers, became sentimental and echoed a recurring theme, emotionally reminding his new protégé: "When you showed up, Danny, you saved my life. You'll never know how much it meant to me when you came around." He repeated, "Now that you are on board, I'm back in form. Thanks to you, I'm out there thrusting again."

Then Conrad would lecture Wilson on his vision for a high-tech, information-age spy network. Stolen documents should be copied by the use of a video camera, he preached, a far more efficient system than a still camera or a copying machine. During one brainstorming session, Clyde described his concept for a video camera disguised as a package that could be carried into an office and used without attracting attention. Once documents were captured on videotape, he chortled, the tape could be mailed anywhere. Payment, Conrad bragged, would be by electronic transfer to Swiss banks, thus eliminating risky, face-to-face meetings. The full vision for his information-age espionage network, he told Wilson proudly, was taking shape in his home computer as Operations Plan 001.

Danny Wilson, an avid hobbyist with a gift for rebuilding clocks and jukeboxes, worked at home to bring Clyde's camcorder concept to life. The prototype he delivered was ingenious. He had created a housing into which a camcorder could be concealed, with a disguised opening for the lens. Outwardly, the device looked like a package destined for the post office. Wilson demonstrated his handiwork to the enthralled Clyde. All you had to do was place the package in a position where the camcorder could image documents that you were reading at your desk. As you paged through the document, its contents would be captured by the camcorder. Clyde was ecstatic. On his next trip to Budapest, he would bring Danny's device to show the Center the inventiveness of his new recruit.

The full-court press also required the development of a plan to locate Conrad's money. If he had indeed earned a fortune in his espionage career, where was it? Conrad had bragged about his Swiss bank accounts and advised Wilson that any self-respecting spy should have at least one.

Finally, the plan contained a gambit to catch Conrad in the company of a card-carrying Hungarian intelligence officer. On at least two separate occasions in 1987, Clyde had taken off for Vienna to meet Miklos, but the wily sergeant had quickly melted into the crowds in the Austrian capital and shaken our hasty and undermanned surveillance effort. The full-court press included a robust surveillance team armed with the latest high-tech equipment, which we hoped would permit the surveillance of a meeting in Austria between Conrad and Miklos. Once again, Gary Pepper and agent Danny Wilson would be the catalysts to make this happen. The next time Conrad ventured to Austria, agents were determined to capture the big event on film.

That was the plan. Its near-term goal was to smoke out Conrad's alleged "V Corps guy" as soon as possible. For the long term, which certainly could not be more than six months, investigators would redouble their efforts to collect information that Department of Justice attorneys insisted was essential to indict Clyde Conrad. Absent this kind of detail, I reported to my superiors, the conservative Department of Justice would not tackle a prosecution of Clyde Conrad. Increasingly, its attorneys seemed to harbor a view that they would prosecute only if the case were an airtight, guaranteed winner.

The medieval city of Heidelberg nestles on the banks of the picturesque Neckar River, overlooked by the steep, wooded heights of a small mountain known locally as the Konigstuhl, the "king's chair." Known for the red sandstone ramparts of its partially destroyed castle and its picturesque, fifteenth-century Altstadt, Heidelberg was also the location of Campbell Barracks, headquarters of the U.S. Army, Europe, for most of the Cold War. There, in a former Wehrmacht *kaserne* that had survived Allied bombing, thousands of soldiers, myself included, had labored over the years with the necessary staff actions required to keep the V and VII Corps manned and ready to defend West Germany in the event of war with the Soviet Union and her Warsaw Pact allies.

I negotiated the sentries and antiterrorist barriers of the familiar main gate, flanked by its distinctive granite carvings of martial figures. It had been almost five years since I had worked on the annual revisions of the war plans in a Campbell Barracks vault, but I recalled enough to know that the Hungarian wish list that Conrad had just passed to Danny Wilson would not be well received by CINC-USAREUR.

In the CINC's plushly carpeted inner office, I introduced myself as Bob Lunt's replacement and moved directly to the business at hand. On a positive note, I informed General Otis, there was progress to report. I then summarized what we had learned from Danny Wilson.

General Otis listened calmly as I turned to the bad news. Conrad was apparently escalating his espionage. Our introduction of Danny Wilson into the case seemed to have given the retired sergeant a new lease on his secret-agent life. Worse, I told the CINC, Conrad had met our controlled source right here in Heidelberg and bragged that he had recruited a "V Corps guy" who was about to provide him with new documents.

I handed General Otis a copy of the Hungarian wish list and waited as he digested it. At the head of the list were two documents: "V U.S. Corps OPLAN 33001, GDP, 1988," and "VII U.S. Corps OPLAN 33001, GDP, 1988." These were the general defense plans of both corps. They were among the command's most sensitive documents. Their betrayal to the Warsaw Pact could cost the CINC and his army a catastrophic defeat in the opening battles of any war. Also on the list was "HQ USEUCOM Emergency Action Plan, Volumes l–V, 1 Dez 1987." Emergency action plan (EAP) documents were top secret and dealt with nuclear release procedures in the event of war. In the event of a NATO inability to stem a Warsaw Pact attack by conventional means, nuclear weapons were the last resort. Emergency action plan documents provided details of this sensitive subject.

General Otis winced perceptibly as he studied the list. His brow furrowed with concern, the four star placed the paper on the table and gazed at me expectantly. Struggling to control my nervousness,

I explained the planned full-court press and concluded with an appeal. "Sir, no one wants to end this case more than we do, but we have to assume that Conrad's claim to have a V Corps source is not empty boasting. We need time to ferret out this guy, so that when we take Conrad down, we don't leave his replacement in the ranks. To do that, we need your concurrence. If we move too quickly, we might yank out the crabgrass and leave the roots in place."

General Otis hesitated briefly, as if he were crafting each word of his response. Then he spoke, calmly but with determination. "The way I see it, if he says that this guy is about to give him these documents, then they are as good as gone already. That's done. Now we need to get on with bringing this thing to an end. I'll support you on this, but you and everyone in Washington have to understand that this can't go on much longer. You need to press as you've described, and get on with it."

I nodded and replied with a crisp, "Yes, sir," assuring the general that we were already gearing up for a maximum effort and that the army senior leadership in the Pentagon shared his view that, one way or another, it was time to end the case. Before I departed, General Otis reminded me that he would give up his command by summer and asked that I explain the investigation to his replacement, Lt. Gen. Crosbie Saint, before his arrival in Heidelberg. He also directed that we confide the bad news about Conrad's alleged V Corps source to the V Corps commander in Frankfurt.

I departed the general's office with more than a small amount of admiration for his patience and steady hand. A lesser man would have taken one look at Conrad's list and called for an immediate halt to the case. At the same time, it was clear from the general's words and demeanor that his patience was not unlimited. Canasta Player was living on borrowed time.

The full-court press we promised General Otis would be orchestrated out of Wiesbaden. Team chief Al Puromaki, who had never aspired to leadership of the effort, had by now worked himself to total exhaustion. By the spring of 1988, Puromaki was increasingly burdened by his own private ghosts, chief among them a nagging fear that Conrad had seen through Danny Wilson's act from the beginning and was toying with FCA investigators. As we prepared to escalate our efforts, it was time to give the hardworking and intense officer a respite. The perfect place for him was at FCA's Fort Meade headquarters, where his keenly analytical mind and unequalled institutional knowledge would be invaluable as we steered the unwieldy case to closure.

The full-court press needed a floor captain. Reenergizing the effort in Europe called for a seasoned senior agent with two qualities: operational experience, in the sense of running source operations of the Lake Terrace–Canasta Player variety, and leadership skills.

Pressures to end the case were real, and fear of failure was palpable among the members of the Wiesbaden team. The danger of a case-fatal compromise had become particularly acute once agents intensified their physical surveillance of Conrad. Danny Wilson continued to boldly wear a concealed microphone and tape recorder during his meetings with Conrad, a dangerous practice if the security-conscious Clyde were to suddenly decide to pat him down. Team members were weary, frightened, and timid. Some agents had come to see Conrad as a looming, ten-foot-tall superspy with eyes in the back of his head and subsources everywhere. The fear of a compromising mistake was particularly acute among members of the surveillance team.

To address these problems, I was initially inclined to seek out Bob Thayer, whose performance in Berlin had shown him to be a proven leader with excellent operational judgment. But Bob was in the middle of a long-overdue sabbatical at the Defense Intelligence College in Washington. He would not be available for duty at FCA until later in the year.

Bob Bell spoke up. If what was needed at the Wiesbaden helm was a strong, charismatic leader with solid operational and leadership skills, Norman Runk, a senior agent in our Munich detachment, was the ideal choice. If anyone could rally the exhausted Wiesbaden team and get the case on track, Bell urged, Runk was the man.

Still a newcomer to FCA, I was nonetheless aware of the key role played by the unit in orchestrating the FBI's 1982 Augusta, Georgia, arrest of Otto Attila Gilbert. The arrest had been one of the more significant counterespionage successes of the decade, and

Runk had featured prominently in it. Once the popular agent's name was tabled as a possible successor to Al Puromaki, a number of FCA veterans enthusiastically seconded the nomination. Runk, they advised, had the right stuff to land Clyde Conrad flopping on the deck.

If spy novels are correct, and success in the intelligence game is guaranteed to the faceless spook who blends comfortably into his surroundings and attracts no attention, Norman Runk would not qualify for spy-of-the-year honors. Stocky, bespectacled, and sporting a thick brown mustache, Runk is a gregarious, upbeat presence, the exact opposite of the inscrutable spook of espionage literature. Blessed with a keen sense of humor and an infectious, room-filling laugh, the veteran case officer and investigator instantly livens up any group as soon as he enters the room. But beneath the light-hearted, fun-loving exterior was a serious, skilled agent with a deep sense of mission accomplishment and a personal code that emphasized loyalty—not only to his superiors but above all to his subordinates.

A retired warrant officer with some twenty-five years in the counterespionage business, Runk had as his trademarks hard work and taking care of his people (whom he was given to calling "these kids"). The forty-four-year-old agent was also known as a low-maintenance professional, not a whiner who required continual stroking. Favor Norman Runk with an occasional "well done," keep him fueled with prodigious portions of German food and beer, and the good-natured agent could function tirelessly, literally eighteen hours a day, seven days a week. With experience in Korea, Hawaii, Japan, and Germany, Norman Runk was rightly seen as the best in our business. The talented agent's ebullient persona and infectious laugh, even under great pressure, made him extremely popular with our German allies.

In mid-March 1988, I flew to Munich. Runk and I promptly adjourned to the Forsthaus, drank some beer, and shoveled down a heavy German meal. The chemistry between us was right. Sipping a beer, his mustache festooned with foam, the retired warrant officer asked questions about the case that were perceptive and on the mark. Runk was positive, confident, and smart.

We quickly struck a deal. When I said that he would have to depart Munich right away—it was essential that he take the helm in

Wiesbaden immediately—the veteran agent didn't hesitate. The following day, he packed his bags and headed north to begin a suitcase existence. His mission was unambiguous: Work toward the day when our counterintelligence investigators could turn the case over to law enforcement authorities, be they German or American.

As is often the case in our business, Norman traveled alone. His wife remained in Munich to care for their two-year-old daughter. Neither wife nor daughter could be permitted to know why Norman had suddenly been yanked away from home. This time around, he would be gone for six months.

Before departing Germany, I met one final time with Runk, this time in Wiesbaden. It was essential that the two of us be in perfect accord on what needed to be done in the delicate case, above all the endgame, which remained unclear. Based upon my meeting with General Otis, it was urgent that we think about the last day of the covert investigation and begin serious planning for the takedown of Clyde Lee Conrad.

That night, in the *ratskeller* under the Wiesbaden City Hall, Runk and I did serious damage to a wooden barrel of Wiesbadener Ratsbrau beer and enjoyed the incomparable German cuisine that the popular locale offered. Late in the evening, I sketched on a napkin a concept for the organization of the growing team that Norman would lead and scrawled some key words of final guidance under the diagram. "Plan for the last day of the foreign counterintelligence covert investigation," I wrote. "Who will do what? Where, & when? To whom?" As distasteful as it was, Norman and I agreed that it was time to think the unthinkable. United States authorities might be unwilling or unable to arrest Conrad, forcing us to deliver the case to our German allies. "What roles will/must be unilateral [U.S. only]?" I penned on the napkin. "What must be bilateral [in concert with German authorities]?" By the time we found our way back to the Hotel Am Brunnen, Norman and I were on the same sheet of music. The case would be closed by summer's end, one way or another, and a role for our German allies was becoming a serious possibility.

# 21: Tightening the Ring

Norman Runk took charge with a firm hand. From new offices in the operations building on Wiesbaden's sprawling air base, he and his expanded team orchestrated the closing ring that we had promised General Otis.

To breathe life into the surveillance effort, Runk put his faith in a uniquely talented, gutsy special agent, Bob "Wally" Gaiter. Gator (his code name) was a twelve-year veteran who had begun his career as an MP before transferring into military intelligence. Like Gary Pepper, he had made the choice with one motivation—to catch spies. By the time he was tapped to play a key role in Canasta Player, the thirty-two-year-old native of Brownstown, Indiana, had served almost seven years as a counterspy in Germany, where he had earned a reputation as an investigative pit bull. Of medium height, with a deceptively benign baby-faced visage, the tenacious Hoosier was schooled and experienced in advanced foreign counterintelligence operations and surveillance techniques. Completely familiar with the roads and terrain around Bad Kreuznach, the Gator was a sound choice for a mission that had the potential for disaster if mishandled.

"From now on," Norman told Gator, "the surveillance mission is yours. You know what we need, and we both know you can produce. Just take care of your people and keep them informed." It was the stuff of leadership—vintage Norman. From that day on, the cowed and dispirited surveillance team's morale climbed.

From my office at Fort Meade, new secure communications equipment permitted support of Norman as if he were next door. When Wiesbaden needed a legal ruling, usually on surveillance-related questions, we could provide answers on short notice. ("Hey, boss, do we have to install the electronic beeper on his car when it's parked on a public thoroughfare, or can we sneak onto his property at night and emplace it while the Audi's in the driveway?") Other operational questions continually surfaced, requiring a Washington decision. ("Sir, the surveillance team's sedans are getting too 'hot'; request permission to have them repainted different colors.")

For more than two years, in the name of security, agents in Wiesbaden had communicated with Fort Meade by message only, using the CIA's communications center at the U.S. embassy in Bonn. No one trusted the army's own telecommunications centers to handle the delicate traffic. As a result, when Al Puromaki had a message for Fort Meade, a courier had to drive more than a hundred miles to Bonn, where the text was encrypted by the CIA station, which transmitted it to agency headquarters in Langley, Virginia. An FCA liaison officer then picked up the traffic and couriered it to my office at Fort Meade. Use of the open telephone from Wiesbaden to Fort Meade was limited to innocuous subjects only since the Soviets monitored overseas calls.

The intensified surveillance of Clyde Conrad soon began to yield results. Their target, agents quickly discerned, was a tireless night owl. His usual routine was to hit the road shortly after dinner—always alone—and prowl the Century and Nahe Clubs, two popular military watering holes in the Bad Kreuznach area. Wherever he went, he was accompanied by Gator's surveillance agents. At his favorite haunts, Clyde followed a standard routine. Downing beer at his usual tempo, the retired sergeant had a penchant for playing pool, usually for money. A gregarious schmoozer, Conrad would sit in a booth or at the bar with whomever was available, conversing in his characteristic subdued tones.

On one occasion, an FCA surveillance agent managed to position herself in a booth adjacent to Clyde, who had zeroed in on an attractive female lieutenant. Conrad literally oozed charm as he effortlessly launched into a cover story, telling the young officer that he was a newly arrived civilian schoolteacher who didn't know much about the army. Perhaps the two could get together and she could help him acclimate to the ways of the military.

Agents concluded that Conrad was trolling for recruits. Each evening, Gator's agents reported, Clyde the Glide would hit the clubs, suck down a few beers, and chat with a number of people, usually ending up one-on-one, engaged in earnest conversation. To the members of the FCA surveillance team, any one of these nocturnal contacts might have been Conrad's shadowy "V Corps guy."

Norman's resourceful agents were able to identify everyone whom Conrad contacted. If they were in uniform, the name tag worn by all soldiers simplified the task. For those in civilian clothes, agents noted their vehicle tag numbers as they departed or elicited identifying information from the bartender or patrons. Gradually, the list of the retired sergeant's contacts and known associates expanded. Everyone on it would have to be checked out.

It was brutal, draining work for Gator and his stalwarts. On a typical evening, Conrad would stay out until well past midnight, then careen home in the silver Audi with a weary and wary surveillance team in cautious pursuit. On more than one occasion, the savvy spy doubled back on himself in a clear attempt to detect a tail.

Another important tactic in the promised full-court press was the development of a watchdog in the headquarters of the 8th Infantry Division—a trusted agent whom FCA investigators could target against Clyde Conrad. Investigators needed to know if the retired sergeant had left a sleeper agent in his former duty section or if he was attempting to regain access to the office's classified document vault by recruiting a subsource. In 1987, anticipating this requirement, FCA agents had spotted and recruited a senior noncommissioned officer in the 8th Infantry Division's G-3 staff section. It was time for the man to produce.

Mike Barnes was the G-3 sergeant major, the highest ranking NCO in the organization. Like Conrad before him, the senior noncom enjoyed access to most of the sensitive documents that would be of interest to Budapest. For security reasons, investigators recruited the gruff sergeant major under the guise of needing a source to assist in a security-related investigation in the headquarters. Barnes was not told that agents suspected Clyde Conrad. Instead, he was told to keep his eyes peeled for security problems.

The sergeant major was nearing the end of a distinguished career, during which he had spent many years in the elite U.S. Army Special Forces, to include combat tours in Vietnam. A powerfully built man who radiated strength and authority, Mike Barnes was one of a dying breed: the square-jawed NCO with a chest full of medals, the old army, tough but fair—most of the time. As FCA investigators checked out their man, a story appeared in the *Army Times.* "Sergeant Major Administers Traditional Discipline," the article trumpeted. Barnes, it seemed, had shaped up one of his soldiers by kicking the man across the parade ground. Agents noted with bemusement that the rugged sergeant major was proud of the publicity. Barnes was most definitely one of a kind.

Mike Barnes had a German girlfriend and planned to retire in the Bad Kreuznach area. If Conrad was looking for a well-connected confederate with access to the goodies prized in Budapest and Moscow, the former Green Beret was the perfect candidate.

In October 1987, special agent Joe Herda was detailed to handle the mercurial sergeant major. The slightly built Herda was a twenty-five-year-old staff sergeant with a keen intellect and a vocabulary to match, the sort of smart-assed, wisecracking young soldier whom NCOs such as Mike Barnes masticate for lunch. Herda was a native Alaskan, the son of a World War II veteran of the Aleutian campaign. In his sixth year of service as a special agent, Herda had been warned by his office mates that Barnes was a tiger. No one "controlled" Mike Barnes.

The investigation was entering a critical phase. Barnes had still not been told that Conrad was a target when Herda drove to Bad Kreuznach to make his first meeting with the FCA source. Herda screwed up his courage. Somehow, he had to keep the fire-breathing NCO under control.

The cigar-smoking sergeant major was waiting at the pickup point by an outdoor cigarette machine. It was raining heavily. When Herda pulled over, Barnes glided into the passenger seat with the agility of a bull elephant.

The young special agent ventured a few words of nervous small talk. It sure was one heck of a rainstorm.

Barnes jumped on the remark. "I love the rain. Made all my combat kills in Vietnam in the rain."

Herda kept his eyes on the road, wondering what he had gotten into.

Barnes pushed a Ziploc plastic bag into Herda's hand. "Here, you might be interested in this," he quipped with a smug look on his craggy face.

Herda glanced at the bag. Inside was a piece of paper on which was written the name, address, and home phone number of Clyde Conrad. The FCA agent stared, unable to disguise his reaction, in the process nearly crashing the German rental car. Barnes was not supposed to know that Conrad was the target.

"What's this? Where did you get this?"

Barnes grinned. "Just thought you might be interested in it. The guy came into my office the other day. Told me that he'd heard I was having supply problems and volunteered to help out."

Herda had to ask. "Why the plastic bag, Sergeant Major?"

Barnes fired back. "Just thought you could lift some prints from it."

Joe Herda recovered from his shock. The street-smart NCO was making fools of the MI spooks. So much for the smoke screen that agents had attempted to put up in the name of security.

Herda tasked Sergeant Major Barnes to be alert for any signs that Conrad was maintaining close contact with soldiers in his former duty section. At the same time, the FCA investigator warned the senior NCO that Clyde Conrad might approach him or one of his soldiers with a nebulous "business offer."

Within a few weeks, Barnes contacted Herda. Conrad, he revealed, had sought him out and initiated a series of probing, suspicious conversations. At first, Clyde had casually offered the sergeant major advice on how to approach his G-3 duties, even providing Barnes with a notebook that included tips on most functional areas, including the safeguarding of classified documents. Later, Barnes related, Conrad launched into an elliptical discussion of the benefits of retirement in the Bad Kreuznach area. Herda instructed the sergeant major to cultivate the friendship and let it develop naturally. Conrad was sniffing the bait.

The sergeant major played his role well. Over beer and pool, Conrad became bolder. There was much to be said for remaining in the Bad Kreuznach area, he pointed out, particularly for a bachelor with a German lady friend. Big money could be made in the information business for a man with the right connections. The patriotic and volatile Barnes was probably capable of killing Conrad by this point, but he controlled his anger and feigned interest. Clyde pushed.

"You could make fifty thousand dollars, even a hundred thousand dollars a year in the business," he enthused, leaving no doubt what he meant. Conrad confided that certain key documents could be marketed to his contacts for between 50,000 and 100,000 deutsche marks. He then told Barnes that he had an immediate requirement from a client for the location of the new northern wartime boundary of V Corps. As for army regulations concerning the security of classified materials, Clyde declared simply, "If I put ten thousand on the table, you'll know what to do about those rules."

An outraged Mike Barnes reported these developments to his FCA case officers. Things were moving rapidly. Conrad, it was clear, was serious when he told Danny Wilson that he was reinvigorated and "thrusting." We had breathed life into the beast.

Even while making his pitch to Mike Barnes, Clyde continued to call Danny Wilson at all hours, often summoning the master sergeant to meetings with progress reports on the business. Clyde confided to Wilson that he was putting the finishing touches on Operations Plan 001. A key element of the concept, Conrad elaborated, was to recruit and train field men, whose job it would be to spot and assess recruitment targets. In the new ring, he explained, field men would focus on the top-secret-document custodians at V and VII Corps; at Headquarters, U.S. Army, Europe (Heidelberg); and at the Headquarters, U.S. European Command, in Stuttgart. (Known as EU-COM, this was the unified command that controlled all army, navy, and air force components in Europe.) These agents, Conrad elaborated, would be the workers, the actual collectors. With his military intelligence background, Conrad continued, Wilson would recruit targets spotted by the field men. Then, as a controller, Danny would function as their superior. Soon, Conrad assured Danny, he would market his opus to Budapest. The charter members of the ring, he noted with pride, were to be himself and Wilson. Big money was in the offing.

In Washington, Department of Justice attorneys continued to push their agenda. Still at the head of their list was the need to smoke out the elusive Miklos. Heeding this guidance, FCA deputy director

Bob Bell contacted a colleague in a sensitive intelligence unit that was working on a compartmented program called Maximum Marvel. Explaining that we needed a classified document so enticing that Conrad would summon Miklos to an emergency meeting, Bob obtained permission to pass a message to Conrad that discussed a secret shipment of material that was due to arrive in Germany within days. A trained agent handler himself, Bob knew that any spy who came into possession of such time-sensitive, "codeword" information would almost surely smell a bonus payment and activate an emergency meeting with his case officer.

We shipped the Maximum Marvel message to Norman in Wiesbaden. Controlled Source 170 would be center stage once more. To kick off the gambit, Gary Pepper would instruct Danny Wilson to notify Conrad that he had latched onto something hot.

Once Wilson had passed the message, the plan was for the surveillance team to track Conrad on what all hoped would be a quick trip to meet Miklos, most likely somewhere in neutral Austria. Hopefully, this would enable the Gator's people to obtain photographs of Clyde Conrad in the act of betraying defense secrets to a known agent of the Hungarian intelligence service. In our haste to orchestrate this drama, we failed to discuss our choice of bait—the Maximum Marvel document—with Department of Justice attorneys. It was a regrettable oversight for which we would pay dearly.

The plan seemed to work to near perfection at the outset. Gary Pepper activated Danny Wilson, who contacted Conrad. The pair met in Heidelberg, midway between Bad Kreuznach and Wilson's government quarters in Stuttgart. Gator and his overworked surveillance personnel, on the ground and airborne, were standing by to take up the chase.

Clyde read the Maximum Marvel message, raised his eyebrows, and told Wilson excitedly, "You just cost me nine hours on the road." Bob Bell had guessed correctly. The message's cryptic reference to an imminent shipment of secret material from the United States to Germany was the kind of tip that any self-respecting spy would see as a chance to demonstrate his value. Conrad departed the meeting site in the silver Audi, Austria bound. Not even a blinding snowstorm stopped him as he sped south, followed by Gator and his team. As

the Audi streaked down the autobahn, it emanated a telltale beep-
ing sound. Overhead, FCA pilot Sky King kept pace with the target.

Experience taught us that Conrad would meet with Miklos in
Salzburg or Innsbruck. South of Munich, the Audi made a turn in
the direction of Innsbruck, where agents knew the favorite meeting
place of the Hungarian intelligence service was the Maria-Theresien
Strasse. Acting on this educated hunch, Gator had positioned a surveillance cell in a rented room that commanded an excellent view
of the area. With luck, Conrad and Miklos would walk by our cameras. As insurance, army counterintelligence agents with hidden
cameras patrolled the area on foot.

Conrad drove with his usual suicidal speed directly to Innsbruck,
parked the Audi, and headed for Maria-Theresien Strasse, still under surveillance. There, in front of the Wienerwald restaurant,
agents observed him link up with a slim, dark-haired, bespectacled
man. The two conspirators then strolled along the busy pedestrian
shopping zone while Gator's camera crew recorded the rendezvous
for posterity. The plan had come together almost perfectly, with one
significant exception. Surveillance team members who had been present during the February meeting in the Mainz Hilton Hotel recognized Clyde's Innsbruck contact as the ubiquitous courier from
Sweden, Imre Kercsik. The resulting photographs of Conrad and
Kercsik were useful, but Clyde's ties to the shadowy Miklos remained
undocumented. Worse yet, although we didn't know it at the time,
our choice of the Maximum Marvel message was about to cause the
investigation to take a bizarre and unexpected turn.

# 22: Kidnapping and Murder

The failure to encounter Miklos in Innsbruck was frustrating, but there was no time for wound licking. The once and future spy was definitely out there thrusting, a veritable dynamo of energy as he continued to prowl the Bad Kreuznach night scene. Shortly after the Innsbruck trip, Clyde excitedly summoned the frazzled Wilson to yet another meeting. This time the subject was the Maximum Marvel document.

The enterprising Conrad was obsessed with the cryptic text of the codeword message. Although the document contained no clue to the identity or use of the Maximum Marvel material that was being shipped to Germany, Conrad noted that among its recipients were an army medical command and an office at Fort Dietrich in Maryland, where research on chemical warfare had been conducted for years. This tidbit was sufficient for the greedy Clyde. Project Maximum Marvel, he concluded (erroneously), dealt with a Defense Department breakthrough to combat Soviet nerve agents or it indicated that the army had discovered a cure for influenza or AIDS. Influenza, Conrad lectured Danny, had killed more soldiers on the battlefields of history than had gunpowder. But whatever the Maximum Marvel project was about, Clyde gushed, big money was involved. Visions of fantastic riches, huge sums of money, appeared in the ambitious spy's mind.

Once airborne on this flight of imagination, Conrad soared to new heights of greed. Suddenly, the opportunistic retired sergeant lost all interest in his budding espionage Operations Plan 001. In meetings with Danny Wilson, all Conrad could talk about was the economic opportunity posed by the Maximum Marvel (MM) message. Whatever the Maximum Marvel material was, he enthused, it was almost surely worth a king's ransom. With dollar signs almost visible in his eyes, Clyde announced to Wilson that his top priority was to cash in on this opportunity by laying his hands on a sample of the material, unlocking its formula, and marketing it to the highest bidder. An action plan to steal the sample was essential.

Now we had a real problem. The entire Maximum Marvel drama had been orchestrated to uncover a specific facet of Conrad's espionage on behalf of Budapest—the identity of Miklos. No one could have envisioned that the nebulous message would launch the impetuous and greedy former sergeant on some wild, criminal enterprise.

Almost overnight, Conrad's speculation about the MM material became truth in his mind. The opportunistic ex-sergeant was convinced that he had hooked into the chance of a lifetime.

During the next several weeks, Clyde Conrad became progressively more obsessed with the Maximum Marvel enigma. What did Danny think the MM project was all about? It had a codeword, after all, Clyde reminded his friend, and that meant it was one of the Pentagon's biggest secrets. Had Danny seen any more classified message traffic containing additional details about the upcoming shipment?

The more Conrad fantasized about Maximum Marvel, the more bizarre his ideas became. During one disturbing conversation with Wilson, he floated a sinister plan. He and Danny could somehow hijack or ambush the convoy carrying the mystery shipment and steal a sample of the obviously priceless material. Or even better, if Danny could determine the route of the convoy, he and Clyde could hide by the side of the road and shoot at the trucks. With luck, the impact of the bullets might cause some of the precious stuff to spill out onto the highway, where it could be retrieved, preserved, and analyzed.

As Norman's messages describing Conrad's wild schemes arrived in Washington, it was evident that the unscrupulous and greedy retired sergeant was spinning out of control. Our Department of Justice colleagues shook their heads in frustration and disgust and urged us to get the investigation back on track.

I relayed the concerns of official Washington, but Norman viewed Conrad's obsession differently. What Department of Justice attorneys regarded as counterproductive, Norman saw as pure opportunity. In his view, Conrad's judgment had become so clouded by greed that we could use the Maximum Marvel caper to overcome one of the biggest obstacles of the case—our lack of jurisdiction to arrest him in Germany. Clyde, Runk insisted, was so overwhelmed at the prospect of overnight millions that we could easily lure him to the United States by convincing him through Danny Wilson that the trip would yield access to the Maximum Marvel formula. Then the retired sergeant could be neatly arrested by the FBI.

Norman argued adamantly that this was the direction we needed to take, reminding me of our conversation in the *ratskeller*. Had I not tasked him to plan for the endgame? This was, he felt, the perfect ploy to bring Conrad before the bar of justice. Mindful of the lenient penalties meted out by German courts for espionage, I had to admit that Norman's aggressive approach to trick Conrad into a stateside visit was not without merit. No one wanted to admit defeat and hand the case to our West German allies, who might not be able to keep it from leaking to their cousins in the East.

Norman pushed. Even if we did manage to catch Conrad in the act of passing documents to Miklos, and uncover his ill-gotten gains as urged by the Department of Justice, unless Clyde set foot on U.S. soil, he could not be arrested and tried in an American courtroom. Convinced beyond a doubt of Conrad's guilt, the savvy agent was positive that any American jury would convict the retired sergeant based on what we had learned to date in the investigation.

Runk's views were compelling. But in Washington, one had to deal with the bureaucratic infighting that had increasingly characterized the investigation. By May 1988, we were encountering serious problems with the Department of Justice's hard-nosed attorneys. Their view, which also had merit, was that we were offtrack. The entire Maximum Marvel affair was distracting Conrad from his espionage pursuits and thereby obstructing progress in our investigation. "You don't want Conrad plotting to steal some formula for sale to a pharmaceutical firm," Justice's John Dion argued. "You want him to be stealing military secrets and selling them to an agent of a foreign power." Like it or not, this was an incontestable argument. Even though we had not intended the Maximum Marvel document to trigger a Conrad-led criminal enterprise, it had happened, and our investigation was sidetracked as a result.

As the officer responsible for the success or failure of the Canasta Player case, I knew that unless we documented Conrad's espionage as demanded by the Department of Justice, they wouldn't authorize an arrest even if the erstwhile spy were to camp on their doorstep on Pennsylvania Avenue at high noon. I firmly told an unhappy Norman that we needed to squelch the Maximum Marvel caper—the sooner, the better—and return to the basics.

This was easier said than done. In Germany, Maximum Marvel had taken on a life of its own. Nothing Danny Wilson could do or say seemed to dissuade Clyde Conrad from pursuing the instant wealth that he had convinced himself resided in the MM formula. By mid-May 1988, Wilson met with Gary Pepper and reported a troubling development. Conrad had set up a summit conference in the German city of Kiel to discuss the Maximum Marvel opportunity. The plan was for Conrad and Wilson to drive to the North Sea port, where they would meet with Imre and Sandor Kercsik. The Kercsiks, Conrad reminded Danny, were physicians. Their advice on the opportunities posed by this medical breakthrough was essential.

In late May 1988, Conrad and Danny Wilson sped north in Wilson's maroon Chrysler LeBaron. Once again, FCA's technical expert Dick Bankston had worked his magic. Knowing Conrad's penchant for drinking in the car and talking about his ambitions, Bankston fitted the Chrysler with no fewer than three separate taping systems. All Wilson had to do was throw a different switch concealed under the dash every two hours, and every word spoken in the car would be captured for posterity.

In Kiel, Clyde and Danny would link up with the Kercsik brothers, who were taking the ferry from Sweden. As usual, the faithful master sergeant was wearing a concealed tape recorder. The actual meeting of the four conspirators would be covered by a handpicked cell of FCA surveillance agents. Their mission was to obtain ID-quality photography of the four conspirators as they discussed the Maximum Marvel plan.

The Kiel summit took place in a waterfront bar. By the time Conrad and Danny linked up with the Kercsik brothers, Conrad, having inhaled his first beer in the car when he and Danny departed Frankfurt, was in an expansive, talkative mood. For the first time, Wilson met the elder Kercsik brother, Sandor, also known as Alex. He was a squarely built, dark-looking fellow whom Clyde had more than once described as a dangerously mean type sometimes used by Budapest as an enforcer. Unlike his high-spirited younger brother, Sandor was serious and low-key.

Sitting around a rough-hewn wooden table, Clyde began the discussion of the Maximum Marvel project, making it clear that this opportunity was not to be shared with Budapest. This would be another case of some opportunistic freelancing, the sort of activity that had long ago led to friction between Conrad and Zoltan Szabo.

Conrad repeated his earlier discussions with Danny. This was the opportunity of a lifetime, he told the Kercsiks. Millions might be at stake. But success depended totally on whether they could conjure up a foolproof plan to lay hands on the Maximum Marvel material. Danny would be the key man, Clyde announced. With his access to classified message traffic, only he could provide specific updates on the impending shipment, its method and route of transport, and its destination upon arrival in Germany. With this information, Conrad suggested, it might be possible to intercept the convoy and obtain a sample of the mystery material, which he insisted had to be a medical breakthrough of some sort that was worth a fortune. As Clyde rambled on, Danny Wilson realized with horror that the man was still seriously thinking about a forceful hijacking of the Maximum Marvel convoy. Not only that, the Kercsik brothers seemed to think that the reckless scheme was a good idea.

Acting on Gary Pepper's instructions, Danny Wilson offered no words of encouragement that he could play such a role. It was a fluke, he explained, that he had gotten his hands on the Maximum Marvel message, a break that was unlikely to be repeated. Undaunted, Conrad conjured up a more devious scheme.

Instead of trying to hijack the shipment to obtain a sample, why not simply steal the Maximum Marvel formula? To accomplish this, Clyde explained, it would be necessary to identify a person in the United States who had access to it. Once we home in our target, he continued, we kidnap the guy. Then we can bribe him with cash or use drugs to force him to reveal the formula. After we've got the secret, Clyde added, we'll have to kill the prisoner in a manner that makes it look like a terrorist act, so no one will know that the formula has been compromised. Of course, Conrad concluded, as a military intelligence guy, Danny would be the logical one to travel to the

United States to locate and identify the target. Implied but not explicit in Conrad's remarks was that he would then travel to the United States to carry out the plan.

An incredulous Danny Wilson glanced at the Kercsik brothers to see if they would attempt to put the brakes on Clyde's ruthless plan. But Imre and Sandor didn't blink an eye at the cold-blooded plot. Wilson would later tell Gary Pepper that the three conspirators were not just making idle conversation. Clyde Conrad, he reported, was deadly serious and prepared to commit murder to obtain the Maximum Marvel formula.

Clyde pressed the two physicians. Was there a truth serum that really worked? Or was there perhaps a drug that caused so much pain when injected that the prisoner would talk but could not be detected in his body by an autopsy? Imre Kercsik speculated that scopolamine, injected directly into the spine, would create unbearable pain.

Conrad and Sandor Kercsik then outlined a scenario that deeply shook Danny Wilson. The best case would be if the bearer of the secret formula was a female who had children. Kidnap the woman together with her children and the rest would be easy. Faced with threats to the lives of her offspring, the captive mother would give up her secret. Once the terrified woman had coughed up the Maximum Marvel formula, Conrad observed nonchalantly, she and the children would have to be eliminated. There could be no witnesses who might warn the U.S. government that the secret formula had been compromised. Taped securely around Wilson's thigh, a miniature recorder captured the outlines of the sick plot.

As for marketing the formula, there were several possibilities, all of them attractive. Sandor Kercsik felt certain that a Swedish pharmaceutical firm would purchase it and the manufacturing rights for several million deutsche marks. Conrad himself leaned toward doing business with a Swiss firm, observing with a smug chuckle that none of these schemes would in any way prevent them from a double return on their investment. We can sell the formula to a commercial firm and also to the Soviets or the Hungarians, Conrad said with a grin. The operation had almost unlimited potential, he crowed.

The discussion in the Kiel bar lasted for several hours. As the conspirators talked, FCA agent Bob Watson deposited a bag containing a concealed video camera on a nearby chair. Had Watson placed the bag on the table, the results would have been perfect. But the view from the chair was useless, yielding table legs and lower extremities. Fortunately, one of Watson's colleagues had moved through the room with a still camera rigged in an FBI-provided concealment device. This time the results were excellent. When developed, the film included a clear photo of the four plotters. Between the tape recorder strapped to Danny Wilson's leg and the surveillance photos, the gruesome Kiel conference was well documented.

News of the incredible plotting in the Kiel bar bombed in official Washington. Conrad and the Kercsik brothers had clearly flipped out in a fit of criminal greed, and it was unsupportable to have an army-controlled source present at meetings where plans were being made to commit kidnapping and murder. Norman Runk had already received marching orders to back away from Maximum Marvel but too late to avoid the Kiel summit conference. This time, I told FCA deputy Bob Bell, the Wiesbaden team must contrive a way to shut down the Maximum Marvel caper.

Bell nodded but reminded me with a characteristic wink that I would have to deal with Norman, who continued to see great opportunities in the Kiel plotters' plans.

Norman and I had one final conversation on the subject. There was no doubt in my mind that Conrad was in the grips of uncontrollable greed; this much of Norman's argument I understood. The persistent agent made his case one more time: "Boss, I'm telling you, this thing will enable us to deliver Conrad to you at JFK Airport." Not only that, Norman reminded me, Maximum Marvel wasn't a total diversion. Had not Conrad himself alluded to selling the formula to the communists? If that wasn't espionage, what was? Espionage related or not, Norman pleaded, Conrad's obsession with Maximum Marvel was the key to arresting him.

I had little doubt that Norman, Pepper, and Danny Wilson could manipulate the Maximum Marvel affair to deliver Clyde Conrad to U.S. soil. But we would never agree on this one. I was in Washington, taking the heat from the lawyers, while Norman was in Wiesbaden, dedicated to the worthy goal of seeing Clyde Conrad in a U.S. courtroom.

We had not yet produced the overwhelming, complete details of Conrad's treason that Department of Justice attorneys insisted were the minimum essential conditions to authorize an arrest. Personally, I thought their conditions were overly demanding and probably unattainable, and I was not alone in this view. Tom Reilly, the senior FBI supervisor on the case, commiserated with our plight. "This is typical for those guys over at Justice," he explained. "DOJ wants to overtry the case, and if they sense that there is even a 1 percent chance they might lose, they won't prosecute." With the Department of Justice unwilling to authorize Conrad's arrest, it was useless to pursue further operational moves to lure him to the United States.

I issued a rare direct order to Norman. Danny Wilson must cease all discussion of Maximum Marvel and offer no encouragement that he might be able to undertake a trip to the United States to locate the keeper of the formula. The Wiesbaden team must return to the original priorities of the case, and that meant identifying Conrad's mysterious "V Corps guy," smoking out details of his ill-gotten financial gains, and capturing Miklos on film.

# 23: The Swiss Connection

In the 1930s, Soviet spymasters reaped major benefits from a wave of idealism that swept the intellectual left in the West. Enthralled by what they perceived to be Lenin's and Stalin's great social experiment, naive students at Europe's finest universities gravitated toward communism. It was the age of the ideological spy, an era that bred Kim Philby, the Rosenbergs, and a host of devotees to Moscow's cause, all in the name of world peace.

By the 1980s, few true believers graced Moscow's spy stable. No longer an affair of the heart to most of its practitioners, espionage had become a business, and a most lucrative one at that. Before he was unmasked in 1985, retired U.S. Navy warrant officer John Walker organized and ran an espionage ring consisting of four persons. In eighteen years, Walker and his confederates earned an estimated $1.1 million from Moscow. If Danny Wilson's reporting was accurate, Clyde Conrad and Zoltan Szabo's enterprise had outdone even the infamous Walker family spy ring. Bushels of money were involved in this case, money that could be Clyde Conrad's undoing, if investigators could locate it.

Department of Justice attorneys harped incessantly on the importance of identifying the money trail. It was, they urged, essential to reconstruct Clyde Conrad's windfall profits made since his recruitment in 1975. If the retired sergeant had gone from rags to riches, FCA sleuths needed to prove it. Like most of the investigative challenges, this one belonged to Norman Runk and his Wiesbaden stalwarts.

The methodology employed by investigators to demonstrate undue affluence is not complicated. Agents begin by establishing the known legal income that the suspect earned during a stated period. For Conrad, this was no challenge. As a noncommissioned officer in the U.S. Army between 1975 and 1985, Conrad had a cumulative take-home pay somewhere in the range of $200,000; this information was no secret.

Next, agents build a balance sheet listing all known assets and expenditures of the suspect during the same period: rent, purchase of an automobile, investments, valuable property (such as Conrad's gold coin collection), and bank balances. At the same time, investigators focus on the suspect's travel during which he might have met an agent of a foreign power and received a significant cash payment. Matching such travel with bank deposits made in its wake is an important part of the process. A trip to Vienna over the New Year's holiday might appear innocent, but a hefty bank deposit made on January 4 could shed light on the trip's clandestine purpose.

The objectives are to correlate travel with money and also establish that the suspect's expenditures and lifestyle far exceed his legal income. Such was the case in the early 1990s when FBI and CIA counterspies examined the finances of CIA agent Aldrich "Rick" Ames. Agents established that Ames had poured serious money into purchasing a house and a luxury car well beyond the means of his salary, and his bank account reflected significant deposits that seemed connected with foreign travel. Once inheritance or other legal possibilities to explain the CIA officer's income were ruled out by investigators, Ames clearly displayed what counterintelligence agents term "undue affluence." The most logical source of his excessive cash flow was espionage.

It was essential to subject Conrad to this kind of scrutiny. In Canasta Player, however, the process was complicated by the fact that the cautious ex-sergeant had taken steps to conceal his assets. By 1986, Conrad was living modestly in Bosenheim. His local bank account had an unremarkable balance, although it did betray several unexplained deposits. Yet more than one witness recalled that the cash-strapped Conrad family had suddenly begun to prosper sometime around the mid-1970s, with several eyewitnesses actually seeing Clyde's infamous gold coin collection that he touted as Europe's finest. Danny Wilson reported to Gary Pepper that Clyde had repeatedly boasted that he had earned a fortune during his thirteen years of espionage, at one time mentioning a figure in excess of a million dollars. During one meeting with Wilson, Conrad proudly told his protégé that in addition to a monthly salary from Budapest, he was able to earn a bonus of between 150,000 and 200,000 deutsche marks (more than $100,000) each time he provided Budapest with a current copy of the V or VII Corps general defense plans. His ultimate goal, Clyde confided in Danny, was to score a $1 million payment for a single delivery of secrets. As an aside, Conrad also confessed to Wilson that the prospect of such windfall profits was the reason that he had rejected the idea of going into the drug business or some similar illegal enterprise. The marketing of classified material, he assured his protégé, was more lucrative and far less risky for a smart operator. Drug lords were mean SOBs.

As with many of Conrad's revelations to Wilson, these admissions were received in Washington with a mixture of astonishment and disbelief. Surely Conrad was exaggerating in order to impress his new recruit. Espionage sometimes paid well, but the sums that Clyde was advertising seemed out of line with what experience taught about East Bloc pay scales for a good agent. Most of us had been astonished at the original report in 1978 from one CIA source who claimed that Budapest's agent had received $50,000 for a single document. Now Clyde Conrad was talking about two and three times as much money for certain key war plans.

If Clyde Conrad had indeed made this kind of money, where was it? We had easily documented the suspect's military earnings; now the challenge was to cement the case for undue affluence by locating his ill-gotten gains. Uncovering a bank account or an investment portfolio that displayed a major cash deposit following a Clyde Conrad venture to Austria or after he had met with the Kercsik brothers was a sound ideal approach. Another logical first step would be to identify the Swiss bank accounts and safe-deposit boxes that Conrad had told Danny Wilson had been in his name as early as 1978. To accomplish this, Gary Pepper would coach Wilson on how to orchestrate a trip to Switzerland.

Pepper met with Wilson to plan the move. After more than a year of dealing with Clyde, Wilson knew the buttons to push. He assured Pepper that he would have no difficulty in conjuring up a trip to Switzerland. A simple appeal for help would do the job.

"I'm on board with your advice that I need to open the Swiss bank account, Clyde," Wilson announced to Conrad, "but I haven't got a clue about how to do it, or which bank is a good bank." Clyde the

Legend, mentor of aspiring spies, took the bait. The two agreed to travel together to Zurich at the end of May.

Not wishing to send army surveillance agents into neutral Switzerland, we contented ourselves with Danny Wilson as a government witness to the trip. For insurance, technician Dick Bankston rigged a long-playing tape recorder in a parcel that Wilson could bring along to record Conrad's words during the three-hour run down the Frankfurt-Basel autobahn. If Clyde the Glide acted in character, he would swill beer during the drive. Who knew what surprises his alcohol-loosened tongue might reveal?

As the two men loaded the Audi with beer and provisions, Wilson experienced a flash of anxiety as Conrad lifted one bag and wisecracked about its weight. The bag contained the long-playing tape recorder. But soon the pair were coursing down the autobahn at Mach speed with Conrad at the wheel, demolishing his first of many beers. Once again, the resourceful Danny Wilson was on his own, with instructions to get Clyde talking for the record.

In Zurich, the plan worked to near perfection. Conrad took his star recruit to the Zuricher Union Bank, which he confided was one of his own banks, and guided Wilson through the simple procedures for opening an account and obtaining a safe-deposit box. This accomplished, the two walked to a nearby square, where Clyde displayed the keys to five safe-deposit boxes he maintained in various Zurich banks. Conrad directed Wilson to wait for him in the square and excused himself for thirty minutes to accomplish unstated business. Certain that Clyde was on his way to service another account, Gary Pepper's well-coached agent prudently resisted the temptation to play spook and follow him. The suspicious and cautious Conrad could be testing him, he knew, or both of them could be under Hungarian surveillance. Better to play it safe.

If nothing else had emerged from the Zurich trip, it would have been rated a success. Once again, the plucky Wilson had come through. Thanks to his efforts, the Wiesbaden team had not only identified one of Conrad's Swiss banks but also confirmed for any skeptics that Clyde's claims concerning Swiss safe-deposit boxes were not idle boasting. The Zurich mission was a solid start at documenting Conrad's ill-gotten gains, even though the banking secrecy laws in Switzerland posed a major barrier to obtaining the detailed data we required.

But the trip was not over. As the silver Audi raced north along the Rhine River, the Zurich mission paid a pair of handsome dividends. Conrad, fueled as usual by beer, occupied himself during the drive by expanding upon his favorite subject, the enterprise. As the well-lubricated spy waxed eloquent on the brilliance of his vision for a high-tech espionage ring, Wilson listened attentively, now and then cooing in admiration and stoking the flames of Conrad's well-developed ego. Mercifully, Clyde's obsessive preoccupation with Maximum Marvel seemed to have receded to the back burner of his active brain. In its place, the mercurial ex-sergeant rediscovered his first love—espionage.

As the south German landscape flashed past, Conrad began to tout the merits of his "V Corps guy." The new source was a real winner, he confided, someone who had the balls to serve as a first-class operator in the new network. On top of that, the man was well placed. He had access to highly classified documents and the smarts to handle the risky job of actually stealing the goodies from under the noses of his superiors. The new recruit, Conrad bragged, was a career NCO with years of experience wearing the elite green beret of the Special Forces. The guy had been through all of the army's most difficult training, Conrad explained, to include Airborne, Ranger, and Special Forces. He'd also served multiple tours in Vietnam with distinction and seemed determined to retire in Germany. As Clyde prattled on about the new recruit, Danny Wilson strove to commit his description to memory, knowing that Gary Pepper would want every detail and feeling certain that the concealed tape recorder had long since run out of tape.

Conrad popped open another brew and turned the conversation to Operations Plan 001. Producing a thick document from his bag, Clyde identified it as a final draft of the plan. Because Danny was a counterspy by training, Conrad directed him to scrutinize each page of the sensitive plan to ensure that it contained no weaknesses that could result in compromise of the envisioned agent network.

As Clyde handed Danny Wilson a copy of his much-touted espionage opus, he confided one additional, priceless fact. He needed

Danny's assessment of the document soon. The reason for the deadline, Clyde added coyly, was that he had an appointment in Vienna to meet Miklos. There, he explained, he would provide his Hungarian contact with the final version of the 001 plan. Miklos would then deliver the plan to the Center in Budapest for a final blessing. Once approved, Conrad beamed, the concept would become the bible for all further operations of the new network. He and Danny could begin to build up a network of field men and workers, stolen documents would begin to flow to Hungary, and the money—big money—would be electronically transferred into their accounts in Switzerland.

As the two parted, Conrad assigned his promising new recruit one additional mission. Danny should return to his unit in Stuttgart and raid the safes. Clyde needed additional classified documents to sweeten the pot for his planned meeting with Miklos. What better way to convince the Hungarian officer that the Legend was back than the delivery of a few fresh secrets?

Norman Runk was justifiably jubilant as he reported the results of the Zurich trip. Danny Wilson had once again performed well, and the stage was now set for a meeting with Miklos. I listened with undisguised excitement as Norman described the triumph over the secure phone. After the dark days of the Maximum Marvel debacle, all of us needed good news, and this was it. The Zurich trip had moved us significantly closer to the long-anticipated day when Clyde Conrad's thirteen-year career of treachery could be stopped.

Norman's report left no doubt that Danny Wilson had outdone himself this time. As Wilson repeated Conrad's description of the "V Corps guy" to Gary Pepper, the efficient master sergeant could not know that he was describing someone with whom the Canasta Player team was quite familiar. Pepper and Runk knew immediately that Conrad was certainly describing FCA's other recruited source, Mike Barnes, the sergeant major in the 8th Infantry Division headquarters. (In keeping with standard tradecraft, Wiesbaden agents had carefully compartmented the Wilson and Barnes operations. Until the case reached its spectacular final stage, neither man knew of the other's relationship with FCA.)

The confirmation that Mike Barnes was probably Conrad's mysterious "V Corps guy" moved investigators a giant step closer to wrapping up the investigation. General Otis and the army's senior leadership in Washington had agreed that it was unwise to terminate the case as long as Conrad had an unidentified, disloyal soldier on his payroll somewhere in V Corps. Now, it appeared all but certain that Conrad's earlier claim that he had a new source in V Corps was a boast, almost certainly grounded in the cocky spy's belief that he could successfully recruit Barnes. Clyde Lee Conrad, Budapest's "Legend," was in the process of relaunching his espionage career with two fresh recruits—Danny Wilson and Mike Barnes—both of whom were double agents under FCA control. It was a delicious prospect.

Norman Runk and Gary Pepper had other reasons to celebrate. Locked securely in the Wiesbaden office safe was a carefully tagged and bagged copy of Clyde's espionage Operations Plan 001, almost certainly traceable to the man's home computer, and equally likely to have his fingerprints on it.

The acquisition of this plan was a major investigative success. The fifty-page road map for treason was surely destined to be a centerpiece in any prosecution of Conrad. Its acquisition by Danny Wilson constituted complete vindication of his role as an FCA source. For more than a year, the dedicated master sergeant had met with Conrad and faithfully related the often bizarre things that his old friend revealed. In Washington, the more far-fetched the master sergeant's reports seemed, the greater the tendency to disbelieve or dismiss them. To one degree or another, everyone, myself included, had gotten into the second-guessing mode that haunts most counterintelligence operations, where healthy skepticism flirts daily with paranoia.

Part of the problem was what one could call the too-good-to-be-true syndrome, and part of it was a gut feeling shared by many that Conrad was surely too smart to be so easily taken in by our operations against him. The cerebral Al Puromaki, who had been with the case from the beginning, had all but convinced himself that the wily Conrad was in the driver's seat. Conrad, he suspected, had known that Wilson was a double agent from the beginning. Could the manipulative retired sergeant be playing with us, cynically using Wilson to shower investigators with false information and keep us chasing our tails, all the while confident that he was immune from arrest and prosecution in his overseas retirement haven?

By the summer of 1988, only in Wiesbaden could one find nearly unbridled confidence in Danny Wilson. Gary Pepper and Norman Runk stood by their man. In Washington, I tried to be objective, but it was easy to argue that the Wiesbaden guys were too close to the problem and were committing the cardinal sin of human intelligence—falling in love with one's agent.

But when Wilson produced a copy of the plan that Conrad had been trumpeting about for a year, even those who harbored the most nagging doubts about the case were impressed. The incriminating blueprint for high-tech spying conformed in every detail to the reporting that Danny Wilson had been rendering for months.

Rivaling this achievement was Wilson's alert that Clyde would soon travel to Vienna for a meeting with Miklos. This tip presented investigators with the possibility of catching the spy from Bosenheim in the act of meeting an agent of a foreign power, without which we had no hopes for an arrest and prosecution.

The results of the Zurich trip revived my flagging confidence that we could ever achieve the difficult agenda being urged on us by the Department of Justice. Persistence was paying dividends. Like Norman Runk and every agent on his team, I dreamed of the day when a judge would eyeball Conrad and inform him that he would be spending the rest of his life in prison. Even more appealing was the realization that a change in the espionage statute during the Reagan administration now permitted the death penalty for spies who betrayed war plans. If Norman's team could prove that Conrad had indeed given his masters in Budapest "everything," the forty-one-year-old retired NCO might be the first test case of the revised statute.

Planning for the Vienna showdown went into high gear. Conrad could not be permitted to slip the noose in Vienna's crowded streets, as he had twice done in 1987. To lay the foundations for success, investigators needed details of the planned trip.

Gary Pepper met with Danny Wilson to prime him for the key rendezvous with Conrad. The Texan's mission was to ferret out Clyde's travel plans. Gator and his small army of surveillance specialists had by now been shadowing Conrad almost without respite for ten weeks, pulling twelve-hour shifts, seven days a week. Now the bleary-eyed agents of the surveillance team would again be center stage. Well briefed by Norman on the progress of the investigation, the Gator's people understood the stakes of a Vienna deployment and were ready to dig deep to end Clyde Conrad's career as a secret agent.

Wilson delivered yet again. During a brief meeting with Clyde to pass a pile of classified documents that Clyde would use to impress Miklos, the FCA agent artfully elicited the day and time that Conrad planned to take the train to Vienna. Armed with this information, Norman Runk and the Gator crafted plans for a foolproof surveillance operation.

For counterspies, the adage that a picture is worth a thousand words is gospel. A clear image of Clyde Conrad hobnobbing with Miklos might enable our CIA partners to identify the Hungarian from their biographic-photo files of known foreign intelligence personnel. That done, we were confident, Department of Justice and Pentagon attorneys would agree that the case was strong enough to justify Conrad's arrest and indictment. Whether this would be done by civilian or military authorities was a matter for the attorneys to determine.

# 24: Compromise

In late May 1988, as FCA investigators planned the Vienna surveillance, someone approached *New York Times* reporter Jeff Gerth at a Washington luncheon. Had Gerth heard that there was a major espionage investigation under way in Europe? Apparently, the tipster confided, some retired military folks were spying for the Bulgarians. Gerth listened attentively. At the *Times,* a good spy story was always popular with his editors. But the source had provided no details, just the cryptic fact that there was a big case under way. The lead was tantalizing, Gerth decided, but it would have to be checked out carefully. Gerth was one of Washington's best-connected reporters; if the tip were true, someone in his Rolodex would know about it.

By the summer of 1988, as the pace of Canasta Player escalated and the investigation moved inexorably toward denouement, the number of people in Washington and Europe who were granted access to the tightly compartmented case had mushroomed. This account of the investigation focuses on where the real action was—in Germany with Norman Runk and his team. But in Washington, orchestrating the complex case was a consuming, full-time job. Each day was a bureaucratic and operational roller coaster ride punctuated by multiagency steering group meetings, conferences with army attorneys, meetings with senior officers, briefings to the secretary of the army or other VIPs, and regular strategy sessions in the Pentagon chaired by the army's ranking intelligence officer, a quick-thinking, demanding three-star general named Sidney T. "Tom" Weinstein. At all such forums, my job was to provide senior officers a status report—where we were in the case, where we were going, and how we proposed to get there.

The meetings in General Weinstein's E-Ring office are particularly memorable. On the average, there were twelve to fifteen people present, including no fewer than four attorneys representing the different levels of the chain of command, the Office of the Army General

Counsel, and the Office of the Army Judge Advocate General. Some might characterize the meetings as intrusive micromanagement, but not me. On the contrary, the sessions were a useful opportunity to enlist support from key senior officers and to elicit advice on a host of issues that surfaced as we moved in fits and starts toward whatever the endgame might be. Involving the senior army leadership in this final eight months of the decade-long investigation made considerable sense to me at the time, and it still does. Nonetheless, the demands of this schedule were great, and the formidable number of people who had been granted access to the sensitive case would have been alarming to my predecessor. Jokingly, I began to refer to a law of inverse security. (In Washington, the greater the sensitivity of a secret, the greater the number of people who feel they have a right to know it.) Ultimately, we paid a price for this.

The shoe fell in early June 1988. It was the forty-fourth anniversary of D day, and I had just checked into a hotel room in Killeen, Texas, outside the gates of the army's sprawling Fort Hood. A red blinking light on the telephone beckoned. Foreign Counterintelligence Activity national liaison officer Jim Whittle had left a message. "Call the office on a secure line, sir. Something's up."

The purpose of the Texas sojourn was to meet with Lt. Gen. Crosbie Saint, the outgoing commander of the army's III Corps, who would soon replace Gen. Glenn Otis as the commander, U.S. Army, Europe. My job was to meet privately with the Fort Hood–based general, inform him that his war plans had been betrayed by Clyde Conrad and Zoltan Szabo, and explain what army counterintelligence was doing about it. Saint, one of the army's most aggressive war fighters, was not likely to welcome such news. To prepare him for the visit, Washington had asked him to grant me a private office call.

I located a secure phone and contacted Fort Meade. Jim Whittle picked up the phone. A native of Richland, Washington, Whittle was a veteran of almost twenty years of service, including a Vietnam tour as an infantry platoon sergeant in the Americal Division. Since the end of the Vietnam War, he had served as a counterintelligence special agent in Germany, Turkey, and the United States. With a background as a case officer and a technician (electronic eavesdropping and related skills), Whittle occupied one of our unit's most vital jobs. As the FCA national liaison officer, he was the director's daily eyes and ears with the national agencies without whom we could not function. Although his principal duty was the coordination of delicate matters with our interagency partners, Jim had an instinctive gift for schmoozing, which made the veteran chief warrant officer perfectly cast to be my eyes and ears in Washington. Daily, Whittle visited with officers of the FBI, the CIA, and other national-level agencies with whom we maintained close ties, always on the alert for scuttlebutt that might enhance our ability to get the job done. As the pace of the Canasta Player investigation escalated, Jim had become the proverbial indispensable man.

Whittle minced no words. He had just come back from his daily trip to CIA headquarters. We had a serious problem.

"Sir, I hope you're sitting down," he began gravely. "The *New York Times* has found out about Canasta Player."

I couldn't believe it. Perhaps the rushing noise in the secure phone had garbled his words. "Say again, Jim," I replied, hoping that I had misheard him.

But it was true. Whittle had just learned in Langley that *New York Times* reporter Jeff Gerth had contacted Bill Baker, the CIA public affairs officer (PAO). The *Times,* Gerth confided, was aware that a major spy case was under way in Europe involving retired military members selling secrets to the Bulgarians. Could Baker confirm this?

Baker told Gerth that he knew nothing about it but would check it out with appropriate CIA officials.

The alert PAO contacted his superiors, who were deeply concerned. Perhaps Gerth was on a fishing expedition for more information, but it was clear that the reporter had somehow latched onto a source who had spilled the beans about Canasta Player. Even though his facts were garbled, there was no mistaking the broad outlines of the information. There was a serious leak somewhere in Washington. If the *Times* went to press with such a story, Clyde Conrad would read it and flee to Budapest, and the CIA's sources behind the Iron Curtain would be endangered. This could not be allowed to happen. The fate of the case now rested on the CIA's ability to influence a member of the Fourth Estate.

Baker contacted Gerth and appealed for restraint. The case in question was fraught with serious national security implications. Breaking such a story would do grave damage.

Nine years later, Gerth recalled the incident. "When I called Bill Baker, I actually only had this cryptic tip dropped to me at a luncheon—not a lot of details, and certainly not enough to publish anything. I needed to develop the story. Since I had a pretty good relationship with Bill Baker, I gave him a call. I didn't have much, but I guess it was enough to shake things up. Anyway, based on Baker's request, I backed off, including I didn't make the usual inquiries around town that I normally would have under such circumstances."

Gerth told Baker that the *Times* would not pursue the matter or break the story for the moment, unless it became clear that its competitors were about to do so. Gerth recalls that Baker told him at the time that when the story did break, Baker would "work with him" in exchange for his cooperation. One hand washes the other.

Jim explained that our agency friends had apparently carried the day. The *New York Times* would sit on the explosive scoop, at least for the moment. But if the competition sniffed out the story and prepared to run it, the *Times* could be expected to break its silence. Unaware of the extent of Gerth's information, we worst-cased the problem. The resourceful reporter probably knew a lot more than he communicated to Baker, speculated Norman Runk. No doubt he had deliberately masked this by referring to Bulgarians rather than Hungarians. Canasta Player was living on borrowed time.

Deeply disturbed, I showed up the following morning to brief General Saint. The devastating news of a leak had changed the situation overnight. Even if the *Times* lived up to its promise and temporarily squelched the story, the timetable of our investigation had been derailed. If the paper broke the story, the Canasta Player investigation would crash and burn just at the point when we were finally closing on the target. Ten years of hard work and more money than I would earn in the remainder of my working days would go down the drain; Conrad and Szabo would elude justice; and national security and the reputation of army counterintelligence would suffer serious blows.

The Gerth leak could not have occurred at a worse moment. In granting General Saint formal access to Canasta Player, I planned to describe the case as the most sensitive and compartmented counterintelligence investigation in the history of the U.S. Army. Now I would have to add that, somehow, reporters from the *New York Times* had penetrated our impenetrable security. Saint could be excused for wondering about our competence.

The leak to Jeff Gerth mapped out our course. With the security of the Canasta Player investigation hinging on the patriotism, fidelity, and discretion of the *New York Times* ("those same wonderful people who gave us the Pentagon Papers," I quipped to Jim Whittle), we had no choice but to wrap up the case, one way or another, ready or not.

General Saint listened attentively and focused on photographs of Clyde Conrad and former armor officer Zoltan Szabo. Saint, a career tanker, pointed to Szabo's picture and shook his head slowly.

"I knew Szabo when he was a captain," Saint observed. "We served together many years ago. He was a good officer then."

The general calmly absorbed the bad news about the leak, which I pointed out would undoubtedly force an end to the marathon investigation within weeks of his assumption of command in Heidelberg. Now that the press was sitting on the story, we could not follow a protracted investigative plan. Conrad would have to be confronted soon.

I jetted back to Washington, still in a dark frame of mind. The long-awaited endgame of Canasta Player was staring us in the face. But other than Norman Runk's assurances that he could use the Maximum Marvel affair to lure Conrad to the United States—a ploy that had been rejected by the Department of Justice—no plan to end the investigation existed.

Inside the Beltway, consternation over the bad news was universal. The inevitable finger-pointing had commenced, although no one had a clue concerning who would leak such a sensitive story. And there was no time to waste on a leak investigation (traditionally the most intractable and fruitless of investigations). Fearful that the *Times* might break the story at any time, there was a collective sense that our backs were to the wall. It was time to make some tough decisions about ending the case.

Three serious options existed to bring Clyde Conrad before the bar of justice. None was overly promising.

One option could be executed by the German government. If the Washington legal community could not devise a foolproof formula to arrest Conrad and try him in a U.S. courtroom, we could always appeal to the West Germans for assistance.

A second option fell squarely into the jurisdiction of the Department of Justice: arrest and trial before a federal judge.

The final option, arrest and court-martial, could be carried out by the Department of Defense.

The German option was the least palatable. With no disrespect intended toward our German allies, we were not enamored of this approach. Conrad needed to feel the hammer of American justice, which was unforgiving of espionage. The German option was fraught with security concerns, and no one wanted to see Clyde Conrad get away with the sort of light sentence that a German court would likely mete out. If, as we felt certain, Conrad was the East Bloc's most successful human intelligence penetration of NATO in history, a sentence of life in prison, or even death, was appropriate. Only an American court could be counted upon to deliver such punishment.

The second option was for Conrad to be tried by Department of Justice prosecutors in a civilian court. This approach was more complex and less certain than the other options, because we could not arrest Conrad in Germany, and the retired sergeant showed little inclination to travel to the United States, where he could be apprehended. And the Germans could not arrest him on our behalf and hand him over; this would be a violation of the treaty that governed extradition. For Conrad to find himself facing a judge in a U.S. courtroom, he would have to make a serious mistake and travel to the United States. Well aware of this, Norman Runk and his Wiesbaden colleagues were ready to revive the Maximum Marvel affair and snooker the greedy spy into buying an airline ticket.

But the most serious obstacle to the Department of Justice option was the Department of Justice. We had thus far failed to convince the DOJ prosecutors that a trial of Clyde Conrad would be successful. Certainly I believed it would be, as did Norman Runk, Gus Hathaway, and most of our FBI colleagues. But the Department of Justice attorneys remained reluctant to sign up to any espionage prosecution that did not offer an airtight chance of a conviction. Timidity was their watchword.

To the investigators in the Foreign Counterintelligence Activity who had spent years on the case and who knew best the magnitude of Conrad's treason, the preferred denouement was option three: recall the traitorous sergeant to active duty and court-martial him. As a military retiree, Sergeant First Class Conrad could be handed orders reactivating him and then be immediately arrested. Justice could then be administered by a court-martial convened by the commanding general of the 8th Infantry Division.

This course of action had considerable appeal. Conrad would face justice from a court of his peers—the fellow soldiers whose lives he had put at risk by betraying war plans to our Warsaw Pact adversaries. The Uniform Code of Military Justice permitted the ultimate penalty for Conrad's sort of betrayal, and putting Clyde back in uniform was the only way that American authorities could legally arrest him in Germany. As long as the retired noncommissioned officer was a civilian living on German soil, he was subject to German civil law, not American.

Surely Clyde Conrad had planned it this way. That's why he had carefully refrained from obtaining postretirement employment with the U.S. Army and why he had avoided frequent travel to the United States. With no ties to the U.S. forces in Germany, the cagey ex-sergeant knew that he was all but immune from arrest by American authorities. The prospect of ringing the doorbell of Conrad's Bosenheim house, handing the disloyal retiree orders recalling him to active duty, then standing aside while two military policemen arrested him for espionage was a vision that had more than minimal appeal.

As the lawyers in Washington focused on these options, FCA investigators in Wiesbaden pulled off yet another major success. This time it happened in Vienna.

# 25: Miklos

On June 25, 1988, Clyde Conrad disembarked from an intercity train in Vienna. Tucked in his jacket was a bundle of secret documents provided by Danny Wilson and a copy of Espionage Operations Plan 001. As Clyde moved along the platform, Gator's agents easily spotted their target's characteristic shock of white hair. True to his cautious nature, the veteran spy moved directly into the crowded pedestrian shopping zone in the elegant Stadtzentrum. On the two earlier occasions when FCA agents had attempted to tail the slippery agent in Vienna, Conrad had shaken his pursuers by darting in and out of stores and diving into crowded places. To Gator's dismay, history repeated itself. The well-schooled spy detoured abruptly into a crowded department store that had several exits and disappeared into a sea of shoppers. Desperate agents covered the store's exits in a vain attempt to reconnect with their man.

Gator was furious but kept his wits about him. Over a small hand-held radio, he flashed a codeword that directed all team members to execute an emergency drill worked out to cope with just such a contingency. A dozen agents flooded the target area and began a pre-planned search pattern of the neighborhood. Gator was convinced that Conrad and Miklos were meeting in a bar or restaurant, probably within a block or two of where Clyde had shaken his tail, because the Hungarians were too cheap to invest in an expensive Vienna hotel room for a short meeting.

Foreign Counterintelligence Activity agents smothered the area and systematically checked out every bar, beer cellar, and restaurant, communicating with Gator by small radios as they canvassed each search grid. Then, just at the point when the Gator was ready to slash his wrists, the tactic paid off. In Vienna's famous Gosser Beer Hall, a basement beer cellar that seats hundreds of people, an alert agent spotted Conrad hunkered in a booth with another man. After alerting her teammates by radio, she moved boldly through the crowded beer hall toward the booth.

The beer cellar was jammed with several busloads of noisy tourists. Across from Conrad sat a heavy-joweled, dark-haired man—Miklos, at last. Gator's agent made several passes by the booth, her concealed purse camera clicking away unheard amid the noisy diners. As she passed the booth, Conrad and his Hungarian companion were engaged in animated discussion. Clyde had laid some papers on the table and was talking rapidly. Miklos seemed to be unreceptive to the pitch and could be seen shaking his head.

Other agents arrived on the scene and settled in at nearby tables to observe the two men. Clyde and Miklos sat at the table for almost an hour. From the manner of their parting and the look on Conrad's face, the session did not appear to have been cordial. The two conspirators paid their bill and departed, escorted at a discreet distance by Gator's triumphant agents.

As Conrad strode briskly in the direction of the railroad station, Miklos linked up with two men on the sidewalk. By now, Gator was enjoying the drama. The three unsuspecting Hungarians were virtually surrounded by FCA agents armed with still and video cameras. Gator chuckled. Miklos's two companions were his countersurveillance team—men whose job it was to keep watch and warn their man of any possible hostile surveillance. This was not their finest hour. The three Hungarians ambled to a nearby park, where Miklos passed around the documents that Conrad had given him for all to inspect. After a few minutes in the park, the three men walked to a small, Hungarian-tagged vehicle—a Soviet-made Lada—and drove off in the direction of the Hungarian border. Foreign Counterintelligence Activity video cameras recorded the action.

The pictures taken in the Gosser Beer Hall came out perfectly. The camera captured Conrad and the Hungarian in animated conversation, with papers spread out on the table in front of them. Other shots showed the pair walking together on the streets of Vienna, and Miklos with his two companions. Our CIA colleagues easily identified Miklos as Hungarian lieutenant colonel Andras Berenyi, a known intelligence officer who had once served in the Hungarian Trade Mission in Hamburg, West Germany.

This was the best possible news. Persistence and hard work had paid off. The photos conclusively documented Conrad's ties to a known Hungarian intelligence officer. In Wiesbaden and Washington, spirits soared. Surely this would satisfy our demanding Department of Justice colleagues. The untimely leak to the *New York Times* was forcing us to terminate the case, but we could now move from a position of strength.

In late June 1988, a critical meeting of the Canasta Player steering group took place at the imposing Pennsylvania Avenue headquarters of the FBI. With ten years of effort hanging by the thinnest of threads, at issue was the urgent need to close the investigation. Army, CIA, and FBI agents sat around the conference table, joined by a lone Department of Justice attorney. All agreed that it was time to apprehend Clyde Conrad. The question that hung in the air was how.

Pentagon staff lawyers had already researched the regulations and delivered a disappointing assessment. Senior army legal officers advised against recalling Clyde Conrad to active duty and trying him by court-martial. Even though the Uniform Code of Military Justice (military law) permitted this to be done, the army had never attempted it. As a result, there were no implementing policies or regulations on the books under which a recall for the purposes of prosecution could be carried out. Theoretically, this problem could be hastily corrected—new policies could be established—but cautious military lawyers were concerned that a smart defense attorney might be able to find fault with the process and successfully challenge it, in which case Clyde Conrad could go unpunished. I understood the argument, even though I didn't like it, and would have voted to accept this risk (had I been given a vote). On the other hand, the thought of Conrad beating the rap because of some procedural glitch was repugnant. If military attorneys felt that the court-martial approach was unacceptably risky, who was I to challenge their expertise?

Because of the Pentagon decision, when the Canasta Player steering group convened, it was clear that the Department of Justice was the sole remaining avenue for prosecution of Clyde Conrad by the U.S. government.

Throughout 1988, the Department of Justice had played unrelenting hardball with army counterintelligence as agents stalked

Clyde Conrad. The process was sometimes difficult, but Justice attorneys had provided valuable guidance and assisted us in keeping the correct focus. We had heeded the DOJ advice, so that by the time the watershed meeting convened, FCA agents in Wiesbaden had accomplished much of what Justice attorneys had demanded. Once we recovered from the unlucky (but revealing) Maximum Marvel digression, Norman and the Wiesbaden crew had faithfully moved the investigation along the path recommended by the lawyers.

As the meeting's attendees raided the FBI-provided coffee and donuts and settled in at the large conference table, army, CIA, and FBI attendees at the pivotal meeting were unanimous that it was time for the Department of Justice to step up to the plate and prosecute Conrad. All knew that the surveillance in Vienna had yielded ID-quality photography of Clyde Conrad as he met with Miklos, who had departed the scene in a Hungarian-tagged car. Added to the vast quantity of information obtained by Danny Wilson, we now possessed compelling evidence of a conspiracy between Clyde Conrad and an agent of a foreign power.

On the eve of the critical session, Norman Runk and I spoke on the secure phone. Runk knew the stakes and fretted over the meeting's outcome. Put politely, Norman lacked full confidence that Department of Justice lawyers would be supportive of our efforts. More bluntly, the Wiesbaden team chief was openly cynical and predicted that the "DOJ bureaucrats" would fail to do their duty.

I reassured the worried agent. When the chips were down, the Department of Justice would surely not miss the opportunity to prosecute a spy of Conrad's notoriety. Intuitively, I knew that the case, when it broke, would expose the Szabo-Conrad ring as one of the most damaging in the history of the Cold War. The Department of Justice would get on board. And when they did, we would have to deliver Clyde Conrad into their arms.

The meeting commenced with a round of mutual hand-wringing about the *New York Times* leak. All agencies—army, FBI, CIA, and Department of Justice—were dismayed at the thought that someone would talk to the media about such a sensitive investigation. Having said this, we all surely had the same thought: Was the leaker among the fourteen or so persons sitting around the long conference table? Which agency harbored someone capable of such a leak, and what was the leaker's agenda? Who at our meeting might have a vested interest in spiking the investigation?

After providing a short update on the Vienna success, I tabled the $64,000 question: In view of the progress made by the FCA Wiesbaden team and the imminent danger of a media story that could propel Conrad on his escape route to Budapest, would the Department of Justice prosecute Conrad if we could somehow manipulate the greedy spy to travel to the United States? All eyes shifted and focused on the Justice representative.

The Department of Justice attorney responded with an artful display of circumlocution. Prosecution of Conrad was possible, he opined, but only under certain conditions. The army's Foreign Counterintelligence Activity had done a truly magnificent job in identifying and stalking Clyde Conrad. However, he added, there were some "uncomfortable dimensions" of the case that worried the Justice Department. Chief among them were the CIA's involvement in the investigation and the army's introduction of the Maximum Marvel document into the case.

The discussion that followed this announcement was of the sort usually described in official Washington as a "frank exchange of views." After several minutes of polarized debate that solved nothing, I repeated my question. What we needed was a commitment from the Department of Justice attorney. Would DOJ prosecute Conrad or not?

The answer was yes and no. Simply stated, the DOJ attorney explained, the Department of Justice desired assurances that the CIA would be willing to testify in court concerning all aspects of its involvement in the investigation. Experience had taught the Justice attorneys that the CIA was normally unenthusiastic about sanctioning the appearance of its personnel in a courtroom.

There was a history to the Department of Justice's demands for a formal CIA commitment to cooperate in the prosecution. In an infamous 1986 case, the Department of Justice had prosecuted Richard Craig Smith, a former army civilian, for espionage on behalf of the KGB. In 1984, a cash-strapped Smith had disclosed the identities of several army double agents to the Soviets in Tokyo. Smith, who had worked as a case officer in FCA before resigning, was arrested and charged with espionage. No fool, he ultimately resorted to the time-honored defense that he was actually working for the CIA. Privately, CIA officials scoffed at Smith's contention. Nonetheless, the issue had to be confronted directly by the government in the courtroom, which required the testimony of someone from the agency. This led to what Department of Justice prosecutors regarded as an unresponsive attitude on the part of the CIA as federal prosecutors and Smith's defense team sparred over how much sensitive information might be released in the courtroom. Eventually, a retired CIA officer appeared on the stand to testify that the agency had never heard of the two CIA agents for whom Smith claimed he was working when he passed information to the KGB. Unfortunately, as the FBI's principal case agent recalls, the CIA witness "came across as an absolute weasel to the Judge and the jury. He just seemed like he was withholding information and not telling the truth, so that the trial converted almost instantly to a trial of the CIA rather than a trial of Craig Smith."

Smith was acquitted, leaving a legacy of hurt feelings and resentment. It was the only time in the history of the Justice Department that the government had lost an espionage prosecution, a humiliating legal debacle at the vortex of which had been FCA (Smith being a former FCA agent) and the CIA. After his release, Smith rubbed salt in the Justice Department's wounded ego by boasting during a nationally broadcast television interview that he was the only person ever to be tried for espionage in a U.S. courtroom and acquitted.

Still smarting from the ill-fated Smith prosecution, the Department of Justice sought assurances that any prosecution of Clyde Conrad would be a 100 percent team effort by the government, the CIA included.

But on this occasion, the CIA would not blink. Gus Hathaway was adamant that Conrad face prosecution in a U.S. court. If required, the agency representative stated, Hathaway would personally appear in court and testify about the CIA role in the unmasking of Conrad, no holds barred. Such testimony could be accomplished under the umbrella of the Classified Information Protection Act, which provided for closed court sessions and the granting of limited security clearances to defense attorneys when sensitive national security issues were likely to surface. Having given birth to the Canasta Player investigation in 1978 (and having lost no small sum of money to Conrad during the David scam), the CIA would not abandon its commitment to put Conrad in jail.

This left us with one outstanding issue: the Department of Justice's discomfort with the Maximum Marvel issue. The Justice attorney demanded firm assurances that the Pentagon would cooperate fully and permit testimony about the project in the event that it surfaced during Conrad's trial.

The Pentagon position was that the project should be kept out of the courtroom by the prosecution, to which the Justice Department representative shook his head vigorously. "The government can avoid mention of Maximum Marvel during the prosecution's presentation," he pointed out, "but when Conrad's defense attorney learns of the project under discovery rules, we cannot prevent him from asking about it. Like it or not, Maximum Marvel has been in this case since the day Colonel Herrington's people introduced that document."

It was the Justice Department's secret weapon to fend off the unwanted prosecution. And my organization had provided it by using the Maximum Marvel message. At the time, we were focused on the need to manipulate Conrad into contacting Miklos—at the urging of the Department of Justice. The one-page message seemed like a good idea. In hindsight, the choice of document had been unwise. Had we explained the Maximum Marvel strategy during a steering group meeting before its execution, the lawyers would have undoubtedly seen the trap and saved us from falling into it. Still, one had to believe that the Department of Justice was overreacting to the problem. If, in a trial, the innocuous message had to be introduced, so be it. After all, the Maximum Marvel people had not had a problem with it being passed to Budapest or Moscow, so what was wrong with its being introduced in a courtroom but limiting discussion of the project's details?

This approach was unacceptable to our DOJ partners. Introducing the cryptic message, they insisted, would open the door to questions concerning the details of the project. No amount of argument could dissuade them from this view, and the Pentagon was unwilling to permit exposure of the project's details in a courtroom, even a closed courtroom. Faced with this dilemma, the Department of Justice attorney announced that his department would not agree to prosecute Conrad. I can still recall his words: "You can't expect us to go out on the football field to play, but not let us have the football. If we agree to prosecute, nothing can be held back." Justice was insisting on overtrying the case, just as FBI agent Tom Reilly had predicted.

This was a bitter pill to swallow in light of the hard work and sacrifice that FCA agents had expended in the pursuit of Conrad, not to mention the more than $500,000 we had spent on the case in the first six months of 1988.

Frustrated and angry, I posed a question: "Are you telling me that in spite of everything we have collected about Conrad's activities—his recruitment of Danny Wilson, the Switzerland trip, the acquisition of the espionage operations plan, and the photographs of the recent Vienna meeting—if Clyde Lee Conrad showed up at JFK Airport tomorrow, the Department of Justice would not authorize his arrest?"

The eyes of all present turned to the hapless Justice attorney, who replied simply, "That's what I'm saying."

Incensed, I fired back, "Is this your personal view, or is it the position of the attorney general?"

"This is our department's view, not mine," the attorney replied.

The meeting concluded on this acrimonious note. We were now at an impasse. It was clear to everyone present that the Department of Justice position was based on the cautious judicial philosophy that it prosecutes only when it has a 100 percent chance of a conviction. Arguments that the case against Conrad was strong and likely to get stronger once he and the Kercsiks were arrested and their houses searched fell on deaf ears. Neither did we encounter sympathy when we attempted to convince Department of Justice representatives that, philosophically, the government should prosecute when it was convinced of the defendant's guilt and when it appeared that a competent prosecutor could marshal significant evidence to obtain a conviction. Sometimes prosecution was the right thing to do, even if the case was not 100 percent airtight.

Foreign Counterintelligence Activity investigators had amassed a mountain of exhibits that could be introduced as evidence. A search of Conrad's Bosenheim home would doubtless lead to the seizure of his computer, likely to contain compromising materials, not to mention his Casio pocket organizer, which Danny Wilson had reported was crammed with other incriminating information. Furthermore, Wilson himself could take the stand and testify about his recruitment by Conrad and their meetings with the Kercsik brothers. And if the Kercsiks were arrested in Sweden, they would likely confess and implicate Conrad. With the exception of the Department of Justice attorneys, those familiar with the case were convinced that the army had amassed overwhelming information pointing to Clyde Conrad's guilt.

But the Justice Department's attorneys held their ground. In their view, the Department of Justice had not refused to prosecute Conrad; the department had merely levied two reasonable conditions on the matter, one of which was unacceptable to the Pentagon. In the annals of the Justice Department's history, it would be written that the army had tainted the case and derailed the chances for prosecution of Conrad by introducing a sensitive program that could not be permitted to see the light of day in a courtroom.

Those of us who were close to the case felt that we knew what was going on. It was the ghost of the Richard Craig Smith humiliation raising its head and reminding our Justice colleagues that American juries could be capricious. True, the case was not as neatly wrapped as any of us would have liked, but it was strong and likely to get stronger. We believed that the American people would never understand it if a spy such as Conrad were permitted to get away with his treachery. Our Department of Justice counterparts were not concerned with such matters. They had found a way out of what they assessed as a potentially messy case, and they took it. As I later told a bitterly disappointed Norman Runk, that was how the game was played inside the Beltway.

# 26: The Rescue: The Germans Weigh In

The opposition in FCA to asking our German allies to roll up Clyde Conrad and his confederates was visceral. No one lacked respect for the German security organs, which could perform with great skill when challenged. But the principal targets of the investigation were two retired American soldiers who appeared to rank among the most damaging traitors in our nation's history. Clyde Conrad and Zoltan Szabo should be held accountable for their treason by the American criminal justice system.

Yet it was also true that Conrad's and Szabo's espionage had undermined Bonn's security as much as, if not more than, that of Washington. After all, West Germany, not Pennsylvania, would be the battlefield in the event of war in Central Europe. Too, among the thousands of betrayed secrets were both German and NATO war plans. Nor could we not ignore cryptic statements made by Conrad to Danny Wilson that strongly suggested the recruitment of at least one member of the West German army by the ring.

We also opposed taking the case to the Germans for technical reasons. The first was security. The same security concerns that had caused us to pursue the investigation behind the backs of our German allies told us that it would be dangerous to bring Bonn into the case before Conrad was safely behind bars. Having said this, it seemed presumptuous, if not outright hypocritical, for us to pontificate to the Germans about security. After all, had not the *New York Times* penetrated ours?

A more serious problem was the discouraging track record of the West German government in meting out punishment for espionage. In the most celebrated and damaging case of espionage against the Germans, Chancellor Willy Brandt's personal assistant, Gunter Guillaume, had received a fourteen-year sentence for passing secrets from the pinnacle of the Bonn government to East Berlin. No one was confident that the West German justice system would be able to satisfactorily sentence a traitor whose acts had put NATO forces at risk of a quick defeat in the event of war in Central Europe.

But all of these considerations were moot. Our investigation had exposed a spy ring that had delivered NATO's war plans to the communists for sixteen years. The American press was poised to break the story, and we couldn't find anyone on our side of the Atlantic Ocean willing to arrest Conrad and take the case to court. In truth, we had no choice but to package up our case file and export it to our German allies, however disappointing this might be. A ten-year sentence would be heavy by German standards, but at least we would stop the hemorrhage of secrets and have the satisfaction of seeing Conrad where he belonged—behind bars. Within days of the frustrating meeting in FBI headquarters, my army superiors instructed me to approach the West German government and request its assistance in wrapping up the decade-long investigation.

As the bureaucratic infighting played itself out in Washington, Norman Runk's Wiesbaden team pressed its pursuit of Conrad. As usual, at the center of the action was Controlled Source 170, MSgt. Danny Wilson.

Within a week of Conrad's return from Vienna, Wilson contacted Gary Pepper and signaled the need for a meeting. As expected, Clyde the Glide had contacted him to report on the Vienna trip. The FCA double agent was bursting with news.

Wilson reported that Clyde had triumphantly declared the Vienna trip to be an unqualified success. His meeting with Miklos, Clyde enthused, had been a positive three-hour session, during which the Hungarian case officer had praised Conrad's vision of a high-tech espionage ring. The grand design was on track. In fact, Conrad boasted, Miklos was so upbeat about the envisioned enterprise that he had given the green light for a Budapest trip, during which Conrad could sell his concept to the Center. In three weeks, Clyde said with a grin, he would be in Budapest, where he confidently predicted he would obtain final approval of his plan. (Norman noted that Conrad's description of the Vienna meeting and that of Gator's surveillance people differed. The meeting had actually been much shorter, and clearly contentious. In character, Clyde was imparting a positive spin to impress his protégé.)

Finally, Wilson told Gary almost matter-of-factly that he had been able to determine Conrad's travel plans. After his normal quota of

German beer, the spy had confided that he would drive to Budapest on July 17.

This was welcome news. If Conrad was Budapest bound in the silver Audi, Gator's team would have the opportunity to photograph the veteran spy as he drove across the Austro-Hungarian border.

The news that Clyde Conrad was on the verge of a pilgrimage to the Center in Budapest also had a downside. The problem was the *New York Times*. If Clyde was savoring gypsy violin music over a bowl of goulash and a glass of Tokay wine in a Budapest restaurant when the *Times* broke the story, the case was finished.

In late June 1988, I boarded a Pan Am 747 for Germany clutching a tubular case containing a map of Europe, around which appeared a cluster of attention-getting surveillance photos documenting the conspiracy of Clyde Conrad and Zoltan Szabo. Arrows led from the photographs to the cities in Germany and Austria where Conrad and his coconspirators had carried out their espionage activities. The highly classified chart was a road map that graphically depicted the history of the complex case. It was not an item that one would want to lose in an airport.

The army leadership had concurred with Gus Hathaway's suggestion that we approach Dr. Peter Frisch, the vice president of the West German counterintelligence service (the BfV). Frisch was a respected and popular professional with whom Hathaway enjoyed a warm relationship. The entree would be arranged by CIA Station, Bonn. Dr. Frisch would be invited to the U.S. embassy for a tour of the facilities, during which he would be diverted into my presence. My job was to unveil the chart and make a formal request for German assistance.

Considerable thought went into the plan for the important meeting. My appeal would require an up-front admission to Dr. Frisch that we had been conducting the Canasta Player investigation on German soil for years. Then would follow a summary of the case and a request for Bonn's assistance in the final phases of the sensitive investigation. This latter point was critical. If we merely tried to drop the case in the Germans' lap and ask them to arrest and prosecute Conrad, they would have no sense of participation in the investigation. If, on the other hand, we requested that Frisch and his agents join us as partners in the final phase of the case, after which they would arrest Conrad, we could better establish the basis for the teamwork and cooperation essential for success.

On the eve of my departure, controversy was rampant in Washington over the decision to ask the Germans to bail us out. Some, myself among them, were haunted by visions of a communist mole in Bonn hustling off to East Berlin and blowing the entire investigation within days of the approach to Dr. Frisch.

Others cautioned that the messenger who carried the case to Bonn would be walking into a political buzz saw; the Germans would be upset that we had conducted the investigation behind their backs and would refuse to buy into a case as complex, risky, and potentially explosive as Canasta Player. We were, after all, telling the Germans that we had not trusted them with the case for years and then, in the next breath, asking them to tackle the landmark investigation as it entered its most delicate stage. In addition to stalking and eventually arresting Conrad, they would clearly be required to coordinate with the Swedes to effect simultaneous arrests of the Kercsik brothers, and also with the Austrians if it appeared feasible to score a clean sweep by apprehending Zoltan Szabo. It was a substantial undertaking, all of which would have to be accomplished quickly to minimize the dangers of a compromise at the hands of an East German penetration agent. Assuming that Conrad's arrest was successfully orchestrated, the Bonn government would then face a costly and complex prosecution.

Airborne over the Atlantic, I silently rehearsed the planned approach and fretted over its possible outcome. If a German colonel were to approach the FBI in Washington, confess that he and his agents had secretly run an espionage investigation for years in the United States, and solicit assistance in wrapping up the case—assistance that would require coordinated arrests in Washington, Ottawa, and Mexico City, followed by a complex and costly prosecution in a U.S. court—how would the Department of Justice and our FBI friends respond?

Then there were the stakes to consider. Failure to obtain Dr. Frisch's pledge of assistance, above all with respect to a prosecution of Conrad, would leave us stranded with a spy on our hands whom no one wanted to arrest. Conrad could not be permitted to walk, I knew, but this was a real possibility if we could not sell the case to someone willing to prosecute. No question about it: Frisch had to be persuaded or Norman Runk and his agents would never forgive me. He and the Wiesbaden team had delivered everything that was asked of them. My job was to find a home for their case.

On June 29, 1988, we executed the overture to the Germans. As Dr. Frisch and his small entourage toured the Bonn embassy's facilities, the senior German official was temporarily split off from the group and ushered into my presence in a CIA office behind a vault door. The Canasta Player chart was prominently displayed on an easel. Bill Lieser, the CIA's deputy station chief and a major supporter of our investigation, introduced me and Norman, explaining that I was an army intelligence officer and friend of Gus Hathaway's who had just flown in from Washington.

For perhaps twenty minutes, I described the investigation, emphasizing that the case was the longest running, most sensitive, most compartmented army counterintelligence investigation since World War II. Using the eye-catching chart, I traced the origins and activities of the Szabo-Conrad ring, emphasizing its years of betrayal of NATO, German, and American secrets. Apologetically referring to the fact that we had run the case without consulting German counterintelligence authorities, I explained the *New York Times* problem. If the *Times* broke its story and Conrad attempted to flee to Austria or Hungary, we hoped for German assistance in the form of an advisory to all border posts to apprehend the retired sergeant on sight.

Dr. Frisch listened patiently without interrupting. I continued. Could the Germans assist in the surveillance of Conrad during the final phase of the investigation? Our own surveillance efforts had been under way since February, and every day brought renewed fear of a mistake by exhausted American agents that might alert Conrad. It would thus be helpful if the Germans could tap Conrad's telephone under their G-10 law. A timely telephone tap would provide another valuable window into our target's activities and state of mind. By listening to Conrad's phone conversations, we would acquire tip-offs that would make surveillance operations easier and less risky.

Finally, I admitted to Dr. Frisch that Conrad's full-time residence in Bosenheim and the cautious spy's deliberate avoidance of civilian employment with the U.S. Army posed a jurisdictional problem that rendered it all but impossible for us to arrest and prosecute him. Army attorneys continued to struggle with legal issues associated with recall to active duty and court-martial, I added, but we were not optimistic that a solution could be found. In such a case, it was likely that we would ask the German government to arrest and prosecute Conrad to the maximum extent permitted by law. Then I held my breath.

Frisch turned his gaze from the chart to me and spoke.

"Have you controlled his telephone?"

I shook my head. "No, sir. That's one of the reasons we badly need your assistance during the final phase of the investigation."

The senior German official expressed a measure of astonishment that we had been able to shadow Conrad for so many months and amass such a revealing collection of surveillance photographs during the man's operational meetings in Austria. Unspoken was the notion that if Conrad was such a top spy, how could we have laid bare his activities so completely?

The money question also disturbed Dr. Frisch. In his experience, it was unheard of for a spy to earn the amounts of money we attributed to Clyde Conrad. (I had used the figure of a $50,000 payment for a single document in the presentation.)

Frisch had another question. "Colonel, how long do you envision this final phase of the investigation to last?"

"That depends, sir," I responded. "Conrad intends to travel to Budapest in July, so we would need to confer on whether or not it is a good idea to permit this trip in view of the danger of a press story. But in no case do we envision the phase to last longer than ninety days."

Dr. Frisch shook his head slowly. "We would see this phase as going no longer than thirty days. As you know, we have our own problems with security. Because of this, we cannot put Conrad's name on a watch list to prevent him from crossing the border. Our experience with such lists has not been good. Often they are passed to our friends in East Berlin within twenty-four hours."

Another matter troubled Dr. Frisch. "You understand that our laws are not the same as yours when it comes to espionage. If you really want this Conrad to be punished severely, our courts are likely to disappoint you. You would be better off arresting him yourself."

This was an awkward moment. Dr. Frisch was preaching to the choir, but there was no reason to dwell on the near bloodletting in Washington over the prosecution decision. Yet it was important to be honest. I explained that military and civilian attorneys in Washington had wrestled with the issue for weeks without a satisfactory solution. Faced with the urgent need to wrap up the case, we were prepared to accept whatever punishment the German courts might mete out, the major objective being to put an immediate stop to Conrad's treason.

The German nodded his understanding. Silently grateful that we had begun to discuss the modalities of cooperation, I explained that my investigative team was operating under cover in Wiesbaden. Herr Runk was the agent in charge, and he was under instructions to open the books of the case to our new German partners. As for the timing of Conrad's takedown, that was a matter for the Germans to determine.

Dr. Frisch glanced at his watch and rose to depart. "We will gladly assist you," he announced, "although you have done an amazing job without us up to this point. But I wish you to please give this same briefing to the two colleagues who accompanied me today, if you could. The case will fall into their area of responsibility."

That was it. Canasta Player was now a joint investigation. The doom and gloom predictions of an angry German backlash had not been borne out. From this point on, Norman Runk and his team would work with the German security organs and prosecutors to create the conditions for Conrad's arrest and prosecution.

Timing was now the key. Runk and his agents would have to explain the complex case to our new partners and convince them that it was a winner. All of this had to be accomplished within days if an arrest were to occur within a month. The meaning of Dr. Frisch's candid admission that "we have our own problems with security" was evident. Our German partners had just signed on and were already worried that a leak to East Berlin could derail the investigation.

• • •

Dr. Peter Frisch's goal to arrest Clyde Conrad within thirty days proved unattainable. The investigation was simply too complex to hand off that quickly to the German authorities. Ultimately, almost two months would race past before our German partners were ready to deliver the coup de grace to Zoltan Szabo's espionage ring. A formidable amount of coordination had to be accomplished to lay the foundation for the arrests, most of it consisting of detailed explanations of every dimension of the case to our willing but incredulous new partners.

Point man for the U.S. government was Norman Runk. Working initially with German investigators of the BfV, the dedicated agent and his team had a major job on their hands merely to convince their German counterparts that the case was real. Whereas Dr. Frisch had been cordial and accommodating, BfV senior investigators Dirk Doerrenberg and Werner Goll were professional, demanding, and justifiably skeptical.

To satisfy the BfV's demands for information, Runk leaned heavily on the institutional memories of Dave Guethlein and Gary Pepper. While Pepper devoted himself full-time to Danny Wilson, Runk and Guethlein ran the wheels off their rental cars in repeated pilgrimages to the BfV's Cologne headquarters. There they faithfully attended meetings, provided documents, explained evidence, delivered briefings, and responded to a seemingly unending host of questions from skeptical German investigators. It was almost surreal. These were people whom a week earlier we had not trusted with the sensitive case. Now Runk and his team were engaged in a nonstop sell-a-thon, struggling to convince Dr. Frisch's investigators that Clyde Lee Conrad was perhaps the worst NATO spy in the history of the Cold War.

The BfV's no-nonsense agents challenged everything. The major problem seemed to be an inability to suspend disbelief. No spy in their experience had ever earned the kind of money Conrad had boasted of to Danny Wilson. Furthermore, if Conrad was the most dangerous and successful spy since World War II, how could he have been so foolish and fallen into every trap that FCA laid for him? The amiable Norman kept his cool and patiently trotted out the many exhibits we had collected that supported the admittedly bizarre story of Conrad's thirteen-year career as an East Bloc spy.

Much later, as German and American investigators bonded into a team, our German partners would confide in Norman that when Dr. Frisch agreed to take on the sensitive case, his subordinates were convinced that the Americans had fouled up a big case and were dumping it on the luckless Germans, who would, of course, take the blame in the event of failure.

Once the German professionals realized that the Americans had hooked into something real, and Runk's team showed its willingness to support the investigation without compromise, relationships between American and BfV investigators improved. The more Dr. Frisch's people learned about the case, the more astounded they were that FCA agents had managed to maneuver so closely to Conrad and expose so much of his secret life. When Norman revealed that the Gator and his people had been tailing Conrad almost twenty-four hours a day for several months, our German colleagues were incredulous. "We would have never attempted such a thing," one admitted. The fact that Danny Wilson had managed to obtain a copy of Conrad's espionage opus was regarded by the Germans as nothing short of miraculous.

As FCA agents in Wiesbaden revealed the various layers of the complex case, they gradually won over even the most skeptical of Dr. Frisch's no-nonsense investigators. The case was solid, our BfV colleagues advised, so much so that it was time to bring in officers of the Bundeskriminalamt, the Federal Criminal Office (known as the BKA). In the German system, the BKA had the responsibility for conducting investigations that were headed for executive *Massnahmen,* or executive measures, defined as arrest leading to prosecution. Once the name of the suspect was revealed to the BKA, the countdown to arrest would commence.

Now Runk and his team had two sets of German partners: the BfV, which had some continuing investigative jurisdiction, and a phalanx of BKA agents from Section ST-13, led by Herr Manfred Rutkowski. When conditions were ripe, Rutkowski and his men would be responsible for the actual arrest of Conrad and the resulting follow-on investigation. Once again, Runk and Gary Pepper were subjected to a thorough grilling about the complex case, this time at the hands of BKA investigators Holger Klein and Peter Debus. In one memorable phone conversation at the end of a solid week of shopping his case to a brace of dubious German counterspies, a deeply frustrated Norman called me at Fort Meade and wailed, "Boss, they don't believe us."

Along with the BKA investigators came yet another group of helpful Germans, a team of methodical attorneys from the Federal Prosecutor's Office in Karlsruhe, the Generalbundesanwalt (GBA). The GBA prosecutors were the counterparts of our Department of Justice. As the cast of Teutonic characters swelled to Wagnerian proportions, Norman found himself at the center of a maelstrom of furious activity by all three German agencies. Each agency, the overburdened agent soon learned, required convincing anew that the Canasta Player investigation was to be taken seriously, and each agency had its own demands for information.

Dr. Frisch's BfV agents pursued certain investigative measures—physical surveillance, obtaining a tap of Conrad's phone, and establishing contact with the Swedish Intelligence Service. At the same time, Manfred Rutkowski's BKA investigators played frantic catch-up ball to master within days the facts of a case that had taken us more than a decade to develop. At the same time, attorneys from the GBA posed a battery of penetrating questions to determine if there was anything about our investigation that might be a showstopper to a prosecution of Conrad under Article 99—*Spionage*—of the German Constitution.

Much of the FCA case hinged upon the reporting of Danny Wilson. Not surprisingly, our new German partners were anxious to meet Controlled Source 170 and conduct their own assessment of the man who would one day be their star witness. Norman Runk rented a suite in the Graf Zeppelin Hotel, across from the Stuttgart main railroad station, where Wilson patiently submitted to a long grilling by the still-skeptical Germans. Emerging from these sessions, the senior German prosecutor (Oberstaatsanwalt), Volkhard Wache, shook his head in amazement and pronounced Gary Pepper's source totally *glaubwurdig* (credible). Norman and his team were carrying the day in the difficult handoff to the Germans.

The resources and effort that the Germans mobilized, and the speed with which they swung into high gear, were nothing short of astonishing. Within a few weeks of the delicate overture to Dr. Frisch, our new partners had mastered the facts of the complicated case and begun to formulate a plan of action.

On the German side, as skepticism gave way to admiration, the verdict was unanimous. The case against Clyde Conrad was solid, albeit complex. It would take many months to prepare for prosecution, but GBA prosecutors and investigators of both German agencies concluded that their American colleagues had pulled off a truly astounding piece of investigative wizardry. Unlike our Department of Justice attorneys, German prosecutors saw no problem with the Maximum Marvel document. Like American law, their law contained procedures to protect classified information in a court of law. These procedures would be followed, German prosecutors assured us. The magnitude of Conrad's treason cried out for prosecution, they ruled. To permit hypothetical actions by Conrad's hypothetical defense attorney to spook German prosecutors from applying the full force of the law was unthinkable.

The many audiotapes that Danny Wilson had bravely made of his meetings with Conrad were a problem. Tapes of concealed monitoring were inadmissable under German law. The GBA prosecutors were wary. Conrad's defense attorney could be expected to raise this issue. But when Gary Pepper explained that he had written reports of all Wilson's contacts with Clyde Conrad based upon Wilson's descriptions rather than on the difficult-to-decipher tapes, Herr Wache and his team relaxed. If nothing from the tapes had found its way into Pepper's reports, then the illegal tapes were a nonproblem.

During the month of July, Manfred Rutkowski's BKA investigators assumed the lead role for the Germans. A camaraderie between Norman Runk's team and the congenial BKA agents soon developed, on and off duty. More than a few steins of beer were raised in the name of the defense of democracy and German American friendship. Bob Bell and I agreed that this was positive but lamented our luck. While we sat at Fort Meade working the Washington end of the case, Norman and his team were having all the fun.

Each day brought fresh reminders of what a wise choice it had been to pull the good-natured Runk from his duties in Munich. In just four months, he had turned the investigation around. When Norman was told that something needed to be done, the task was efficiently accomplished. The Gator and his stalwart surveillance folks were blindly loyal to Runk, and now the high-spirited and amiable agent had won over the Germans. Years later, our German partners would still fondly recall Norman's cheerful response to their myriad, rapid-fire requests for support. "No problem," Norman would sing out and then do whatever was required to fulfill the German request. Manfred Rutkowski's BKA investigators were impressed. They had worked with Americans in the past, but not Americans like this crew.

Several important issues had to be dealt with to prepare the way for Conrad's arrest. These included a plan for coordinated arrests of the Kercsik brothers, a plan for the arrest of Zoltan Szabo, and the particularly delicate question of how to cope with Clyde Conrad's upcoming mission to Budapest.

Coordinating with the Swedes should have been a routine task. As often happens in the counterintelligence business, simple things can become complex. With the countdown to Conrad's arrest under way, the Germans planned a trip to Stockholm to coordinate the simultaneous arrests of the Kercsik brothers in Goteborg and Conrad in Bosenheim. More than a year earlier, FCA agent Al Puromaki had discreetly visited the Swedes after the Kercsik brothers surfaced in the FCA investigation. Officers of SAPO, the security element of the Swedish National Police, had been told only that we had a major case under way and that tip-offs on the Kercsiks' planned travels to Germany would be helpful. The neutral Swedes had cooperated but asked us not to reveal their role. Thus, when we took the case to Dr. Frisch, we respected the Swedish request, telling the Germans that the case was so sensitive that we had told no one about it. Now, as the BfV laid plans for their trip to Stockholm, we alerted our colleagues in Sweden of the impending German overture and reassured them that we had respected their desires and not revealed their assistance to the Germans. For obvious reasons, the Swedes should act surprised when the Germans briefed them on the sensitive case.

Initially, all went well. The BfV's Werner Goll traveled to Stockholm and explained the case to the Swedes. The two services agreed to roll up Conrad and the Kercsiks on the same day. Stockholm and Bonn would share whatever they learned from their prisoners and from searches of their homes. But before Goll departed, one of the Swedes let the cat out of the bag. Perhaps it was over aquavit or beer—we never learned—but one Swedish officer misspoke and mentioned Al Puromaki's name. Dr. Frisch's man knew immediately what had happened. By the time BfV agent Goll returned to Germany, we had received a warning about the miscue in Sweden. Norman soon reported that a perceptible coolness had descended over his BfV colleagues, who were understandably miffed at what they saw as our lack of candor. Later, Werner Goll made his point politely to me. There must be genuine trust and openness between partners, he urged. Goll was on the mark, but we had found ourselves in a box. The Swedes had asked us not to reveal their complicity, and we had agreed. If the Germans had asked us for a similar consideration, they would certainly expect us to respect their request. The issue had nothing to do with trusting the Swedes more than the Germans. Goll was a gentleman about the matter, but all of us regretted that the BfV had reason to doubt our sincerity, particularly because we had developed great admiration for their investigative acumen.

Laying legal hands on Zoltan Szabo was a trickier planning challenge. Shrewdly ensconced in neutral Austria in the shadow of the Hungarian border, Szabo was a tough target.

Pentagon international lawyers researched Article 256 of the Austrian Criminal Code and advised that espionage was not against the law in Austria unless the spy was collecting information about Austria. To the best of our knowledge, Szabo had used Austria as a base of operations, but his spying had focused exclusively on the NATO target. There was not a big market on the other side of the Iron Curtain for information about demilitarized and neutral Austria. It was thus not at all clear what we could ask the Austrians to do about Szabo were we of a mind to approach them, which we were not.

The Germans expressed admiration for the abilities of the Austrian Staatschutz but shared our doubts about the wisdom of approaching Vienna, however desirable a clean sweep seemed. Once again, the issue was security. Just as we had been reticent to approach the Bonn government with our case, we were uncomfortable about taking the sensitive case to Vienna, the former glittering capital of the Austro-Hungarian Empire.

Continuing close ties existed between communist Hungary and neutral Austria. If we confided in the Austrians and a well-placed Hungarian agent learned of our plans, Conrad and Szabo would be alerted. This fact, together with our belief that Szabo had committed no offense in Austria, caused us to conclude that any effort to orchestrate the arrest of Zoltan Szabo by the Austrians at the same time the Germans grabbed Clyde Conrad was too risky.

As a compromise measure, we prepared a Szabo dossier that contained a summary of all available information concerning Szabo's activities, with emphasis on his use of Austria as a base for Hungarian intelligence operations. As soon as Conrad was safely behind bars, I would travel to Vienna and deliver this information to the Austrian Security Service. Perhaps they could move against Szabo. Like other judgments we made during this case, caution was the ever-present watchword.

Clyde Conrad's impending mission to Budapest was the sole remaining issue that we and our German partners had to address prior to his arrest. The American side of the partnership was understandably nervous about the planned trip because of the *New York Times* angle. For our part, prudence argued that Conrad should be taken down before his Budapest travel.

But Manfred Rutkowski and his investigators held a contrary view. Conrad must be permitted to go to Budapest. The Karlsruhe-based prosecutors of the GBA concurred. A Budapest trip was worth the risk. Photographs of Conrad's Audi as it crossed into communist Hungary were highly desirable, our German partners explained, and any information about the trip that he might share with Danny Wilson upon his return would enhance the prosecution's case.

The Germans proposed to permit Conrad to travel to Budapest and arrest him shortly after his return. As for the surveillance effort required to document the actual border crossing, Bonn's agents would not violate Austrian neutrality. Norman Runk assured Manfred Rutkowski that the Americans would undertake one final Austrian mission. It would be left to me to mend fences in Vienna after the arrests.

In Washington, it was necessary to alert key civilian and military officials who had a need to know that the Conrad case was on the verge of making headlines. These included Maj. Gen. Ed Soyster, the commanding general of the Intelligence and Security Command, as well as senior FBI and CIA officials. In the Pentagon, the list included Lieutenant General Weinstein; Secretary of the Army John O. Marsh; the four-star Chief of Staff of the Army, Gen. Carl Vuono (who had once been Conrad's commander at the 8th Infantry Division), and his four-star vice chief of staff; and a small circle of other officials, in particular those from the legal side of the house—the Office of the Army General Counsel and the Office of the Army Judge Advocate General. As a professional courtesy, I visited Lt. Gen. William Odom, who by 1988 was the director of the National Security Agency. As the officer who had demanded a maximum effort to smoke out the unknown spy, Odom deserved to know the results of the order he had issued to Col. Bob Lunt three years earlier.

On Capitol Hill, key members and staffers of the House and Senate Intelligence Committees were also apprised of the impending arrests. Accompanied by the CIA's Gus Hathaway, I also made a pilgrimage to the Department of State to brief Ambassador Morton Abramowitz to ensure that the department was not taken by suprise when the *New York Times* broke the story, which it surely would.

In Europe, Norman Runk paved the way for the impending arrest by making similar rounds to major American headquarters in Heidelberg, Frankfurt, Munich, and Stuttgart. The players were in place for the last act.

Clyde Conrad departed for his Budapest summit conference on July 17, 1988. As the once and future spy streaked down the autobahn in his Audi, Manfred Rutkowski and his agents put the final touches on a plan to ensure that this would be the last travel of any kind that Conrad would undertake for many years.

Thanks to Danny Wilson's acquisition of Clyde's travel plans, FCA agents were on the scene at the Nicholsdorf border crossing east of Vienna when Conrad's silver Audi pulled up to the barrier. Disguised as a married couple on a tourist outing, agents Meg Reilly and Bob Watson snapped several excellent photographs as Clyde Conrad crossed into Hungary, the license plate of his Audi clearly legible.

At their final meeting before his departure, Conrad had shared an intriguing detail with Danny Wilson. Miklos had given him explicit travel instructions, to include the exact hour he should enter the checkpoint. The Hungarian, Clyde confided, had boasted that one of the Austrian border guards on duty at that time was a Hungarian agent who would ensure smooth passage.

It was a timely, useful tidbit. When I visited Vienna in the wake of Conrad's arrest to request assistance on the Szabo matter, a tip concerning a possible disloyal Austrian official would interest the Austrian Staatschutz.

Clyde Lee Conrad lingered in Budapest for a week, during which few of us got an abundance of sleep. Norman and I drowned our apprehensions regularly at the Wiesbadener Ratsbrau as we kept vigil and brainstormed the rapidly approaching next phase of the case. Stalking the target was about to end. As soon as Conrad was behind bars, exploitation and rollup would begin. This phase would be equally difficult. Headlines would surely trumpet the arrest, alerting any other coconspirators. Speed and careful planning were essential.

Yet we dared not fail. A well-planned and swiftly executed postarrest investigation would not only ensure the successful prosecution of Conrad, it might also enable agents to identify other conspirators. The espionage ring had been functioning since the early 1970s. No one believed that Clyde Conrad was Zoltan Szabo's sole recruit, or that Conrad's only coconspirator was Danny Wilson.

Once the Germans had arrested Conrad, dozens of army special agents would deploy around the world to conduct hundreds of interviews, working from the long lists that agents had developed of Conrad's former superiors, fellow soldiers, associates, and close friends. In Europe, most interviews would be done in partnership with the Germans. In the United States, when interviewees were civilians, FCA agents would team up with the FBI. The goal of these interviews was to identify other suspects on whom spin-off investigations could be opened, and to obtain additional information about Conrad's espionage to support the German prosecution.

Chief candidates for spin-off investigations would be soldiers who had worked in the division G-3 during Conrad's service, and a number of others whose ties to Conrad had been uncovered through interviews or by the FCA surveillance team. Earlier interviews had established that the charismatic Mr. Plans had been a role model for many of the younger soldiers in the Bad Kreuznach headquarters over the years. Investigators strongly suspected that the smooth-talking Conrad had exploited his position of authority to involve some of them in his enterprise. One in particular, former sergeant Rod Ramsay, had worked with Conrad in the G-3. Cashiered out of the army for drug use, Ramsay was living in Tampa, Florida, where he was a busboy at a local restaurant. He was already in the FBI's sights.

Norman would continue to be the focal point in Germany. His job was to make sure that whatever the Germans required, they got. Our attitude was that the Germans were doing us a considerable service by joining in the quest to bring Clyde Conrad to justice, although our proud partners did not see it that way. As GBA prosecutor Volkhard Wache repeatedly reminded us, his country would arrest and prosecute the retired sergeant because of what he had done to harm German security, not as a favor to Washington. It was a valid observation. But to the end, Runk and I were acutely aware that our German comrades had saved the day by entering the fray, for which they had earned our gratitude and loyalty.

Clyde Conrad returned from Budapest on July 25, 1988, to spend time with stepdaughter Sonja, who had arrived from California with her new husband. On August 3, 1988, he summoned Danny Wilson. The two men met in a Stuttgart *gasthaus*.

Conrad was psyched up, telling Danny jubilantly that the Center had blessed his plan. The way was now cleared for the recruitment of the top-secret-document custodians in Heidelberg and Stuttgart. Like a kid with a new toy, Clyde showed off an electronic device that the Hungarians had provided. The size of an elongated VCR remote control, the high-tech device was a Textlite PX 1000 data-encryption–burst transmitter-receiver. Conrad explained the sophisticated gadget. He could type a message on the keyboard and encrypt the copy by a series of keystrokes. This done, he need only dial up a phone number in Budapest where someone sat with the same type of instrument. By placing the device against the telephone headset and pushing a button, the encrypted message would be burst-transmitted to Budapest in a microsecond, immune from interception or decryption. Clearly enthralled with his new toy, Clyde overflowed with boyish enthusiasm as he contemplated what lay ahead for him and Wilson.

This August 1988 meeting was to be Clyde Lee Conrad's final encounter as a free man with star pupil Danny Wilson. The next time the self-styled master spy would meet the man he had groomed to anchor his reborn espionage empire would be in early 1990. But instead of sipping beer in a *gasthaus* and plotting treason, the two would confront each other in a German courtroom.

# 27: Takedown

With Teutonic thoroughness, our German partners in the BKA laid the groundwork for the arrest of Clyde Conrad. Manfred Rutkowski's seasoned agents were not novices in takedown tactics. Not only was Section ST-13 responsible for counterespionage cases, it had an impressive track record of dangerous terrorist apprehensions involving Germany's ruthless Red Army Faction.

The FCA Wiesbaden team worked closely with Rutkowski and his men as the day of arrest neared. From Gary Pepper's extensive debriefings of Danny Wilson, FCA agents were able to offer detailed tips in support of the arrest plan. From Wilson, the Germans knew that Conrad kept information about his espionage enterprise in an Apple computer and that he had used a video camera to copy documents, carefully sandwiching stolen secrets between scenes of innocuous movies. All videotapes in Conrad's home would have to be seized and previewed. Thanks also to Danny Wilson, BKA agents knew the password to Clyde's Casio hand-held calculator with its encrypted and incriminating contents. It was high on the list of items to seize. Rutkowski's agents also knew from Wilson that Clyde sometimes used stepdaughter Heidi's nearby apartment as an alternate office, where yet another computer could be found. It, too, would have to be confiscated. Clyde also had a hobby room in the basement of his Bosenheim home where he kept business-related materials, Wilson revealed. At one time, Conrad had spoken of a radio receiver issued by Budapest, which he could use to monitor a special frequency to obtain instructions from the Center; all radios would have to be seized. Also high on the evidence list was Conrad's recently acquired new toy, the Textlite burst transmitter-receiver, a beautifully incriminating example of what prosecutors called "espionage paraphernalia," which would be difficult for any defense attorney to explain.

The big day was to be August 23. As the long-awaited event approached, Rutkowski's agents exuded confidence. The Stockholm connection was secure. As handcuffs were placed on Clyde Conrad, Swedish authorities would arrest both Kercsik brothers on their way to work.

The BKA plan was thorough and effective. At dawn, Rutkowski and his men would quietly surround the Bosenheim home. A locksmith would pick the lock on the front door, permitting Rutkowski's agents to quietly flood the residence. Once agents were in place in each room to ensure total control, the doorbell would be rung. When Clyde the Glide opened his eyes, he would be staring into the muzzle of a Sigsauer automatic pistol.

The BKA agents would convey Conrad and Annja to the Bad Kreuznach police station. Annja Conrad would most likely be questioned and released, unless evidence surfaced during the search that she had committed positive acts in the furtherance of her husband's illegal enterprise. Under German law, merely being aware of her husband's espionage did not constitute a criminal offense. Nonetheless, detaining Annja had considerable merit. Apart from getting her out of the house so that the planned search could proceed without interference, who knew what the frightened woman might reveal under the stress of apprehension?

Rutkowski assigned one agent to rouse Conrad's thirteen-year-old son, Andre, and spirit the teenager gently out of the house. Once the Conrad family was secured, an army of agents would search the home and seize evidence. Down the road, at twenty-eight-year-old Heidi's apartment, an almost identical operation would be carried out. Heidi would be detained, her apartment searched, and her computer seized.

This was a 100 percent German operation. As the plan unfolded, Norman, myself, and the entire Wiesbaden team would be standing by in our offices on the air base. To flash word of Conrad's arrest, FCA agents Mike McAdoo and Dave Guethlein were posted at the Bad Kreuznach police station. We were comfortable with this arrangement. We could teach the efficient Germans nothing about such operations, and our presence at the arrest was inappropriate.

As a final part of the planning, we had asked the Germans for a press blackout. If there were no press releases concerning the arrest for twenty-four to forty-eight hours, this would give us the opportunity to approach the Austrians about Zoltan Szabo. With luck, we might bag the ring's founder before he learned of Conrad's capture. Our German colleagues agreed not to issue a press release but could make no promises of press silence. One or two days of blackout might be possible, they advised, but no more.

Then there was the Swedish connection. The arrests of the Kercsik brothers by Swedish security officials would no doubt hit the press. With luck, the international wire services might not pick up the story. If they did, Szabo would surely smell the danger and dart across the Hungarian border with his opera singer wife.

In Washington, Pentagon and State Department public affairs officers were under orders not to issue a press release. Only if queried would press officers confirm the arrests, stating that it would be inappropriate to comment on cases being conducted by the Germans or Swedes. The wild card that no one could control was the *New York Times*. If Jeff Gerth went to press with the story too soon, our rollup efforts could be jeopardized.

That was the plan. As German and Swedish agents closed in on their targets, teams of army, FBI, and German agents deployed to cities in Germany, Korea, Hawaii, and the United States to interview their assigned targets as soon as the word was flashed that Clyde Conrad was behind bars. Each interview team carried a chronological case summary of the Canasta Player investigation that showed whether the person they were to interview was a witness or a possible suspect. Carefully researched areas of inquiry accompanied these summaries.

Gary Pepper would lead a German-American team into the Bad Kreuznach headquarters of the 8th Infantry Division. Its mission was to sequester all classified files in the division G-3 safes and conduct an inventory of their contents. If Conrad had indeed provided the Hungarians copies of everything to which he had access, the resulting inventory would be a good starting point to determine the extent of his treason.

Properly done, these postarrest measures would provide a wealth of information to uncover the full dimensions of Zoltan Szabo's espionage ring.

• • •

On August 23, 1988, five days before his forty-first birthday, Clyde Conrad was awakened at dawn by the doorbell of his Bosenheim home. Annja's familiar form was on the bed beside him. Clyde's arm was draped over her hip under the sheets.

No doubt wondering who could be calling at such an early hour, Conrad groggily opened his eyes and stared into the muzzle of an automatic pistol. There were two armed men in the room, one on each side of the bed. The officer closest to Clyde, BKA investigator Holger Klein, spoke. As Klein later related, he used his rusty English to protect against any possible misunderstanding.

"You vill take ze hands out of ze vife and place zem vere vee can see zem," Klein ordered, not realizing that he had just uttered words that were to become legendary in the retelling of the great arrest scene for years thereafter.

The stunned Conrad saw no humor in Klein's unique rendering of the command. Eyes fixed on the black weapon, he carefully unwound himself from the bedsheets without uttering a word. Annja, no doubt terrified, donned a robe while her husband put on a gray sweatsuit emblazoned with the Puma trademark. When the master spy finally spoke, it was to meekly offer coffee to the invaders. Agent Klein ignored the gesture and swiftly retrieved Conrad's Casio hand calculator from the nightstand. Conrad lapsed into silence. The day he had feared for more than two years had arrived, and the savvy spy knew better than to open his mouth.

Son Andre was traumatized by the early morning invasion and attempted to flee the scene, screaming. *"Der Junge hat ausgeflippt,"* BKA agents later recalled. Rutkowski's men gently restrained the frightened boy and vainly attempted to calm him down as his parents were taken to the Bad Kreuznach police station. There the man suspected of being the most damaging spy in the history of NATO was booked on charges of suspected espionage, a violation of Article 99 of the German Federal Constitution. Mug shots taken that day show a somber, chubby Conrad (five feet, ten inches, and two hundred pounds) clad in the Puma sweatsuit and high-top tennis shoes.

In the neighboring village, BKA officers entered the apartment of Clyde's stepdaughter Heidi. The twenty-eight-year-old blonde, who worked as a television camera operator, had an overnight guest. Rutkowski's officers rousted the couple and searched the apartment, seizing a computer and other items as possible evidence in the case.

In custody and after her release, Conrad's wife expressed shock when asked about her husband's espionage. She insisted that she knew nothing about it. In a conversation with a neighbor, Annja explained that Clyde had told her that he worked for a computer firm, and she had no reason to doubt this. When he was gone from home for several days, he explained that he was at a convention in Frankfurt. As to the name of the computer firm, Annja contended that Clyde had never shared this information.

German and American investigators knew better. German intercepts of the Conrad telephone had made it clear that the woman was well aware of her husband's Hungarian connection. Annja could be heard coaching Conrad, asking him if "they" had paid him and complaining to her daughter Heidi that a planned vacation to a Hungarian intelligence service–owned villa on Lake Balaton had to be cancelled because her daughter Sonja was coming from the United States. Unlike sister Heidi, Sonja apparently was not aware of the source of the family's extra income.

German investigators knew that Annja was a liar, but their hands were tied by the law. Only if the woman had committed positive acts to aid her husband, such as serving as a lookout or copying documents, could she be prosecuted. By this yardstick, unless evidence to the contrary surfaced, Annja Conrad could not be touched.

The search of the Bosenheim home took several days. Agents confiscated the Apple computer, financial documents, and hundreds of other items that would later enable prosecutors to reconstruct their prisoner's espionage career. Agents seized the Textlite burst transmitter-receiver that Conrad had acquired in Budapest, as well as several hundred videotapes and computer disks. Rutkowski's searchers also snatched up a formidable collection of photographic equipment, including a video camera later confirmed to be the one that Conrad and one of his enlisted protégés had used to copy classified documents.

Various tourist brochures, train tickets, maps, and hotel receipts painted a picture of extensive travels to Austria and Hungary, as did a cup containing Austrian and Hungarian banknotes. One airline boarding pass stub bore the name "Kercsik, Imre." Agents from the BKA were pleased with the haul. Before moving Clyde's computer, Rutkowski's technicians sketched a diagram of its wiring to make sure that the device could be reconnected in the BKA laboratory. Any secrets the Apple contained would have to be recovered by experts.

Still, one of the most notable results of the search was what agents failed to locate. Gone was the stash of classified documents that Conrad had reputedly built up before his retirement. The shortwave radio that he had mentioned to Danny Wilson was also conspicuously missing, as was the gold coin collection that several sources had described to FCA agents in 1986. Records from local banks showing modest resources were present, but no statements or correspondence were uncovered that pointed to Swiss accounts. In this sense, the search was disappointing. The cautious Conrad had once told Danny Wilson that he had taken protective steps in the event that something went wrong. "If anything happens to me," he intoned in a somber voice, "I've taken measures to ensure that Annja and Andre will be well taken care of." It appeared that he had been true to his word.

At the Wiesbaden airfield offices, the telephone rang. The FCA lookouts at the Bad Kreuznach jail jubilantly reported the long-awaited good news. A sullen and dispirited Clyde Lee Conrad had just been led into the police station in handcuffs. I shook Norman Runk's hand and told him the truth: We could not have done it without him. Runk grinned. Pointing to the gaggle of backslapping, triumphant agents who had gathered around when the phone rang, he responded with another truth. "No, boss, we couldn't have done it without these kids."

As Rutkowski's search teams prowled the Conrad home, Swedish authorities apprehended the Kercsik brothers as they arrived at the Goteborg clinic. SAPO officers also detained Klara Kercsik, Imre's wife. Older brother Sandor was initially defiant and uncooperative, but thirty-four-year-old Imre was frightened out of his wits and began to talk freely about his life as a Hungarian agent.

As the Swedish authorities searched Sandor Kercsik's home, they noted a screwdriver on the bedroom nightstand—a strange place to keep tools. Curious investigators quickly discovered that the implement had a hollow handle, which contained decryption ciphers. Agents followed the scent. Where there was cipher material, somewhere there had to be a radio. In the attic, searchers uncovered a two-way radio used by Sandor to communicate with the Center in Budapest. Searchers also recovered a pair of thick ring binders in which the elder Kercsik had foolishly saved virtually every decrypted and translated message he had received from Budapest for the better part of his twenty-year espionage career.

Confronted with this evidence, Sandor joined younger brother Imre and began to sing like the proverbial canary. The melody the two produced would be music to German investigators' ears. It was the ballad of Zoltan and Clyde, and how the physician brothers had served as Budapest's go-betweens for the two American agents. A quick glance at Budapest's communications with Sandor found them replete with messages from the Center instructing Imre and Sandor to meet "Charlie" in various German and Austrian towns in order to pick up documents, render payment, or meet his Hungarian case officer. Charlie was Budapest's cover name for Conrad.

Buoyed by this latest good news, I departed for Vienna. Perhaps the press might not pick up on the arrests, and we could net an unsuspecting Zoltan Szabo.

Our luck did not hold. In Stockholm, the Swedish prosecutor broke the story at a press conference, followed shortly thereafter by the *New York Times*. The *Times* story was a detailed scoop under the byline of Jeff Gerth.

Gerth recalls the circumstances. Once the Swedes broke the story, he relates, he received a call from "someone in the U.S. government" advising him that the story was out and that he should feel free to publish his. "U.S. and Europeans Reportedly Break a Major Spy Ring—8 Detained by 2 Nations" was the *Times* page one headline, followed by a story containing details that had to be coming from someone with access to much of what we had been doing for the past seven months.

In the wake of the Stockholm press conference and the *Times* story, the arrest quickly blossomed in the European media. Soon Europeans were reading about a long-running investigation that had involved American counterspies shadowing Conrad in Germany. In Vienna, the media broke the electrifying news that American counterintelligence agents had boldly stalked their suspect in neutral Austria. This on the eve of my departure to request Austrian assistance.

Once the print media seized on the story, Conrad's arrest was reported on virtually every German and Austrian radio station. In Austria, Zoltan Szabo and his wife were en route in their Mercedes to their vacation home in Spain. Hearing news of Conrad's arrest on the car radio, Szabo turned the Mercedes around and raced back to their small home in Weiden am See. Within hours, after salvaging what they could from the house, the couple fled into Hungary.

In Vienna, the chief of the Austrian Staatschutz, Dr. Schulz, was contacted by his superior, the minister of the interior. The minister was displeased. According to the media, he thundered, American agents were running around with impunity on Austrian soil. Staatschutz officials in Vienna were blindsided by these press accounts and complained to CIA officials in the American embassy. Agency officers explained that an American colonel was en route from Germany to explain the whole affair. Before I departed Germany, Bill Lieser in the CIA's Bonn Station gave me a heads-up. Fence mending would be the first order of business in Vienna.

We had always known that cross-border surveillance operations would cause a problem in Vienna but hoped we could make our peace with the Austrians discreetly. Now, with the newscasts blaring out reports of American counterspies coursing about the Austrian countryside, all I could do was meet with Dr. Schulz, explain what our agents had done, and apologize.

This I did. Accompanied by a CIA officer and the FBI legal attaché, whose job it was to request assistance in law enforcement matters, I made a pilgrimage to Dr. Schulz's office. The Austrian official turned out to be a wise and realistic gentleman who quickly grasped the dilemma we had faced each time Conrad crossed into neutral Austria. I described the Canasta Player investigation and informed Dr. Schulz that until the recent arrest, the case had been the most sensitive and compartmented investigation in our history. We had stalked Clyde Conrad in Germany for years before being forced to tell our German allies. I apologized profusely for our abuse of the principle of "hot pursuit" and assured the Austrian official that only Americans had been involved in surveillance operations on Vienna's soil. Our German allies had insisted on respecting Austria's borders.

Schulz responded graciously. "Let's forget this matter now. What can we do for you?"

I produced the Szabo dossier. The file described Zoltan Szabo's role as the ring's progenitor, his activities during the 1980s as a recruiter for Budapest—operating out of his Austrian residences—and Conrad's broad hint that Budapest had recruited an Austrian customs officer.

Dr. Schulz and his associate, Dr. Blumauer, shook their heads. We should have coordinated with them sooner.

I attempted to explain. Our reluctance to approach Vienna sooner was based not only on security concerns but also on our understanding of Austria's espionage statute, Article 256. "We knew that you could not do anything to him under your law."

Dr. Schulz eyed me as if I were a truant schoolboy. "But haven't you heard about Article 319?"

I had not, and sheepishly confessed as much. No one, including Pentagon international lawyers, Department of Justice attorneys, or our German partners, had ever mentioned the existence of this article. In planning possible arrest scenarios, we had focused solely on the Austrian espionage statute.

Article 319, Dr. Schulz explained patiently, forbade any and all military intelligence operations on Austrian soil, regardless of by whom they might be conducted or against whom the intelligence activity was directed. Because the 1955 Austrian State Neutrality Treaty established a demilitarized Austria, a special article forbidding all military intelligence operations was included in their criminal code. Under that proviso, the Austrian official declared sternly, Szabo's activities as an agent of the Hungarian Military Intelligence Service were clearly illegal and punishable by a prison term. The gracious Dr. Schulz resisted the temptation to add that Article 319 also applied to the activities of Colonel Herrington's military intelligence personnel, but I received the message.

Schulz barked an order to Blumauer, and the Austrian Staatschutz swung into operation. First priority was to mount a manhunt for Zoltan Szabo in the unlikely event that he had not heard the news of Conrad's arrest and remained on Austrian soil. To everyone's disappointment, but no one's surprise, the Austrian dragnet came up empty-handed. Szabo maintained an apartment in Vienna. It was vacant. Agents showed up at the Weiden am See house by sundown, only to learn from neighbors that the couple had hastily departed a day or two earlier. The landlady reported that after Szabo and his wife had fled, a Hungarian man with the key had entered the house and removed some things, including the telephone book.

Dr. Schulz's agents reported that Szabo's house was crammed with military surplus clothing and artifacts. Szabo seemed to have been establishing some sort of militaria business—an enterprise that enables the entrepreneur to network with military men—a perfect cover for a recruiter.

We had narrowly missed snaring our man. Had I traveled to Vienna on the eve of Conrad's arrest and met with Dr. Schulz at dawn on August 23, the Austrians could have staked out the Szabo house and intercepted the veteran spy as he attempted to cross the border. But this was Monday-morning quarterbacking. Such an approach would have been an option only if we had known about the existence of Article 319, which we hadn't. The next time around, the attorneys needed to do better homework.

In Bad Kreuznach, as Clyde Conrad was being booked, Gary Pepper and BKA partner Werner Zeitler arrived at the Rose Barracks headquarters of the 8th Infantry Division. The two investigators set about sequestering and inventorying all classified files in the G-3 staff section.

Pepper and Zeitler started in Conrad's former duty section, where two or three safes contained the classified documents required by the division. Then one veteran member of the staff reported an important fact. Three years earlier, in the wake of Clyde's retirement, the G-3 Plans office had been almost wall to wall with safes, all of them stuffed with sensitive secrets, most of which did not pertain to the division. The overwhelming collection of classified files, all accumulated by Conrad, had since been destroyed.

Then a major break. A helpful NCO, SFC Fredrick Johnson, led Pepper to the G-3 emergency action console (EAC) vault. "You might want to look at these," the noncom drawled, pointing to a sizeable cardboard box. The container was stuffed with classified document accountability logs, transmittal documents, and destruction certificates. Most of the vital records had Clyde Conrad's signature on them.

Pepper grinned at his German colleague. "This is it," he remarked to Zeitler. Conrad's collection of documents may have been gone, but the dusty box of records contained an audit trail of the disloyal sergeant's espionage wares. Its contents were destined to be a centerpiece in the German prosecutor's contention that Sergeant First Class Conrad, whose duties as top-secret-document custodian required him to safeguard classified documents, had instead betrayed secrets that would have led to the defeat of NATO in the event of a war with the Warsaw Pact.

# 28: Santa Claus Is Here

In the United States, news of the arrests in Europe dominated the print and broadcast media for several days before being pushed from the headlines by the spectacular and tragic crash of the Italian air force's aerobatics team during an air show at Ramstein Air Force Base in Germany. *Newsweek* did a cover story on the Conrad story within two weeks of the arrests, attributing the investigation to the CIA, FBI, and West Germans. In the Pentagon, one army official reassured the public that it was "doubtful that major portions of NATO and Army defense plans were involved." The spokesman added, "Conrad worked for the 8th Infantry Division, [which] doesn't have details of the war plans at the V Corps level." Other pundits were equally off the mark. The deputy director of the Center for Defense Information, Eugene Carroll, opined in *The Stars and Stripes* that "the spy case is more significant politically than militarily."

*New York Times* reporter Jeff Gerth knew better. As the investigation unfolded, Gerth and colleague Stephen Engelberg's stories were so crammed with details that it sometimes seemed as if my secret daily updates to Washington were finding their way directly to their desks. There was simply no doubt about it: Someone with inside access to our investigation had established a pipeline to the *Times*.

In Sweden, Dr. Sandor Kercsik sat in his cell and contemplated his situation. His wife was pregnant, his life had come crashing down, and the inside of a Swedish jail was not the lifestyle to which he was accustomed. The forty-eight-year-old physician made a decision. If selling out Budapest and his friend Clyde would get him a lenient sentence, he would tell the authorities whatever they wanted to hear.

The Swedes would prosecute the brothers under a law that forbade citizens of their neutral country from committing acts prejudicial to the security of another state, in this case Germany. The statute was intended to ensure Sweden's traditional neutrality. Under this law, if convicted, the brothers could be sentenced to eighteen to twenty-four months in jail.

At the BKA's Meckenheim headquarters outside of Bonn, German investigators had encountered an obstacle. The BKA lab technicians were unable to break into Conrad's Apple computer. Word flashed across the Atlantic, and within two days special agent Alex Dei arrived from FCA's Fort Meade headquarters. The gifted noncommissioned officer was our premier automation expert and an accomplished hacker. The architect of FCA's Canasta Player automated database, Dei was confident he could crack Conrad's security codes.

Dei arrived in Meckenheim and plopped down in front of Conrad's elusive Apple, surrounded by a bevy of curious German technicians. Loading a piece of software that we had jokingly labeled "How to Break into Anyone's Apple," the FCA agent executed a rapid sequence of keystrokes. The Apple began to chirp. Within minutes, a menu appeared on the monitor. The good-natured automation addict flashed a victorious grin.

"Shall we print something out, sir?" he asked me.

By now, the group around the computer included Manfred Rutkowski, special agent Klein, and a growing assemblage of enthralled BKA technicians in white lab coats. I glanced at the menu entries.

"Try 'Letter,' Alex. Let's see what kind of letter Clyde has saved."

Dei deftly punched several keys. Text appeared on the monitor. It was a twenty-four-carat offering—a wordy, passionate appeal from Conrad to Miklos complaining about the lack of cooperation he was experiencing in his efforts to gain the acceptance of Danny Wilson as a new recruit. One of the English-speaking German officers read the first paragraph of the deliciously incriminating letter, then called out joyfully: *"Um Gottes Will. Der Weihnachtsmann ist angekommen"* (My God. Santa Claus is here). The crowd around the computer swelled. Alex keyed the computer to print the letter. More German agents flooded the room as the printer whirred and cranked out Conrad's compromising frustrations. Dei was enjoying the limelight. "Try another one, sir?" he quipped with a wide grin. I nodded again.

The second offering from Clyde Conrad's computerized safe was even better than the first. It was a long letter from Charlie to the Center in Budapest. In its text, the frustrated spy complained bitterly about the bureaucratic and arbitrary treatment that he felt he was being subjected to by Miklos. Slow payment, timidity, lack of vision, and other sins that Conrad felt were being committed by his handler paraded across the pages of the damning letter. As Conrad's frustrations stuttered from the printer gate, Germans and Americans alike celebrated the moment. It was the kind of hard, incriminating evidence that one dreamt about.

The Apple computer also spit out the latest revised edition of Conrad's cherished Operations Plan 001. The names and addresses of Clyde's key targets—document custodians in Heidelberg and Stuttgart—were recorded in this final draft of the grand design, complete with the home telephone numbers of prospective workers. Our BKA colleagues were ecstatic. Conrad had managed to sanitize his house, but the computer contained information that he could never explain. The letters to Budapest were fully corroborative of what future star witness Danny Wilson had diligently reported during 1987 and 1988. Not only that, in Stockholm the Kercsik brothers were regaling their Swedish interrogators with details concerning Clyde Conrad's deteriorating relations with Budapest. Having scammed and freelanced behind the backs of his Hungarian superiors for years, Conrad was seen by his Budapest bosses as an over-the-hill espionage genius whose achievements had gone to his head.

For weeks thereafter, Alex Dei and patient BKA agents systematically searched hundreds of floppy disks seized from the Bosenheim home and Heidi's apartment. Most contained electronic gibberish; their cautious author had employed a degausser to erase them. But once again, fortune smiled on the tenacious BKA investigators. On several of the disks, entire sentences or fragments of sentences had survived the erasure attempt, including one complete passage that was marked "(S)" for "secret." Ultimately, Norman and his team were able to identify this entry as a direct quote from classified 8th Infantry Division war plans. The irony of this discovery was worthy of savoring. Clyde Conrad, the self-styled high-tech spy, had been compromised by the very technology he sought to embrace.

In Karlsruhe, at the Bundesgerichtshof (Federal Palace of Justice), prosecutors followed these developments closely. As the dimensions and duration of Conrad's espionage came into focus, a new legal possibility arose. In discussions with Volkhard Wache, the senior state prosecutor who was engineering the prosecution, Norman Runk learned that serious thought was being given to elevating the charges against Conrad from Article 99, Espionage *(Spionage)*, to Article 94, State Treason *(Landesverrat)*. The difference? Convicted of an Article 99 violation, Conrad could be sentenced to a few years in jail. Under Article 94, in especially grave cases, a sentence of life in prison was possible.

Wache cautioned against undue optimism. With the sole exception of a single in absentia life sentence levied against a West German defector, no spy had ever received such a sentence in the history of the Federal Republic. Having said this, Wache added that he knew of no case as grave as Conrad's, nor had he ever seen an investigation in which the investigating agency had provided prosecutors with such voluminous and compelling evidence. After our less-than-satisfying experiences with Department of Justice attorneys in Washington, the German prosecutor's upbeat assessment was a timely and welcome show of confidence.

Languishing in his jail cell, Clyde Conrad continued to refuse to talk to his German captors. After hearing Herr Wache's assessment, Norman Runk and I adjourned to the Wiesbadener Ratsbrau for consultation over a few steins of beer. Wache's counsel that we should not elevate our hopes was fruitless. The possibility that Clyde the Glide could actually be put away for the rest of his life in an unforgiving German prison was too tantalizing not to savor. As the evening wore on, other agents from the Wiesbaden team joined us. Gallons of beer fell victim to the celebration, after which the high-spirited group migrated to the town of Bosenheim, which was celebrating its annual Weinfest. After a ritual pilgrimage past Conrad's home, we wound up in the village fest tent. Suddenly, someone remembered that Clyde had just celebrated his forty-first birthday. With the villagers of Bosenheim gawking at our merry group, we did the only civilized thing, raising our voices in a rousing rendition of "Happy Birthday" to the once and future, would-be spy turned prisoner.

A decade later, these antics seem silly, but to us as military intelligence agents, Conrad's willingness to sell out his country and his fellow soldiers by hawking his command's most sensitive secrets to the enemy was repugnant. Here was a man who had actually sold the location of his own wartime position to the enemy, whose greed had jeopardized the forces assigned the mission of defending his own wife and children, and who could rationalize his actions by declaring the entire Cold War a "big game." In our hearts, we loathed Clyde Conrad as all soldiers loath traitors, and we shamelessly gloated over his plight. Had the disgraced sergeant died that week in jail, we would have danced on his grave.

Ten years transpired between the CIA's warning about a traitor in our ranks and Clyde Lee Conrad's arrest. In 1978, few would have suspected that stalking and apprehending the spy would consume an entire decade. In August 1988, as German prosecutors began to build their case against Conrad, no one would have predicted that by 1998, FCA and FBI investigators would remain engaged in the follow-up phase of Canasta Player.

When the cuffs were finally put on Conrad's wrists, special agent Gary Pepper and his FCA colleagues were poised for the exploitation phase of the case. Rolling up coconspirators, after all, was standard fare in espionage cases. But as investigators swung into action on the day of Conrad's arrest, none could have foreseen how deeply into the fabric of the U.S. Army Zoltan Szabo and Clyde Conrad had penetrated.

But before the agents of FCA could concentrate fully in their pursuit of Clyde Conrad's coconspirators, a new investigation had to be tackled—a case so sensitive that its national security implications rivaled those of Canasta Player.

# Part III
## The James Hall Investigation

# 29: Sir, We've Got Another One

*When the special phone rang on August 22, 1988, in West Berlin, Foreign Counterintelligence Activity agents Pete Kelly and Roger Clifford exchanged looks. Probably another wrong number, both men thought. The phone was a source line, its number given only to agents as a means of emergency contact. Kelly picked up the receiver. The tense voice on the line was familiar, a voice that the FCA agent had long since decided he would never hear again. The source stammered. He needed to meet someone, quickly. Something urgent had come up . . .*

The news that the agents of FCA would be denied a long-overdue rest came early on the day of the Conrad arrest. In Norman Runk's Wiesbaden office, agents drank coffee and wolfed down donuts, awaiting word that Manfred Rutkowski's agents had taken Clyde Conrad into custody. When Runk's phone finally rang, the Canasta Player team hovered expectantly in the area.

But the voice on the phone belonged to Bob Bell, the FCA deputy director, calling on a secure line from Fort Meade.

"Sir," Bob led off cryptically, "get ready for this one. You know that thing you're doing? Well, we've got another one."

Bell had operated for years without reliable scrambler phones and often used double-talk even when on the latest high-tech encrypted lines.

"What do you mean, 'another one'?" I queried impatiently.

"Well, sir, Kelly just called from Berlin. One of our sources, Canna Clay, has come out of East Germany with a hot one. Clay claims to have been present twice this year at meetings in an East Berlin safe house during which the East Germans met an American spy. Apparently the guy's a soldier who's been giving away the store to the East German MfS and getting big bucks for doing it. We're working on it hard at this end, trying to identify him based on Canna Clay's description, and we think we can do it. This one looks like the real thing, sir. I think we're in for a double header—two in one year."

The FCA deputy commander's estimate was on the mark. The allegations of an obscure agent in West Berlin were about to propel the Foreign Counterintelligence Activity into an investigation that, although totally different in character from the Conrad case, was equally sensitive and challenging. When unmasked, Canna Clay's spy would emerge as the perpetrator of one of the most costly and damaging breaches of security of the long Cold War. Those of us in FCA's "Berlin Mafia" were about to be confronted with characters out of our past, in a case that would remind us in stark and humbling terms of how thin our counterintelligence lines of defense in the Divided City had actually been.

A well-trained, disciplined spy can usually operate undetected with impunity. Counterintelligence agents don't like to be reminded of this, but it is true. Even in an organization with the most stringent security measures, the determined spy can raid his office's secrets, particularly if he is smart and cautious. Sometimes it takes sheer luck to expose a penetration. Such was the case in the recruitment of FCA's East German source, Canna Clay. A mole had penetrated the American signals intelligence establishment and systematically looted its secrets for six years. Thanks to a single act of poor judgment by an obscure academician, American counterintelligence was handed the identity of the traitor.

The stroke of luck that led to the breakthrough was a routine arrest for shoplifting by the West Berlin police in 1986. Employees in West Berlin's giant Kaufhof department store had observed a balding, middle-aged man as he stuffed merchandise into his clothing. Unlike professional shoplifters, this man was not furtive in his actions. Security officers detained the inept shoplifter and summoned the police. It was an everyday occurrence in a city of two million but for one fact. When accosted, the fifty-two-year-old culprit produced papers identifying him as a resident of communist East Berlin.

During the Cold War, East Berliners in the detainee's age group were forbidden to travel to West Berlin. Alert West Berlin *Kriminalpolizei* knew at once that their prisoner was someone special and summoned their Staatschutz colleagues. Only members of the East German State Security Service, privileged party officials, or other politically reliable fat cats in Erich Honecker's communist regime were permitted to travel through the Berlin Wall to sample the fruits of capitalism. The would-be shoplifter, Karl, was a low-level academician, yet his papers indicated that he enjoyed travel privileges. Something didn't add up. German Staatschutz agents confronted the prisoner with their suspicions.

Karl admitted that he had ties to the East German State Security Service, hinting boldly that he had deliberately staged the aborted shoplifting ploy to create an opportunity to talk. Even more intriguing, the East German volunteered that he had been working for the Stasi, or MfS, intermittently for several years, using his academician's credentials to travel to the West in the performance of low-level operational missions.

Representatives of the West German counterintelligence service met with the suspicious detainee to assess his claims. German interrogators soon noted a significant fact. Karl had supported East German espionage operations not against West Germans but against the Americans. This one had the interests of the Amis written all over it. Through well-worn liaison channels, the word flashed to the Americans. Within an hour, an agent from Berlin's CIA base showed up at the Tempelhof police headquarters.

Ever on the alert for an operational opportunity, CIA officers hoped that the detainee was a bona fide line officer of the MfS. If he were, his embarrassing predicament with the Berlin police was made-to-order for exploitation. But the agency officer who answered the call was quickly disappointed. The prisoner seemed to be exactly what he said he was—a private citizen recruited by the East German intelligence service to perform support missions in the West. Karl was an *instrukteur*, MfS jargon for a low-level agent who could travel unnoticed in the West to case meeting sites, service dead drops, or perform other operational support missions.

In the wake of a damaging defection in the late 1970s by MfS lieutenant Werner Stiller, the East Germans had become more cautious about compartmentation and travel privileges. It was far safer to recruit someone such as Karl and grant him only the limited access he needed to support one operation than it was to dispatch card-carrying MfS officers to the West, where they might be tempted to follow in Stiller's footsteps. A single disloyal, card-carrying line officer could wreak havoc on many sensitive operations. The damage that someone such as Karl could do if he were apprehended or if he defected would be limited to the sketchy details of the one operation he was supporting. Karl was a small fish.

The CIA base contacted FCA's West Berlin team and offered the army a chance to handle Karl. The shoplifter's information was dated, agency officials observed at the time of the handoff, but if it could be confirmed, who knew what his next mission might be? It was, in our parlance, a "freebie," with little investment required. Yet, like all opportunities, this one had a downside. Karl could be an East German provocateur, a dangle dispatched by the devious East German service to identify our operatives, feed us useless or deceptive information, or force us to pursue an investigative wild-goose chase.

The FCA's West Berlin team chief was skeptical about accepting the agency handoff, freebie or not. No fewer than four German agencies had been exposed to Karl since his arrest, hardly ideal if one desired to mount a clandestine operation. Fort Meade nonetheless directed that the East German be hastily recruited and provided a telephone number. Nothing ventured, nothing gained.

Assuming that Karl was genuine, it would be dangerous for him to be absent from East Berlin for too long. The normally cautious, step-by-step recruitment process would have to be accelerated. During a brief interview with FCA agent Pete Kelly, the academician expressed intense bitterness against the communist regime of Erich Honecker. Having traveled to West Germany on behalf of his East German masters, Karl explained resentfully, he knew better than most how corrupt and stultifying life was under Honecker's Stalinist Socialist Unity Party. His goal, he told Kelly, was to bring his wife and family to the West. In exchange for resettlement, he was willing to reveal secrets about his life as an agent of the feared Ministry of State Security.

Within an hour of Canna Clay's August 1988 call, Foreign Counterintelligence Activity agent Kelly explained reality to the East German. To obtain sponsorship of his aspiration, Karl would have to contribute "something significant" to his new American masters.

The East German raised an eyebrow. "Exactly what," he asked in his British-accented English, "would qualify as 'something significant'?"

In the counterespionage business, there is a hallowed maxim: "The best way to catch a spy is to recruit a spy." Our man in Berlin looked Karl in the eye and replied without hesitation, "You bring us an American traitor, and we'll do all we can to support your aspiration to resettle in the West."

Karl nodded his assent. By virtue of this simple bargain, he had crossed the bridge. He was now an American agent, which in East Germany could bring him the death penalty.

Kelly handed Karl a slip of paper with a telephone number on it. The new agent's first mission was simple. "When you return to East Berlin, keep your eyes peeled for us—you know what we want—and call this number from a phone booth in West Berlin when you've got something hot. Your call will activate a meeting with one of us within an hour."

Karl nodded his understanding. He would memorize the telephone number, destroy the slip of paper, and keep his eyes open for "something significant." Reassured by the FCA men that his legal problems with the West Berlin authorities had been taken care of, the East German disappeared into the night.

Now known by the code name Canna Clay, the disaffected academician would not place a call to Kelly for almost two years. The call would trigger a manhunt that would tax the talents and endurance of the team that had just broken up the Szabo-Conrad ring.

The news from Berlin that Canna Clay had resurfaced triggered mixed reactions. Some, myself included, didn't even know that the long-silent source existed. At the time of his 1986 recruitment, I was still in command of the Opsec Support Detachment at Fort Meade, with no need to know about FCA recruitments.

Within an hour of Canna Clay's August 1988 call, Foreign Counterintelligence Activity agents Kelly and Clifford met the East German on a West Berlin street corner and hustled him into a car. Canna Clay nervously announced that he could not linger. He was en route to West Germany on a reconnaissance mission for the MfS and had a train connection to make.

The FCA men drove aimlessly around the city and debriefed their source. As Canna Clay spoke, agents captured his words on a cassette recorder. The excited East German reminded Kelly about their conversation two years earlier. He was now ready to provide "something significant."

Twice during 1988, Canna Clay confided, he had been drafted by his MfS superiors to serve as an interpreter at secret meetings in an East Berlin safe house. At each meeting, Stasi officers debriefed an American soldier who was spying for the communists. The initial rendezvous took place over a long weekend in January. The American, code-named Paul, handed over classified documents from his workplace and submitted to a lengthy debriefing about his duties and the activities of his intelligence unit. The same routine was followed during the second session, which had taken place in July. The spy, Canna Clay told Kelly and Clifford, was a signals intelligence specialist.

The East German described several codeword projects that the American agent had discussed with his MfS controllers. All were secret or top-secret signals intelligence initiatives that neither Kelly nor Clifford had access to. The FCA men exchanged glances. If Clay was telling the truth, this was grave.

The FCA agents pressed for specifics. Tell us everything you can remember about the American spy, they urged. We need details. Give us his description, anything you recall about his personal life, his assignments, or other facts that will enable us to locate him.

Canna Clay was skittish. The operation was one of the best that the East Germans had going, he fretted, and he was one of the few who had been exposed to it. If the American spy were suddenly arrested, Clay himself would be in immediate danger, particularly because he had just returned from a mission into West Germany.

Reassured that nothing precipitous would be done to jeopardize his position, Canna Clay recounted details he recalled from conversations between the American spy and his MfS superiors during the January and July clandestine meetings in the communist capital.

"Paul's MfS contacts, Horst and Wolfgang, referred to him a couple of times as James," he recalled, "so this might be his real name."

"He seems to be married to a German woman who is from West Germany, in the vicinity of Bayreuth," Clay advised. "Maybe he has one—no, two children, I think, but I'm not certain of this. But I am sure about Bayreuth, because when I leave West Berlin, my mission is to travel there to select meeting sites for possible future use with him, in case he cannot get back to East Berlin."

While Clifford drove, partner Kelly took frantic notes. The East German's revelations were too important to place sole trust in the Sony recorder.

Canna Clay continued, the sounds of West Berlin traffic sometimes drowning out his voice. "The man is in his thirties, of average height, a bit stout. I seem to recall something about his hobby being flying. He speaks some German, but not well enough to describe his intelligence duties. I had to interpret during both meetings."

Kelly interrupted. "What about his rank or unit?"

The East German hesitated. "He is, I think, some kind of sergeant, but he has recently been transferred to the United States for professional training. After he finished this training, he said he would be assigned to a base somewhere in the southeastern United States—Fort Benning, Fort Stewart, or somewhere, I can't exactly recall. It seems there was talk of a Fort Sill, or possibly some other post—I'm not certain. But I think he was assigned in Germany for some time in Berlin, and also in Frankfurt, but I can't be specific. You see, I was only introduced to him this year after another man was taken off the operation."

Pressed on this point, Canna Clay was vague. "All I can tell you is that before me, there was some other chap who acted as interpreter for Horst and Wolfgang. Somehow I have the feeling that this fellow left the operation because he departed the country. I don't know anything more specific, but I have the sense that he might not have been German."

Kelly flipped the tape. "Let's get back to these two meetings. Can you be more precise about their dates?"

After some back and forth, it appeared that Canna Clay was describing the Martin Luther King holiday weekend in January, and the Fourth of July. This was consistent with the modus operandi of our adversaries. In order to allow their American agents time to travel to and from East Berlin and still have sufficient time to conduct operational discussions, Soviet and East German case officers favored meetings during three-day weekends.

Roger Clifford pressed. "Tell us everything you can remember about the discussions between the American and the two MfS officers," he instructed.

Canna Clay launched into a lengthy recounting of everything he could recall from the two meetings, to include codenames and classified details of sensitive American signals intelligence operations. From his descriptions, it was clear that whoever the American agent was, he was revealing some of our most sensitive signals intelligence secrets to his communist controllers. Equally obvious was the fact that the traitor had served in Field Station Berlin.

Canna Clay was certain of one thing. His East German superiors appreciated the high value of their man. Stasi case officers Horst and Wolfgang had issued the young American agent a dark blue nylon gym bag with a false bottom in which he could conceal stolen documents. The bag did double duty. Stuffed with greenbacks, it was used by the American spy to clandestinely transport his espionage earnings. At each meeting, Clay told the astonished FCA men, the two East German officers had paid the spy $30,000 in cash. Also, he added, during one of the sessions in East Berlin, the American and his East German masters had stood at attention as Canna Clay solemnly read a citation awarding Paul East Germany's Silbererkampforden (Silver Struggle Medal) in recognition of his service to peace and socialism. A $5,000 cash bonus accompanied the medal. The citation had been personally signed by East German minister of the interior Erich Mielke. The spy, Canna Clay revealed, had also been presented with a large, crystal flower bowl, a gift that the American was told he could present to his wife, although he was cautioned never to reveal its true origin to her.

As their car wended its way through West Berlin's traffic, the FCA men pushed for more information. What about future plans for the operation, now that the American was stationed in the United States?

By now, the nervous East German was compulsively glancing at his watch, fearful of missing his train. He replied with precision. "In July, before he left for the United States, Horst and Wolfgang instructed him to lay low and take no chances in his new assignment for six months or so—just check out his possibilities. They also told him that we would not be meeting him in the United States—that would be too dangerous. Instead, they provided him a phone number to call in East Berlin. When he can come to Germany, he is to call. The safest thing would be if he can come again to East Berlin. But if he cannot do this, then he is to visit his German in-laws near Bayreuth. In such a case, I will be dispatched to meet him there."

The FCA men dropped Canna Clay near the Bahnhof Zoo. Before bidding their source farewell, Clifford and Kelly arranged to meet him once again within a few days, this time in West Germany. During the interim, every available resource would be used at Fort Meade to identify the traitor.

In Wiesbaden, the jubilation at the news of Clyde Conrad's arrest was tempered by the sudden reappearance of Canna Clay. If the East German's information was correct, while the agents of the 766th MID were fending off Soviet attempts to penetrate Field Station Berlin, the East German agent Paul had been systematically looting the sensitive installation of its secrets.

# 30: Paul

The task to identify Canna Clay's alleged spy and tackle the new case fell to FCA's newly arrived chief of investigations, Bob Thayer. Fresh from his studies at the Defense Intelligence College, the experienced veteran was well cast for the role. With eighteen years of investigative experience under his belt, he had credentials that few could match.

Thayer and a skeleton staff tackled the new quest. The immediate challenge—identify Canna Clay's spy—was not daunting. After all, how many signals intelligence specialists could there be who were NCOs, had recently spent time in Berlin and Frankfurt, were married to a German, had transferred to the United States for training in January 1988, and were bound for an assignment to the southeastern United States? Throw in an aviation hobby, a possible first name of James, and the physical description provided by Canna Clay, and the result ought to be a quick hit. This one was not a Conrad-style needle in a haystack. It should be possible to run Canna Clay's profile against the army active-duty roster and smoke out the traitor with dispatch.

That's precisely what happened. By the end of the day, Bob Thayer and his men were looking at a black-and-white ID-card file photo of a round-faced junior warrant officer who closely matched Canna Clay's description. His name was James W. Hall.

Agents studied the suspect's service record. Born in 1957 in the Bronx, New York, James Hall had joined the army in 1976 after one undistinguished year at a junior college. Bright, with an army aptitude (GT) score in the high 120s (almost identical to Clyde Conrad's), the New Yorker had been trained in the signals intelligence field. Assigned initially in 1977 to Schneeberg, a remote communications intercept site on the border between East and West Germany, the twenty year old had done well as a soldier, making his promotions swiftly.

Off duty, agents later learned, James spent time consuming copious quantities of German beer at a local *gasthaus,* the Jagerhof.

There, the young GI met and fell in love with his future wife, Heidi Gabriella Guenthner, a waitress in the popular GI watering hole. By 1981, nineteen-year-old Heidi was pregnant, and her boyfriend was on orders to a new assignment in Field Station Berlin. In March 1981, Hall, still single, departed Schneeberg and moved to West Berlin. Security regulations precluded soldiers in sensitive positions from marrying a foreign national, although a waiver provision existed. Sergeant Hall obtained the waiver, which permitted him to marry Heidi and retain his top-secret security clearance. By 1982, Heidi and newborn daughter Jessica joined Hall in Berlin. In the corridors of Field Station Berlin, James Hall quickly established a reputation as a diligent and talented analyst.

Foreign Counterintelligence Activity investigators scrutinized Hall's assignment history. If he was the spy whom Canna Clay had met in an East Berlin safe house, it had to be assumed that wherever Hall had served, he had probably looted his unit's secrets. Hall, investigators noted, had departed the Berlin Field Station in 1985 at the same time that Vasily was pursuing SSgt. Lowry Wilcox. Hall's new assignment was the 513th Military Intelligence Brigade at Fort Monmouth in New Jersey. There, the record revealed, the young sergeant had a staff job that gave him access to sensitive war plans, including those for U.S. military intervention in the Persian Gulf.

Like Clyde Conrad, Hall seemed to have no stomach for stateside duty. In the spring of 1986, after a one-year stint in New Jersey, Sergeant Hall volunteered to return to Germany. No doubt his superiors thought this normal. After all, Hall (again like Conrad) had a German wife, and it was only natural that he should volunteer for duty in her homeland.

In Germany, James Hall was assigned to yet another signals intelligence unit, the 205th MI Battalion, which supported the headquarters of V Corps in Frankfurt, the same corps that Clyde Conrad had been targeting in his operations since the mid-1970s. Unlike Hall's duty in New Jersey (where he had dealt largely with war plans), he now enjoyed almost unrestricted access to top-secret codeword information. If Hall were the spy, duty in Frankfurt would please his East German handlers.

Investigators noted that Staff Sergeant Hall had remained in Frankfurt until January 1988, at which time he departed for the

United States to be groomed for appointment as a warrant officer—a conspicuous honor and a testimony to his talents. Between January and July 1988, the thirty-one-year-old warrant officer candidate attended intensive training at Fort Sill in Oklahoma, Fort Huachuca in Arizona, and Fort Devens in Massachusetts, the latter two posts being the twin homes of military intelligence at the time. In June 1988, James Hall pinned on the silver and brown bars of a warrant officer. His specialty was signals intelligence. Leave records told Thayer's investigators that their suspect had spent the Fourth of July holidays with his parents in Sharon Springs, New York, far from East Berlin. This was a problem. Canna Clay had been certain that he had seen the American agent in East Berlin on this weekend.

After the holidays, the newly minted warrant officer reported to Fort Stewart in Georgia. There he would work in the G-2 (Intelligence) staff section of the 24th Mechanized Infantry Division. The 24th was part of the famed XVIII Airborne Corps, headquartered at Fort Bragg in North Carolina. The 24th's Fort Stewart–based units were involved in the planning and execution of many sensitive missions, from Persian Gulf contingency deployments to real-world operations in Central America.

Thayer was concerned. This was serious business. With his top-secret security clearance and access to compartmented special intelligence products, the new warrant officer would enjoy daily access to these and many other sensitive military secrets. If Canna Clay identified James Hall as the man he had met in East Berlin, Thayer and his agents would have to prove it, and prove it quickly.

A copy of James Hall's file photo was flown immediately to Germany, along with an array of photos of other soldiers. In a Frankfurt hotel room during the last week of August 1988, Canna Clay again met FCA agents Kelly and Clifford. Shown the lineup of photos, the East German operative did not hesitate. Pointing to the picture of Warrant Officer Hall, he quipped, "If this man's name is James, then he is your man."

But what if Canna Clay was a pawn in an elaborate East German plot? Could the East Germans be orchestrating the entire affair to tie down and ultimately discredit army counterintelligence? Kelly and Clifford, both seasoned veterans, were convinced that their source was genuine. Nonetheless, before launching a major investigation, it made sense to further validate Clay.

Canna Clay submitted to a polygraph examination. Asked if anyone from the East German intelligence service had instructed him to approach the Americans with his story, the academician replied with a firm "no." The stylus on the polygraph machine did not twitch. Canna Clay seemed genuine. A single polygraph examination is insufficient vetting of any source, but it was the best that Kelly and Clifford could accomplish in the limited time before their man was due to return to East Berlin.

Once Clay had identified James Hall, it seemed highly likely that the new warrant officer was disloyal. Now this would have to be proven. In the short space of one week, FCA agents had arrived at a point in the new investigation that it had taken eight years to reach in Canasta Player.

Before Canna Clay returned to East Berlin, agents Kelly and Clifford reassured their nervous source, explaining that they would develop a plan to bring him and his family out of East Germany while concurrently launching a discreet investigation of the suspected traitor. Before American authorities moved against Paul, Kelly promised, Canna Clay would be spirited to safety in the West.

Clay was instructed to memorize a set of instructions. If it became urgent that he depart East Germany, he would receive a phone call from a Mr. Schmidt, during which Schmidt would refer to gardening. This would be the signal that Clay should prepare to depart. In the meantime, Kelly advised, return to East Berlin and go about your business. Above all, he cautioned, tell no one—not even your wife—about these arrangements.

The news that Canna Clay had identified James Hall and passed the polygraph prompted my immediate return to Washington. If we indeed had a disloyal officer in the G-2 of an XVIII Airborne Corps unit, the resultant investigation would rival the Conrad case in its demands for Pentagon and interagency coordination. My place was at Fort Meade, orchestrating the new investigation inside the Beltway while Bob Thayer and his investigators stalked the suspected spy.

Within hours of Hall's identification, Thayer dispatched special agent Bob Watson and a cell of agents to Savannah, Georgia, the nearest large city to Fort Stewart. Captain Watson, twenty-seven, was a native of Miami, Florida, and a distinguished graduate of Furman University's ROTC program. The slim, fair-haired officer had already served a lengthy tour as a counterintelligence agent at Fort Bragg in North Carolina, the home base of the XVIII Airborne Corps. He had also been stationed at Savannah's Hunter Army Airfield, where he had made what would be a useful connection with special agent Doc Mobley of the FBI's Savannah office. Watson was the best choice to head the FCA advance party in Savannah. He knew the turf and appreciated more than most the damage that a traitor in the G-2 of the 24th Division could inflict.

To lay the groundwork for the investigation, Watson would have to coordinate with the Savannah FBI office, meet with the 24th Division's commanding general and its G-2 staff officer, and contact the local police. His job was to prepare the way for the arrival of a sizeable contingent of FCA agents, because suspect Hall would have to be taken under surveillance as soon as possible.

Bob Thayer soon followed Watson to Savannah. Within two weeks, the FCA contingent in the quaint city's motels would swell to more than two dozen, and then double in size as the Christmas holidays approached. In Washington, a cloak of secrecy was draped over the new FCA case. From the beginning, the case was referred to only as the 1126 investigation, a name derived from its Department of the Army case control number.

In Washington, Canna Clay's allegations had created a sensation among the tight circle of Pentagon senior officers who were aware of the investigation. Among the anointed few were Lt. Gen. Tom Weinstein, who had been so supportive during the Conrad case; Army Chief of Staff Carl Vuono; Secretary of the Army John O. Marsh; and a small cadre of attorneys.

Fresh from the Conrad success, FCA enjoyed the confidence of the army leadership. As soon as I arrived in Washington, General Weinstein passed on guidance from Secretary Marsh. Under no circumstances should Hall be permitted to travel overseas and pass additional secrets to the East Germans. If he were to head for an airport, FCA agents were to apprehend him, even if the investigation was incomplete. James Hall was an active-duty soldier with daily access to top-secret codeword information. Foreign Counterintelligence Activity was to take him down as soon as possible. The case could not be allowed to drag on the way Canasta Player had.

This edict effectively put a sunset clause on the 1126 investigation. Canna Clay alleged that Hall was told in July to report to his new assignment and wait approximately six months before traveling to Germany to deliver his first installment of secrets from Fort Stewart. Bob Thayer's best estimate was that James would most likely travel to Germany sometime between Thanksgiving and Christmas. If Thayer were correct and James Hall headed for the Atlanta airport, we would have to roll him up, ready or not. From the beginning, we assumed that we had until Christmas to make the case for espionage.

This was a formidable challenge. In the bureaucratic and methodical world of army counterintelligence, almost nothing could be accomplished in four months. In early September, James Hall was merely a suspect in an espionage investigation. All we knew for certain was that Canna Clay had made a set of serious allegations. Recent experience had underscored dramatically the difference between a set of allegations and the development of concrete information that would support an espionage indictment. It was the Conrad dilemma all over again. Having identified a man who might be a spy, investigators had to prove it. That meant, I reminded my Pentagon superiors, an exhaustive look at Hall's money, travel, activities, and associations. With luck, we might quickly uncover information that would enable us to apprehend and court-martial the junior warrant officer for espionage. But if James Hall were the spy, and if he had been well schooled by the East Germans, we might not find a money trail: Witness the Conrad case. Worse yet, if the newly appointed warrant officer had been clever and traveled discreetly, and if we were unable to catch him in the act of stealing classified documents at Fort Stewart, it was not difficult to envision Christmas coming and going with little major progress on the case.

In the counterintelligence community, an oft-quoted truism counsels, "You're only as good as the one you're working on." For FCA, there could be no resting on the laurels of the Conrad success. A full-court press would have to be immediately mounted, based upon the assumption that Warrant Officer Hall was a spy.

When FCA tackled the Hall investigation, the deputy command-ing general of the Intelligence and Security Command was Brig. Gen. Floyd "Larry" Runyon, a career signals intelligence officer. We at FCA would depend upon General Runyon to run interference for the complex investigation whenever required. Larry Runyon was a cerebral, soft-spoken Indiana Hoosier. Himself a former field station commander, Runyon knew all too well from his own career the kind of havoc a disloyal officer of Hall's specialty could wreak. In the stress-ful months to come, Runyon was a rock.

General Runyon made two immediate decisions. First, knowledge of the case would be closely held within his own headquarters, where the investigation would be referred to only as "1126." No men-tion of Hall's name was permitted unless essential for legal affidavits or other close-hold correspondence. Most of the Intelligence and Se-curity Command staff would be excluded from the case. The gen-eral would deal directly with me or through Lt. Col. Dave Owen, a talented and hardworking counterintelligence staff officer who had played an indispensable role as the headquarters focal point for the Conrad case.

More importantly, Runyon gave guidance to his staff that whatever FCA needed to conduct the investigation—resources or otherwise—would be forthcoming on a priority basis. This latter edict proved to be critical. From August until December 1988, the Foreign Coun-terintelligence Activity spent nearly a half million dollars on the case, this on top of the $850,000 that we had thrown at the Conrad in-vestigation since January. Almost none of this money had been pro-grammed for in the FCA budget. If the kitty ran low, I, as FCA di-rector, would summon my principal miracle worker, budget officer Pat Griffin. As she had done during Canasta Player, Pat cheerfully and smoothly networked with her contacts in General Runyon's headquarters, and it rained dollars, usually at the expense of one of FCA's less fortunate sister units.

From the outset, one of the most troubling dimensions of the Hall case was the obligation that we had undertaken to protect Canna

Clay. It was indisputable that James Hall, if disloyal, posed a serious threat to national security. No one could quibble with Secretary of the Army Marsh's firm guidance that the junior warrant officer should not be allowed to betray more secrets.

But the secretary's edict created an intractable dilemma. Hall was to be apprehended at an airport if he attempted overseas travel, yet a sudden arrest of James Hall would place Canna Clay in mortal peril. Special agent Bob Watson recalls the airport problem this way: "We lived in daily dread that Hall might head for the airport and force us to apprehend him on the spot. The gut-wrenching prospect that haunted us was that we might be forced to grab Hall, and in the process kill our East German source, only to learn that James was merely on his way to visit his mother."

To prevent such a disaster, Thayer's men implemented the Pentagon guidance with an elaborate array of hasty plans prescribing actions that agents should take if James Hall headed for the airport. Foreign Counterintelligence Activity agents coordinated with security officials at the Savannah airport, and with U.S. Customs at the Atlanta airport. If Hall were to steer toward the Savannah airport, investigators realized, he might merely be on his way to rent a small plane to pursue his flying hobby. But if he entered the main terminal and purchased a ticket, agents would have to quickly determine his destination. If their man had booked a domestic flight, someone would attempt to accompany him. If overseas bound, James would have to be apprehended, regardless of whether Thayer's team had collected sufficient incriminating information to establish espionage, and regardless of the consequences in East Germany to Canna Clay. If this were to occur, every attempt would be made to conduct the apprehension without fanfare, in hopes that the press would not pick up on it immediately. With luck, this might buy time to spirit Canna Clay out of East Germany.

Few were comfortable with this plan. Everyone knew that there was still a leaker in Washington with a connection to the *New York Times*. We had been unable to keep the Conrad arrest a secret for even one day, and the event had taken place in Germany.

But Canna Clay's safety was not the sole reason that an airport arrest was undesirable. Emergency apprehension of Hall would deny

FCA investigators the opportunity to end the case on the government's terms, at a time and place of our choosing. Already in 1988, the army had been forced to hastily terminate the Conrad investigation because of a leak to the media. This time around, agents wanted to make an overwhelming case against Hall that would justify the first use of the death penalty in the recently revised Uniform Code of Military Justice. The recently arrested Conrad, we feared, faced a possible ten-year sentence from the Germans. No one wanted the same to happen with Hall.

In a worst-case airport apprehension, Canna Clay would most likely be trapped in East Germany, eliminating him as an eyewitness, and with him would disappear one of the strongest proofs that James Hall had sold documents to the East Germans. In the wake of a hasty airport arrest, even if Hall had classified documents concealed in his luggage, attorneys might be forced to charge him with violation of the regulations governing the security of classified documents, the penalty for which would be a slap on the wrist.

For legal and moral reasons, it was imperative to protect Canna Clay. We needed a foolproof plan to exfiltrate the academician and his family out of East Germany on short notice and resettle them in the West. To accomplish this, FCA would require advice from the CIA.

Once again, Gus Hathaway, John Whiteley, and Martha Graves were supportive. Hathaway and I were of one mind that the commitment to Canna Clay would have to be honored; otherwise we were no better than our communist adversaries. From the outset of the tricky case, Gus Hathaway pledged the advice and assistance of his agency. This was a not inconsiderable advantage, given the CIA's extensive experience operating in Germany and given its specialized resources, for which we could foresee a need. Hathaway, Whiteley, and Graves were the unsung heroes of the Conrad investigation—all of us knew that—and the 1126 case was shaping up as yet another opportunity for them to make a difference.

# 31: Rags to Riches

Bob Thayer and his team moved quickly to put James Hall under observation. If the warrant officer at Fort Stewart were indeed a spy and the East Germans somehow learned of Canna Clay's betrayal, a warning could flash across the Atlantic and the suspect would flee. In Savannah, the FBI made room for FCA agents in their austere offices. Fort Stewart, some thirty miles away, was a sprawling post, jammed with armored vehicles, trucks, and artillery pieces, all decked out in desert camouflage. More than 20,000 soldiers in battle dress uniforms trained on the installation. It would not do for the post to begin buzzing with tales of spooks in civilian clothes driving dark colored rented sedans. For the delicate investigation to remain nonalerting, Thayer's investigators could not operate out of Fort Stewart.

To ensure compliance with the army senior leadership's mandate that James Hall not be permitted to travel to Germany, Thayer focused initially on surrounding the suspect with several tiers of security that would make it impossible for him to slip the noose.

An all-out physical surveillance was manpower intensive and risky. To minimize risk, FCA investigators decided to rely upon technical surveillance as much as possible. Alone in the army, FCA had the talent and equipment to carry out such operations. Bob Thayer and a small team of technicians would orchestrate these efforts on the ground in Savannah; agents at FCA's Fort Meade headquarters would work with army attorneys to prepare the necessary requests for legal approval of intrusive technical means. Phone taps, hidden video cameras, microphones, and tracking beepers could not be employed against an American citizen without demonstrating convincing probable cause.

Soon, thirteen surveillance agents joined Thayer, Watson, and a trio of technicians. Many of the new arrivals had just returned from Germany. By September, the FCA surveillance effort would expand to twenty-seven agents and a small fleet of vehicles, backed up by

Sky King, who flew the FCA surveillance aircraft from Fort Meade to Savannah.

Foreign Counterintelligence Activity investigators would be forced to operate in a tricky environment. James Hall lived in Richmond Hills, a remote, rural area in Chatham County. Surveilling their suspect in the Richmond Hills subdivision was at least as difficult as trying to keep track of Clyde Conrad in the small village of Bosenheim. Each time I spoke with Bob Thayer, I badgered the harried senior investigator. We could not wake up some morning only to find that Hall had flown the coop. Make sure the surveillance team doesn't slip up.

Initially, the FBI had a small role in the investigation, because the suspect was an active-duty soldier. The investigation was destined to take an unexpected turn, which would turn our FBI colleagues into full partners; but for the moment, under special agent-in-charge Bill Clancy, the bureau provided office space and the benefits of their local law enforcement contacts to the growing FCA contingent. We would depend on the FBI not only for operational support, such as a tap on Hall's home telephone, but for their pursuit of any possible civilian coconspirators who might surface in the investigation. For the duration of the delicate case, the partnership was cordial and productive.

The commanding general of the 24th Infantry Division was Maj. Gen. Pete Taylor, a demanding officer with a reputation as one of the army's premier experts on training. With glasnost in full swing, Taylor had recently journeyed to the Soviet Union to observe the training techniques of the Red Army. One of the first tasks accomplished by agents Thayer and Watson was to enlist the two star's support. Investigators would require Taylor's repeated assistance as well as that of his G-2, Lt. Col. Bill Peterson, for whom James Hall worked. Peterson, a wiry, addicted jogger with a Yul Brynner look, began his military intelligence career as a human intelligence officer (Huminter)—a break for investigators. When a phalanx of FCA spooks descended on his turf, the one-time Huminter embraced the task at hand, telling Thayer and Watson that they could count on his discretion and support. Counterintelligence agents bearing bad news are rarely as well received as Thayer's men were on Fort Stewart.

Agents assiduously kept General Taylor abreast of the unfolding investigation. The stern two star was an attentive listener and strong supporter, although from the beginning it was evident that he was incredulous and deeply hurt that one of his officers might have betrayed the army and the nation. As the investigation moved inexorably closer to an arrest, the sometimes gruff general would express deep concern for Hall's wife and two daughters, whose lives were about to be turned upside down. We needed to be sure that our plan included provisions to take care of them, Taylor counseled.

I met briefly with General Taylor in early September, reaffirming Bob Thayer's pledge that he would be kept informed as the investigation proceeded. We needed the general's assistance in keeping the delicate investigation compartmented. This meant that the two star could not even tell his own superior, the commander of the XVIII Airborne Corps at Fort Bragg. In the world inhabited by combat arms officers, loyalty to one's chain of command is a dominant value. Division commanders don't spook around behind the backs of corps commanders. Requesting General Taylor to keep his commander in the dark was asking a lot.

Taylor didn't blink. "Keep me in the loop," he counseled, "and remember, if and when an arrest takes place, I'll need early warning so I can alert my boss. It wouldn't do for him to read about something this significant in the morning paper." For the duration of the case, working with General Taylor and his G-2 was smooth and uncomplicated.

It is not always so. Sometimes, apprising a commander that one of his soldiers is under suspicion can lead to a compromised investigation. For every understanding and professional officer such as General Taylor, others exist who can react in a manner that jeopardizes the case. This happened in the Hall case, but not at the hands of General Taylor.

As FCA agents began stalking James Hall, Brigadier General Runyon, a consummate team player, felt that he had to notify a general officer colleague who was the senior intelligence officer in the headquarters of the U.S. Forces Command in Atlanta. This was a violation of Runyon's own "strict need-to-know" edict. If General Taylor's Fort Bragg–based corps commander had no need to know, certainly a staff officer at Fort McPherson should have been kept in the dark.

All understood why Runyon desired his Georgia-based colleague to be in the loop. Conducting such a sensitive investigation on the turf of a fellow senior intelligence officer without informing him was not a wise way to do business. Well aware of the case's sensitivity, General Runyon placed a secure phone call to Fort McPherson and expressly cautioned his colleague that no one else was to be briefed on the case.

Within hours, Bob Thayer received a frantic phone from Bill Peterson, the division G-2. The cat was out of the bag, Peterson warned in an alarmed voice. Apparently someone had told general so-and-so in Atlanta about the case. That general then felt he had to tell his boss, a two star, who in turn felt compelled to alert the Public Affairs Office that a high-profile spy arrest of a warrant officer was about to go down on Fort Stewart.

The situation coursed rapidly downhill. An espionage arrest would be a headline-producing event. The public affairs people in Atlanta, worried that they were about to be deluged by media queries, placed a call to their press officer counterparts on Fort Stewart. What was going on? Was a big spy bust about to occur on Stewart? Blindsided by what sounded like a sensational story about to break on his turf, the Fort Stewart public affairs officer rang up the logical person, the division G-2. Surely Peterson would know if a spy was about to be arrested on post.

It fell to Bob Thayer and Bob Watson to put the genie back in the bottle. After silencing the Fort Stewart public affairs officer with stern security admonitions, Thayer traced the leak back to the caller in Atlanta and hit the road. At Fort McPherson, he was able to locate every person who had become aware of the news, admonishing each that they had received an inadvertent disclosure of highly classified information. Under no circumstances could they repeat what they had heard to another soul. General Runyon, whose sense of team play had triggered the incident, vowed with a wry grin that he would never again trust another general with a secret. The near debacle reminded everyone why it was essential to practice strict compartmentation in counterintelligence investigations. If the Fort Stewart public affairs officer's call to the G-2 offices had been fielded by James Hall, or if Bill Peterson's secretary had chatted about the rumored arrest at the coffeepot, the entire case could have been blown.

Thayer's advance party promptly established a safety net to preclude Hall's departure to Germany. The first line of defense was G-2 Peterson, the only person in the suspect's office who was witting of the investigation. But it was unrealistic and imprudent to rely upon Peterson to keep track of the newly assigned warrant officer. A lieutenant colonel in a division headquarters does not hover around a junior warrant officer.

The FCA Savannah team took a page out of the Conrad case and sought approval to recruit a source in Hall's office who could discreetly keep an eye on James. The logical candidate for this sensitive role was Hall's office mate, WO Jeff Weddal, the man whom James was actually replacing. Because Weddal was not scheduled to depart Fort Stewart for some time, he was available to report on Hall's day-to-day moods and activities.

Agents met with the young officer without initially revealing FCA interest in James Hall. Describing what we called "the profile of a spy," agents asked Weddal if he had ever met anyone who fit the mold. The profile included signs of undue affluence, working late at night, and excessive curiosity about classified information beyond one's legitimate need to know.

The warrant officer replied without hesitation: "The new guy, Hall, comes to mind," he exclaimed.

Why did he think this?

"Well, Hall and I are the same rank and make the same money. I know what I can and can't afford. This guy's just bought a house in Richmond Hills. That's officer country—beyond my means. He owns a Ford pickup that I'd love to have but can't afford; he's talking about taking flying lessons; and just today he mentioned he'd like to get a big sailboat. How does he do it?"

Weddal had broken the code. Thayer's men recruited the perceptive soldier and apprised him that his replacement was a suspect in an espionage case. Foreign Counterintelligence Activity agent Bob

Watson tasked the new controlled source. Be sensitive to Hall's moods, Watson counseled. Report any signs that he might be planning a trip, particularly if he mentions overseas travel. Avoid doing anything that Hall might see as excessive curiosity. Just keep your eyes and ears open and report everything you hear, see, or suspect.

To supplement the new agent's reporting, Bob Thayer recommended the installation of hidden video cameras in the G-2 offices. If Hall were collecting information for the MfS, the cameras might catch him in the act. Tapes of the young warrant officer stealing classified documents would be persuasive exhibits in a courtroom.

Assisted by Bill Peterson, FCA technicians entered the G-2 offices late one night in early September. It would take two hours to rig concealed cameras that would provide continuous coverage of Hall's desk and nearby safe. The "black bag" job almost ended in catastrophe when FCA tech agent Frank Duffer slipped from a rafter in the G-2 attic and crashed through the plywood ceiling of the World War II barracks building. Agents worked feverishly throughout the night to repair the damage. By dawn, the cameras were installed and the ceiling was repaired. G-2 Bill Peterson had a ready-made cover story for the new ceiling panel: Clumsy post electricians had summoned him overnight to access the attic and caused the damage.

Duffer's cameras transmitted their images to a monitoring site located in a guest cottage across the street from the G-2 offices. For the next three months, patient FCA investigators would man the site and observe every move that James Hall made in his office. If suspect Hall stole classified documents, the concealed cameras would capture the event on videotape.

The FCA surveillance team established itself in Savannah, and its members set about orienting themselves to the area. Drive-bys of Hall's new home were revealing. Located across the street from a lake, the Richmond Hills home was an attractive ranch house in an upscale neighborhood. Parked in the driveway was a Volvo 760 GLE sedan—Heidi's car—next to which was a new Ford F250 XLT pickup truck. Bob Thayer's men made a note to check on how their suspect had managed to pay for $40,000 worth of new vehicles and a Richmond Hills home.

In Washington, army attorneys sought permission to tap Hall's duty and work phones. Affidavits to establish probable cause that James W. Hall was an agent of a foreign power included Canna Clay's depositions and information that pointed to a pattern of undue affluence.

Foreign Counterintelligence Activity agents could install and carry out the tap of Hall's office phone because it was on an army installation. Bill Clancy's FBI agents took care of the home phone. If Hall were on the East German payroll, he might use the telephone to contact case officers Horst and Wolfgang in East Berlin or to make travel arrangements in preparation for an overseas meeting. The phone taps would also make the daily task of the FCA surveillance team far easier.

With these and other measures in place by mid-September, I reported to the army leadership that Hall would not be able to plan a trip to Germany without our knowing about it. With the safety net secured, we could devote all of our efforts to establishing the elements of the crime of espionage.

Bob Thayer and his men had begun to focus their investigation on their suspect's finances from the moment Canna Clay pointed his finger at James Hall's photograph. Unlike the recent experience with Clyde Conrad, reconstructing the warrant officer's personal finances would prove to be easy. One of the first facts to surface was a long-forgotten interview of Hall done in West Berlin by Ron Sidwell, then an agent of the 766th MI Detachment, now an FCA investigator. That interview, recounted earlier in this book, established that James Hall was in financial trouble shortly after bringing Heidi and his new daughter to West Berlin. That was 1982. Now, agents noted, the junior warrant officer was taking flying lessons, had just bought a new home, and owned two expensive vehicles. It was the rags to riches phenomenon all over again.

Foreign Counterintelligence Activity investigators constructed a matrix displaying Hall's army earnings since his West Berlin assignment, then zeroed in on his expenditures. The results of their patient digging were revealing. Hall's total available cash from his army pay for the five-plus years scrutinized was about $78,000. Agents calculated that during the same period, the soldier's major purchases and investments amounted to approximately $90,000. The warrant officer's average checking account balance was $10,000. He had purchased the 1985 Volvo in November 1984 at a West Berlin dealership for $20,580, making a cash down payment of $13,500. The Ford pickup truck, an $18,000 toy acquired during Hall's 1988 training in Arizona, was paid for in cash. James also had $15,000 worth of mutual funds, and in August 1988 he had made a $26,000 deposit into a money market account. To purchase the $92,000 ranch house in Richmond Hills, suspect Hall had put down $6,000 cash in July. At closing, he had tossed in another $28,000 by writing a personal check.

Thayer's men cinched the case for undue affluence when they gained access to Hall's mortgage application. On it, neatly arrayed for the bankers, James had listed his assets. Investigators were instantly attracted to a column entitled "Other assets." There, in Hall's handwriting, was the startling entry, "$30,000 in a box at home."

The newly appointed warrant officer could not possibly have accumulated such riches from his army pay. Still, there was always the possibility, however remote, that he had legitimately acquired the cash. If the man's grandmother had passed away and left him an inheritance, investigators would look like fools if they alleged undue affluence due to espionage. To further muddy the waters, FCA agents located one soldier who recalled that James had confided to coworkers in Frankfurt that Heidi's father was a wealthy farmer. His father-in-law, Hall told friends, was selling off plots of land and sharing the proceeds with his children.

Agents exhaustively scrutinized Hall's finances, even checking courthouse records in New York State, looking for any evidence of an inheritance or other legitimate source for the couple's sudden prosperity. Two FCA investigators traveled to Sharon Springs, New York, and nosed around. Upon their return, the men reported that James Hall clearly did not come from wealthy roots. His parents lived modestly, in consonance with his father's employment as an auto mechanic.

Thayer's investigators also had to explore the suspect's contention that he had wealthy and generous German in-laws. But an official inquiry of the German security services was fraught with risk. Our interest in the finances of the Guenthner family in Kemnath might be discovered by an East German penetrator, who could alert East Berlin. So apprised, the MfS might easily deduce that their star agent was threatened.

Norman Runk solved this problem by contacting FCA's trusted German friends. Soon we had the results of discreet inquiries into the background and finances of Hall's father-in-law. To no one's surprise, the story that his wealthy in-laws were donating cash to Jim and Heidi Hall turned out to be fiction. Records at the Kemnath Standesamt revealed no land sales by the Guenthner family.

Ultimately, investigators could uncover no legitimate explanation for James Hall's sudden wealth. To Thayer and his men it was obvious. The $30,000 that Canna Clay saw Paul stuff into the false bottom of the dark blue gym bag in an East Berlin safe house in early July was almost surely the same $30,000 that James Hall had listed on his mortgage application one week later.

# 32: The October Surprise

Having established that James Hall and his family were living a lifestyle more appropriate to a major or a lieutenant colonel than a junior warrant officer, Savannah investigators pressed for proof that their prosperous suspect was collecting documents for eventual passage to the East Germans. Recalling Canna Clay's description of a dark blue gym bag with a false bottom, agents had been on the lookout for the incriminating bag from the beginning—without success. If Hall was our man, he was not using the East German–issued concealment device.

From the moment James Hall arrived at his office until he donned his camouflage hat and departed, he was under observation by FCA investigators. In the tiny white clapboard cottage across from the G-2, bored agents fought off fatigue as they watched their target leaf through documents, read the newspaper, chat with his office mates, and talk on the phone. Five weeks into the video surveillance, the results were disappointing. If Warrant Officer Hall was stealing documents, he was a master of concealment.

In early October 1988, sitting at his desk in FCA's Fort Meade headquarters, deputy commander Bob Bell received a secure phone call from the Savannah team. Something was up.

"Sir, they may have the big one in Savannah," Bell called out. "Thayer says that the cameras captured Hall taking a document out of his desk drawer and hiding it in the folds of a newspaper before leaving the room."

The Savannah team had worked out a coordinated plan to cope with such a case. If the agent monitoring the video spotted what looked like a theft, he was to alert the surveillance team, which always had at least one cell of agents standing by. If James Hall concealed documents on his person and departed the headquarters, the surveillance team would tail him to his home or other destination. This was essential so that investigators could later testify that the suspect had removed the documents from a government facility and taken them to an unauthorized area.

The alert proved to be a false alarm. Hall had left his hat hanging on a hook and had gone somewhere else in the building out of camera range. Ten minutes later, he returned and replaced the unidentified document in his desk. Because it was against regulations to store classified documents in a desk drawer, agents instructed Warrant Officer Weddal to wait until Hall went home and check the drawer's contents.

Weddal complied. The drawer, he reported to his FCA case officer, contained a well-worn issue of *Playboy* magazine. Agents surmised that Hall had made a trip to the men's room. "Frailty, thy name is James," I quipped with a grin to Bob Bell.

In Savannah, the nonstop monitoring of Hall's office continued. Sooner or later, Thayer and Watson felt sure, their suspect would slip up.

In late October 1988, the FBI-administered tap of the telephone in Hall's Richmond Hills home picked up a suspicious conversation. The caller was Hall's mother in Sharon Springs, New York, with a message for Jim. A man named Mike Jones had called from Florida. Speaking accented English, Jones had asked Mrs. Hall to pass on his Florida telephone number to her son. Perhaps Jim could call him?

"Who is this Mike, anyway?" Hall's mother asked.

"Oh, he's just some guy I knew in Berlin who taught me how to weld," James replied nonchalantly. "I'll give him a call."

At the FBI's Savannah office, investigators crowded around a console and listened as the telephone drama played out. Shortly after the conversation with his mother, Hall dialed the 813 number in Florida that Mike Jones had provided. A woman answered the phone.

"Is Mr. Yildirim there?" Hall queried. Agents exchanged surprised glances. Mike Jones had suddenly become Mr. Yildirim. Foreign Counterintelligence Activity veterans of Berlin duty knew at once that there was only one Yildirim in the world who taught welding in Berlin to American soldiers: the Meister.

With the Meister's unexpected appearance in the 1126 investigation, the pieces began to fall neatly into place. Canna Clay had told agents Kelly and Clifford in West Berlin that his predecessor, as the link between Paul and the MfS, was someone who "might not have been a German" and who "might have left the country."

The female voice that answered the Florida phone was Peggy Bie, the matronly music student whom the Turk had used as his ticket to the United States. Of this I was certain. I could still hear the Meister in 1986 extolling Peggy Bie's elusive virtues. "She love me too much," the Turk had said with a roguish wink and a nod. "She veerry rich. Maybe I go Florida for good."

Mike Jones came on the line. The voice was unmistakably the Meister. The Turk was skittish, obviously uncomfortable talking on Peggy Bie's line. After obtaining Hall's home phone number, he signed off hurriedly. "I call you back, Jim, soon."

Within thirty minutes, the Richmond Hills phone rang. Heidi picked up the receiver. It was Yildirim. Could he speak with Jim?

"Yes, just a moment," replied Heidi. "Is this Mike?"

"Yes, I am Mike," the Meister said. For whatever reason, the Turk was known only by his cover name to Hall's wife. In the background, the telltale clicking of coins being digested by a pay phone was clearly audible. Yildirim had left Peggy Bie's home and driven to a pay phone. Cover names, the use of pay phones—the call was cloaked in conspiratorial trappings.

Yildirim wanted to meet with his friend.

"I go to New York," the Meister asserted cryptically. "Have lots of diamonds, precious stones, other things, very interesting. We can get together?"

Hall replied guardedly. "Yeah, I'm in Savannah, you know where that is."

"Yes, in Georgia," said the Meister. "When can I meet you?"

The two made an arrangement. Meister would stop by Savannah on his way back from New York within one to two weeks.

"Just give me a call and I'll meet you somewhere," Hall advised. James did not invite the Turk to the house, hardly normal behavior for social friends. Apparently the two men had business that they were keeping from Hall's wife.

This unexpected twist in the case raised troubling questions. Was the Meister an East German courier who would service Hall and remove the need for him to travel to Germany? Or were the two working some sort of smuggling operation, a documented proclivity of the Turk? The Meister had an unproven record of contacts with the

East German service. In a worst case, Yildirim could be to Hall what the Kercsik brothers had been to Clyde Conrad. If this were true, investigators now had a grave problem. What if Hall seized a load of classified documents and ventured to a roadside meeting with the Meister? The secretary of the army had ordered that James Hall should not be permitted to betray additional secrets.

The recollection that our new suspect had twice been in my home was painful. The unannounced visits took on new meaning if the ebullient Turk were indeed an agent of the East German MfS.

As a civilian suspect, Huseyln Yildirim was an FBI target. Within hours of hearing the Turk's voice on that tape, I prepared a detailed memorandum of everything I could recall about my association with him, commencing with our initial meeting five years earlier in Berlin's auto craft shop. As FCA's new full partner in the case, the FBI needed to know everything we knew about the manipulative Turk.

At Fort Meade, investigators retrieved the case file on the stillborn West Berlin investigation of the Meister, a case that had been kicked off when jailed former soldier Jackson had denounced Yildirim as an East German agent. Now that the irrepressible Turk had been detected sniffing around James Hall, Jackson's revelations required a second look.

The review of this file yielded bad news. Viewed with the advantage of hindsight, it looked as though the Berlin investigation had been a lost opportunity, a polite way of saying that it had been mishandled. With Yildirim now linked to James Hall, Jackson's allegation that the Turk had once brokered a debriefing of Ella Pettway by the East Germans made more sense. At the time, the smooth-talking Meister had passionately denied any wrongdoing, professed his love of America, and volunteered to take a lie detector examination. The case had been closed by Bob Thayer's inexperienced predecessor without polygraphing Yildirim. And agents had not tracked down Ella Pettway and confronted her with Jackson's accusations. The brash Turk had smoothly talked his way out of trouble.

With Hall and the Meister planning a meeting, Thayer and his Savannah investigators faced the very real prospect that another hemorrhage of classified information might be imminent—an event that was unacceptable in Washington.

Even with Hall's undue affluence established, FCA agents were weeks, if not months, away from proving espionage. If James met the Turk with the intent to give away a stack of secret documents, he would have to be confronted on the spot. Canna Clay would have shuddered at the prospect.

The FCA surveillance cameras had thus far failed to detect James Hall looting his duty section of classified documents. Video coverage, reporting from Warrant Officer Weddal, and insights from the telephone taps indicated that if the suspect was an East German agent, he was doing exactly what his MfS case officers had told him to do: Report for duty, lay low, and check out the situation for up to six months. Furthermore, nothing Yildirim had said on the phone could be interpreted as an order or invitation to Hall to hand over any documents.

In Washington, I appealed for breathing space. Thayer's team should permit the Turk and Hall to meet without taking any hasty action. The FBI had just opened a preliminary investigation of Huseyin Yildirim. Bureau agents had almost nothing on which to base an apprehension of the Turk. This was a time for patience.

These arguments carried the day. Foreign Counterintelligence Activity should not make any precipitous apprehension, senior army officials agreed, but if agents received any indication that Hall was about to hand over a satchel of secrets to Yildirim, a decision would have to be made at the highest levels about how to react.

During November and December 1988, Huseyin Yildirim called James Hall several times to arrange nocturnal meetings. Tipped off by the telephone tap, FCA surveillance agents twice shadowed Hall as he departed his home in the late evening and drove in the direction of Interstate 95. The Turk arrived from Florida in a dilapidated Cadillac. On both occasions, Hall and the Meister conducted late-night meetings at the Cracker Barrel restaurant at the intersection of I-95 and state highway 206. During the second rendezvous, as waitresses prepared for closing, an FCA agent carrying a camera concealed in an attaché case boldly entered the restaurant and obtained a photograph of the two men as they sat in a booth and conversed in low tones. The agent observed the Turk pass a brown envelope to Hall during the meeting. The photo and the brown envelope later proved to be critical pieces of evidence in demonstrating the conspiracy between the two men.

By now, an FBI surveillance squad was shadowing Yildirim in Belleair Beach, Florida, where he was living at Peggy Bie's ranch house, sometimes using the alias Huseyin Bie. The bureau's investigation had already yielded one telling fact: Shortly after his first meeting with James Hall in Savannah, the Meister had made a quick round-trip to Berlin. Still, because the FBI had gotten a late start in the case, they had little on the Turk other than some doublespeak phone calls, the trip to West Berlin (where he had a wife and children), and his vague relationship with army suspect James Hall. It was not much to go on. Federal Bureau of Investigation desk officers in Washington reminded us of Yildirim's police record for smuggling. Perhaps that was what the two were doing.

All of us understood what FBI supervisors were facing. The bureau could arrest Yildirim only with the agreement of the Department of Justice, whose conservative judicial philosophy we had recently experienced during the Conrad case. The FBI was impaled on a dilemma. If it wanted to make the case for espionage against the Turk, it would have to open a full field investigation. But to take this important step, it would have to establish credible probable cause that the Turk was a hard espionage suspect—and do so promptly. With a two-month head start, the FBI's army partners were looking at December as the target date for arresting James Hall.

By November 1988, FCA investigators had made significant progress in two of the four investigative spheres: money and associations. Their suspect was rolling in cash and was conducting furtive meetings with a suspected East German agent. Across the street from the G-2 offices, frustrated agents continued to man the electronic observation post, but Hall had made no mismoves since the *Playboy* false alarm in October. As the Christmas holidays drew nearer, Bob Thayer fretted. If James Hall followed the orders of his East German handlers, he should be stealing documents and planning a trip to Germany.

Thayer enlisted the assistance of G-2 Bill Peterson to guard against a sudden holiday trip to Germany. If Hall followed the rules, he would have to obtain permission for out-of-town travel. Peterson circulated a Christmas leave projection roster throughout his staff section. James Hall did not sign up.

Captain Bob Watson met his source. As of December 1, Warrant Officer Weddal reported, Hall had said nothing about any holiday travel plans.

The telephone taps and the surveillance team likewise revealed no travel plans. James continued to maintain contact with Huseyin Yildirim, but he made no calls to airlines or travel agents. And his daily routine had not varied. Agents regularly observed their target as he made stops at the PX, the post laundry, and the officers' club. Hall drove past the airline ticket office frequently but did not stop.

Thayer and Watson knew that investigators had to establish when James Hall was planning to travel to Germany. If Savannah investigators could confirm this date, their planning challenge would be clear. Canna Clay would have to be out of East Germany by the day of the flight, paving the way for Hall to be apprehended as he boarded the aircraft. With luck, a search of his luggage would reveal classified documents.

There had already been two tense false alarms. On a Thursday in mid-November, Hall suddenly announced to his office colleagues that he would take Friday off. Agents reacted. G-2 Peterson had just circulated the leave roster, and James had made no entries on it. Now the suspect was abruptly arranging a three-day weekend. What was up? Had Hall detected the FCA surveillance and decided to flee the country? Or was he on his way to a rendezvous with Horst and Wolfgang in East Berlin? Twice during 1988, Hall had met his MfS masters on three-day weekends. If Hall were overseas bound, he would have to be arrested. Investigators began to plan for an airport apprehension.

After several tense hours, the telephone tap resolved the brewing crisis. Hall's daughter, Jessica, was ill. The day off on Friday was to take her to the family doctor. Agents stood down from the airport alert.

Investigators had experienced a similar scare in October, over the Columbus Day holiday weekend. Foreign Counterintelligence Activity surveillance agents had arrived on station in Richmond Hills in the early morning, only to discover that their target's silver and black truck was not in the driveway. Thayer's men were dismayed. Continuous surveillance since September had established that James was a late starter, rarely leaving the house before 9:00 A.M. on weekends.

The surveillance team immediately reported the bad news to Bob Thayer in his motel room. Hall had slipped the noose. No one knew how long he had been gone. With a head start of an hour or two, James could be anywhere, possibly on his way to the Savannah or Atlanta airport. Bob Thayer shared the unwelcome development with my Fort Meade headquarters while the surveillance team patrolled Hall's known weekend haunts and cruised the parking lot at the Savannah airport in search of the Ford pickup.

As agents scrambled to locate Hall's distinctive truck, I vented to FCA deputy director Bob Bell. Hadn't we repeatedly told the Savannah team that they could not give Hall too much space and let him out of Savannah? Now the suspect was on the loose, possibly on his way to Germany. If Hall was Germany bound, breaking the news to the secretary of the army would not be easy.

Bell counseled moderation. Thayer's men understood the guidance, he argued, but had attempted to implement it intelligently. It was simply too risky and too exhausting to place their suspect under around-the-clock surveillance. Arriving in Richmond Hills shortly after sunrise and departing in the late evening when both of Hall's vehicles were in the driveway and the house was dark was a prudent compromise. Between the telephone taps and the source in the G-2, Savannah investigators thought they had a good feel for James Hall's moods as well as his intentions. The surveillance team was husbanding its strength for when it would be ordered to tail James Hall twenty-four hours a day.

In Savannah, FBI agent Bubba Yoemans reviewed tapes of Hall's home phone. The telephone tap yielded reassuring news. James had just called Heidi to report that he was at the local Sears store. One of his daughters was with him, and he had other errands to do before returning home. Yoemans notified the FCA surveillance base, which vectored a pair of vehicles to the Sears Roebuck store. Word flashed to Fort Meade. The emergency was over. James had merely broken his routine and gotten an early start on his Saturday errands. The target was under control.

The episode exposed an unacceptable vulnerability. The surveillance net would have to be drawn tighter around Hall. If a fresh crop of agents had to be dispatched to Savannah, I told Bob Bell, so be it. If James Hall had departed his home at 10:30 the prior evening and caught the late flight to Atlanta, by the time the surveillance team discovered his empty driveway the following morning, he would have been in Germany.

Foreign Counterintelligence Activity agent Nick Pokrovsky had spent an eternity in the tiny guesthouse across from the G-2. With nothing to do but watch his man, Pokrovsky studied Hall's every move, looking for patterns of behavior or signs that he was about to undertake some illegal action. Agents manning the cramped observation post were certain of one thing: Hall was terminally lazy. The slightly rotund warrant officer could sit for hours at a time behind his gray metal government-issue desk doing nothing other than reading a newspaper and chatting with his office mates. Every now and then, James would paw through his in-box, glance at a document with a red secret cover sheet, then cycle it into his out-box.

For more than three months, Pokrovsky and his colleagues had been on the lookout for the dark gym bag that Canna Clay described in Berlin. If James carried the bag with the false bottom to the office, agents surmised, it could signal his intention to steal a stack of documents. For three months, the elusive bag was nowhere in evidence.

In early December, investigators keyed on something of possible significance. Their man had begun to carry a clipboard to work. Clipboards are common in a place such as the G-2 office of an infantry division. The typical GI-issue clipboard is a slab of masonite with a steel clasp at the top. But Hall's clipboard was a civilian model, much like the style used by an electrician or a plumber. Made of aluminum, it had a half-inch-deep storage bin built into it, intended for the carbon copies of receipts. By lifting up the hinged writing surface, the user could drop documents into the hidden bin.

Across the street in the observation post, Pokrovsky and his coworkers agreed that if James was going to pilfer documents, he would conceal them in the aluminum clipboard. The investigators shared their hunch with Bob Thayer. Something might happen soon.

Nick Pokrovsky was no stranger to intrigue. The son of a former Red Army officer who had voted with his feet after World War II and settled in Paris, the thirty-year-old sergeant first class had already served fourteen years in the Cold War trenches. In 1978, as a twenty-year-old military policeman, the Russian-speaking Pokrovsky had been assigned to checkpoint duty on the Berlin-Helmstedt autobahn, where his duties put him face-to-face with Soviet officers. Confrontations between American and Soviet officials over access rights to Berlin were frequent. Pokrovsky was often in the middle, handling matters that normally would have been the purview of someone much senior.

Soviet checkpoint officials included officers of the KGB's Third Chief Directorate. It was inevitable that the Russian American sergeant would attract their attention. When the six-foot-five NCO reported to counterintelligence officials that a Soviet officer was becoming chummy, he was put under the control of case officers from the Foreign Counterintelligence Activity. Play along, the FCA men counseled.

By 1981, Nick Pokrovsky was a double agent, recruited by the KGB and under control of the Foreign Counterintelligence Activity. Pokrovsky soon informed Mischa, his KGB handler, that he had decided to transfer to military intelligence. His first assignment was at Fort Huachuca in Arizona as an instructor in interrogation techniques. Before his newly recruited agent departed Berlin, Mischa urged him to collect classified information at the sensitive post. If possible, the KGB officer instructed, Pokrovsky should travel back to Berlin to deliver stolen documents. The continental United States was out of the territory of KGB Third Chief Directorate handlers.

Pokrovsky balked. American counterspies might notice such travel. Flying to Berlin was risky. It was a response manufactured in the Fort Meade corridors of FCA.

Once in Arizona, Pokrovsky and his FCA handlers artfully manipulated the KGB. Traveling to Mexico City, the quick-thinking NCO visited Moscow's embassy and spoke with a Soviet named Konstantin. The Soviet worked for the KGB's First Chief Directorate, which staffed Soviet embassies with language-trained agent handlers.

Your people in Berlin, Pokrovsky lectured the Soviet, are amateurs. If he followed their advice and traveled to Europe to deliver

documents, he would surely be identified by American counterintelligence and arrested. "I want to work for genuine professionals,"
Pokrovsky told the poker-faced KGB officer across the table. "Those
guys in Berlin will get my ass caught."

Then Pokrovsky played his trump card, telling Konstantin that he
had just received orders reassigning him to a sensitive human intelligence unit at Fort Meade in Maryland. The spook outfit was a priority collection target of the KGB.

The Soviet officer struggled to calm the headstrong American.
"Do not worry," he purred sympathetically. "We will work it out. Go
to your new unit at Fort Meade, get settled in, and return to Mexico
City in three months."

Pokrovsky reported the Soviet officer's instructions to his FCA case
officers and moved to Fort Meade. Three months later, he returned
to Mexico City to meet with Konstantin. But the KGB had a surprise
for the brash sergeant. Standing at the embassy gate was Mischa Bogdan, his Third Chief Directorate controller from Berlin.

"I ought to cut your balls off," Bogdan growled as he led the hor-
ror-stricken Pokrovsky across the courtyard of the beige-walled compound. It was, the NCO later recalled, the most terrifying moment
of his life. As the pair passed through the embassy portals, it crossed
Pokrovsky's mind that he might not emerge. This was clearly a time
for contrition.

Pokrovsky mumbled a penitent mea culpa to the grim-faced Russian. He hadn't meant anything personal by his complaints to Konstantin; he was simply afraid. One stupid move and Nick Pokrovsky
would spend the rest of his life in an American prison.

Bogdan became conciliatory. If Pokrovsky was too frightened to
travel to Berlin, a courier could meet him in the United States. The
Soviet pushed a photo across the desk. It was a snapshot of sixty-
seven-year-old Alice Michelson, an East German woman who taught
at East Berlin's Humboldt University.

"She will be your courier," Mischa explained. "She is above re-
proach. The FBI would have no reason to suspect an elderly female
academician."

Mischa introduced another Soviet. The man was the KGB's resident expert on the army's Intelligence and Security Command. The
two Russians explained that Pokrovsky's Fort Meade unit was high

on Moscow's list of priority targets. Pokrovsky's mission was to steal its secrets.

The two Russians provided their agent a phone number and six packs of Marlboro and Winston cigarettes. Several of the cigarettes in each package were hollowed-out concealment devices designed to accommodate spools of exposed film. Mischa instructed his American agent to photograph classified documents and place the film in the bogus cigarettes. When you have accomplished this, Mischa ordered, call courier Michelson at this phone number. She will meet you and pick up the pack of cigarettes.

Pokrovsky nodded his understanding and departed the embassy. Outside, the sergeant took a deep breath and composed himself. Even the polluted air of Mexico City was a pleasure to breathe.

When he returned to Maryland, Nick Pokrovsky informed his FBI and FCA case officers that the Soviets had swallowed the bait. He was about to meet with a clandestine courier of the KGB.

On a Saturday morning in early October 1984, FBI agents affixed a tiny tape recorder around Pokrovksy's thigh. He drove to Baltimore's BWI Airport. The FBI-FCA double agent sat in the lounge, where a concealed FBI camera would record his meeting with the East German woman.

Alice Michelson arrived and sat down. Pokrovsky identified himself by a KGB parole, referring to his Uncle Peter. Michelson relaxed. Pokrovsky was tense. Rivers of sweat flowed around the tape machine strapped near his groin.

For an hour, the two sat in the airport lounge. The American double agent delicately led the conversation in the direction of the stolen documents he was turning over in the pack of Marlboros. His instructions were to induce Michelson to incriminate herself. He handed the gray-haired woman the pack of cigarettes.

Michelson put the Marlboros in her purse, admitting wryly that even though she didn't smoke, she had matches in her purse to complete the image of a smoker. Then she stood up and headed for the concourse to catch a plane to New York City. Federal Bureau of Investigation surveillance officers boarded the flight.

Back at FCA headquarters, Pokrovsky's handlers discovered that their man had sweat so much that electrical leads to the tiny tape recorder had shorted out. Most of the conversation with Alice

Michelson had been lost. Fortunately, the machine had picked up the East German courier's remark about the matches. In a court of law, her comment would be difficult to explain.

Alice Michelson lingered for a week in New York City under around-the-clock FBI observation. When the KGB courier attempted to board a Prague-bound Czech airliner at JFK Airport, she was arrested in a headline-making operation. The incriminating films of classified documents were found on her person.

Michelson was ice cold in captivity, refusing to utter a word to her FBI captors. Convicted of conspiracy to commit espionage, she languished for three years in federal prison before being exchanged in 1987 as part of a trade to obtain the freedom of seventeen incarcerated western agents. Considerable credit for the liberation of the seventeen agents belonged to Nick Pokrovsky and his FCA-FBI handlers.

On December 5, 1988, Nick Pokrovsky sat in the FCA monitoring post at Fort Stewart, fighting off boredom and watching Warrant Officer Hall sluff his way through yet another undistinguished day at the office. As duty hours drew to a close, nothing remarkable had happened. The curious aluminum clipboard was sitting on Hall's desk. The warrant officer thumbed absently through some documents and tossed them on the desk.

One of Hall's subordinates approached and pointed to the documents. "Do you want me to lock these up, sir?" she queried.

James shook his head. "Nah, I'll take care of them."

Pokrovsky straightened up. What was this? Why hadn't Hall permitted the woman to secure the documents? It was her job.

James glanced around the room and leafed through the documents. Then, ever so casually, he opened the lid on his clipboard and dropped them inside.

Across the street, Nick Pokrovsky stifled a shout of triumph as the video recorder captured the action for posterity. Then he seized a hand-held radio and alerted the surveillance team. The target was hot.

Pokrovsky grinned at his colleague. If James Hall carried that clipboard out the door and brought it to his home, another investigative milestone would be achieved.

Unaccountably, when duty hours ended, Hall locked up his safe, grabbed his hat, and departed, leaving the clipboard on his desk. Pokrovsky replayed the videotape. No doubt about it, whatever James had placed in the makeshift concealment device was still there. And since his subordinate had volunteered to lock them up, the documents were almost certainly classified.

A debate ensued. Was it safe to check out the clipboard? Had the warrant officer trapped the device by placing it in a certain manner or by putting a microscopic piece of litter on it that would tell him if someone had inspected the clipboard? A frame-by-frame scrutiny of the tape revealed no such precautions. Hall had acted normally, exhibiting no actions that might convey nervousness or suspicion. Assured by attorneys that it was legal to check out the contents of the suspicious clipboard, Thayer's investigators called on G-2 Peterson for assistance. With utmost caution, Peterson opened the compartment gently, just enough to observe that it contained classified documents.

Throughout the following day, the loaded clipboard rested undisturbed on suspect Hall's desk. Outside, the full surveillance team was poised to do its job. Nick Pokrovsky fixed his gaze on the monitor's screen as the end of duty hours approached, feeling a bit like a cheerleader. "Come on, James," he muttered to himself, "Pick up the goodies and take them home."

At 4:30 P.M. on December 6, 1988, James Hall locked his safe, nonchalantly picked up the clipboard containing the contraband cargo, and headed out the door for his truck. As the Ford pickup departed the G-2 parking lot, FCA surveillance vehicles shadowed it from a distance. Overhead, Sky King radioed his comrades on the ground each time their target took a turn. Hall was faithful to his daily routine. He made a brief stop at the officers' club, leaving the clipboard on the front seat of his truck. Thirty minutes and two drinks later, the pickup was speeding down the highway toward Richmond Hills. An FCA surveillance agent observed the warrant officer carry the clipboard into his house. Another investigative objective had been fulfilled.

By the first week of December, three of the investigation's four objectives had been met. The thirty-one-year-old warrant officer was rolling in illicit money, he had a conspiratorial business association with suspected East German operative Huseyin Yildirim, and he was removing classified documents from his office. The case against James Hall was all but overwhelming, with one important exception. Investigators had failed to document their suspect's espionage-related travels.

Canna Clay had told agents Kelly and Clifford that the spy Paul had been in East Berlin during the Martin Luther King holiday in January 1988 and over the Fourth of July weekend. If Clay's memory was accurate, and if James Hall was the spy, we should be able to place him in East Berlin on these two weekends.

But there was a problem. During the January period, Hall's leave and travel records indicated that he was in the middle of travel from Germany to the United States. During the Fourth of July weekend, records reflected that James was on leave with his parents in Sharon Springs, New York, probably celebrating his appointment as a warrant officer.

At the Pentagon, I briefed the vexing challenge to General Weinstein and senior army attorneys. What would we do, I asked rhetorically, if we moved against Hall, only to learn that he had indeed been with Heidi in Frankfurt on that particular January weekend? Or worse yet, what if it turned out that Hall had attended a family reunion in Sharon Springs over the Fourth of July, for which there were fifty witnesses?

I returned to my FCA offices and ordered that no stone be left unturned to unmask Hall's travels.

# 33: The Plan Comes Together

Establishing that James Hall had twice managed to sneak to East Berlin in 1988 proved to be the most elusive challenge of the 1126 investigation. Since September, FCA agents on both sides of the Atlantic had devoted countless hours to the task—all without success.

Part of the problem was that the starting point was vague. At Fort Meade, investigators repeatedly played the tape that agents Kelly and Clifford had made of their August interview with the East German professor, a tape that was often nearly impossible to decipher due to the din of West Berlin traffic in the background. When asked how the American spy had traveled from Frankfurt to Berlin, Canna Clay waffled. He was certain only that East German border guards had sneaked the American agent through the wall from West to East Berlin. For both visits, he recalled, the American had appeared at a prearranged time at a remote spot on the west side of the wall, where East German border guards unlocked a maintenance door to admit him. From there, Horst and Wolfgang brought their agent to the safe house. But Clay was uncertain how the American agent had traveled to Berlin. Perhaps, he suggested at one point in the interview, the man had flown to West Berlin from Frankfurt. It was also possible, he added, that the American may have rented a car in West Germany and driven on the autobahn through East Germany to West Berlin.

It was not much to go on. In New York City, FCA investigators once again screened thousands of customs landing cards filled out by arriving passengers. If James had flown to Germany in July, he would have filled out such a form during the return flight. The quest uncovered nothing.

In Germany, investigators checked the records of arriving passengers at Berlin's Tegel Airport. Agents focused on American passengers for the Friday and Saturday of both weekends in question. West Berlin customs police maintained such records and routinely photographed passports of passengers. Agents checked thousands of records for January and July 1988, without success. It was a long shot. If Hall had traveled using a false passport under an alias—not unheard of for East German agents—the chances of recognizing his photograph among the thousands of passport photographs were slim.

Security was also a major concern. If one of the German police officials with whom investigators had coordinated was reporting to East Berlin, the MfS could easily deduce from the Americans' focus on January and July that their target was James Hall. It was a calculated risk that had to be taken.

Norm Runk's FCA investigators in Germany screened the records of German and American rental car agencies, hoping to discover a rental car contract in Hall's name for the January or July weekend. Striking out in Frankfurt, agents expanded their quest to rental car agencies located in the border town of Helmstedt, where the autobahn route through East Germany to West Berlin terminated. This, too, proved to be a dry hole.

Frustrated investigators considered dispatching an agent to Sharon Springs, New York, to determine whether Hall had been at home on the Fourth of July weekend. It would be a risky mission in such a small town. Bob Thayer was skeptical. What could the agent do? Sleuth about and try to elicit the information from neighbors? Any attempt to approach Hall's family or friends, however clever and disingenuous, was out of the question. Investigators had learned the hard way during the Conrad case the consequences of getting too close to the target.

Persistence finally paid off when investigators noticed that James Hall displayed a partiality for Pan American World Airways. If he had flown to Berlin from either Frankfurt or New York, perhaps he had done so on his favorite airline. In such a case, Pan Am's corporate records might be revealing.

In early December 1988, special agent Dave Guethlein departed on the morning shuttle flight to New York City carrying an official letter signed by me enjoining the assistance of Pan Am officials. If Guethlein could smoke out a deserter on a remote Caribbean island, perhaps he could unravel the mystery of James Hall's travel.

Around midday, the phone rang. It was Guethlein.

"Sir, the airline folks were most helpful, and I'm on my way back," he reported. "The word is *bingo!*"

Later that afternoon, the jubilant agent strode into my Fort Meade office. Pan Am's chief of corporate security had given army counterintelligence first-class service. Guethlein beamed as he unveiled a computer printout of James Hall's airline travels for the past four years. It was good news and bad news.

The good news was that Guethlein's quick trip had unlocked the stubborn travel mystery. The Pan Am record revealed that a passenger named James Hall had indeed made a round-trip flight between Frankfurt and West Berlin on the Martin Luther King holiday weekend. Six months later, in early July 1988, passenger Hall had made a quick round-trip on Pan Am flights from New York's JFK Airport to West Berlin.

The bad news was that the Pan Am printout was ominously lengthy. Hall's Pan Am flights were so numerous, Bob Bell quipped, that he should have bought stock in the airline.

One flight listed on the printout was particularly alarming. In June 1985, when Hall was assigned to the 513th MI Brigade at Fort Monmouth, he had flown to Vienna, the preferred meeting place of many intelligence services, particularly the Soviets. Once Hall was in our hands, we would have to discuss this trip with him.

Even more telling was the long list of Staff Sergeant Hall's weekend flights to Berlin during his service in Frankfurt's 205th Military Intelligence Battalion. Between the summer of 1986 and January 1988, the FCA suspect had regularly plied the air corridors between Frankfurt and West Berlin. Each weekend trip, agents had to assume, marked a delivery of secrets to his East German controllers.

Canna Clay had participated in only two 1988 weekend meetings between James Hall and his case officers. In each case, Clay reported, the American sergeant had pleased his MfS controllers by delivering heroic quantities of top-secret information. If Hall had done the same thing each time he had flown to Berlin, the FCA suspect was probably one of the worst spies in the history of the U.S. Army.

The 1126 plan called for investigators to prove or disprove Canna Clay's allegations by Christmas. This Bob Thayer's agents had done. There was now no doubt that James Hall was the traitor whom Canna Clay had met in East Berlin. In less than four months, FCA agents had accomplished what it had taken two and a half years to do in the Conrad case.

But progress had not come without its risks. Chief among these were the security pitfalls posed by a surveillance squad of strangers lurking in the rural Georgia communities surrounding Fort Stewart. Bob Thayer's men had coordinated at the outset with the Richmond Hills Police Department, which pledged discretion and assistance. But this was rural Georgia. By mid-November, the secrecy of the surveillance was in jeopardy at the hands of what intelligence officers call the "friendly opposition."

Investigators confronted several problems. There were limited stakeout positions to cover Hall's comings and goings from Richmond Hills. One was a centrally located small park, which the FCA surveillance control element adopted as one of its field command posts. Unbeknownst to the Yankees from Fort Meade, the park was a local rendezvous for the area's gay residents. Agents realized their poor choice of real estate only when a Chatham County sheriff's deputy rousted them late one evening. The FCA men produced their badges and explained that they were on official Department of Defense business that had been coordinated with the Richmond Hills police. The deputy promptly called local police on an unsecure radio to confirm the story, thereby advertising the FCA presence to anyone who might own a police scanner. Shortly thereafter, when agents made a regular 5:30 A.M. stop at a donut shop, the clerk eyed them and inquired if they were "some of the CIA folks who were in the area."

It was simply impossible to hide in rural Georgia, yet FCA agents had no choice but to cling more closely to Hall as Christmas approached. As coverage of his movements escalated, the citizens of Chatham County took increasing notice. It was only a matter of time before Jim or Heidi Hall would pick up on the local gossip while doing errands in the neighborhood. From my Fort Meade office, I chided Bob Thayer. There was a lesson to be learned from all of this: Instead of relying on look-alike four-door sedans, some of which had been driven to Georgia from Fort Meade, the surveillance team should have leased pickup trucks and four-wheel-drive vehicles.

By Christmas, James Hall would be in his sixth month at Fort Stewart. Horst and Wolfgang had instructed their agent to lay low for six months before scheduling a trip to Germany. With all 1126 case objectives fulfilled, it was time to put an end to Hall's espionage career.

Consultations with army and Department of Justice attorneys were encouraging. Based upon the information that Thayer's team had collected, even the conservative Department of Justice concurred that Hall could now be arrested.

The army chain of command was supportive of an arrest before Christmas. All agreed that it was important to apprehend the warrant officer at a time and place of our choosing. No one was enthusiastic about the hasty airport bust that would be triggered if James Hall decided to fly to Europe.

Two significant impediments to a Christmas arrest had to be removed. The first problem concerned FCA's FBI partners. Army investigators were ready to move against Hall, but the bureau's case against Huseyin Yildirim remained soft. Ideally, the best way to end the investigations would be synchronized arrests of the two conspirators.

Bob Thayer traveled to Washington, and the two of us visited FBI headquarters. Supervisors there made it clear that a double arrest would be facilitated if FCA could delay the apprehension of James Hall. This would permit the FBI's Tampa office to make a stronger case against the Turk. This we could not do.

At Fort Meade, FCA planners faced one final task. With Thayer's agents ready to move against Hall, Canna Clay had to be gotten out of harm's way, which meant spiriting him and his family to the West. Army counterintelligence had made a commitment to the East German professor, and a promise was a promise. It was unthinkable to leave our source in East Berlin and condemn him to arrest, torture, and possible execution by the MfS.

There was also a compelling legal argument for rescuing Clay. Twice the East German had been present as Hall peddled top-secret information for large amounts of cash. Even though the case against Hall was now sound, what better frosting could there be on the legal cake than the testimony of an East German eyewitness at Hall's court-martial?

Persuasive operational reasons also mandated that Canna Clay be removed from harm's way. Jim Whittle, the FCA national liaison officer who had performed so skillfully during the Conrad case, hatched a tempting idea. Whittle outlined his plan to me in early December as we were en route to yet another summit conference at FBI headquarters. Why not bring the East German professor to the United States, Jim argued enthusiastically. Fly the guy to Savannah and use him in the final arrest scene.

Whittle elaborated. Canna Clay could call Hall on the phone and summon him to a meeting to exchange documents for cash. Hall would no doubt recognize Clay's distinctive bass voice from his recent meeting in East Berlin. "Just imagine it," Whittle said, chuckling. "Clay summons Hall to a meeting. Hall shows up, hands over those documents we saw him steal on the video, and rakes in a pile of money—all for the cameras."

I liked the idea so much that we fleshed it out on Washington's infamous Capitol Beltway. Whittle drove and described his vision. I wrote as fast as my hands would permit. Within twenty minutes, the arrest scenario for James Hall was born. We would use Canna Clay to lure the disloyal warrant officer to a Savannah motel. There, Clay would introduce Hall to a "Soviet" officer, who would actually be a skilled FBI role player.

The gambit was a classic "false flag" sting. The FBI role player would praise James Hall for his superior service to the cause of socialism and announce that Moscow had directed the KGB to assume control of the operation. Like most spics, Whittle knew, James Hall was motivated by ego and greed. The false flag showdown would exploit these weaknesses.

Exfiltrating Canna Clay from East Germany would not be easy. Had the disaffected academician been single, the challenge would have been manageable. But Clay was happily married, which permitted his East German superiors to control him. Any time Horst's and Wolfgang's man traveled to the West, his wife remained behind the Iron Curtain. To further complicate matters, the East German couple had several grown sons. At Fort Meade, FCA deputy director Bob Bell raised a good question. Would the East German expect us to bring out the entire clan?

This was an operation that FCA could not accomplish unassisted. There were several methods to get people out of East Germany. All were risky or required sophisticated methods beyond the means of army counterintelligence. One could smuggle the person "black" across the border, concealed in some kind of vehicle (very risky); one could employ the "gray" approach and provide false documentation that would make it appear that the people crossing the border into West Berlin were West Germans (less risky); or the escapees could travel to another East Bloc country, where they would be met and provided with forged identity documents turning them into western tourists, after which they would simply board a plane to West Germany (least risky).

In discussions with Gus Hathaway, we worked out what all felt would be a nearly risk-free way to get Canna Clay to the West. To kick off the operation, a Berlin-based agent would place a phone call to Clay from an East Berlin phone booth. The caller would employ the recognition code that agents Clifford and Kelly had provided our source in August. Mr. Schmidt would mention gardening, then set up a meeting to explain the escape plan to Clay and his wife. Documentation would be prepared using photographs obtained by Mr. Schmidt, and a special flight from Germany to Washington would be arranged. With Canna Clay safely in the United States, Hall could be taken into custody. If all went smoothly, the plan was to have Canna Clay and Mrs. Clay in the United States one week before Christmas, just in time for the academician to perform his last mission.

The exfiltration operation was far from smooth. When called by Mr. Schmidt—a CIA officer—Canna Clay seemed disoriented and abruptly hung up the phone. Later, when Schmidt reestablished contact, he learned that Canna Clay had been seized by indecision. His strong-willed wife knew nothing of his grand design to leave their sons behind and flee communist East Germany. Worse yet, Christmas was just around the corner, and the family was planning a late December wedding. In an intense and risky meeting in Clay's East Berlin residence, the distraught couple bargained with Schmidt and confronted him with a plan to bring out their entire family—thirteen people. Told that this posed an unacceptable security risk, Clay and his wife produced their fallback position. They could not depart East Germany without their large and beloved dog, King. The dog, a seventy-five-pound brindle boxer with a fearsome visage, was present for the negotiations.

In his message regarding the tense meeting, Schmidt described the scene. Throughout his visit, he reported, Canna Clay and his wife, Ingrid, had conversed with their dog as if he were human. King was like a fourth son to the couple. Any exfiltration plan that did not reckon with this stood no chance of acceptance.

Schmidt persevered. After a second emotional discussion, the couple compromised. Canna Clay, his wife, and King would be brought to the West. Once the three were safely out of East Germany, we would use Washington's influence in Bonn to push for family reunification. (At the time, the Bonn government was paying hard currency to the financially strapped East Germans—ransom money, some said—in the name of family reunification.)

The "canine annex" to the exfiltration plan turned more than a few heads in Washington, but Schmidt's famous "dog message" was later proven to have been prescient. Weeks later, when it was possible to laugh about the whole thing, Canna Clay reminisced about the tense negotiations. The Americans should give Schmidt a medal, Clay noted with a chuckle as he stroked King's thick neck. Schmidt had been right, he added: "No King, no Karl."

The arrangements required to move Canna Clay, his wife, and King from Germany to Washington and thence to Savannah would themselves constitute a book. Here are several examples.

A dedicated U.S. Air Force plane to fly Clay and his family to Washington was required. A German-speaking person familiar to the couple would have to be on board to alleviate the anxieties of the newly liberated family.

Once the aircraft arrived at Washington's Andrews Air Force Base, our jet-lagged guests had to be paroled into the country by the Immigration and Naturalization Service (requiring the intervention of the CIA), and they needed a comfortable place to spend their first night in freedom. The Foreign Counterintelligence Activity prepared for the couple's arrival as if a general officer were coming. Agents arranged for a VIP guest suite on the base, which was stocked with flowers, wine, beer, and dog food. A simple note accompanied the flowers: *"Herzlich Willkommen!"*

Timing and security were vital. Once Canna Clay failed to show up at work in East Berlin, the MfS would certainly check his house and discover that he was missing. Worst-case planning was essential here. At most, investigators estimated that they would have only a few days before Clay would be missed. Arranging for the professor's departure on a Thursday or Friday might give us an extra day. Once Clay and his wife were safely in the United States, they would have to be kept under wraps, and the plan to arrest Hall in Savannah would have to be swiftly executed. When the MfS realized that Canna Clay was missing, Hall could be expected to receive a warning call from Horst or Wolfgang. With our recent experience at the hands of the *New York Times* during the Conrad case, few had confidence that we could keep the Canna Clay defection a secret for long. If the East Germans didn't warn Hall, the *New York Times* might.

Once Schmidt had resolved the "who goes, who stays?" debate in East Berlin, which took three precious days, the detailed exfiltration plan worked to perfection. Canna Clay, his wife, and King were spirited to West Germany and boarded a U.S. Air Force jet, accompanied by FCA agent Kelly, whose relationship with Clay was solid. The Andrews Air Force Base welcome was a big hit. Within twenty-four hours, the couple was ensconced in a remote VIP guest lodge on Fort Stewart, courtesy of Major General Taylor.

It was December 19. Foreign Counterintelligence Activity agents had been shadowing the disloyal warrant officer for twenty-four hours a day from the moment the CIA's Schmidt had established contact with Clay in East Berlin. If something were to go wrong and Hall received a warning, we had to be ready to collar him before he could flee. Ears were glued to the telephone taps, listening for a warning call from the MfS.

The chief of the FCA surveillance team objected. His agents were exhausted. Someone was going to fall asleep at the wheel or, worse, someone might make a mismove and alert Hall. Bob Thayer understood the problem but repeated the firm guidance from headquarters. Agents must summon all their strength. Until James Hall was behind bars, we must have eyes on the target at all times. The investigation was in the home stretch.

With Canna Clay on tap in a Fort Stewart guest house and ready to perform one more mission, Bob Thayer moved into high gear with his FBI partners. It was time to execute what promised to be the greatest sting in the history of army counterintelligence. But to pull off Jim Whittle's ingenious false flag sting, additional detailed planning was essential. The actual arrest scenario would have to be legally and operationally sound—no room for error. We were well aware that the case would make headlines. Should something untoward mar the ending, the world would read about it in the *New York Times*. Even as the frustrated Schmidt sat in Canna Clay's East Berlin living room and haggled over the terms of his exfiltration from East Germany, senior army officials were gathering in the Pentagon office of Lt. Gen. Tom Weinstein.

Seventeen people crowded the E-Ring office. Five were general officers or the civilian equivalent. At least four attorneys sat around the conference table or in the second tier of chairs. The final coordination session was an all-army affair with one exception: CIA's Gus Hathaway had come over from Langley. As always, my job was to provide the show, in this case a detailed recounting of precisely how FCA agents planned to arrest suspect Hall.

The step-by-step review of the approaching apprehension was a useful opportunity to subject the plan to one final sanity check. If FCA planners had overlooked something, however minute, this was the best place to find out. Laying out the arrest concept for our Pentagon superiors had an additional advantage. If something did go wrong, no one could accuse FCA of winging it without appropriate approvals.

After a quick review of the status of the Canna Clay exfiltration, I turned to the heart of the plan: the approach to Hall and how Thayer's men planned to deal with their target in the hours prior to and after his arrest.

"Sir, the plan is simple," I led off, addressing General Weinstein, the senior officer present. "But to succeed, it does require attention to a host of details." Weinstein, who had once supervised a counterintelligence field office, nodded. He and the attorneys around the table expected to hear about those details.

I continued. "We will employ Canna Clay in a false flag scenario. Shortly after supper, Clay will telephone Hall from a room in the Days Inn located near the Savannah airport. We expect Mr. Hall will recognize Clay as one of his East German contacts. Clay will summon Hall to a meeting that night, intimating that he is to bring classified materials and that the meeting will be a payday. The lawyers have reviewed the exact words he will use to ensure that we cannot be accused of entrapment."

The briefing continued in this vein for more than thirty minutes. I explained that we expected Hall to respond positively to Clay's phone call. Ideally, he would retrieve the documents that the video cameras had seen him steal and drive directly to the motel, where the East German would introduce him to a "friend." The friend would be an ethnic Russian FBI agent who would introduce himself as a Soviet intelligence officer. The FBI agent's Russian accent was authentic, right out of central casting. His track record of successful stings was legendary.

To overcome any suspicions or discomfort that Hall might harbor, the script called for the "Soviet" to tell the disloyal warrant officer that Moscow was assuming control of the operation to tighten up security and better remunerate him. During the remainder of the meeting, our bogus KGB agent would maneuver Hall into discussing his espionage on behalf of the East Germans, accept whatever documents Hall might bring with him, and pay the disloyal officer handsomely—all for the benefit of a hidden array of cameras and microphones that FCA technicians had installed in the motel room.

When James Hall departed with the cash on his person, FCA agents would arrest him and read him his Miranda rights. Care would be taken to handle the actual arrest in a manner that would encourage Hall to waive his rights. We did not want the prisoner to lapse into a Clyde Conrad–like defiance. Skillfully handled, and convinced that his KGB contact had also been arrested, Hall might attempt to ingratiate himself with his captors by cooperating. The actual apprehension would be done professionally and be low-key. Agents of the army's Criminal Investigation Division (CID) would assist to ensure a clean arrest. Lawyers, FBI agents, technicians, and surveillance personnel would round out the cast of characters at the motel.

Thayer's investigators had rented eight contiguous rooms in the remote rear wing of the motel. One room was the video-sound stage where Hall would meet Canna Clay and the "Soviet." The two adjacent rooms were rigged as monitoring stations. Two FCA arrest teams had been handpicked—four veteran agents carefully selected for their experience and demeanor. Depending on which direction Hall took when he departed the motel room, one of the two teams would apprehend him. Once Hall was in custody, veteran special agents Chuck Pickens and Bill Dwyer would interrogate him. If they did their job well, James Hall would waive his Miranda rights and discuss his espionage without an attorney present.

Finally, I noted, we had reserved a cell for Hall in the Fort Stewart stockade. The post provost marshal had been briefed and would not be surprised when we showed up with a late evening guest for his jail.

There were questions. "What will you do if Hall gets suspicious when Canna Clay calls?" was one of the best.

Savannah investigators had agonized over this possibility and come up with an array of countermeasures if Hall were overcome by suspicion and fear—a not unlikely outcome. After all, Horst and Wolfgang had expressly told their agent that he would not be met in the United States. Canna Clay's phone call could cause him to phone East Berlin, or he could conclude he was in great peril. In such a case, our target might decide to stay home and destroy evidence, beginning with the classified documents he had stolen under the watchful eye of the FCA-installed video cameras.

If Hall attempted to call East Berlin, I explained, technicians would divert the call. A German-speaking army intelligence agent would answer and play the role of an MfS officer. "Horst and Wolfgang are not available," Hall would be told, "but everything is okay. You should go to the meeting."

If Hall panicked and began to destroy evidence, an FCA agent concealed in the trees behind the warrant officer's house would provide warning. Clad in black from head to toe and equipped with binoculars and a radio, the man would have as his sole mission sounding the alarm if things looked bad in the house. The couple had just moved in and there were no curtains on the rear windows. It would not be difficult to observe James and evaluate his actions when he hung up the phone.

If Hall began to dash about and destroy evidence, the lookout would alert an FBI-army search and arrest team concealed in a vacant house across the street. The team, equipped with a battering ram, could be inside the Hall residence within thirty seconds of receiving the alarm. If necessary, the warrant officer would be arrested on the spot, even though it would mean forgoing the enticing sting operation planned for the Days Inn.

The questions continued. What if Hall attempted to flee?

Thayer's plan had taken this into consideration. If Hall headed down I-95, observers in the FCA surveillance aircraft would sound the alarm. Our FBI partners had agreed to alert the Georgia Highway Patrol prior to the planned arrest. Troopers would be on station to assist in case the operation degenerated into a high-speed chase. If it became necessary to arrest Hall under such circumstances, an ad hoc interrogation could be conducted in a motel room near the interstate that special agent Bob Watson had rented for this contingency.

Last, if Hall decided to collect incriminating evidence and stuff it in a pillowcase for deep sixing in the lake across the street from his home, he would be intercepted by two sturdy FCA agents lying in ambush on the path leading to the waterfront.

If all went well and our target traveled to the Days Inn, the FBI would serve its search warrant on Heidi. Because the house was off post, the search was an FBI mission. While James Hall was meeting in the Savannah motel room, the FBI would be in his home. An FCA officer and a German-speaking female FBI agent would escort Heidi and their two daughters to a Fort Stewart guest house. From what investigators had learned, it seemed clear that Hall's wife was an unwitting victim in the case. From a humanitarian and an operational perspective, treating her with consideration made sense. The search of the house would be moderately destructive, better done outside the presence of a German housewife.

At the end of the detailed briefing, General Weinstein waited until the office was empty before giving me one fatherly piece of guidance and sending me on my way to Savannah. His words, delivered with a grin, were vintage Weinstein, the sort of encouraging mentorship that we had come to expect from the earthy general. "Hey, Stu," the general quipped, "just don't fuck it up."

• • •

In the wake of the Pentagon meeting, one nagging issue remained unresolved: what to do about the Meister. As FCA prepared to arrest James Hall, FBI investigators continued to circle the Turk, digging tirelessly for hard information to justify his arrest. In Belleair Beach, Florida, an FBI surveillance squad had been on the scene for weeks, shadowing the Meister's movements in search of incriminating conduct. During this period, Yildirim had made one trip to Germany, where he had family, and two trips to Savannah to meet James Hall. On the telephone, the Turk had talked about diamonds.

Bob Thayer and I were 100 percent certain that Yildirim was dirty. The Hall arrest would blow the case wide open, we were convinced, by unearthing a mountain of incriminating facts about the clever Turk. But in Washington, the FBI supervisor responsible for the case was playing it close. At times it seemed that the bureau man didn't value what we were telling his organization about the Meister's activities in West Berlin. Now that investigators had linked the Turk with James Hall, the facts cried out that Huseyin Yildirim had been an East German agent for at least six years.

It wasn't lost on me that perhaps the FBI supervisor lacked confidence in the army. After all, the 766th's investigation of Yildirim in Berlin had been badly handled, and the Turk had even made two visits to the home of the Berlin Command's senior counterintelligence officer, now the director of FCA. Regardless of the reason, each time the subject surfaced of what to do about the Turk, Bob Thayer and I were not on the same wavelength as our FBI partners in Washington. As late as the middle of December, the army saw Yildirim as a spy; FBI supervisors saw him as a spy or a smuggler, neither of which they felt they could prove.

We understood what the FBI was facing in its efforts to convince cautious Department of Justice attorneys to authorize a move against Yildirim. Arrests are based on facts, not suspicions. Nonetheless, there were compelling reasons to apprehend Hall and Yildirim at the same time. With both men in jail, the chances of capitalizing on a falling-out among thieves were great. Not only that, synchronized arrests would result in concurrent searches of the two conspirators' homes, searches that would surely yield incriminating evidence. But when Bob Thayer and I visited FBI headquarters to lobby for coordinated arrests, we got nowhere. Army counterintelligence was within days of arresting James Hall, but the FBI officer in charge of the case in Washington clung to his insistence that no action would be taken against the Turk when the army made its move.

Central Intelligence Agency counterintelligence chief Gus Hathaway accompanied me to FBI headquarters, where we met with Intelligence Division chief Tom DuHadway. Hathaway appealed to DuHadway. His case supervisor was getting it all wrong. Yildirim may be a smuggler, the CIA official argued, but more importantly, he is most certainly a spy. When the army arrests Hall, Hathaway pointed out, Huseyin Yildirim will be on the next plane out of the country, and the FBI will have egg on its face for permitting him to slip the noose.

DuHadway summoned his case supervisor and reviewed the bidding on the Turk. During the ensuing debate, which became passionate, Hathaway's arguments carried the day. Convinced that Yildirim would attempt to flee as soon as the news broke that Hall was in custody, DuHadway directed that the Turk be apprehended as a material witness as soon as Hall was in custody. If Hall then implicated Yildirim, or if the search of the two men's residences established an espionage conspiracy, the FBI could quickly prepare a new affidavit for federal magistrates and obtain approval to change the Turk's status from witness to suspect.

With the situation in Washington now clear, the sole remaining task to be accomplished before the Hall arrest was coordination between Canna Clay and the FBI agent who would impersonate a KGB officer. The more the FBI's role player knew about James Hall's espionage as it appeared from East Berlin, the more convincing his performance would be.

On the afternoon of December 20, in a Savannah motel room, the FBI man and the East German met. Canna Clay described the pair of meetings in East Berlin and shared his impressions of James Hall. The bureau role player, Vladimir, emerged from the surprisingly brief meeting brimming with confidence. If the plan worked, in a matter of hours he would face James Hall at the Days Inn. A more cautious man would have pumped Canna Clay's brain unrelentingly,

fearful of committing a blunder when face-to-face with Hall. Not
Vladimir. The FBI agent's demeanor conveyed supreme confidence.
"Everything will go fine," he assured Bob Thayer and me. "You will
see. I'll know what to say when the time comes."

With the East German and Vladimir on one sheet of music, and
the Airport Days Inn all but owned by army counterintelligence, the
stage was set. For the second time in four months, multiple arrests
by different agencies would signal the roll-up of an espionage ring
involving disloyal soldiers. At the center of the action once again
would be agents of the Foreign Counterintelligence Activity.

# 34: "Moscow" Takes Over

The legendary German field marshal von Moltke was fond of reminding his staff officers, "Even the best plan doesn't survive the first shot in combat." The Prussian's prescient words have withstood the test of time. Those who fail to plan for the unexpected court disaster.

On the night of December 20, 1988, the timeless maxim was again demonstrated. As army and FBI agents prepared to carry out the arrest operation, the unforeseen intruded. Warrant Officer Hall didn't play his assigned role.

Every duty day for almost four months, FCA surveillance agents had observed James Hall depart work, do an errand or two, pay an occasional visit to the officers' club bar, and head for his Richmond Hills home. By 6:30 P.M., the distinctive Ford pickup was almost always in the driveway. But on this late December day, what was to be Hall's last day of freedom, the East German spy was overcome by the holiday spirit and decided to go Christmas shopping.

At 6:30 P.M., Canna Clay sat nervously on a bed in the Days Inn, psyching himself up to play his greatest role. Foreign Counterintelligence Activity technicians Dick Bankston, Frank Duffer, and Ron DeComo bustled about the room, completing a last-minute shakedown of their hidden cameras and microphones. In a nearby room, attorneys caucused one final time with the agents who would arrest and interrogate James Hall. Nothing could be left to chance.

The plan called for the East German to call James Hall at 7:30 P.M. and summon him to the motel. If all went well, James should arrive at the Days Inn by 8:30 P.M. Clay would immediately introduce him to Vladimir, "a KGB agent from the USSR's Washington, D.C., embassy." Hall would then star in a videotaped discussion, during which we hoped he would make incriminating admissions about his espionage career. An hour or so into the meeting, the FBI's KGB impersonator would orchestrate the coup de grace for the cameras: The suspect would hand over classified defense documents, for which he would be compensated with a mountain of cash. The actual arrest would take place after the planned one-hour meeting, somewhere around 10:00 P.M.

Timing was all-important. Intelligence and Security Command attorney Col. Fran O'Brien was on the scene and warned that agents Chuck Pickens and Bill Dwyer would have to accomplish their interrogation before the hour became too late. We dared not provide an aggressive defense attorney with a credible claim that his client had been subjected to an all-night third degree.

In Richmond Hills, army and FBI agents were in place, as were FCA surveillance vehicles, and the FBI search team was poised to take down the house. Overhead, Sky King and his observer were on station. At sundown, a lone FCA observer had taken his position on the cold ground in Hall's backyard.

In Florida, FBI surveillance agents bearing arrest and search warrants kept watch on Peggy Bie's ranch house.

But now the entire timetable was thrown off. Foreign Counterintelligence Activity surveillance personnel reported to Bob Thayer that their target was meandering through the crowded malls along Savannah's glitzy shopping strip and showing no indication that he was in a hurry to get home. Still worse, the throngs of holiday shoppers made it difficult for agents to keep suspect Hall in sight. Each time he departed a store and climbed into his truck, the surveillance team would report the target on the move—homeward bound. Several such reports reached us, with each subsequently declared a false alarm. Hall stopped at several stores, then pulled into a Western Sizzlin' steak house for a meal. By 9:00 P.M., the warrant officer was unhurriedly browsing through rows of Christmas trees.

Bob Thayer and I huddled. It now appeared that the earliest Hall might arrive at his home in Richmond Hills was 10:30 P.M., an extremely late hour to receive a telephone summons to a meeting at a distant motel. Some among the FBI and army people at the motel suggested a postponement—a reasonable position to take, given the late hour. But a day's delay was unacceptable. The surveillance team was truly at the end of its endurance; a postponement would mean another risky day of stalking our man. Still riskier was the ticking time bomb in East Berlin. Canna Clay had been gone for four days. Each day that passed increased the chances that Hall would receive a warning from the East Germans.

I dug in my heels. The sting would go down that night. Clay would call James as soon as he walked through his front door.

Bob Thayer took measures to counter the problem of a late phone call by Canna Clay. At around 8:00 P.M., Thayer instructed Clay to call the Hall residence and ask for Jim even though we knew that he was not home. This way, Thayer reasoned, when Hall came through the door, Heidi would tell him that someone had called and would likely call again. The East German made two such calls between 8:00 and 10:00 P.M., dry runs that had the additional advantage of giving the nervous professor the opportunity to practice his English-language telephone technique.

Finally, at 10:30 P.M., the surveillance team reported that their man had pulled into his driveway in Richmond Hills. We waited two minutes, then gave Canna Clay the green light. The East German dialed the number.

"Hello, Jim. Paul calling. I'm in town now and would like to get together with you if you have time."

Hall replied in a subdued, confused voice. "Paul? Paul who?"

Canna Clay replied, "You know, a friend of Horst and Wolfgang."

Hall perked up. "Oh!" Within a few minutes, the pair had agreed to meet at the Days Inn. Hall insisted that it would take an hour or so to get there.

Canna Clay delivered his key line. "Oh, by the way, if you have anything for me, please bring it. I have something for you. And don't forget to bring the bag." The bag in question was the East German–issued gym bag with the false bottom. Its mention told James Hall that it was payday, just in time for Christmas.

With money in the offing, James revised his estimate. It would take him "forty-five minutes or so" to make the trip. As the conversation ended, he called Clay "sir." He had heard his master's voice.

The black-garbed FCA surveillance agent in Hall's backyard reported that the warrant officer was out of the house and on the road within minutes of hanging up the phone. Overhead, Sky King checked in. The target was driving the family Volvo, speeding north in the direction of the Airport Days Inn. On the ground, FCA sur-

veillance vehicles kept their distance from the Volvo, relying on their
aerial observer's reports.

James Hall arrived at the motel wearing a light gray jacket. Canna
Clay greeted him in the parking lot and walked him to the motel
room, making small talk along the way. Once inside, with the cameras rolling, Hall shook hands with a man who introduced himself
as Vladimir Kosov, from the USSR embassy in Washington. Those
watching the drama unfold on the monitor noted that the warrant
officer seemed ill at ease.

The FBI impersonator launched into his pitch. There was "something very important" to discuss, Kosov explained, "private business,"
which should be done between the two of them. On cue, Canna Clay
left the room. Distancing the East German from the action was important. It impressed upon Hall that the Soviet agent was calling the
shots, and it minimized the defector's need to testify about the meeting at Hall's court-martial.

Vladimir began with an appeal to James Hall's ego. His superiors
in Moscow were most impressed with Jim's contributions, which the
East Germans were sharing with their ally. "They think you're a very
valuable person, and the material you've been giving is very valuable," Kosov cooed. Nonetheless, Vladimir continued, "to speak
frankly with you, my superiors in Moscow, they thought that the way
our friends handled the whole thing could have been done much
better—much better for two important reasons. One is your personal
safety and security, which is number one for everybody involved, of
course, as you understand; and the second one, we think that because the material that you have provided was so good and so valuable, we think that they [the East Germans] should have taken—how
you say in America—better care of you." For these reasons, Vladimir
informed James, Moscow intended to assume control of the operation. Hall nodded his understanding. He was a superstar; the East
Germans had been shortchanging him, and the good guys from
Moscow were determined to correct this injustice.

Vladimir's artful stroking of James Hall's prodigious ego was effective. Prior to Vladimir's praise and hints of generosity, Hall had
sat stiffly, his hands gripping the arms of the chair, still wearing his
jacket. It was body language that bespoke caution. At the mention

of money, the transformation was immediate. Hall relaxed visibly, removed his jacket, and settled back in the chair. Soon he was reclining comfortably, legs crossed, his hands clasped behind his neck, a willing listener for whatever the man he believed to be a Soviet KGB agent might say.

But the real challenge lay ahead. Somehow, the FBI agent had to get Hall talking about his espionage for the record. To do this, Vladimir emphasized the need for a smooth handoff of the case. "I have received some messages from Moscow," he told Hall, "but you will excuse me if I don't know everything about the case."

Having thrown out a plausible reason for his curiosity, Vladimir raised the subject of Hall's business relationship with the East Germans.

"We're not sure how much Horst and Wolfgang paid you and, again, my superiors thought that if they did not pay you enough, we can make up the difference, and I'm sure probably at this time of the year you can use a little bit more difference," Vladimir said with a chuckle. "I think everyone at this time of year needs a little bit more." Hall laughed amiably and nodded his agreement.

"Anyway, as we understand it, you've had two meetings with the East Germans this year. At least this is what I know—and please forgive me if I don't have all the facts because I'm still new on this case."

This was the key moment. In the adjacent rooms, army and FBI agents sat breathless in front of the monitoring equipment. So far, Vladimir had done all the talking. There was a brief pause. James was evidently thinking.

Within seconds, Hall took the leap. He had, he acknowledged, met "two times, maybe three times" with the East Germans in 1988. Then a breakthrough for the FBI: "Okay, do you know about the Turkish man, Yildirim?" said Hall.

"Um, does he have another name?" Vladimir asked.

"Meister," replied Hall.

"Oh! We've heard about him," said Vladimir.

Silent cheers and vigorous thumbs-up signs were exchanged by everyone in the adjacent rooms. "We've got him." The FBI agents in the monitoring room grinned as Hall launched into an explanation of his relationship with Yildirim, and how the Turk had been his intermediary with the East German State Security Service since the autumn of 1982. "I've met Yildirim since I've been here and gave him a note to take to the East Germans with some operational considerations in it," Hall told Vladimir. "Then, when he came back, he brought me some money from them."

For the next two hours and forty minutes, James Hall engaged in a wide-ranging conversation with the man who he was convinced was his new KGB case officer. Sometimes in response to Vladimir's questions, but often on his own initiative, Hall recounted his career as a communist agent, salting his account with helpful pointers on how the Soviets might obtain better results from his espionage. With little prompting, Hall willingly described for Vladimir six highly classified signals intelligence projects in great detail—the same array of sensitive programs described by Canna Clay in West Berlin.

It was well past midnight when Hall ventured into the parking lot to retrieve the documents he had stolen from his office. He returned to the room within minutes, carrying a plastic bag. He apologized that the requisite dark blue gym bag was on the washing machine at home, still full of sweaty workout clothes. "This stuff isn't much," he said as he took the documents from the plastic bag. "What I tried to do was a quick roust of my open desk to show you what I can get." Then Hall patiently described each stolen document.

The first was a classified trip report written by Major General Taylor upon his return from a visit to the Soviet Union, during which the general had observed a Red Army training maneuver.

Hall handed Vladimir another document, a classified intelligence summary from Europe. "This one's from EUCOM; that's the European Command," he explained to Vladimir. "Some of the stuff in this one may have come from the CIA."

The FBI role player thumbed through the document, noting that it had two duplicate pages.

Hall laughed. "When you're copying stuff, man, you're just copying. You know how it is."

Then the finale. Vladimir put the betrayed documents in his bag and spoke. "Now it's my turn to give you something. This is money from the USSR for a change, not from East Germany. So if you will hold out your bag, each of these stacks is five thousand dollars."

With that, the FBI officer dropped six bundles of $5,000 into Hall's sack. Vladimir fixed his gaze on Hall and spoke.

"Now, I want to emphasize that this sum is for what you did before, because we think that our friends, the East Germans, they didn't pay you enough, so we are making up the difference."

Hall nodded his assent. On the other side of the wall, the attorneys who had suggested this approach were pleased. Hall's acceptance of this sum was important additional proof that he had betrayed secrets prior to this particular meeting.

As James closed his sack of easy money, Vladimir produced yet another gambit from his bag of tricks. "Now I have to get you to sign a receipt for this," he explained apologetically. "You know, bureaucracies are the same on both sides. I have written it out for you. All it says is that you received money from me for something you did." The FBI man placed a receipt in front of Hall, who meekly signed it.

There was more. Vladimir produced another armload of cash. "Now I have some more for you. But this money is different. That other money was for what you did in the past. Since you also gave me information this evening, this is for what you gave me tonight. These are also five-thousand-dollar bundles, so if you will again hold out your bag . . ."

Once again, investigators were treated to the ludicrous spectacle of Hall holding the plastic bag open with two hands while an FBI agent counted out $30,000 and dropped it in the bag. As each $5,000 bundle landed in the sack with a plop, I muttered to myself, "Ten years, twenty years, thirty years, forty years." Then, just when it seemed that the whole thing was too good to be true, it got even better.

As Hall again closed the plastic bag, Vladimir produced a piece of blank paper and a pen. "Unfortunately," he purred, "I have to get you to sign another receipt. But this time perhaps you can write it out for me yourself?"

Vladimir handed James the paper and pen. "Just make it simple," our FBI colleague coached in his perfect Russian accent. "You know, just so my superiors in Moscow, they do not think I take the money and run off to Valt Deesney Vorld," he quipped. In the adjoining rooms, agents stifled their laughter.

Hall groused as he wrote out the receipt and signed it. "You guys are really getting tough on this. I used to just have to scribble my name."

Before the warrant officer rose to depart, he levied two demands on his new handler. If Moscow was going to be in the driver's seat, he said, "You guys are going to have to get control of Yildirim." Also, James added, he needed a better concealment device. "The bag your people gave me only holds a small amount of documents," he complained. "Some of those Oplans get really thick. What I need is something large, something that will hold a thick document."

The pair discussed a means of clandestine communication as James prepared to depart. It was past 1:00 A.M. on December 21 when the spy donned his jacket and headed for the door. Carrying $60,000 in his plastic bag, with Christmas only a few days away, James must have felt that life was treating him well. There just might be enough cash left over after the holidays to buy that sailboat he'd been wanting.

The last sound made by James Hall as a free man was a resounding thump as he was spun against the wall of the Savannah Days Inn by agents Chuck Pickens and Bill Dwyer.

"Army intelligence. You're under arrest," Dwyer barked as his partner relieved James of the plastic bag and patted him down. The prisoner meekly submitted without a word. Firmly but gently, Pickens and Dwyer marched their man thirty feet to the room that was set up for interrogation.

Agents politely read their captive his Miranda rights. No one said a word about the fate of Vladimir. As far as James Hall knew, his Soviet accomplice and the East German had also been apprehended. And Hall was not informed that the entire meeting had just been videotaped.

The prisoner sat at the table in a deep funk, his head bowed. When asked if he would waive his rights and talk to his captors, he replied in a timid voice. "What can you do for me if I cooperate?"

The question was not unexpected. Bill Dwyer responded.

"We can't make any deals with you, but we will make your cooperation known to proper authorities."

Hall countered: "What if I refuse to cooperate, or if I lie to you?"

Dwyer's reply was polite but firm: "We don't advise you to do that, but if you do, then we will make that information known to proper authorities."

The veteran FCA agent's responses were not spontaneous. Earlier in the day, Dwyer and Pickens had met with army attorney Fran O'Brien. O'Brien's guidance was specific. It was vital that Hall understand that no deals would be cut with him in exchange for cooperation. Most importantly, his interrogators had to avoid saying anything that could be later twisted by a defense attorney to imply that the arresting agents had tricked his client into confessing.

Hall shrugged his shoulders in resignation and signed the rights waiver form. He would talk without an attorney present. Chuck Pickens slipped out of the room to convey the good news. The concept of a soft arrest had borne fruit. Had Dwyer and Pickens pushed weapons into Hall's face, treated him roughly, strip-searched him and dressed him in a prison jumpsuit, the outcome would no doubt have been different.

Dwyer and Pickens played their parts perfectly. Because they approached Hall with finesse and compassion (however feigned), the two agents were able to obtain fourteen hours of quality interrogation time with the unnerved and depressed warrant officer before he gathered his wits and obtained an attorney. Not surprisingly, the defense attorney's first move was to tell his client not to say another word.

James Hall sipped a glass of ice water, hung his head, and gazed at Chuck Pickens. "I'll bet I know what you're thinking of me right now," the warrant officer murmured.

Chuck Pickens is a bear of a man, a retired master sergeant whose imposing appearance belies his soft-spoken and introspective nature. A veteran of three decades of intelligence service, the shrewd, experienced operator sensed opportunity in Hall's hangdog demeanor. Gazing across the table at the disgraced warrant officer, Pickens responded in a low voice. "Tell me what you think I'm thinking."

Hall replied softly, eyes downcast. "You think I'm a rotten traitor—the scum of the earth."

Chuck Pickens shook his head. "No," he replied gently. "You shouldn't think that. I've been doing this for years, and it's just business with me. I recognize that we all sometimes do things under stress and pressure that are wrong, and I don't attempt to judge someone. So don't think that, because it's not true. Everyone makes mistakes."

Pickens's low-key response seemed to visibly relax Hall. His interrogators had quickly divested themselves of their weapons and established at the outset a nonthreatening environment. Chuck Pickens's display of understanding was inspired. It established an almost father-son bond between the two men that was to persist for months, ultimately enabling the government to learn far more from the junior officer than would have been possible if macho agents had terrified and humiliated him upon arrest. The hard-nosed approach to arrests common to many law enforcement agencies might work with a career criminal or a sociopath such as John Walker, but for James Hall, honey rather than vinegar resonated.

Dwyer and Pickens soon had James prattling openly about his six years as a communist spy. As the dialogue continued, FBI agents in Richmond Hills were loading twenty boxes of evidence into a truck. Among the seized items were more than $10,000 in U.S. banknotes, several thousand deutsche marks, and a collection of cameras and film that rivaled Clyde Conrad's (all provided by the Soviets and East Germans, Hall later admitted). Searchers located the dark blue gym bag where Hall told Vladimir he had left it—on the washing machine—still full of sweaty workout clothes. Concealed in its false bottom was an East German–issued bogus British passport bearing Hall's picture and the name Robert Hillier. Agents also recovered a Soviet-issued black attaché case with a hidden compartment that concealed a variety of bogus British documents that supported the identity on the British passport.

Two recovered items were particularly revealing. The first was a folksy "Dear Friend" letter from the East Germans found in the attaché case. In the letter, the East Germans tasked their source to steal specific war plans and signals intelligence directives. From under the seat of Hall's pickup truck, delighted FBI agents retrieved a brown envelope, the same one that FCA surveillance cameras had caught as the Meister handed it to James during an early December meeting at a restaurant. The envelope still held most of the $5,000 that Hall would soon confess the Meister had brought to him from the East Germans.

The brown envelope was vital. Bagged and dispatched to the FBI's crime lab, it bore the fingerprints of Huseyin Yildirim—important evidence of a conspiracy between Hall and the Turk.

The apprehension of James Hall was a major counterespionage victory. But as the badly shaken warrant officer talked, the sense of triumph was tempered by the magnitude of the damage he had done. Canna Clay's description of Hall's espionage in Berlin had been on the mark, as far as it went. But the East German academician had observed only a small part of the young officer's espionage career. During the evening in the Savannah Days Inn, investigators learned the rest of the story.

James Hall first crossed the bridge of treason while serving as a twenty-five-year-old sergeant at Field Station Berlin. Depressed, strapped for cash, and responsible for a new wife and baby, he became fed up with waiting for the things he wanted in life. It was the fall of 1982 when the overstressed buck sergeant simply decided one day to become a spy. The decision was strictly business. He had a commodity that someone would pay for. James Hall was no communist.

To our great surprise, James began his espionage not with the East Germans but with the Soviets. To launch his new career as a KGB agent, he dropped a letter into the mail slot of the Soviet consulate in West Berlin's Grunewald district.

As a cover to deliver the fateful letter, Hall had borrowed a neighbor's dog and walked it by the Soviet consulate. The letter's text, which he later reconstructed for his FCA debriefers, concluded with an offer to the Soviets. If they were interested in doing business, they should meet him at 7:30 that evening at a well-known West Berlin restaurant. To facilitate recognition, Hall told the KGB that he'd be wearing a red pullover with a black stripe.

With that act, the young sergeant joined the growing ranks of espionage volunteers, of whom the infamous U.S. Navy warrant officer John Walker remains the most notorious example. To the KGB, an espionage volunteer was the best kind of spy, assuming that he

was a genuine traitor and not an American double agent. John
Walker's treason epitomized the damage that could be inflicted by
a motivated espionage volunteer. After walking into the Soviet embassy in Washington in 1968 and volunteering his services, Walker
operated continuously until 1985, recruiting along the way his best
friend, his brother, and his son. Before the ring was broken up by
the FBI, Walker and his confederates had provided Moscow the capability to decipher millions of American top-secret military communications. By 1982, when James Hall dropped his offer in the mailbox of the Soviet consulate, no Soviet intelligence officer could
afford to lightly dismiss a volunteer who might turn out to be another
John Walker.

The Soviets responded to Sergeant Hall's overture. At the appointed time, a casually dressed KGB officer approached him at the
restaurant. "We received your letter," the Soviet told Hall. "It is necessary for us to go where it is safer to talk." Having taken the leap, a
nervous James Hall meekly followed the KGB man to the subway,
where the train made a stop at East Berlin's Friedrichstrasse Bahnhof. Soon James found himself in a safe house near the Soviet compound in the Karlshorst district. There KGB officers questioned the
aspiring agent in some detail about his duties at Field Station Berlin,
much as Vasily would question SSgt. Lowry Wilcox three years later
during Operation Lake Terrace.

The young sergeant's willingness to cross into East Berlin and his
forthright replies to their questions persuaded the KGB that he was
the real thing, not an American provocateur working for the 766th
MI Detachment. By the time James Hall returned to West Berlin that
evening, he was a recruited source of the Soviet KGB. The officer
in charge of the KGB's Karlshorst Detachment could report a major breakthrough to the Moscow Center. Penetrating the mountaintop electronic eavesdropping site of the Americans was his
unit's top priority.

The rookie spy's Soviet superiors had a long wish list. Hall's case
officer instructed him to copy and deliver highly classified documents from the Teufelsberg Field Station. Soon Hall would have the
opportunity to meet with a Soviet signals intelligence expert from
Moscow—someone who understood the complexities of electronic

warfare. But such face-to-face contact with KGB officers, he was told, would be rare. Actual deliveries of stolen secrets would be via dead drops in West Berlin. Later, Hall would drop packages of documents through the partially open window of a parked Soviet sedan, reminiscent of the tactic attempted by Vasily during Operation Lake Terrace. When James Hall returned to West Berlin, he was carrying a thick stack of crisp $100 bills. "There will be a lot more than this," he was told, "if you deliver what we need."

Hall admitted sheepishly that he soon began to engage in double-dealing. Peddling copies of stolen documents to the KGB and the East Germans was an easy way to multiply his profits. Money, after all, was the whole idea.

The East German connection, he explained, had gotten started almost by accident. Within two to three weeks of his trip to East Berlin, Hall was chatting with Huseyin Yildirim in the auto craft shop when the subject turned to the Turk's major obsession—how to make easy money. James described the scene.

"As a passing joke—and I really shouldn't have done this—I mentioned during a conversation about making money, 'It's easy to do, you sell secrets.' A week later, the Meister announced that he had made contact in East Berlin—at first he said it was with the Turks, but it turned out to be the East Germans."

Hall continued his amazing saga. "So, from that point on, each time I made copies of documents for the Soviets, I made an extra copy for the Meister. Meister would pick up the ones for the East Germans, and later deliver my share of the money."

It was easy money, Hall recalled. There was a large photocopying machine in his duty section. He merely had to select documents for theft and make two copies of each. Eventually it became difficult to make copies at the field station, because the copying machine was leased based upon a certain level of use, and with James feverishly cranking out stacks of secrets for Moscow and East Berlin, the machine began to exceed its quota. Soon his superiors designated a soldier to control access to the machine—not for security, Hall said with a laugh, but to save money. After that, James smuggled documents out of the field station and photographed them in a step-van in the parking lot.

Then came his transfer in the spring of 1985 to Fort Monmouth. Once in New Jersey, dealing with Moscow became too difficult. James decided to sever communications with the KGB and deal solely with the East Germans through the Meister.

Hall elaborated. "I had good stuff, but communications were too difficult. You know, I was in Long Branch, New Jersey, and the Soviets had given me detailed instructions to dead-drop sites in Queens and Long Island, with complicated and time-consuming requirements about driving up from New Jersey, making chalk marks on telephone poles, and all that stuff. I tried to make one such run, but it took an hour and a half, and that was one way. I just couldn't do it. I was a sergeant. They'd ask questions at work about where I was for three hours, questions for which I had no answers."

Yildirim made spying easy, James admitted. The Turk would fly in from Germany, take whatever documents he had acquired, and pay him, all in one neat and convenient operation.

Hall's description of his conspiracy with Yildirim was unsettling to me personally. In 1983, while the Meister was cheerfully mentoring me through a crash course on auto restoration, he had been plundering the secrets of the command's most sensitive intelligence unit, which my unit was charged to protect. In this context, the Turk's strange visits to my quarters took on new meaning. (Later, after the collapse of East Germany, East German intelligence officers would reveal that the uncontrollable Turk had attempted to impress his handlers with his access to the local counterintelligence commander, even going so far as to smuggle a tape recorder into my home to record one of his brief social visits. To the brash Turk, snuggling up to me and other American intelligence officials in West Berlin was useful. He could use the contacts to impress the East Germans and the gullible Peggy Bie, who apparently believed that he was a star agent for U.S. intelligence. Not only that, if something ever went wrong and he were apprehended, ties to the American intelligence community might be useful.)

The discovery that Hall had worked on behalf of the Soviets and the East Germans was the major surprise of the evening. But there was additional unwelcome news. The motel meeting confirmed that

James had indeed betrayed an array of highly sensitive signals intelligence projects to the Soviets and the East Germans. The projects
discussed by James with Vladimir were so sensitive that one thirty-
minute portion of the Days Inn tape had to be classified "top secret,
codeword."

During the Days Inn meeting with Vladimir, James explained why
he had embarked on espionage.

"I wanted to be able to afford some of the things I wanted and
when I wanted them," he admitted. When James boasted to Vladimir
that he had given information on a certain high-tech electronic project before it was fielded, Vladimir countered: "So before you even
turned it on, our side knew already?"

Hall replied with a chuckle, "I hope so. As long as I get my money."

"So you did it for money?" said Vladimir.

Replied Hall, "What you guys do with whatever it is I give you is
up to you. Sure. I'm not anti-American. I wave the flag as much as
anybody else."

Lest the KGB man misunderstand, James elaborated. "It's dollars
and cents to me. . . . You guys tell me what you want, and like before,
I'll get it." He added with a tone of finality, "If I've got it and you guys
want it, it's yours."

While James Hall prattled on to agents Pickens and Dwyer about
his six years of espionage, the FBI made its move in Belleair Beach,
Florida. Agents knocked on the door of Peggy Bie's ranch house
armed with a search warrant and a warrant to arrest the Turk as a
material witness in the Hall investigation.

The deeply suntanned Meister appeared at the door wearing a
splashy blue surf shirt. Peggy, he insisted, was not at home. Agents
flashed their warrants, entered the house, and escorted the Turk to
the kitchen for a chat. Other FBI personnel swarmed into the house
and began a methodical, room-by-room search.

In the master bedroom, agents heard a muffled noise in the closet.
What happened next has become legend. Opening the closet doors,
surprised agents discovered Peggy Bie, naked as a jaybird. She
shrieked. A quick-thinking female agent grabbed a sheet from the
bed and wrapped it around the hysterical woman. Peggy screamed

even louder, cast off the sheet, and streaked through the house to the kitchen, screaming like a banshee. "Don't say a word," she shouted at the shocked Yildirim, who was sitting at the kitchen table talking with an agent. "I've seen this all on television. You have a right to an attorney. Don't say another word."

With that, any chance for a friendly chat with the Turk evaporated. In Savannah, special agents Dwyer and Pickens were schmoozing with James Hall at the Fort Stewart post stockade, but in Florida, our FBI colleagues would be forced to go about their work without conspicuous help from the Meister. Frustrated agents hustled the Turk out of the house and paraded their prize in front of the media, who had been tipped that an arrest was going down in the quiet suburban neighborhood. It was well-earned advertising for our publicity-conscious bureau partners.

Once Yildirim was out of the house, agents searched it with professional zeal, recovering evidence that would help make a strong espionage case against the Turk. This included a small passport photo of James Hall, identical to the picture that appeared on his East German–issued bogus British passport. Agents recovered travel records confirming that Yildirim had traveled to Berlin between his meetings with Hall in November and December.

By sundown on December 21, 1988, army and FBI agents had done a credible day's work. Between them, FCA and FBI investigators had netted two spy suspects and seized dozens of boxes of evidence that could be used to develop airtight cases against the pair.

Bob Thayer's investigators had one more job to accomplish. Donning coats and ties, and without time to catch up on lost sleep, they descended on Fort Stewart to conduct two days of intensive interviews of James Hall's coworkers. It was unlikely that Hall had recruited any associates during his six months at Fort Stewart, but the interviewing had to be done. Perhaps James had mentioned the names of close friends in Frankfurt or Berlin or expressed interest in classified materials that might point toward his collection targets. The only way to learn the answers to such questions was to ask, even if it was but four days until Christmas.

By Christmas Eve, with these interviews accomplished and with Heidi Hall and the couple's two daughters in the care of Bill Peterson and his wife, the last of Bob Thayer's triumphant and weary FCA agents redeployed to Fort Meade.

James Hall also spent Christmas at Fort Meade—in the post stockade. Because the court-martial of the signals intelligence specialist would require a secure courtroom in which classified information could be discussed, the army had decided to transfer him to Washington. Instead of being court-martialed by the 24th Infantry Division, the accused warrant officer would face a judge from the military district of Washington.

As James Hall settled in to life in the Fort Meade stockade, we reflected on our good fortune that the press had not intruded on the Savannah investigation. The specter of *New York Times* reporter Jeff Gerth's well-placed Washington source had haunted the four-month investigation of James Hall. Still smarting from the near disastrous leak that had almost derailed the Clyde Conrad investigation, the army had enforced draconian limits on need to know during the Fort Stewart case.

And rightly so. In Hall's own words, even the slightest hint that he was under investigation would have caused him to use the bogus British passport and flee the United States. "I'm somewhat paranoid," James told Vladimir during their Days Inn meeting. "If for any reason I suspect I'm being investigated, I'm leaving the country. If I suspect I'm in trouble, I'm gone, I'm history."

If Jeff Gerth or Stephen Engelberg had floated a story in the *Times* to the effect that the army or the FBI were stalking a spy somewhere in the southeastern United States, James Hall would have been history. After the two reporters wrote about the Conrad case, it was clear that they had developed at least one well-placed and talkative source somewhere in Washington. No one doubted that the two reporters' deep throat could have derailed the 1126 investigation.

That we were able to carry out our four-month investigation of Hall and the Meister without a major leak was thus a source of some satisfaction. Whoever the *Times* source was, either we had succeeded in keeping him out of the information loop or he was lying low in the face of a leak investigation that had been mounted by the FBI after Clyde Conrad's arrest.

The need for total secrecy was not over merely because James Hall

and the Meister were behind bars. Canna Clay and his wife were se-
questered in a Maryland safe house, and the couple was deeply concerned for the safety of their sons in East Berlin.

On December 21, news of the Hall and Yildirim arrests broke in
the national media. In Savannah, FBI Special Agent-in-Charge Bill
Clancy invited Bob Thayer and me to join him at an FBI news conference to release details of the Hall arrest to the local media. Bob
and I politely declined. The case had been a truly joint effort, and
the bureau was free to deal with the media as it chose. As in the
Conrad case, FCA preferred to dodge the media spotlight and maintain a low profile that would permit us to quietly pursue follow-on
leads.

The public affairs guidance of the arrest plan had been sharply
debated before I traveled to Savannah for the arrest. Pentagon public affairs officers, whose job it was to maintain cordial relations with
the media, made the case for a limited release of information surrounding the arrest. As counterintelligence investigators in the middle of a sensitive case, we considered it inappropriate to comment
on an ongoing investigation. Any queries about the case were thus
directed to the Department of Defense Public Affairs Office in the
Pentagon. Their officers released information concerning Hall's arrest and service record but little about our investigation. Above all,
the fact that an East German defector had tipped army counterintelligence had to be protected.

But the Savannah and Tampa arrests were big news, although they
were overshadowed by the tragic sabotage of Pan Am Flight 103 over
Lockerbie, Scotland, the following day. Still, persistent reporters
mounted an aggressive campaign to uncover what official Pentagon
spokespersons were not releasing. Viewers tuning in CNN or the network news shows were treated to footage of a scowling and hand-
cuffed Yildirim being led from Peggy Bie's Florida ranch house to a
waiting FBI sedan. Camera crews swarmed into Richmond Hills,
Georgia, and interviewed James Hall's astonished neighbors. "STEW-
ART OFFICER HELD AS SPY" trumpeted the headline of the *Savannah Evening Press*. Quoting Pentagon public affairs officers in
Washington and the Savannah FBI, the paper reported that James
Hall was a "signal intelligence–electronic warfare specialist stationed

at Ft. Stewart" with a top-secret clearance who had spent his entire career in the signals intelligence field.

The media began to dig. At Fort Meade, FCA insiders ran an informal pool. How long would it take the press to uncover our secret? The *Washington Post* reported within days of the arrest that "Army officials began investigating [Hall] last summer after being tipped that Hall, recently promoted from staff sergeant to warrant officer, was living above his armed services salary of $20,200 a year." To everyone's delight, this misleading version of Hall's demise was carried by *Newsweek* and the print media in Georgia.

That the army had stumbled on Hall because of his high living was a convenient version of the events in Savannah. This was not totally untrue. Foreign Counterintelligence Activity had in fact been tipped, and part of the tip was that a spy was being paid large sums of money. That the FCA tipster had been a double agent who had penetrated the East German State Security Service was no one's business at the time. Our immediate concern was the protection of Canna Clay and his family in East Berlin. If the media was reporting an incomplete version of the truth that served this end, so much the better.

But within a day of the arrests, it became clear that we were not going to be able to keep the details of our investigation a secret. By December 22, industrious reporters began to piece together the story. *Washington Post* wire reporters Ruth Marcus and Molly Moore quoted "a person familiar with the case" as revealing that "investigators conducted closed circuit television surveillance on Mr. Hall's office at Ft. Stewart and saw him putting documents into a case that had a hidden compartment." The lengthy story drew heavily on the detailed affidavit submitted by the FBI to a U.S. district judge in support of its warrant to arrest Huseyin Yildirim. The unclassified affidavit contained a detailed summary of our successful sting of Hall in the Days Inn, to include the fact that we had captured him on videotape selling classified documents. Reading the *Post* story, one could only wonder how long it would be before our friends at the *New York Times* reactivated their deep throat source and learned of Canna Clay's role.

The *Times* was not far behind the competition. In its lead story on the day after the arrests, reporter Michael Wines described Hall's career as a signals intelligence analyst. Quoting unnamed "American officials," Wines advised the *Times*'s readers that "The operation may have seriously damaged American intelligence efforts in Europe in part because Hall held a sensitive Army post in West Berlin, a center for electronic eavesdropping that is directed by the supersecret National Security Agency, based in Ft. Meade, Maryland." Quoting other U.S. officials, reporter Wines observed, "While Hall was in West Berlin and Frankfurt, he was probably in a position to receive valuable information about the types of electronic signals the United States was collecting and how they were analyzed." The impact of Hall's betrayal, Wines opined, was no doubt serious.

Michael Wines and colleague Stephen Engelberg then began to plumb their sources in Washington for the story behind the story of the Hall-Yildirim arrests. At the same time, ABC television news assigned reporter James Bamford, author of a controversial expose of the National Security Agency, to uncover whatever it was about the case that the Department of Defense wasn't telling. The results of these two efforts were significant, albeit completely different in character.

At the *New York Times*, Wines and Engelberg once again established their paper as the premier penetrator of government secrecy. Within a few months, the enterprising pair had successfully pieced together most classified dimensions of the case, to include the role of Canna Clay.

*ABC News*, on the other hand, made the mistake of trusting the impetuous Bamford, with the result that the network's news staff was successfully manipulated by the spacey and unreliable Peggy Bie as she told any lie, however big, in a desperate attempt to obtain Yildirim's freedom.

While the press struggled to uncover the truth behind the Hall investigation, at Fort Meade, James Hall's attorneys began to speak of a possible plea bargain. At FCA, we initially dismissed this as unthinkable. Why would the government bargain when its case was so strong? James Hall was looking good to be the first test of the death penalty.

# 35: Devasting Revelation

On a rainy day in early March 1989, James W. Hall III stood in uniform before a military judge in a Fort McNair courtroom and tearfully pleaded guilty to espionage. His actions, he told Col. Howard C. Eggers in a soft, mournful voice, had left him with "a feeling of betrayal which goes to the bone." Present in the courtroom to plea for mercy for his son was James W. Hall, Jr., a fifty-seven-year-old auto mechanic from Sharon Springs, New York. "What can a father say about his son?" the elder Hall told the judge. "He just loves him. . . . When I first saw him, I felt like I would punch his lights out. I threw my arms around him instead."

As the judge sentenced Hall to forty years in prison, a $50,000 fine, and a dishonorable discharge, teary-eyed Heidi sat silently in the courtroom. Earlier, Heidi told the judge that she had not known that her husband was spying, then tearfully insisted that she loved him in spite of his mistake and would wait for him, regardless of the length of his sentence.

Foreign Counterintelligence Activity investigators present in the courtroom felt truly sorry for the shy German woman. Hall, they knew, had explained the sudden flow of extra money to his naive wife by spinning a tall tale. The Meister, he told Heidi, was a spy for American intelligence. But because the Turk didn't trust the American spooks fully, he insisted on using James as a middleman. To show his gratitude, James told his wife, the Meister, whom she knew as Mike, shared his CIA earnings.

Hall's brief appearance in the Fort McNair courtroom lacked the drama of witnesses and sparring attorneys. Thanks to a surprise pretrial agreement between the defendant and the army prosecutors, there was no need for a protracted court-martial. On the advice of his attorneys, who knew a lost cause when they saw one, the admitted spy made a bargain to avoid the death sentence.

For his part, the disgraced warrant officer promised to cooperate with government experts to assess the damage he had inflicted on his nation's vital signals intelligence capabilities. He would also co-operate fully with FCA agents in a lengthy series of counterintelligence debriefings to document his Soviet and East German contacts. Hall would not exploit his crime in the future by granting interviews or writing a book, and he promised to cooperate with the government in the prosecution of Huseyin Yildirim. All revelations by the convicted spy would be verified by government-administered polygraph examinations.

The agreement contained something for everyone. It assured the FBI and the Department of Justice that Hall would be available to testify in the trial of the Meister; it ensured that the damage inflicted by the disloyal officer to America's signals intelligence effort could be evaluated and kept low profile; and it provided army counterintelligence the opportunity to exhaustively debrief Hall concerning how the Soviets and East Germans had handled him—vital information for future counterintelligence operations. An ancillary benefit of the plea bargain was to eliminate the need for Canna Clay to testify at a drawn-out court-martial.

The army's decision to bargain with Hall made sense, but that didn't make it popular in the corridors of FCA. Even though agents desired to keep Canna Clay's role discreet, there could be little doubt that Horst and Wolfgang had long since discovered the academician's absence and concluded that he was involved. In East Berlin, American sources reported that a swarm of MfS agents had descended on Clay's small bungalow shortly after James Hall's arrest. Authorities had swept up the couple's grown sons and interrogated them about their parents' whereabouts. Those familiar with the East German service had no doubts that an in absentia death sentence would eventually be pronounced on the missing professor.

Certainly the pretrial agreement would make the task of the convicted spy's debriefers easier. By mandating Hall's total cooperation in debriefings, the bargain would enable FCA and National Security Agency specialists to do a better job of assessing how he had spied and what he had given to the Soviets and East Germans.

Nonetheless, when Hall walked out of that Fort McNair courtroom with a sentence that would make him eligible for early release in as few as ten years, more than one FCA agent branded the whole thing a sellout. "He should have been the first one to be executed," some argued bitterly. "How can we stop this kind of thing when the stiff punishments are not meted out?" It was a valid question.

Subsequent discussions with Hall's jubilant defense attorneys were revealing. The army could have won Hall's cooperation by merely agreeing not to press for capital punishment, they confided. After all, the prosecution had an absolutely airtight case against him. James Hall's army-appointed defense attorney bluntly told Bob Thayer and me that he was incredulous when the prosecution agreed to bargain.

The controversial agreement between the government and James Hall had little to do with crime and punishment. Any time counterintelligence agents unmask a traitor who has looted the government of its secrets, the resulting revelations are embarrassing and unwelcome. The quicker the story drops out of the media, the better. Public exorcisms of security lapses caused by sloppy to nonexistent controls are unwelcome by the government. And when the case deals with the hypersensitive subject of signals intelligence, even greater impetus exists for the government to wrap it up as quickly and quietly as possible.

Twice in four months I had briefed the army chief of staff on major espionage arrests. On both occasions, the four star accepted the bad news like a patient who had just been told that his biopsy revealed malignancy.

In the wake of the court-martial, a team of FCA debriefers tackled the challenge of documenting James Hall's treason. For several weeks, they retrieved the convicted spy from his cell at the Fort Meade stockade and conveyed him to a debriefing facility. The task was to completely reconstruct the convicted spy's six-year espionage career, reviewing every contact that Hall had made with the East Germans and Soviets, from his first trip to East Berlin in 1982 until the final meeting with the Meister in a Savannah restaurant a week before his arrest.

The FCA men were not conducting a formal damage assessment (that is, determining with precision which secrets Hall had peddled to the Soviets and East Germans). Because of Hall's signals intelligence specialty, these determinations would be made by debriefers from the National Security Agency.

Hall was generally cooperative as he searched his memory for the details demanded of him. As debriefers pieced together the saga of his six years of betrayal, they reported their preliminary findings to my office. These reports were bleak and made it clear that the self-centered spy was surely one of the most productive agents that the KGB and MfS had ever recruited.

Hall's revelations were devastating—for what they told us about our security and for what he recalled about the materials that he and the Turk had given away to the Soviets and East Germans. As the specifics of Hall's espionage became known within FCA, those who had characterized the plea bargain as a sellout were confirmed in their conviction. Like Clyde Conrad and his confederates, Hall had looted his unit with impunity, all but unhindered by security measures. As for moral compunctions, there were none. At first, he revealed, he had felt he could outmaneuver the Soviets and East Germans by selling them material that was of little value. After all, the Soviets knew what their units in East Germany were doing, didn't they? So what was wrong with selling them information that they already knew? Reminded that each compromise of secrets told the communists much about our signals intelligence capabilities, James hung his head. It had gotten out of control as the Soviets pressed for more sensitive secrets. Eventually, he caved in and gave them everything.

Hall described in detail his operations in West Berlin when assigned to the field station. He had dutifully obeyed his KGB handlers and deposited thick packages of secret and top-secret intelligence documents and war plans in prearranged dead-drop sites in the city. On one occasion, Hall recalled, when a three-inch-thick envelope bulging with stolen secrets would not fit through a one-inch opening in the rear window of a Soviet sedan, he had moved on in frustration, still gripping the envelope. Then he heard a clucking noise to his rear. "A little guy scampered out of the nearby bushes," Hall told his debriefer, "unlocked the car and rolled down the rear window a few more inches. Then he disappeared into his hiding place while I backtracked and dropped the envelope into the car."

But most of Hall's adventures were not funny. On at least two occasions, the convicted spy admitted that the KGB had dispatched a signals intelligence expert from Moscow to debrief him on technical matters that his KGB agent handlers could not grasp. Granted access to a top-secret black program in 1984 of great interest to Moscow, the disloyal sergeant traveled to Vienna in June 1985 and described the project to his Soviet debriefer. Unnamed "government officials" later told reporters Stephen Engelberg and Michael Wines that the program had cost the U.S. government hundreds of millions of dollars to develop. The German magazine *Quick,* which in 1990 recovered documents from the MfS files that had no doubt originated with Hall, identified the project and printed revealing excerpts from the Stasi documents.

*Quick* also provided its readers with a rare glimpse into the inner circles of the East German MfS. Editor Paul Limbach had obtained top-secret Stasi files that showed how the East Germans had handled the material betrayed by James Hall and Huseyin Yildirim. Among the *Quick* documents was a letter from the notorious head of the HVA (the foreign intelligence arm of the East German State Security Service), Markus Wolf, to the deputy chief of the MfS, Lieutenant General Neiber. Written at the time that James Hall and the Meister were handing over the secrets of Field Station Berlin to the East Germans, the Wolf letter and other documents in *Quick*'s possession were Hall's MfS report card.

"By order of the Comrade Minister," Wolf wrote, "I am sending you 13 original documents of the U.S. intelligence services. The material deals with vital information concerning the basic organization of signals intelligence collection by the U.S. intelligence services in peace and in war, about specific plans for the European theater of war, and about the special role of West Berlin in the enemy's electronic warfare." Wolf advised his superiors that a Major General Mannchen, the director of Hauptabteilung III, which focused on enemy signals intelligence units, was personally responsible for evaluating the newly acquired documents and recommending countermeasures that might be taken to frustrate the American electronic snooping.

*Quick* had also obtained Major General Mannchen's evaluation of the windfall documents and published a portion of the first page. Entitled "Initial Estimate and Evaluation of HVA Material from the U.S. Signals Intelligence Arena," Mannchen's document is a revealing commentary on Hall's treason. "The material consists of some of the most important American signals intelligence directives," wrote the East German general. "The material is current and extremely valuable for the further development of our work, with high operational and political value. It deals with directives and working documents of the NSA, the leading organization of the USA for signals intelligence, as well as with plans and analysis of the DIA and the Intelligence & Security Command. The contents, part of which are global in nature, some very detailed, expose basic plans of the enemy for signals intelligence collection into the next decade."

General Mannchen then expressed a major concern. The material was of such a high value that extraordinary measures to protect its source should be taken. "Any sharing of these documents with others who have a signals intelligence mission—for example, with partner services [that is, the Soviets], should only be considered possible if the material is fully restated [disguised] and combined with other sources, with the consent of the HVA." Mannchen was unaware that the MfS star agent was generously sharing everything with the Soviets.

When asked by his debriefers about his motives for giving away such clearly sensitive secrets, Hall was ambivalent. Yes, money was a motive, he admitted, but there was more. Hall lashed out in angry frustration at his military superiors, leading us to conclude that some of his betrayal was done to get even with the chain of command for whatever grievances were on his mind at the moment. Bitter at superiors who he felt were frivolous in their management of him and his colleagues, Hall ridiculed the field station's sponsorship of an ice cream sales booth during the Berlin Command's annual German American Volksfest. "Here we were manning an ice cream booth," he railed, "at a time when we should have been devoting our full attention to tracking the summer training activities of the Soviet forces."

This theme of being smarter and more dedicated than his officers was not unfamiliar to investigators. Clyde Conrad had repeatedly told

Danny Wilson that his officers were either dumb, or self-serving "ticket punchers" inferior to a man of Clyde's intelligence and wit. James Hall and Clyde Conrad were textbook illustrations of KGB doctrine. When recruiting Americans, the KGB taught, ego is second only to money as a motivator.

As Hall unburdened himself to his debriefers, he put a self-serving twist on his decision to sell out his country. Gone was the young sergeant impatient for the toys of life and frustrated with incompetent officers. In his place was a reinvented James Hall, a troubled young soldier in need of counseling for personal problems, ignored by an insensitive chain of command and an army that lacked the mechanisms to recognize and deal with soldiers' problems. His own ambition and greed were not the root causes of his fatal decision, Hall seemed to be saying. The real problem was the army's failure to assist a troubled NCO.

In general, Hall revealed, the army's physical security measures were easily overcome. Spying was all but risk free. While stationed at the 205th MI Battalion in Frankfurt, he stole so many war plans and other secrets that the enterprising Yildirim purchased a Canon PC-25 copier and installed it in an East German–financed apartment near the headquarters. The flat was used strictly as a processing center for stolen secrets, just as Clyde Conrad and Rod Ramsay had done in their Bad Kreuznach rental unit. To explain to fellow soldiers why he rented an apartment in Frankfurt when his wife and children lived in a nearby suburb, Hall said he used the apartment to take a shower after his daily noontime exercise. To those who wondered how a sergeant could afford such a luxury, James had a variety of explanations. Heidi's parents were wealthy; his family had money; he had inherited money from a deceased relative. The inconsistency of his claims was not challenged.

There had been one close call. In 1987 Hall had gone out of town. While absent, he had lent the family Volvo to a fellow NCO. The friend discovered a paper bag bulging with hundred-dollar bills in the car's trunk. "What's with the cash?" the nonplussed NCO asked James.

"Oh," Hall replied, "Heidi's a German and doesn't know how to write checks, so I keep some cash in the car so she'll have it when I'm not around."

No fool, the suspicious sergeant reported the incident to the V Corps special security officer. Hall, he opined, was surely doing something illegal.

A lieutenant received the mission to check on Hall's unusual wealth. After several days of snooping around, including a talk with Hall's company commander and first sergeant, the lieutenant found herself face-to-face with Staff Sergeant Hall.

Hall was polite and cooperative. "My first sergeant says you're asking around about my money," he began. "You see, I inherited it from my grandfather, who was a tire magnate. I'll be glad to provide proof of the inheritance."

Stymied, the lieutenant sought guidance from her superiors. Apprised of the inheritance story, officers decided to drop the matter. Hall was not asked to submit proof of his alleged inheritance, and army counterintelligence was not informed of the matter.

James Hall also admitted that he had passed the V Corps war plan to the East Germans. When we learned this, Bob Thayer and I had the same reaction. Clyde Conrad had passed this plan to the Hungarians, who had shared it with the Soviets. And Zoltan Szabo had sold a copy of it to the Czechs. Surely the top-secret V Corps war plan was the Cold War's worst-kept secret.

Some of Hall's exploits were bold to the point of recklessness. In 1987, James had deployed with his unit to a remote West German training area for the annual Reforger exercise. The largest of the annual NATO exercises, Reforger simulated the NATO response to a Warsaw Pact attack across the inter-German border. The East Germans tasked James Hall to provide a copy of the exercise's classified communications electronic operating instructions (CEOI), which would permit communist signals intelligence collectors to more easily eavesdrop on the weeks-long exercise.

Hall and the Meister cooperated to satisfy the East German requirement. James obtained a copy of the sensitive document and hurriedly met the Turk at a small *gasthaus* near the training area. The resourceful Yildirim copied the document in his room using the Canon PC-25. While James returned the original document to his unit before it was missed, the Meister headed to East Berlin and peddled the copy to the MfS for a healthy profit.

Perhaps the most distressing revelation made by James Hall had to do with the mystery surrounding the killing of Maj. Arthur Nicholson by a Soviet sentry in March 1985. While stationed in West Berlin, Staff Sergeant Hall represented the field station at a periodic meeting of the various American intelligence collectors. The forum was a part of the Berlin Tip-off System, whereby, for example, the human intelligence people might pass on a tidbit from an agent that might assist the signals intelligence effort—or vice versa. Each of Berlin's numerous intelligence collectors sent a representative to these show and-tell sessions, including the field station and the U.S. Military Liaison Mission (USMLM), to which Nicholson belonged.

At one tip-off meeting, Hall told his debriefers, the USMLM analyst had unveiled proof of his unit's most sensitive collection success, proudly displaying a stack of eye-catching, close-up interior photographs of the Soviet T-72 tank, pictures that could have been obtained only by someone actually sitting inside the tank. The USMLM analyst confided that one of his unit's bolder tour officers had indeed penetrated and photographed the interior of a warehoused Soviet T-72 tank near Ludwigslust, on the outskirts of Berlin, virtually under the noses of the Soviets, whose sentries were not manning their posts.

Hall saw gold in the startling photos. To ingratiate himself with his Soviet superiors, he sounded the alarm by passing Moscow a copy of the mission's intelligence report, thereby giving the Soviets the details of the American officer's success, including the time of the American penetration and the exact location of the poorly guarded tank warehouse.

Within a matter of months, USMLM tour officer Nicholson lost his life on a repeat visit to the same tank warehouse in Ludwigslust. In 1985, during my debriefing of Nicholson's driver, the distraught NCO had shaken his head in disbelief. An alert Soviet sentry on a Sunday afternoon who would shoot to kill didn't add up.

It did now.

As Hall confessed his betrayal of the USMLM mission, he hung his head. After Nicholson was killed, he told FCA debriefers, it had occurred to him that he might be responsible, and he had become depressed. Eventually, he added, he managed to put the whole affair out of his mind and continued to pass secrets to the Soviets and East Germans.

Hall had every right to feel depressed. He had tipped off the Soviets in January or February 1985 that their security was weak. The Sunday afternoon shooting had occurred on March 24. His tip to Moscow would most certainly have resulted in the issuance of a stern warning to the Soviet commander at Ludwigslust about his lax security. A Russian commander in such a position could be expected to take strict corrective measures, to include a shoot-to-kill order.

This scenario had crossed James Hall's mind, he admitted, but he had coped with the nagging burden by merely dismissing it from his memory.

But air force intelligence officer Bob Sherry was not about to dismiss the matter so lightly. In 1985, Bob was assigned to West Berlin in an air force technical intelligence unit. Sherry's memory of the meeting in Berlin when the USMLM analyst tabled the highly sensitive tank photographs is vivid. Hall, he recalls bitterly, was present and able to make copies of the sensitive reports.

"I feel that he's the one who nailed Nicholson," Sherry volunteered. "He didn't pull the trigger, but in every other way, he did it."

Sherry's impressions of the young staff sergeant from Field Station Berlin remain clear.

"He was well respected for his professional expertise and people valued his opinion," Sherry admits. "But he was arrogant and cocky—sometimes seeming like he had a chip on his shoulder. The tip-off gathering was a tightly knit circle. Its members were regarded as insiders—members of the team—and saw everything. Hall was a regular, and nothing was discussed about the various intelligence units' sensitive collection operations that he wasn't aware of. Anywhere he wanted to be, he was there. The door was open for him."

In 1989, Bob Sherry told the authorities that he would enthusiastically testify at Hall's court-martial. But as the trial approached, he learned that the evidence against Hall was so overwhelming that his testimony would not be required.

"I never saw him after he was picked up," Sherry recalls, "and maybe that was just as well. But he killed Major Nicholson—that's one conviction I'll take to my grave."

• • •

Foreign Counterintelligence Activity debriefers also reconstructed Hall's earnings from his espionage activities. Based upon Canna Clay's testimony and Hall's own recollections, analysts calculated that from late 1982 to 1988, the Soviets and East Germans paid their star agent at least $300,000—and probably more. Hall himself was unable to attest to his earnings with precision, although he acknowledged receiving some $60,000 from the East Germans in 1988 alone. There were, he admitted, somewhere between thirty and sixty other deliveries of classified documents over the years. He had wallowed in cash, most of which he had frittered away on high living, flying lessons, prostitutes, and expensive toys such as his $18,000 Ford pickup truck. The $30,000 annual retainer from the East Germans alone, supplemented by cash bonuses for production, was telling. To garner that kind of money, the young NCO was delivering the goods, no question about it. This Hall himself conceded to his debriefers. "If I had it and they wanted it," he affirmed, "they got it."

Between 1983 and 1985, James Hall had double-dipped, serving the Soviets and the East Germans. Foreign Counterintelligence Activity debriefers were intrigued by this. Even though the intelligence services of the Warsaw Pact allies cooperated with each other, it was obvious that when they had a particularly good mole in their stable, strict compartmentation made them vulnerable to this kind of opportunism.

In Berlin, while the hyperactive Yildirim was shuttling back and forth through the wall laden with documents for the MfS that James had stolen, James was loading Soviet dead drops in West Berlin—often, he confessed, with the same documents he had just provided to the Turk. Remarkably, the illicit business thrived for more than two years before someone in Moscow picked up on the scam.

The Soviets eventually confronted Hall about his double-dipping during a June 1985 secret trip to Austria. In a Vienna hotel room, after the usual exchange of information for money had taken place, Hall's Soviet handler fixed the twenty-eight-year-old sergeant with a firm stare and confronted him. "Have you been dealing with another organization?" the Russian inquired in a stern voice.

Hall recalls experiencing a sinking feeling as he unconvincingly denied any contacts with another intelligence agency. The Soviet officer firmly rebuked him. Moscow knew the truth about his contacts with the Turk and the East Germans. This was risky and unacceptable, the KGB officer decreed. Yildirim, the KGB officer warned, was an unguided missile whom Hall should avoid. If you want to work for us, the KGB officer decreed, you must sever all ties to the Turk and his East German sponsors.

Hall responded with an appropriate show of contrition. Promising the Soviet officer that he would heed Moscow's advice, he silently vowed to cut all ties with the paranoid Russians. From now on, James would stick with the East Germans and Yildirim. To the cocky young spy, Yildirim's door-to-door service was far preferable to the complex and time-consuming security precautions demanded by the KGB.

As soon as the KGB case officer departed, Hall contacted Yildirim, who had flown to Vienna from Berlin. The two met, and when the Turk headed back to Germany, he was carrying the same information for the East Germans that Hall had just sold to the KGB. This included a highly classified plan for the annual deployment by Central Command forces to Egypt—Exercise Bright Star—and a bundle of top-secret information on ultrasensitive electronic warfare projects.

From the day of the Vienna encounter in mid-1985 until he met Vladimir in Savannah, Hall told FCA debriefers, he had dealt only with East Berlin through the Meister. It was a decision for which he was paying dearly. Had James heeded Moscow's warnings about the uncontrollable Turk and broken contact with the East Germans, he might be a free man today.

# 36: The Meister

To this day, more than eight years after Huseyin Yildirim's conviction for conspiracy to commit espionage, separating myth from reality about the man remains a challenge. Nonetheless, once the Meister's secret life was unmasked by FCA, some aspects of the enigmatic Turk came into focus. Yildirim's coveted Berlin scrapbook, for example, was more than mere evidence of his ego. The glowing letters the clever Turk had solicited from numerous officers whose ailing autos he had restored to health were a spy's stock-in-trade, not unlike the portfolio of an aspiring model. It strutted his unusually good placement and access—credentials that he surely displayed to the East Germans. Not by accident were so many of the letters in the Meister's collection authored by senior officers, many of them intelligence officers, myself included. You had to hand it to the cheerful Turk; he had mastered the art of self-promotion.

One also had to wonder about the facts contained in the 1981 article in the *Berlin Observer,* the command newspaper, which described the Meister as a former officer in the Turkish field artillery before he resettled in Germany and became a trained automotive mechanic. All very impressive, if it were true.

When Yildirim suddenly appeared in James Hall's life in October 1988, the CIA's Gus Hathaway made discreet overseas queries about the mysterious Turk who used the alias Mike Jones and had a penchant for nocturnal meetings at roadside restaurants. Just who was Huseyin Yildirim?

Within days, Hathaway's queries produced results. The Meister, we learned from the Turks, had indeed served in the Turkish army, but not as an officer. A low-ranking enlisted man, Huseyin Yildirim had been disciplined and discharged after he attacked one of his officers during a dispute. Undaunted, the Turk migrated to Beirut and became embroiled in a smuggling racket. Arrested by Lebanese authorities, he was jailed and served time before eventually settling in Germany.

And there was more. In the mid-1980s, Yildirim had apparently approached Turkish intelligence and offered to sell classified NATO documents. Explaining that he was able to obtain them from a well-placed American source, the Turk was obviously trying to maximize profits from his Berlin operations. But Istanbul wasn't buying. Turkish intelligence officers dismissed their countryman as a kook and sent him packing. Turkey was a member of the North Atlantic alliance and had no need to purchase NATO documents from a bad actor such as Yildirim. Whether deliberately or through inefficiency, the Turkish intelligence service made no mention of his offer to its American allies.

Much later, after the fall of the Berlin Wall and the reunification of Germany, Wolfgang Koch, one of the Meister's former East German case officers, told an American journalist that Yildirim had actually volunteered to work for East Berlin in 1978. At the time, the East German officer recalled, the Turk was employed by a German automotive firm near Stuttgart—hardly one of the Stasi's priority intelligence targets. The East Germans told the ambitious volunteer that they were uninterested. He had no placement or access to their targets. Find yourself a job with the Americans in Berlin, the MfS counseled, then come back and see us.

The enterprising Yildirim wasted no time. By 1979, he had parlayed his *Meisterbrief* (master mechanic's license) into the job at the Andrews Barracks auto craft shop. Christened "the Meister" by the fawning Americans, Yildirim looked up the MfS. This time, East German intelligence officers welcomed him aboard—for sound operational reasons. West Berlin's Andrews Barracks was the garrison of Field Station Berlin. Hundreds of the highly trained and underpaid single soldiers of the unit lived in the former barracks of the Hermann Goering Division, all of them with daily access to literally millions of pages of top-secret information at the nearby mountaintop installation. Surrounded by recruitment targets and endowed with personal magnetism and mechanical gifts, Huseyin Yildirim was perfectly placed to troll for disgruntled American soldiers who might betray their country.

Wolfgang Koch (of Horst and Wolfgang fame) recalls that the Meister's initial performance was impressive. Yildirim had a gift for identifying vulnerable targets among the soldiers assigned to the field station. But East German handlers soon developed mixed feelings about their bold and enterprising recruit, although no one could accuse the Turk of not delivering the goods. In 1982, he had escorted former field station soldier Ella Pettway to a secret door in the Berlin Wall located in a remote, wooded part of West Berlin. There, the two were escorted through the wall and taken to a safe house, where the East Germans debriefed Pettway about the field station (the infamous incident that the 766th MI Detachment had investigated and determined to be a nonevent).

Later the same year, Yildirim outdid himself when he conveyed James Hall ("Paul") into the arms of the East Germans. The "Paul" operation, which was to run six years, yielded so many sensitive secrets that former Stasi officers still proudly regard it as one of their most successful penetrations of the Cold War.

The East Germans could also not ignore the fact that the Meister, code-named Blitz, operating from his auto craft shop perch, was aggressively proselytizing other disgruntled field station soldiers, sometimes convincing them to provide classified material for money. Later, Ella Pettway, one of the Meister's recruits, told an ABC reporter that the Turk had selectively sought out disaffected field station soldiers, many of whom were lower ranking African American enlisted men—an allegation that was later borne out. The credibility of the heavy-drinking Pettway was far from perfect, but the woman was well qualified to comment on the Meister's operations. She had lived with Yildirim in 1982, and she herself had once been a disgruntled African American soldier assigned to the field station.

Wolfgang Koch later lamented that the problem with the Meister was that although he was an aggressive agent with perfect placement and access, he was also a loose cannon. "The Turk was uncontrollable," Koch was to remark. "He was driven by greed. If there was money to be made from something, he would pursue it recklessly without thinking of the security implications."

But it was not until 1985 that Yildirim's shenanigans caught up with him. The source of the complaint was Moscow. One former East German case officer remembers the disagreement. Soviet KGB officers assigned as liaison to the East German service approached their colleagues with the news that Hall and Yildirim were engaged in a swindle. Hall was a KGB source, the Russians informed the MfS. The Moscow Center had confirmed that the American sergeant was double-dealing, and Huseyin Yildirim was square in the middle of the caper. Hall's contacts with the reckless Turk would eventually compromise him, KGB officers warned, which would be a serious blow to the cause. East Berlin, the Soviets insisted, must yield operational interest in Hall to the KGB. After all, Moscow's agents had recruited him in the first place.

The East Germans ignored the Soviet warning and continued to meet with Hall. In their view, the young sergeant had voted with his feet in 1985 when he severed contact with the KGB. As long as the secrets he was betraying were sanitized to disguise their source and shared with "the friends," as the East German service called the KGB, Moscow had no complaint.

When Huseyin Yildirim quit his job at the auto craft shop and headed for Florida in 1987, his East German handlers breathed a sigh of relief. The Turk was finally out of their hair. While Yildirim was exploiting the gullible Peggy Bie in Florida, Wolfgang Koch activated "Hagen" to replace the Turk as Paul's contact. Hagen was an English-speaking professor who could travel to the West without attracting undue attention. Hagen was known to FCA as Canna Clay.

Knowing that Hall, too, was stateside bound, and all too familiar with the opportunistic Turk's nature, Koch and his partner, Horst Schmidt, anticipated that the Meister might attempt to reestablish himself as Paul's go-between. The two East Germans cautioned their top agent. Once in the United States, he must "cool off and assess his possibilities." Above all, they warned, he must avoid contact with the impetuous Turk.

Now the Meister had gotten himself nailed by the FBI. Worse yet, James Hall was in the hands of army counterintelligence, and the frightened warrant officer was spilling his guts. Between the damning Days Inn videotape and Hall's agreement to cooperate, Yildirim knew that his situation was desperate.

Once James Hall pleaded guilty and agreed to testify against his former confederate, a reasonable person would have read the handwriting on the wall and made his best deal with federal prosecutors. But Huseyin Yildirim he was not your average, reasonable person. Always figuring the angles, the Turk was convinced that he had cards to play, and play them he did, recklessly and with serious consequences.

Tactic number one adopted by the Meister was to refuse cooperation with his captors. Stonewalling all attempts to induce him to confess, he initially maintained his innocence—and his silence. Like Clyde Conrad, Yildirim surely thought that this approach would entice his East German sponsors to arrange a spy trade that would make him a free man. Because most of us familiar with the case assumed that James Hall and Ella Pettway were not the only soldiers whom the Meister had recruited since 1978, we interpreted Yildirim's stubborn silence as an attempt to send a signal to East Berlin. Depending upon what the Meister had in his head, the East Germans might want to bargain for his freedom in order to preclude him from identifying other East German agents.

Yet one had to wonder. Would the East Germans squander a precious bargaining chip to exchange a Turkish national who had been a serious control problem for his handlers?

If the Meister's silence was a signal to East Berlin to rescue him by a trade arranged by the famous spy broker Wolfgang Vogel, he would wait in vain. By November 1989, when the Berlin Wall came down, Yildirim had been in prison for a little more than a year. Any hopes that he might have entertained that Horst and Wolfgang would come to his rescue evaporated with the scenes of jubilant Germans dancing on the hated wall.

Tactic number two in the Meister's array of defenses was ingenious but hardly original. He was, he insisted, a hero of the Cold War who had been working for the Americans all along. To support this claim, Yildirim unleashed his secret weapon—Peggy Bie. The desperate and calculating woman trumpeted this defense on the Turk's behalf. "Her husband," she told the FBI, the fact-starved media, and the Meister's attorney, "was really a double agent working for American military intelligence in West Berlin." Huseyin, Peggy insisted, was a patriot who was working directly for "the head of military intelligence in Berlin, Colonel Stuart Herrington." As proof, the inventive woman conjured up vivid memories of shadowy meetings in West Berlin, claiming that she had repeatedly witnessed Yildirim rendezvousing with me, during which the Turk would pass information to me in exchange for envelopes full of cash.

During the summer of 1989, as Yildirim's trial date approached, Bie frantically shopped variations of this story to the FBI and anyone who would listen. Her poor, brave Huseyin was an American agent who was being callously hung out to twist in the wind by the U.S. government. Desperate to protect her man, Bie told magnificent but malicious untruths about the Meister's alleged operational and social contacts with me. After learning of her fabrications from amused FBI colleagues in Washington, I was unamused. From then on, I reclassified the loquacious woman. In my lexicon, she had graduated from being merely naive and gullible to being naive, gullible, and a malicious liar who would say anything to get Yildirim out of jail. In the Fort Meade corridors of FCA, good-natured banter about the colonel's Turkish agent was heard.

Then followed one of the most ill-advised and ludicrous acts of self-incrimination in the annals of counterespionage history. Desperately seeking to convince federal agents that he was a true American patriot, Yildirim decided to play his hole card to prove this claim. The spy, Hall, was betraying America, Yildirim explained earnestly. He, Huseyin Yildirim, dedicated defender of democracy, had detected Hall's shameful plot and prevented serious damage to U.S. national security by taking Hall's stolen documents and concealing them in West Berlin. The purloined documents, Yildirim assured federal agents, were in secure hiding places, safe from prying communist eyes. He had stashed them "where even Satan would not have access." To back up his claims, the Turk provided his attorney, Lamar Walter, with detailed directions to the cache sites, apparently convinced that by permitting the government to recover their contents, he would demonstrate the heroic role he had played.

In late April 1989, attorney Walter and Department of Justice prosecutors traveled to West Berlin. Following the Turk's instructions, they recovered two caches of documents, one in a basement storage room and the other concealed in plastic water jugs buried in a cemetery near West Berlin's Innsbrucker Platz. The contents of the Meister's stashes were mind numbing: thousands of secret and top-secret defense secrets—10,000 pages in all—most of which appeared to have originated in Field Station Berlin, James Hall's duty assignment.

Federal prosecutors could hardly believe their good fortune. Yildirim's delusional assessment of his plight may have told him that such documents were exculpatory and proved him a hero, but to the FBI and federal prosecutors, the documents were a legal godsend. It didn't take a high IQ to realize that Yildirim had no doubt used the vaunted Canon PC-25 to produce copies of everything that he had obtained from James Hall and his other GI contacts. Having peddled the sensitive documents to the East Germans (and shopped them to the Turks), the opportunistic Meister had salted away backup copies for a rainy day. Perhaps the Bulgarians might pay for them down the road?

Ultimately, of course, Yildirim's "I was working for Colonel Herrington" tactic, and its companion line, "I protected Hall's stolen documents from the communists," failed to impress federal officials. The more the Turk talked, the deeper he dug himself into a slick-walled hole, at the bottom of which was a life sentence.

In Washington, FCA and FBI agents familiar with the case viewed the Meister and Peggy's amateurish lying with bemusement. Claiming upon arrest to be a secret agent of U.S. intelligence was the most shopworn defense in the *Handbook for Spies*. Shopworn, indeed, but veterans recalled that it had worked for Richard Craig Smith in 1986.

In Tampa, FCA's Gary Pepper was concerned. As the army investigator with the best firsthand knowledge of the complex Conrad case, Pepper was heavily involved with the FBI and the assistant U.S. attorney in the roll-up of the Conrad ring. Pepper and special agent Bob Watson, who was working the Tampa end of the Hall investigation, both reported that Tampa-based FBI agents, unfamiliar with the whole case, were openly expressing their doubts to anyone who would listen over the extent of the FCA director's relationship with the Meister. The FCA men raised the flag of caution. At least some of Peggy Bie's assertions about my ties to Yildirim were being talked about in Tampa as if they had merit. At the time, I dismissed their concerns lightly. Our FBI colleagues in Washington were well aware that I had known Yildirim in Berlin, but they were equally cognizant of the role I had played in his identification and arrest. Surely no one would listen to the spacey woman's emotional prattling.

But I had not reckoned with the media. Apparently ABC television news thought highly of their investigative reporter James Bamford. The persistent reporter had visited Berlin and Tampa, sniffing out whatever he could about the high-profile case. Inevitably, his curiosity led him to Peggy Bie. Peggy, Bamford must have sensed, had a sensational angle.

In the Pentagon, public affairs officers received a query from ABC and contacted me. Would I consent to the release to the network of my photograph and personnel file for its use in an impending story on the Hall case? My answer to this and any other media queries was always the same. I would not talk to the media, nor would I consent to the release of information about me, particularly my photo. Sensing that the ABC request bode ill, I gave this answer to the Pentagon public affairs officer and prepared to depart on a duty trip to the Far East.

In Hawaii, fresh from a seafood feast at the Pearl Harbor officers' club, I received a phone call from Bob Bell at Fort Meade. It was May 31, 1989, the twenty-fifth anniversary of my commissioning.

"Sir, get ready. We just got a tip-off from the Pentagon that ABC is running their story on the Hall case on the evening news, and you aren't going to be pleased with it."

I glanced at my watch. The show would air on the East Coast soon. Bell had no details but offered a pithy, unprintable assessment of reporter Bamford coursing about in Florida trying to make a name for himself. Ironically, I had known Bamford when we were kids growing up in Natick, Massachusetts. We were neighbors at the time, and I remembered him well, even though he obviously did not remember me. By publishing his 1982 book on the National Security Agency, *The Puzzle Palace*, Bamford had done damage to national security, of that I was sure. Sadly, the book had sold well, and in the process, little Jimmy Bamford of Surrey Lane had become a media darling, a self-appointed guru on the intelligence community. That evening, I turned on the television in my hotel room and braced myself for whatever was to come.

Peter Jennings delivered the lead. *ABC News* had learned, Jennings began, that the network of spies uncovered by the Hall-Yildirim arrests "may have done far more damage than originally thought." Correspondent Richard Threlkeld had the story.

Threlkeld quoted "U.S. security officials" as his source. "So far, authorities have found more than ten thousand pages of classified documents Yildirim had hidden away." True.

Then the Meister's former girlfriend, Ella Pettway, spoke. Pettway told ABC's viewers that she had personally accompanied the Meister to his safe-deposit box and seen an envelope containing top-secret material from the Department of the Navy.

Then a photograph of me appeared on the screen. ABC had failed to obtain a picture from the Pentagon, but enterprising reporters had clipped my picture from the flyleaf of a book I had written about the Vietnam War. Threlkeld narrated:

> Since Yildirim's arrest, there's been some friction among the various U.S. agencies investigating this case, and concern among some investigators who point to a possible conflict of interest involving the man who's now heading the Army investigation, Colonel Stuart Herrington. Peggy Bie, another of Yildirim's girlfriends, says the accused spy and Herrington were friends in Berlin.

Then Peggy Bie offered her contribution: "Colonel Herrington, who was the chief of military intelligence there, invited us to a catered Christmas Day dinner, my entire family, my son, my mother, Huseyin, and I."

Threlkeld followed her statement with this comment: "Colonel Herrington did not respond to efforts by *ABC News* to contact him, and U.S. Army spokesmen refused to make any comment on the case."

My parents, at their Florida retirement home, suddenly saw their son's picture flashed on the screen as Threlkeld revealed his scoop. Peggy Bie had used Bamford and his ABC superiors to air her fictitious stories in defense of "her husband" in prime time, at my expense. Not only had I not invited Bie and Yildirim to a catered Christmas party in Berlin, there had never been such a party. Peggy was manufacturing and peddling her statements in desperation, unrestrained by any considerations of truth. ABC, in the finest traditions of television journalism, was buying.

My Pentagon superiors complained to ABC's Pentagon correspondent, but the network stood behind its story. Several weeks
passed. I received a phone call from retired colonel Bill LeGro, whose
son had contacts in ABC. Bill's son had shared lunch with an ABC reporter who announced that his network was about to do yet another
Yildirim-related story. "We've got a colonel named Herrington in our
sights, and he isn't going to like it," the ABC official confided.

This time I complained to the Office of the Army General Counsel. Didn't I have any rights or protection from this kind of defama-
tion? A few weeks prior to the Threlkeld story, I had accepted an
honor from my alma mater, Duquesne University, and delivered the
commencement address. ABC's unfair innuendoes had hurt, I complained to the sympathetic attorney as I recalled the embarrassment
of having to call the dean of the college to assure him that the ABC
story was spurious and untrue.

This time the army reacted. The deputy chief of staff for intelligence, Lt. Gen. Tom Weinstein, summoned ABC's Pentagon correspondent to express his displeasure with the network's aggressive attacks on my reputation. "Stu Herrington was responsible for the
successful investigation," he told ABC, "and the Army has full confidence in him."

ABC agreed to set up a meeting between Weinstein and Bamford
at which the reporter could lay out his case against me. At the meeting, General Weinstein confronted the ABC reporter and challenged him to produce something substantive about me or cease his
unfair attacks and innuendoes. Bamford had nothing, and retreated.
ABC would not be duped again by Peggy Bie, but the network never
retracted its story.

Huseyin Yildirim was deeply depressed. As his July 1989 trial
drew near, the Turk could see disaster approaching with dizzying
speed. All of his efforts to stave off the coming catastrophe had
backfired. His attorney, Lamar Walter, had just delivered terrible
news. Government prosecutors had located Ella Pettway and
planned to fly her to the United States. If both Pettway and Hall
testified, the Meister knew, he was lost, because he had personally
escorted each of them through the Berlin Wall for meetings with
the East Germans.

Aware that Pettway had been an eyewitness and participant in Yildirim's East German operation, prosecutors dispatched two FBI agents to West Berlin to escort her to Savannah. Agents Tom Crossen and Larry Whitaker drew the Pettway mission.

After arriving in Berlin, the two G-men conferred with German police officials. The Germans were only too glad to give the Americans a crack at Pettway. Days earlier, the unpredictable woman had physically attacked German police officers who had been dispatched to locate her.

Crossen and Whitaker were undaunted. They could handle the likes of Ella Pettway. Their orders were clear. They should establish contact with the potential witness and somehow groom her to play a role in the prosecution of the Turk. If possible, they should persuade Pettway to accompany them to Savannah.

Crossen and Whitaker tackled their mission with enthusiasm. Somehow, the pair managed to tame the explosive Pettway, even cajoling her to take them to the remote, wooded area along the Berlin Wall where she admitted that the Meister had ushered her through a door into East Germany in the early 1980s. The smooth-talking FBI men were also able to convince Pettway that an all-expenses-paid trip to the United States to discuss her contacts with Yildirim was a good idea. Pettway, unpredictable but not dumb, signed up for the trip only when promised that she was being interviewed as a witness, not as a suspect. Yildirim had indeed escorted her to a meeting with the East Germans, she admitted warily, but she had told Horst and Wolfgang nothing and refused their overtures to sign her up as a spy.

Crossen's and Whitaker's problems started on the Pan Am flight from Germany to Washington's Dulles Airport. During the eight-hour ride, Pettway astounded the FBI men and flight attendants by drinking no fewer than seventeen cans of German beer without once excusing herself to visit the rest room. It was a new Pan Am record. Over the mid-Atlantic, Pettway, who weighed all of ninety pounds, grinned at her escorts. "If you want to get the Meister to talk," she leered drunkenly, "just give me one hour with him in a hotel room and he'll tell you anything you want to know."

By the time the Pan Am flight arrived in the States, Crossen recalled, agents all but carried the anesthetized Pettway aboard the connecting flight to Savannah.

At midmorning in Savannah, the exhausted Crossen and Whitaker deposited the fiercely hungover woman in a hotel room with instructions to sleep it off. Within two hours, the phone rang at the Savannah FBI office. It was the hotel manager. "Is it okay for her to be putting all of this on room service?" he queried. Pettway, agents learned, had already ordered two bottles of vodka, polished off one, and was embracing the second.

The Pettway caper, prosecutors decided, was a definite no-go. "Even a mediocre defense attorney would have destroyed her," agent Crossen recalled. "You never knew what she'd say, and no one—no one—could keep her sober."

Unaware of the Pettway fiasco, Huseyin Yildirim languished in his cell and imagined the worst. Struggling to come up with a way to save himself, the Turk hit upon an idea. With that, he reached out in desperation, telling Lamar Walter, his attorney, that only Colonel Herrington could deliver him.

Walter contacted me at Fort Meade in June 1989, a month before his client's trial in Savannah, a trial at which I was scheduled to testify for the government. Walter's mission was to bring me a desperate, rambling appeal for assistance from the Meister.

The Meister's attorney and I met in a motel room outside of Fort Meade. Walter was uncomfortable with his mission. His client, he led off, considered himself innocent but was in near despair over his legal plight. Yildirim, the attorney added, always spoke of me with great admiration and respect. Would I read the letter and provide whatever advice I thought appropriate?

The Meister's appeal was three pages long, printed neatly on legal-sized paper. Its fractured English guaranteed that Yildirim had composed the text unassisted.

Savannah, May 89

Dear Colonel Herrington,

Thank you for allowing that my lawyer visit you. Still I like you very much, because of not only your military grade but I believed all the times with my heart, that you are cleanest, real honorable best American I ever knowed. I told this several times to my lawyer and he who has mentioned of your name.

You know that's truth I like American people, fall in love with an American woman and I love America so much. One of my biggest dream—one day I'll married American woman and I'll be able to tell that proudly, "I'm an American." In spite of my present bad situation, I never be ashamed. Because I know and Lord God knows that all the times, even many critical situations, I had protect American interest against my own life and my lovely daughter's life. I was fall in communist TRAP. I hope Mr. Walter will explain to you in details how he get the several thousand pages of classified documents relating to the national defense of the United States. I fought for American interest. I never willingly gived to communist's hand. I hid the documents, a big parts of them buryed in the graveyard in Berlin, that so safety—no devil be able to find them. (I was planning to give them to you or Colonel Shearaton [Sheridan].) Communist side was desparade of this documents. They was very skepticle and in a suspicion that I'm hiding and I'm cheating them. Each page of real classified documents offer me $100—no matter it's original or readable copy. So that time was easy for me make a fortune. My own conscience and my love for America never allowed that.

Many times I decided bring those documents your office in Berlin, put on your desk, and explain the truth to you. But I didn't because one of the main reason, that times I believed our friendship not ripe enough do that, maybe you will badly disappointed me and arrest me immediately. If you check your recollection, I'm sure you will remember that I was trying to gain your friendship, coming close to you, give little cristal desk decoration one dollar melted in plastic. All this purpose to dare myself and explain the situation and give documents to you. It was not easy for me. I believed you are the highest responsible intelligence commander of America in Berlin, even important than general, I believed.

Some of other reasons I was skepticle when I gived document to you against my good willing for America and my self-sacrifice maybe your MI service protect me and my family against communist threatening. One other thing, I don't want to burn son of American James Hall and his family. It was a promise I'll never burn any American. In this circumstances, I'm confused that, what is the correct solution of the problem? I think best way my own country will help me, but I got a bitter answer. When I came to States I thought I'm going to find Hall and stop him a peaseful way and find a fake ID for me. After that, somehow, without danger, [bring] the documents back to America. It was not too easy. Perhaps the problem one number bigger than my size.

You know and many other high rank American officers and entellectual civilians knows that my heart is American more than real American. Many of them write good letters to my boss, I didn't even ask them. So many real good people can't be wrong? One of the good example: The last day in the auto craft shop, just my goodwill, I helped to fixed a person's car. He was in trouble and hopeless. I did a good job for him. He was in work clothes. I didn't know who is he. He was so happy wants to pay me, I refused him. Then he told me write an appriciation letter to my boss. I told him this is my last hours here, I'm leaving forever, it's not necessary to waste your time. I was surprise, he write good letter to my ex-boss and my ex-boss send me by post. He was an MI Lt. Colonel. [The officer, whose name is unimportant, turned out to be the deputy commander of Field Station Berlin.]

It's a pitty if those people read in paper my terrible case maybe some of them will disappoint about me. But I'm sure soon or later the reality will be clearly intelligible and they will not resent and shame to know me. Very perhaps somebody write my life in a spy book. [Here he was correct.] I'll give to the writer every details of mysterious dark shadowed side of my life—will be possible to make a film, too. That will happen, I'm sure. Then, maybe people sorry for a misfortune about me. Maybe too late for me and friends. Even Jesus didn't do any bad things but crucify. God help only eternal life. I'm asking you— why not only one government for the planet Earth before two thousand years.

Dear Honoured Colonel,

I swear of God, that willingly and my best ability I did not any bad thing for America. On the contrary, I protect American interest. I'm not able to explain that to Jury and Judge. I'm feeling with all my heart I'm innocent. I hope my lawyer will explain to you, in details. I'm in a nightmare, a stranger. Completely helpless, alone, very depressed. If you still didn't disappointed about me (Hope not have a prejudgement), please advise to my lawyer that in a legal way to help me. I believe you are a person who knows me very well. I couldn't able to do any bad things for America. You are the very wise man that I know it. You are a person able to give advice President of the country in fact. You are a person that see the war, understand the humanity. Thanks in advance. God bless you. H. Yildirim.

The handwritten appeal signaled that the Meister was his old, manipulative self. Walter shot me an embarrassed grin when I finished reading the letter. "This is what I'm dealing with every day," he confided, "so any advice you have for him is welcome."

I reminded the frustrated attorney that his client and Peggy Bie had defamed me by their malicious fabrications about our relationship in Berlin, yet now the Meister was asking for my help—and piling insult upon injury by salting his appeal with lies. Clearly he had learned nothing from his demise. Nonetheless, I would try to assist.

"Tell the Meister that I was pleased to hear from him," I instructed Walter. "But tell him that if he really wants to get out of the dilemma he is in, he must stop the lying and manipulating and tell the FBI the unedited, true story of his espionage—to include the identities of soldiers other than James Hall whom he recruited. Tell him that I can do nothing for him—nor can anyone—if he continues to lie. As far as I can tell, he is on the road to a life sentence, so he would be smart to make a deal. He's a very astute fellow when he wants to be, so he'll know what I'm talking about. If he's not willing to do this, he's a dead duck. Tell him if he really looks up to me as he says, he'll take my advice."

The Georgia lawyer, a former assistant U.S. attorney, was not optimistic that the Meister was ready for such candor. The Turk had
probably lied to Peggy Bie about most of his activities; this fact alone
would keep him from telling the truth. If he lost Peggy's support, he
had nothing, even though we all knew that the spacey widow was not
doing him any good. Yildirim, we agreed, seemed to have an un-
erring instinct for doing things that were harmful to his case. (Earlier in the spring, while awaiting trial, the Meister had made the mistake of plotting a jailbreak, only to be betrayed by a jailhouse snitch.
As clever as Yildirim was in many ways, his conduct after apprehension was simply dumb. There was no other word for it.)

Huseyin Yildirim finally had his day in court in July 1989. Predictably, he took no one's advice and insisted to the end that he was
innocent, a patriot who had tried to protect his adopted country
from the despicable traitor James Hall. Defense attorney Lamar Walter's job was a mission impossible. If he put Yildirim on the stand,
government prosecutors would maul him. And there was no single
credible witness who could speak for the Turk's transparent fiction
that he was an American double agent.

The Meister's harem haunted the corridors outside the courtroom, but Walter knew that it would be catastrophic to put the unstable Peggy Bie or the alcoholic Ella Pettway on the stand. In the
opinion of many, both women had been witting of the Meister's espionage and assisted him, protected only by the fact that they were
so unstable and mentally incompetent that no self-respecting judge
would have presided over their prosecution for longer than a day before throwing out all charges.

Huseyin Yildirim's stellar espionage career thus ended on a flat
note. The defense was defenseless. A parade of government witnesses
trotted out an overwhelming array of evidence and laid it at the feet
of judge and jury.

Denied the opportunity to argue the Meister's case to the judge,
Peggy Bie and Ella Pettway stood by their man. The strange pair
granted interviews to news-hungry reporters, including representatives of the *New York Times,* and emotionally insisted that the poor
Turk was innocent. Bie and Pettway told *Times* reporter Stephen En-

gelberg that they had seen Yildirim refuse to pass classified documents to the East Germans and actually destroy sensitive documents to keep them from falling into communist hands. Ella Pettway told Engelberg that she had personally witnessed the Meister carrying a briefcase containing classified documents that described an American system for bugging telephones in the East Bloc. Rather than betray the information to the communists, the patriotic Yildirim had given the briefcase to her and she had tossed it into a canal. Peggy Bie collared reporter Engelberg: Poor Huseyin had been pinched between the Americans and the East Germans. Her brave, patriotic Turk had told her in near despair, "They're kicking me back and forth like a rubber ball, back and forth."

The women also introduced a new theme. The Colonel Herrington story had apparently become passé. Now the pair insisted that they had witnessed the heroic Huseyin turning over documents to an unnamed American intelligence officer, who doctored them to remove damaging information and gave his blessing for their passage to the East Germans. But alas, Bie and Pettway lamented, the American officer was now deceased.

On July 20, 1989, a Georgia jury convicted Huseyin Yildirim of conspiracy to commit espionage. In the courtroom sat Peggy Bie, who promptly condemned the verdict to the waiting press as the grim-faced Meister was led off in handcuffs. The distraught and flighty woman was furious. The true story, she told reporters, has yet to be told. "This is a big cover-up and lynching."

In September 1989, Judge B. Avant Edenfield presided over the sentencing of Huseyin Yildirim. The Turk, who had not testified during his July trial, told Edenfield that he was an innocent man, a double agent working for the United States. "I am not a spy," the Meister insisted. "I am just dropped in a trap. I am not guilty. I know I work for America, but today nobody believes me."

Prosecutor Fred Kramer labeled Yildirim's claim "ridiculous" and "the standard drivel you expect in an espionage case, the old double agent story."

The Meister's defense attorney did the best he could, calling the court's attention to the fact that James Hall had already been sentenced to forty years' imprisonment. His client, Lamar Walter told Judge Edenfield, was the courier. Surely the courier should not receive a stiffer sentence than Hall, who was the real spy.

Judge Edenfield was unimpressed. "I didn't sentence Hall," he told Walter, in a tone dripping with contempt. "The only proper sentence for Hall would have been death and a firing squad. Hall did not get justice and was the greater traitor, but someone else did that."

Standing in the lobby of Savannah's graceful courthouse awaiting the final act of the Meister's sentencing hearing, I chatted amiably with Lamar Walter. Peggy Bie's name came up, and I chided Walter about the strange woman. "She did more harm to the Meister than good," I observed. "The woman is a complete space cadet."

Walter chuckled. "Here comes your old friend Peggy now."

I glanced toward the security checkpoint at the main doors. Sure enough, Peggy Bie had just been searched and was striding toward us. I grinned at Lamar. "She says she saw me repeatedly with Meister, that I was at her apartment, and that she came to a Christmas party at my home, right? If that's true, she should recognize me, shouldn't she?"

The attorney nodded.

"Watch what happens," I suggested, certain that the woman would never remember my face from the single, brief visit she had made to our home in Berlin five years earlier.

Peggy joined us for a cup of coffee in the courthouse snack bar. The Meister's secret weapon was subdued and polite. She had no idea she was sitting with the Great Satan who was leaving "her husband" twisting in the wind. Attorney Walter shot me a knowing glance.

After I departed, Walter told Peggy that she had just had a cup of coffee with Colonel Herrington. Within minutes, as I sat in the courtroom awaiting the formal sentencing, the distressed woman sought out a seat on my immediate right and fixed me with a withering glance. I had tried to get Bob Thayer to occupy that empty seat, but he seemed to think I deserved better company. I heard him snickering at my discomfort from his seat directly behind me.

The Meister entered the room. When he passed Peggy's aisle seat, she reached out to him with a moonstruck look. As Judge Edenfield read the sentence—life in prison—Peggy said aloud, "No, no," then elbowed me in the ribs and growled in an audible voice, "You can stop this."

I smiled benevolently, determined not to say a word that rhymes-with-witch who I knew had done her best to destroy me to keep the Turk out of jail. As we left the courtroom, Bob Thayer ineffectively attempted to contain his mirth.

Federal authorities remanded the Meister to the custody of the Bureau of Prisons. Soon the talented spy and auto mechanic was a resident of a federal penitentiary in Tennessee, still silent about how many other Americans he had recruited in West Berlin. National Security Agency (NSA) and FBI investigators beat a well-worn path to his door in their quest to uncover details of his Berlin operations, but the Meister continued to dissemble and lie.

Throughout 1989 and 1990, the persistent Peggy continued to haunt the FBI with her shopworn array of bizarre fictions centering around Yildirim's activities on behalf of the unnamed American intelligence officer who had doctored documents (and was now deceased) and the coldhearted Colonel Herrington. From his prison cell, Yildirim railed out at the injustice of his plight, telling the authorities in an impassioned letter that he was a former employee of the U.S. intelligence community who had once been their star agent and was now an innocent victim of U.S. injustice.

In 1992, the sixty-three-year-old Turk was apprehended during his second unsuccessful escape attempt, this time from the Brushy Mountain Federal Penitentiary. A pair of bolt cutters that the resourceful mechanic had fabricated failed just as he was about to clear the prison's perimeter. The Bureau of Prisons promptly transferred him to the more secure Lompoc Federal Penitentiary in California, from which he continued to tantalize federal agents with phone calls and letters laden with hints that he possessed information vital to U.S. security.

In mid-1992, when I relinquished command of the Foreign Counterintelligence Activity after four and a half years at the helm, I never expected to hear from the Meister again. But then, I had thought the same thing when I left Berlin in 1986.

# 37: Keeping a Promise

The U.S. government kept faith with Canna Clay. The East German professor had risked his life by betraying the East German communists and ending the espionage careers of James Hall and Huseyin Yildirim. Given the adventures that agents had experienced in the four months since Canna Clay's Berlin phone call, arranging a new life for the couple and their beloved boxer dog hardly seemed daunting. Yet even this mission was to take a strange turn.

The couple desired to resettle in West Germany to be as close as possible to their sons in East Germany. This required coordination with our friends in the German security service. After that, the task was routine: Make travel arrangements, escort Clay and his family on the transatlantic flight, and assist them in arranging for temporary housing in Germany. Special agent Nick Pokrovsky drew the mission. In the brief time since the couple had joined us at Fort Meade, Pokrovsky had developed a warm relationship with them. Even the ever-alert King had ceased to growl at Nick.

Weighing in once again with an important assist in the relocation operation was Dr. Peter Frisch, the vice president of the German Federal Office for the Protection of the Constitution (BfV). Canna Clay and his wife had no legal papers, and Clay himself had been an agent of the East German State Security Service. The Federal Republic of Germany was a sovereign ally. If we wished to resettle the East German professor in their country, permission would have to be sought.

I traveled to Cologne in the spring of 1989. Fatal events were about to rock East Germany, but no one sensed this at the time. During a brief meeting to request assistance, I acquainted Dr. Frisch and his staff with the magnitude of the Hall betrayal and the importance of Canna Clay's contribution in putting the warrant officer and his Turkish courier behind bars.

I extended an invitation to our German partners: A team of BfV agents could visit FCA's Fort Meade headquarters at our expense and meet Canna Clay. Our goal was to resettle the homesick couple in

West Germany as soon as possible. At the conclusion of my secret briefing, I requested that Dr. Frisch's organization provide support with German government authorities to press for a reunification of the Clays with their trapped sons. This would require a negotiated deal with the East German government.

Dr. Frisch was supportive. He understood how sensitive the case was and pledged to send two of the BfV's most seasoned East German experts to Fort Meade. Before the West Germans would welcome an admitted agent of the Stasi into their country, he would have to be debriefed in detail about his former East German State Security Service ties. The BfV leader was not optimistic about the chances of reuniting the family. It was unlikely that the government in East Berlin would be in a charitable mood. The BfV would attempt to assist, but Dr. Frisch could make no promises.

Within a few weeks, Dr. Rudi Servos and Herr Klaus Kuron arrived at Fort Meade. In my office, I briefed Dr. Frisch's two trusted experts on the Hall case, with an emphasis on the role played by Canna Clay. For the next two days, Servos and Kuron met with Clay and picked his brain about his contacts with Horst Schmidt and Wolfgang Koch in East Berlin.

It was not a pleasant two days for Clay. After his first meeting with the two West Germans, the hero of the James Hall case told Nick Pokrovsky that he didn't trust the pair. The visitors were likewise skeptical about our star source. Neither Kuron nor Servos felt that the East German was being totally open with them (which he surely wasn't, given his instinctive mistrust of the West German visitors).

"It's the German question—the Cold War," I told Bob Bell. "No East German is going to trust two West German spooks—and vice versa." The most important thing was that the mission had been accomplished. The Germans were ready to receive Canna Clay and his wife and would do their best to assist him in resettlement and the emotional challenge of family reunification. On Servos's and Kuron's last evening in Maryland, we served cocktails at my Fort Meade quarters in their honor, a lively affair attended by army, FBI, and CIA officials.

Canna Clay, his wife, and King, escorted by Nick Pokrovsky, boarded a Pan Am flight for Germany in early 1989. King had prospered on American dog food. Consigning the barrel-chested boxer to a cage in the belly of the aircraft was traumatic but necessary. Pokrovsky comforted the couple. The flight would last but eight hours.

Soon the trio was settled in Bonn, on the banks of the Rhine River. I visited them in their modern apartment, which Canna Clay had already begun to stock with his obsession—books about politics. King continued to rule the roost in the Clay family, but the fearsome-looking beast had long since decided to accept me. Both husband and wife were homesick and ill at ease in fast-paced West Germany. As cracks in the Soviet Union's Eastern European empire began to show, they yearned for a miracle that would somehow reunite them with their sons.

Later that year, a miracle happened. In November 1989, the couple joined all Germans in the heady optimism that accompanied the unexpected collapse of the hated Berlin Wall. With the wall gone, and communist East Germany on its way to becoming an ugly memory of the Cold War, Canna Clay, his wife, and King returned to their beloved Berlin and reclaimed their family home.

Shortly after the dramatic scenes of the wall's dismantling, enraged and angry citizens of East Germany broke into the headquarters of the hated MfS on the Normannenstrasse, plundering its files and scattering millions of pages of formerly secret documents on the floors of the massive building. Former Stasi officers now write their memoirs of the period. The interested student of Cold War espionage may read their version of the careers of Canna Clay, the Meister, and James Hall, known to Stasi veterans in Berlin as Hagen, Blitz, and Paul.

But the joy in West Germany at the collapse of East Germany was not unanimous. Thousands of East German agents in the country had bet on the wrong horse. Most were low-level sources, but some occupied influential and sensitive positions in the government. Such persons now faced difficult choices: Flee to Moscow—about the only safe haven left—or face exposure and prison sentences.

One of the moles who had worked eight years for Markus Wolf's Stasi was Klaus Kuron. Six months earlier, Kuron had been considered by his BfV superiors to be one of their premier experts on the

East German intelligence service, so trusted and respected that they dispatched him to Fort Meade to debrief Canna Clay.

Kuron was petrified. The veteran counterintelligence officer knew that he could never withstand the detailed analysis of confiscated MfS files that would surely be done by his service. In desperation, he traveled to East Berlin for a meeting with the Soviet KGB, his only remaining hope.

The KGB's Karlshorst headquarters was not a fun place in the spring of 1990. Its occupants, once the Soviet Union's most privileged class, watched in dismay as Mikhail Gorbachev—whom many were certain was a CIA agent—presided over the evaporation of their Eastern European empire. Some no doubt sensed that the events were a precursor to the dissolution of Soviet power in the homeland. The grim mood and humorless Russian *chekists* sulking around the KGB's Karlshorst offices overwhelmed and discouraged Kuron. The KGB would take care of him, Kuron realized, but it would be no life. Better a temporary German jail cell than permanent exile in the Soviet Union, the distraught and depressed Kuron told his wife. With that, the disloyal agent surrendered to his shocked colleagues in the BfV.

Klaus Kuron confessed that he had been an East German agent since 1981. Like James Hall, Kuron felt that he was underappreciated and underpaid. And like Hall, his solution to this frustration had been to volunteer his services as a spy for the other side. In Kuron's case, he volunteered his services to the MfS by dropping a letter into the mailbox of the East German permanent representative in Bonn. Kuron, the resulting investigation determined, had been paid 730,000 deutsche marks by the East Germans (more than $375,000). Like James Hall, the disaffected officer performed his agent duties well—so well, in fact, that the East Germans awarded him the Silver Struggle Medal, as they had done with James Hall in 1988.

The disgraced Kuron was sentenced to a heavy fine and twelve years in prison.

The news of Klaus Kuron's arrest raced through the corridors of FCA's Fort Meade headquarters. The initial reaction was astonishment, but astonishment soon gave way to savvy head shaking. During the Conrad and Hall cases, we had avoided premature revelations to our German allies, always invoking the security risks that stemmed from a divided Germany. Kuron's arrest was vindication for that position.

We soon determined that the Kuron affair had been a near miss in the Hall case. In December 1988, hours before Canna Clay was due to depart East Berlin, Norman Runk performed a delicate mission. "Visit the BfV," I had instructed Norman, "and inform them that we are bringing out an East German who will transit West Berlin on his way to the United States." Technically, we had no obligation to make this notification; West Berlin was run by the four allies. But the Runk mission was more than mere courtesy. Eventually, we would require the assistance of our German colleagues. Better to heed BfV officer Werner Goll's admonition during the Conrad case. Trust among allies was important.

In Cologne, the BfV official whom Runk was scheduled to visit was detained by other business. Runk briefed the officer's deputy. The absent official was Klaus Kuron.

At Fort Meade, FCA personnel who had dealt with Canna Clay shook their heads. We could picture Clay strolling along the banks of the Rhine River, clucking his tongue and recalling his distrust of Kuron during the Fort Meade debriefings. Within FCA headquarters, there was some good-natured banter about the colonel's choice of social contacts. In Berlin, it was the Meister, hobnobbing in the boss's quarters. At Fort Meade, it was a cocktail party for Klaus Kuron. For a counterintelligence officer, my social choices were abysmal.

# 38: The Meister—One More Time

Five years passed. Occasionally I would hear from colleagues in FCA or NSA that the Meister, still unreconstructed, was once again yanking the chains of federal agents about his diligent efforts as a secret agent in the service of Uncle Sam. At one point, referring to the stash of classified documents that he had turned over to federal authorities, the Meister told authorities that the East Germans would have paid him a hundred dollars a page for the documents, but still he refused to betray America. "Despite all these happenings," Yildirim insisted passionately, "even today and at this very moment, if I had this possibility, I would not have passed those documents to the enemy for gaining financial benefits. My character coupled with my true Turkish blood running in my veins would not have permitted me to commit such a thing."

In 1994, after one final mission to the former Soviet Union in search of information on the fate of American personnel missing in action, I joined the faculty of the Army War College in Carlisle, Pennsylvania. If I could no longer be an operational intelligence officer, I preferred teaching.

In late October 1995, the Meister reentered my life for the third time. This time, the mischievous Turk was represented by the voice of a California attorney calling from Santa Barbara. My photograph had recently appeared in the *Los Angeles Times* as I presented long-overdue medals to the family of a missing aviator. The attorney, Jamie Nichols, had seen the story.

"I've been searching for you for months," Nichols explained. "I represent Huseyin Yildirim, who is in prison here in California, and he needs your assistance."

Yildirim, the Santa Barbara attorney explained, was now a sixty-eight-year-old "pathetic victim of the Cold War." Nichols was representing the Turk pro bono in an attempt to obtain his freedom. All Huseyin wants, the attorney advised, is to work for the U.S. intelligence community or to return to his family in Germany and live out his years.

Nichols explained his client's status. The hapless Meister was an inmate in Lompoc penitentiary, a rough place for such a poor old fellow. Tragically, Huseyin had recently been attacked by a Cuban prisoner. Allegedly, when the Meister refused to turn over his cup of coffee on demand, the Cuban had jammed a prison shiv into his throat, almost killing him. "Peggy Bie thinks it was a hit to shut him up," said Nichols, "but I don't think that's the case. The main issue is that his situation is tragic, and he needs help, Colonel Herrington. Hall may soon be paroled, and it just isn't fair for poor Huseyin to languish in prison while Hall goes free."

It flashed across my mind that the irrepressible Turk had again worked his magic. James Hall was not on the verge of parole, and it appeared that the Meister had found a live one and cranked up his throttle to full manipulation.

Nichols continued. The Meister had assured him that James Hall was the real spy and that he, Huseyin Yildirim, had actually worked for the U.S. government. When arrested by the FBI, the Turk swore to Nichols, he was completely out of the game and inactive. His trial had been unfair, Nichols opined, although he realized that there was no hope for a new trial. Only clemency by the president of the United States could free Huseyin Yildirim.

As one who had himself been snookered by the Meister's disingenuous good nature, I empathized with the well-intentioned attorney. "What does Huseyin want of me?" I asked.

Nichols explained that he had been in touch with the pardon attorney's office in the Department of Justice. If I would support a petition requesting clemency for Huseyin Yildirim, it would raise his chances of success.

Jamie Nichols was a decent man who had fallen for the Meister's affable nature, personal magnetism, and a barrage of artful lies. In California, Nichols was known as an uncompromising defender of the underdog, a pure idealist who generously donated his talents in the name of worthy causes. When the K-Mart Corporation decided to erect a store on a former native American burial ground, Jamie Nichols had single-handedly fought the giant firm to a standstill. When the store was finally built, K-Mart had included in the parking lot a memorial park to the land's first owners.

It took me ten minutes to burst Nichols's bubble. "The Meister was an active agent when arrested," I explained. "He had volunteered to the East Germans and provided his services to them for almost nine years. When the FBI arrested him, he was actively working on behalf of the East Germans. Once caught, he did his best to pin the blame on me—using Peggy Bie as his tool. He's lying and using you now," I warned, "and clearly hasn't changed his ways."

Then an inspiration. Could the Meister's near-death experience and thirst for freedom be exploited? It was worth a try.

"Tell the Meister that I send him my greetings and wishes for a speedy recovery. Tell him also that I would be willing to consider supporting him only if he provides me a detailed written account of his life as a spy—holding nothing back. Tell him we have talked to Horst and Wolfgang and seen his East German file [a white lie], so if he lies or holds back, I'll know it. If he does this for me, I'll be open minded about possible assistance to his clemency request."

Nichols agreed that this was a fair offer and promised to relay it faithfully. Then the disillusioned attorney vented his chagrin at having been the victim of the Turk's lies. I wondered how he would confront the Meister.

I didn't have long to wait. Within a week, Jamie Nichols sent me a long letter.

I confronted Huseyin last Thursday with the truth about himself, his case and his future. It was not a pleasant task, to say the least. However, for the first time in my numerous discussions with him this last year, I finally sense he is willing to "come clean," even if that means he must admit to a lifetime of lying (or at least as long as he has been in the spy business, since dishonesty seems to be one of the necessary qualifications for that profession). He seems also willing to admit to exceedingly bad judgment in his prior dealings with you, the FBI, and other U.S. authorities, and to deception in his relationship with Peggy.

The Meister would write an account of his espionage career for me, Nichols advised. It would be useful, he added, if I would inform him if his client's literary effort failed to pass the sincerity test. "If Huseyin is still playing games with me or showing disregard for the truth," Nichols explained, "I do not intend to help him further."

I waited for the Turk's reply. With luck, he might just tell me things that he had hidden from our FBI and NSA colleagues. In such a case, I would pass the information to investigators.

In mid-November 1995, I received the Meister's response to my request in the form of a neatly printed letter. I could tell from its brevity that Huseyin Yildirim had not followed instructions. A full description of his espionage career would have filled at least a hundred pages. The Meister's letter was written in uncharacteristically smooth English prose, probably thanks to the good-hearted Jamie Nichols.

Lompoc, November 12, 1995

Dear Colonel Herrington,

I would like to begin by apologizing for any embarrasment or inconvenience that you may have had to endure because of the nature of my past actions.

In 1988 a few days before Christmas, in Tampa, FL, I was arrested in a country foreign to me. Without any one to help me, I felt totally isolated and desperate. After I was transferred to Savannah, GA, I was questioned by the FBI and the prosecutor for five straight days. They tricked me with misleading questions and deceptive promises which were tainted with false hopes. It was a very difficult time to say the least. I became very depressed and was overwhelmed with a feeling of total hopelessness. I reached a point I couldn't think clearly or logically anymore. I realized, too late, that my court-appointed attorney, a Mr. Walter, handed me over to the FBI and prosecutor to question me without any written agreement on my behalf. He also turned over to the government the 10,000 pages classified documents that I had buried in a graveyard in Berlin, with no benefit to me any kind. Obviously his defense was aimed at helping the prosecutor. The information the government gleaned from me had thus caused not only my self-incrimination but was also used against me in court.

Regretfully at this time, because of the constant pressure, your name was mentioned. The facts were misrepresented and insinuations were wrongfully made. I'm sorry if there was any semblance that you might have had anything to do with or any knowledge of my operative conduct; nothing could be further from the truth. I can't imagine the tremendous degree of frustration and embarrassment all my friends must have felt, at the time of my arrest. I can only ask both them and the eternal God for forgiveness.

Today the Cold War is history, Germany is unified, the Soviet Union is no longer. All of the Cold War antagonists have released the spies. I am a relic of the past.

Mr. Herrington, I'm 68 years old. The seven years behind bars has been extremely physically and emotionally distressful! To keep me incarcerated for the rest of my life serves no national interest in this changed world. I would hope that America would be more virtuous than vengeful.

I would like to thank you for accepting the phone call from my attorney Mr. Nichols. Perhaps you know from talking with him I had reiterated demonstratively that you never had any knowledge or any involvement whatsoever in my activities. And finally, I would like to put to rest any possible questions about my forthrightness by stating categorically that I have given all information of people and places in my life to the FBI, and also have given the 4 locations to where I hid the classified documents of which were in my possession. I have nothing left to hide.

Please if in the future my attorney Mr. Nichols should have any misunderstandings or questions in my case I would greatly appreciate it if he were allowed to contact you to clarify any of these.

Thank you and God bless you.
Huseyin Yildirim (Meister)

PS: Please excuse my bad English

I contacted Jamie Nichols and told him that the Turk had failed the final exam. I had not sought the Meister's apology. I wanted the truth about his espionage career. Further dealings were a waste of time.

My uncompromising reaction to the Meister's plight was based on the certitude that the Turk recruited many more agents than James Hall in the course of his nine years of service to the East Germans. Short of an unlikely offer of cooperation from Horst Schmidt or Wolfgang Koch, the only way to bring down the curtain on the Meister's entire organization was the stubborn Turk's unbridled cooperation, which he had withheld since his arrest. Why the Turk continues to toy with federal investigators is difficult to fathom. Perhaps he doesn't trust the authorities, who, after all, dug up his caches of documents and used them against him. Or perhaps he is motivated by honor, not wishing to condemn others to suffer as he is. Only the Meister knows.

Attorney Jamie Nichols continued his campaign to obtain mercy for the man he continues to regard as "the last prisoner of war of the Cold War." I would like to have him on my side if I were in trouble.

In 1996, *Los Angeles Times* senior writer Paul Dean visited Huseyin Yildirim in Lompoc penitentiary. Aware of Jamie Nichols's efforts on behalf of the Meister, and an admirer of Nichols's determined and generous spirit, Dean had decided to do a story on the Turk's campaign to obtain his freedom. A former pilot in the Royal Air Force, Dean has been a professional journalist for thirty-five years, during which time he has earned a reputation for fairness and objectivity. If the Meister was an unfortunate victim who had been railroaded by the criminal justice system, as Jamie Nichols contended, Dean would not hesitate to expose the government's excesses.

As the pair began to converse, the Meister was humble and repentant. "I was spy, yes," he told Dean, "but that time was war. . . . I am heavily punished. I want to forget all past. I would like to apologize to the American people."

Dean probed skillfully, enticing Yildirim into a dialogue about his espionage. As the Meister reminisced about his career as an agent of the East German intelligence service, Dean noted that he became animated and engaged. More than a faint note of pride crept into his voice.

He had trolled through the ranks of "intelligence teletypists, cryptographers, analysts, officers, and enlisted men," the Meister told Dean. Most did not respond positively to his overtures, which included gifts, free auto parts, and requests to provide information "for a rich relative in Turkish Consulate." But some, Yildirim admitted, at least six, swallowed the hook. "Their weakness is money," the Meister recalled as he warmed up to the subject. "I tell them: Join the moneymakers, your salary is no good, so get the money." Sometimes the first payment would be a thousand dollars, the Meister told Dean, "big money for a little soldier . . . next, two, three thousand dollars cash and is a big surprise."

To prepare for the prison interview, writer Dean had located and interviewed retired FBI special agent Barry Colvert. In 1989, Colvert had administered several polygraph examinations to the Turk. The FBI agent recalled the encounters. "I told him: 'There were other players involved in this with you.' And he said, 'Absolutely not.' I said: 'What if I tell you about a couple of players who have already told me about their involvement with you?' And he said, 'Oh, oh.'"

The two discussed several other suspects known to have provided classified documents to the Turk. Colvert then conducted a retest. "I asked: 'Now, other than these players that I've told you about, is there anybody else?' He said: 'Absolutely not.'"

The polygraph needles jumped. Yildirim was still holding out. To this day, he has never passed a polygraph examination.

Paul Dean's *Los Angeles Times* feature, "The Waiting Game," was not sympathetic to the cause of clemency. The Meister still sits in Lompoc penitentiary while Jamie Nichols continues to champion his cause. In 1996, Nichols filed a formal pardon request and wrote a letter to President Bill Clinton requesting clemency for Huseyin Yildirim.

I have not heard from the Meister since 1995, but I still watch the mail.

# Part IV
## Rolling Up
## the Conrad Ring

# 39: German Justice

Clyde Conrad sulked in prison for seventeen months before his trial convened. Each time Manfred Rutkowski's investigators attempted to interview him, he defiantly declared himself innocent and refused all cooperation. It was a grievous error. Perhaps the imprisoned spy thought that his grateful communist masters would exchange him if he remained silent—a custom not uncommon during the Cold War—but the Cold War was all but over and such stonewalling was self-defeating. Under the German justice system, the key to a lenient sentence was admission of guilt and remorse. Conrad did not understand this. Unwisely, he retained a pedantic Bonn law professor with little trial experience to defend him. Like his client, the defense attorney seemed not to grasp the importance of remorse in determining an offender's fate.

Conrad thus played into the hands of his accusers, whose case was so strong that the defendant's cooperation would have been almost unwelcome, serving only to make it more difficult to mete out a harsh sentence. During many months between his arrest and trial, BKA investigators lined up the testimony of the defendant's closest collaborators for use against him.

The BKA's first major break was the unexpected surrender of Zoltan Szabo. After seeking sanctuary in Hungary in 1988, Szabo had earned his keep by translating documents for the Hungarian intelligence service. In the spring of 1989, weary of life in communist Hungary, Szabo proposed a deal to the Austrian government. He would turn himself in and cooperate with Dr. Schulz's investigators if Vienna would guarantee that he would not be turned over to the Germans or the Americans, and if the Austrians would permit him and Ilona to reside in Austria. Szabo's goal was to "clean his slate." He wanted no more of the life of a secret agent.

The Austrians consented. On May 21, 1989, nine months after Conrad's arrest, Zoltan Szabo surrendered to Austrian authorities, who charged him with the conduct of illegal military intelligence activities, for which he could be sentenced to serve up to two years in prison. Cooperation with Austrian authorities could minimize his sentence. Szabo, whose loyalty to Conrad was about as firm as his loyalty to the United States, did not hesitate. To secure his future, he would sell out the spy from Bosenheim.

The Germans had issued a standing warrant for Szabo's arrest. No fool, Zoltan refused to cross the frontier. If the BKA wished to speak with him, they would have to do so in Vienna. In June 1989, BKA agent Holger Klein, famous as the man who arrested Clyde Conrad, traveled to Vienna.

For three days, Klein debriefed the man who had recruited Clyde Conrad and who himself had spent seventeen years on Budapest's payroll. Szabo was forthcoming.

Szabo admitted that his first contact with the Hungarians had occurred in 1971 while he was serving as an officer in Germany. He had first spotted Clyde Conrad when the two men were stationed together in Bad Kreuznach and quickly assessed the bright NCO as one who was excessively motivated by money. In 1975, he offered Conrad the chance to join him in espionage. Clyde, he confirmed, had accepted and promised that he would provide Budapest "everything" from his office safes.

This Conrad did, delivering so many classified documents that anyone in the Budapest headquarters who touched the case benefited.

Szabo confirmed that Clyde, without informing his Budapest controllers, had recruited Rod Ramsay to be his collector once he no longer had direct access to classified materials. Ramsay had disappointed Clyde by being mustered out of the army for drug use.

This did not stop Conrad from creating opportunity out of the Ramsay matter, Szabo recalled. Clyde, who had never told Budapest about Ramsay, announced that he had recruited a replacement in his former workplace. "Mike," he lied, was a soldier in the 8th Infantry Division headquarters who was highly motivated to make extra cash. To impress Miklos, Clyde dipped into a cache of documents stolen by Ramsay before his separation and delivered them to Miklos. Conrad's plan was to collect and pocket a monthly salary for the nonexistent agent.

Conrad had a fertile, devious mind, Szabo quipped, but the Hungarians were not stupid. Clyde was directed to bring the new recruit to a meeting in Austria, where Miklos could meet and assess him.

Conrad stalled, telling Budapest unconvincingly that his new recruit could not obtain time off. Then he dipped again into his stash and delivered additional documents from "Mike" to Miklos. More suspicious than ever, Budapest demanded to meet the new agent.

Szabo smiled as he recalled Conrad's reaction. "He contacted Ramsay in Florida. The young man jumped on a plane and flew back to Bad Kreuznach in December, only a month after he had left the Army. Clyde brought him to Innsbruck and introduced him as 'Mike.'"

Rod Ramsay's quick trip from Florida fooled the Hungarians and saved Conrad, Szabo explained. During 1986, Clyde regularly dipped into the mother lode and passed classified documents to Budapest through Sandor Kercsik. Sandor, always game for one of Clyde's moneymaking schemes, reassured the Hungarians that he was obtaining the documents during periodic meetings with Mike. For almost a year, Budapest paid a salary to the nonexistent agent, as well as bonuses for production. All of the money wound up in Sandor's and Clyde's pockets.

Szabo discussed the Mike and the David scams in detail, labeling them reckless. Szabo admitted that he had informed Budapest of Conrad's freelancing, which was risky and had the potential to get everyone in trouble. Conrad had not appreciated this, Szabo told Klein.

Szabo confirmed Danny Wilson's report that he and Conrad had also spied for the Czechs. He himself had been at the heart of this venture. The operation was audacious: The pair simply made duplicates of some stolen secrets and marketed them to the Czechs as well as to Budapest. Szabo, using the cover name Alan, launched the Czech operation in March 1982 by delivering classified documents to the Czech embassy in Bonn, including the general defense plans of the 3d Armored Division and V Corps, and war plans for the intervention of the French on the side of NATO in the event of war. Prague, duly impressed, paid him $30,000. A deal was cut. In exchange for a monthly salary of 3,000 deutsche marks, plus a bonus for production, Alan would make regular deliveries of stolen secrets. For four years, the Czechs demanded and received war plans and information about the American military's procedures to authorize the use of tactical nuclear weapons in the event of war. By the time the double-dipping came to an end, Szabo and Conrad had pocketed a neat 200,000 deutsche marks in profit (about $130,000).

Szabo betrayed three American soldiers whom he had recruited during his seventeen-year career as an agent of Budapest. Investigators tracked down the three men, all of whom were no longer in the army and were living in Europe.

Szabo's first tip concerned Thomas Mortati, an Italian-born former American paratrooper. Szabo told the Austrians that he had brokered Mortati's recruitment in 1981. Mortati was in his early thirties at the time and had a wife and four children. He had left the U.S. Army after six years of active duty and was unemployed. Convinced that the Italian American veteran would agree to betray secrets, Szabo arranged for a chance encounter between Mortati and two Hungarian intelligence officers in Austria. The Hungarians recruited Mortati. The ex-soldier agreed to reaffiliate with the American military and provide documents from his new unit about U.S. and NATO forces in Italy. Zoltan Szabo received a bonus of 15,000 deutsche marks for the recruitment.

The Austrians shared Szabo's deposition with their Italian neighbors, who promptly arrested Mortati. Mortati confessed. He had spied for Budapest for $500 a month plus a bonus for each report he passed to Budapest. An Italian court found him guilty of espionage and sentenced him to twenty months in prison.

Szabo fingered two other retired U.S. Army noncommissioned officers, both of whom, like Conrad, were married to German women and upon retirement had elected to remain in Germany, outside the reach of U.S. law enforcement. In each case, the retirees had served with Szabo during his twenty-year career. Szabo told German officials that he had recruited the men in the late 1970s and early 1980s. On orders from Budapest, he related, one of the sergeants, a tanker, stole a round of high-explosive antitank (HEAT) ammunition that Soviet scientists could use to develop armor for Red Army tanks.

German investigators located the two men. One of them, retired master sergeant Eckart Steininger, was a Vietnam veteran who had served with Szabo during a tour with a U.S. Army engineer battalion in Germany. German investigators picked up Steininger and confronted him with Szabo's allegation that he had stolen tank ammunition. Steininger admitted to knowing Szabo and did not deny that the two had discussed business opportunities. No fool, he would not admit to espionage.

Szabo had told his Austrian interrogators that Steininger had hidden the stolen projectile under an anthill on the Grafenwoehr tank gunnery range, where Zoltan had personally retrieved it and smuggled it into Hungary. Eventually, Szabo told the Austrians, Steininger had met with the Hungarians in Vienna and Budapest, where the Hungarian service had provided him with expensive dental care and a bonus of 10,000 deutsche marks. It was not the kind of story that one would invent. Certain that the man was guilty but lacking sufficient evidence to prosecute, BKA officials released Steininger.

Rutkowski's investigators picked up the second suspect, retired sergeant first class Gunar Amolins. Szabo claimed that he had spotted Amolins in 1974, when the NCO was in financial difficulties due to a divorce. He offered Amolins a well-paying second job but warned that the new job would be illegal and require someone who was fearless and could keep his mouth shut. If Amolins were interested, he would have to travel to Vienna to meet his new business associates. Amolins agreed to Zoltan's conditions, met the Hungarians in Vienna, accepted recruitment, and was given the code name Gary.

Amolins admitted to the relationship with Zoltan Szabo, but because his last mission for Budapest had been in 1979, the statute of limitations had expired and he could not be prosecuted.

Confessions to Swedish authorities by Imre and Sandor Kercsik were particularly damaging to Conrad. Sandor Kercsik's depiction of Conrad's recruitment in a German *gasthaus* corroborated Zoltan Szabo's account. Both Kercsiks admitted that they had delivered secrets from Conrad to Budapest. Imre Kercsik admitted that he had twice peeked at the contents of Conrad's pay envelope. One payment had consisted of 50,000 deutsche marks; the other was 25,000.

The Kercsiks also confirmed Conrad's recruitment of Roderick Ramsay, regaled their interrogators with details of Conrad's ingenious Mike scam, and described the David swindle of the CIA that had netted more than $100,000. Imre Kercsik had written the David letter and made the phone calls. Imre also acknowledged that he had made three trips to Switzerland to meet the CIA's operatives.

The brothers described Clyde Conrad's severe reaction to his falling-out with Budapest over his obsessive wheeling and dealing. By 1986, out of favor with Budapest and fearful that he was under investigation, the usually upbeat Conrad had become deeply depressed, even suicidal. Certain that the next knock on the door would be the authorities, Conrad destroyed his stash of classified documents and disposed of his shortwave radio.

Particularly devastating to Clyde were the contents of the two thick ring binders seized by the Swedes in Sandor Kercsik's home. The binders were a damning archive of the conspiracy—hundreds of decrypted messages from Budapest instructing the Kercsiks on how to deal with Charlie.

In late 1975, Budapest radioed instructions to Sandor Kercsik to be passed to Conrad on the eve of his departure for espionage tradecraft training in Hungary. "We received your telegram. The session should result in you having the capability to photograph more than 100 pages. You should bring a light source. The timing of the meeting we have not yet established. Acknowledge receipt of this communication in the usual manner."

In April 1982, the Center radioed: "The next event is to be on 9 May. Mission: Procure a description of the weapons, communications, infrared equipment, maintenance, fuel consumption, nuclear protective capabilities of the M1 Abrams tank."

In the spring of 1983, Clyde faced a transfer to the United States to train new recruits. Budapest instructed Sandor to meet with "Charlie" to discuss ways to avoid the assignment. "He [Conrad] should demonstrate by repeated medical visits that he is only suitable for office work," the Hungarians proposed, "or possibly complain of unstable blood pressure or blood sugar problems." Kercsik disagreed.

These conditions would be impossible to fake convincingly. It would be better, the physician advised the Center, if Conrad feigned chronic back pain, a complaint that no doctor could challenge.

The Kercsiks also told their Swedish interrogators that Conrad once boasted that he had obtained better access to his unit's classified document control vault by seducing the female sergeant who was responsible for it.

In Washington, FCA agents were tasked to check out the Kercsik allegation. Foreign Counterintelligence Activity investigator Bob Gaiter teamed up with a female agent of the FBI to conduct the interview. The woman was located at her duty station in Washington, D.C.

The administrative specialist admitted that she had bent the rules by letting Conrad keep highly classified documents in his office overnight, although she had no idea he was copying them. Clyde was handsome, charming, and highly respected. As the noncommissioned officer in charge (NCOIC) of the G-3 Plans section, he had a valid need to know. Permitting him to keep documents in his office seemed to be a harmless winking at the rules.

Interviewers gently tabled the Kercsik allegation. Had she slept with Clyde Conrad? The woman nodded. Married at the time of her Bad Kreuznach service, she described how Conrad had persistently propositioned her and admitted sheepishly that she had finally succumbed to his advances. The two had gone to Clyde's small office in the G-3 Plans section for a "nooner."

"We did it," she confessed, "but it only happened once."

The Gator pressed. Was she certain it had happened only once? And if so, why only one time?

The woman eyed her interviewers. "You really want to know? It was because he was so bad, I mean, really bad." Apparently Clyde Conrad was no James Bond.

Later in the interview, the embarrassed sergeant emphatically denied that Conrad had attempted to recruit her or that she was aware that he was selling secrets to a foreign intelligence service. She passed a polygraph examination on the substance of her deposition.

Another significant breakthrough buttressed the German case against Conrad. At its center was FBI agent Joe Navarro, a talented

Cuban American with a degree from Brigham Young University. As German prosecutors labored over the case against Conrad, Navarro—known as a skilled interviewer—was working his magic with the man whom Conrad had handpicked to be his successor.

Former sergeant Rod Ramsay was a mercurial twenty-nine year old with a genius-level IQ. Raised in a suburb of Boston in a broken family, he had joined the army directly after high school. Assigned to the 8th Infantry Division, Ramsay served in the G-3 staff section, where he worked directly under Clyde Conrad. With his longish dark hair, granny glasses, and unconventional lifestyle, Ramsay was unpopular with the lifers in the headquarters. Real soldiers drank in the NCO club. Ramsay studied Japanese in his spare time, or did drugs.

But Rod was talented—so talented that Sergeant First Class Conrad permitted him to brief senior officers and protected him from details that did the dirty work on Rose Barracks. During his final year on active duty, Conrad arranged for Rod's appointment as the alternate top-secret-document control custodian. Under army regulations, the destruction of classified information had to be certified by the signatures of two persons. In Bad Kreuznach, the two authorized signatures were Roderick Ramsay and Clyde Conrad.

Navarro located the former sergeant working as a busboy in a Tampa restaurant. Certain that Ramsay had committed espionage, Navarro cultivated the ex-soldier, avoiding any confrontational moves that might drive him to seek an attorney. Ramsay seemed compelled to reminisce about his close relationship with Clyde Conrad. Navarro had seen subjects like this before—tortured people whose deeds eventually drove them to seek a sympathetic sounding board, someone in whom they could confide.

The smooth FBI man was only too willing to accommodate the confused ex-GI's need to talk. During a series of interviews conducted over many months, Navarro patiently assisted the former soldier in unburdening himself. Throughout these meetings, Ramsay played an ineffective game of cat and mouse as he attempted to avoid self-incriminating admissions that might land him in jail. In the process, the ex-sergeant who had once worshipped Clyde Conrad provided a wealth of information that was damaging to himself and the spy from Bosenheim.

Early in their relationship, Ramsay provided Navarro with a small piece of water-soluble paper on which a phone number for the Hungarian Military Intelligence Service was printed. Conrad had given him the paper, he admitted, just in case he needed to contact Budapest. Without specifically admitting guilt, Ramsay obliquely acknowledged that "hypothetically" Conrad might have recruited him in the fall of 1983 with promises of partnership in his enterprise. If the ex-soldier had prudently sought legal advice, which he had not, admissions such as this would have caused Ramsay's attorney to slash his wrists. Any law school student could have warned the naive former sergeant not to say anything to Joe Navarro.

Eventually, Ramsay discussed his theft in 1985 of the infamous "mother lode" from the 8th Infantry Division headquarters. In a Bad Kreuznach apartment rented by Conrad as a safe house, he had personally videotaped hundreds of pages of documents for passage to the Czechoslovakian intelligence service. For his efforts, he had received approximately $20,000 from Conrad before flunking the urinalysis test and leaving the army in November 1985.

Under German rules of evidence, virtually everything that the Kercsiks, Zoltan Szabo, and Rod Ramsay told their confessors was admissible in court. In the cases of Ramsay and Szabo, German prosecutors could simply subpoena agents Navarro and Klein and put them on the stand to describe what they had been told. As for the Kercsiks, because their confessions had been obtained in accordance with Swedish law, which was substantially in consonance with German law, everything the brothers had told their Swedish interrogators was admissable in the impending trial. It was a prosecutor's dream. Without setting foot on German soil, four of the accused spy's coconspirators could testify against him. As the full scope of the conspiracy took shape, Americans and Germans alike began to think the unthinkable: Clyde Conrad might yet be sentenced to life in prison.

Between Clyde Conrad's arrest in August 1988 and the beginning of his trial in January 1990, the world had changed dramatically. None of the changes was favorable to the defendant. While Clyde sulked in investigative custody, the Berlin Wall fell, East Germany be-

gan to implode, and 80 million Germans stood on the threshold of
the cherished goal of reunification. The communist government in
Budapest was history, the Soviet Union was on the verge of dissolution, and the feared Warsaw Pact was crumbling. The bipolar world
that the self-professed "independent information broker" had exploited for thirteen years had ceased to exist. The great ideological
showdown known as the Cold War was over. Clyde Conrad had cast
his lot with the loser.

The setting for Conrad's day in court was an imposing, fortresslike
stone edifice in Koblenz, Germany. The building, which housed the
Oberlandesgericht Koblenz (the Koblenz State Superior Court), was
situated close to the picturesque junction of the Rhine and Mosel
Rivers. Koblenz is known for its carefree people and the annual
spring ritual known as Fasching, a carnival-like celebration during
which the Rhinelanders don outlandish costumes and let their hair
down in mirthful celebrations.

There was nothing mirthful about Koblenz for Clyde Conrad. Efficient German prosecutors had the former agent squarely in their
sights. Prosecutors Friederich Hecking and Volkhard Wache had devoted almost a year and a half in the preparation of their case. The
state's challenge was so complex, Wache told FCA agent Mike
McAdoo, that the trial could take months. Testimony would be
heard by a panel of five experienced judges. In Germany, there could
be no question of a high-powered defense "dream team" duping a
gullible jury.

Conrad was accused of violating Article 99, Espionage, and Article 94, State Treason—"an especially grave case." The Article 94
charge, if substantiated, would permit the government to ask for an
unprecedented sentence of life in prison. History was being made.
No other foreigner had ever been tried in the German courts for
state treason. Federal prosecutor Rebmann described the impending proceedings as "the most serious treason case in the history of
the Federal Republic."

Mike McAdoo was the FCA director's full-time liaison officer to
the court. The son of a former U.S. Navy radar technician who had
fought in Korea, the twenty-nine-year-old native of Granite Station,
California, was perfectly fluent in German. McAdoo's job was to

make sure that our German allies lacked for nothing as the trail progressed, and to keep me informed daily on developments in the courtroom.

McAdoo reported that the once-handsome Conrad appeared in court on the first day looking frail and aged. A beefy 200 pounder when arrested, Budapest's legend now weighed less than 150 pounds, and his shock of white hair had thinned visibly. Spectacles added to the image of a harmless, wasted creature. German prosecutors told McAdoo that since Conrad's arrest, they had monitored his deteriorating physical condition with some alarm. For a time, the prisoner had embarked on a hunger strike and seemed to become depressed and suicidal. Not that the concern of German prosecutors was humanitarian. They were preparing the most spectacular espionage trial in German history, and Conrad was the featured attraction. In their view, his hunger strike and radical change of appearance was at least partly demonstrative, a feeble attempt to put on a facade of mistreatment. Although such courtroom theater might have played in Peoria, it would not work in Koblenz.

The complex trial dragged on for more than five months, during which the defendant clung to his insistence that he was not guilty. Herr Hummerich, Conrad's law professor attorney, filed one procedural motion after another in an attempt to derail the prosecution—without success. Some of Hummerich's convoluted motions flirted dangerously close to impugning the integrity of the panel of judges, an ill-advised tactic that could hardly engender sympathy for his client.

Prosecutors Hecking and Wache paraded before the judges witness after witness, all of whom testified precisely and credibly that Conrad had served the Hungarians from 1975 to 1988 and that he had violated the trust of his position as the top-secret-document custodian by forwarding to his communist superiors "everything that passed through his hands."

Danny Wilson and Gary Pepper testified at length about Conrad's recruitment of Wilson. Wilson's testimony was objective and precise. Prosecutors told Mike McAdoo that Gary Pepper was the most persuasive, professionally competent witness they had ever encountered in a court of law.

Sergeant Major Mike Barnes, whom Conrad had attempted to recruit for $50,000 in the spring of 1988, made a particular hit with
the court. The hard-charging former Green Beret took the stand clad
in his dress uniform with a Pattonesque chest full of ribbons. Those
who knew him held their breath. Would the volatile combat veteran
be able to maintain a poised, professional demeanor on the witness
stand?

At first, Barnes did well. Prosecutor Wache established the highly
decorated NCO's battlefield experience by asking him about some
of his ribbons. When he came to a red, black, and white ribbon,
Barnes explained that he had received it for "the occupation of
Berlin." Then, catching himself, the sergeant major turned to Judge
Schuth and quipped, "Sorry about that, Your Honor." Even the staid
panel of judges had difficulty controlling their mirth.

Wache asked the sergeant major if he had ever been in the Conrads' Bosenheim home. Barnes acknowledged that he had indeed
visited Clyde at home in 1988. Prosecutor Wache wanted to underscore Conrad's alleged lavish lifestyle. To make the point, he asked
Barnes to describe the furnishings and decor of the Elfelderstrasse
residence.

Barnes gazed momentarily at the courtroom ceiling. "Well, sir, I
guess the best way to describe it is that Clyde's home looked like King
Ludwig's bedroom."

When the laughter subsided, Wache led Barnes in a recitation of
Conrad's attempt to recruit him. The line of questioning triggered
something in the man who had risked his life so many times in Vietnam. Barnes's face twisted into anger as he exploded. Face-to-face
with the man who had tried to get him to betray his country, the decorated combat veteran pointed his finger at Conrad and shouted,
"What you done was wrong, Clyde, and you know it."

Conrad cringed. Judge Schuth and his colleagues recoiled. Mike
McAdoo blanched at Barnes's loss of control, but not federal prosecutors Hecking and Wache. The two attorneys basked in the spontaneous but not unwelcome breach of courtroom decorum, admitting later that it was one of the high points of the grueling trial.
("*Grossartig,*" exclaimed Wache later with a wide grin. Splendid.)

Joe Navarro took the stand. Conrad sat silently at the defense table,

eyes downcast, as the youthful and darkly handsome FBI agent testified to Rod Ramsay's role as an apprentice spy at Conrad's feet.

Federal Criminal Office (BKA) investigator Holgar Klein and a
Swedish investigator piled additional damaging facts onto the prosecution's impressive case as they introduced details of Conrad's espionage obtained from Zoltan Szabo and the Kercsik brothers. A
BKA analyst told the court that the defendant had earned approximately 2 million deutsche marks ($1.7 million) during his thirteen
years of betrayal.

But perhaps the high point of the proceeding was a bonus piece
of evidence, something that no one on the prosecution team could
have expected. In the wake of the fall of communism in Budapest,
Hungary's democratic government elected to apologize for Conrad's
espionage. Budapest dispatched a telegram to Bonn:

> It is the position of the Hungarian government that the case
> involving former U.S. Army Sergeant Clyde Lee Conrad, who
> presently stands trial in the Federal Republic of Germany, was
> part of the mistaken policy of the former political and military
> leadership that failed to properly reckon with the national in-
> terest of the country. The government [of Hungary] unequiv-
> ocally renounces the case, which started about 15 years ago.

The remarkable telegram was the last nail in Conrad's legal cof-
fin. After it was read in court, the depressed and demoralized spy
seemed to visibly retreat into himself. Unmasked by Danny Wilson,
sold out by mentor Zoltan Szabo, betrayed by the Kercsik brothers
and protégé Rod Ramsay, and abandoned by the Hungarians, the
once and future spy must have sensed what was coming as the day
of the verdict approached.

The man who was arguably the worst traitor in the more than two-
hundred-year history of the U.S. Army was sentenced on June 6,
1990. Presiding from the seat at the center of the elevated bench was
Chief Judge Ferdinand Schuth, a career jurist who had learned the
English language from friendly American soldiers in a U.S. Army
prisoner-of-war camp in the wake of World War II. Now, forty-five

years later, the judge was to pronounce sentence on a different type of American soldier.

A pair of bailiffs escorted Clyde Conrad into the courtroom. His handcuffs had been removed. Clad in a dark suit and betraying no emotion, Clyde took his place at the defense table with his attorney and gazed at the elevated bench before him. The five unsmiling German judges wore dark judicial robes. Judge Schuth shuffled a stack of papers and began to read the lengthy sentencing document to the crowded courtroom.

Conrad was "ice cold and unscrupulous," the judge asserted. His treason had endangered not only the security of the Federal Republic of Germany but "the entire defense capability of the West." All of this, Schuth added, was motivated by "pure greed." Ultimately, the judge concluded, because of Conrad's treason, if war had broken out between NATO and the Warsaw Pact, the West would have faced certain defeat. Specifically, Schuth proclaimed in a stern voice, "NATO would have quickly been forced to choose between capitulation or the use of nuclear weapons on German territory." Conrad's treason, the judge intoned gravely, had doomed the Federal Republic to become a nuclear battlefield. Norman Runk elbowed me and grinned. This was sounding better by the minute.

The judge continued:

> Based upon the duration of the state treason and espionage, the quality and quantity of the betrayed documents, the intensity and professionalism of the espionage, as well as the amount of money earned thereby, the espionage of the accused must be assessed as the most significant, and for the West the most crippling, since the Second World War. The accused stands at the top of the worldwide list of all known spies. His Hungarian case officers characterized him as "the best," and as "a legend." One of them even received a Russian medal and was promoted because of the significance of the accused as a source.

Judge Schuth sentenced Clyde Lee Conrad to life in prison for state treason on behalf of the Hungarians, and tacked on an additional four years for espionage on behalf of the Czechoslovakians. In addition, the judge fined Conrad the sum of 2.2 million deutsche marks ($1.7 million), the amount that methodical German investigators calculated he had earned from his treason since 1975. Last, the judge decreed that Conrad must pay the costs of his own prosecution. For almost two years, our German friends had conducted an exhaustive but unsuccessful search for Conrad's ill-gotten assets. The judge's stiff fine was an attempt to ensure that any money Conrad had managed to stash away could not be used by him or his family.

Judge Schuth adjourned the historic proceeding. Never before or since has a convicted spy received a sentence of life imprisonment from a German court. Clyde Conrad betrayed no reaction to the crushing sentence as he rose and meekly departed the courtroom. When the convicted spy exited the courthouse in handcuffs, Mike McAdoo captured the moment on film. The gratifying photo hangs to this day in a place of dishonor on the walls of the Foreign Counterintelligence Activity, a testament to the fate of FCA's once and future spy.

A spontaneous, festive German American victory party developed at a local *gasthaus*. Prosecutors Hecking and Wache, investigators from the BKA, and our FCA delegation repeatedly raised glasses in jubilant salutes to one another, to German American friendship, and "to Clyde, the man who made all this possible."

Norman Runk was in orbital joy. We had done it: the only life sentence in the history of the Federal Republic. The Germans heaped well-earned praise on Norman for his undying loyalty, assistance, and good humor for more than two years. Prosecutor Wache declared that Gary Pepper was the witness who contributed most to impressing the judges by his computer-precise, objective testimony. Foreign Counterintelligence Activity's Mike McAdoo had saved the day during the trial phase by his perfect record of response to every request from harried prosecutors. For our part, we toasted the judges, our BKA and BfV colleagues, and, above all, the thorough and devastating case mounted by the prosecution orchestrated by Friederich Hecking and Volkhard Wache.

# 40: Clean Sweep

In late 1989, FBI agent Joe Navarro and Greg Kehoe, an assistant U.S. attorney in Tampa, Florida, joined me and several of my agents in the FCA conference room for a strategy conference. Kehoe was emphatic. He was certain that Joe Navarro would prevail in his battle of wits with Rod Ramsay, but we could not settle for a confession by Ramsay as an end to the case.

"If all we do in Tampa is put Rod Ramsay into jail," the government attorney argued passionately, "we've failed in our job. The goal here is a clean sweep."

Kehoe's declaration of war launched FCA and FBI investigators on a protracted manhunt. Navarro was supremely self-confident. The bond he had forged with the mercurial Ramsay would unlock additional mysteries. We all nodded enthusiastically, never suspecting that Kehoe's objective would consume nine years.

Navarro had glued himself to Ramsay for months, knowing that as long as Conrad's former apprentice kept talking, the government was winning. If he had to work hard for every tidbit of information, so be it.

Under Navarro's gentle but unyielding pressure, Rod Ramsay admitted that to assist in accumulating the "mother lode" and spiriting it safely out of Rose Barracks, he had recruited two fellow soldiers—Jeff Gregory and Jeffrey Rondeau. Had Clyde known this, he would have been furious; Ramsay's role was that of a worker, not a controller. Only a controller could recruit, he told Navarro; that role Clyde reserved for himself.

The day after Conrad's conviction and sentencing, FBI agents in Tampa arrested Ramsay, whom we quickly dubbed "the spy who talked himself into jail." Ramsay's admissions to Joe Navarro could cost him the rest of his life behind bars.

As part of a plea bargain, the former sergeant agreed to cooperate with the government and reveal everything he knew about Conrad and provide evidence against Gregory and Rondeau. In return, he would receive a sentence of from one year to life in prison. The deliberately open-ended sentence was intended as an incentive. The more cooperative Ramsay made himself to the government, the better his chances of a light sentence.

Investigators closed in on Rod Ramsay's two accomplices. Because Gregory and Rondeau were soldiers on active duty, agents of the Foreign Counterintelligence Activity took the lead. Armed with Ramsay's admissions, FCA agent Bob Gaiter received the nod to make the case against the two suspects.

Even though soldiers accused of espionage would normally face trial by court-martial, Pentagon and Department of Justice attorneys agreed that if and when arrested, the two sergeants would stand trial in the same U.S. court that would handle the Ramsay case.

Working with FBI counterparts, Gator decided to begin with SSgt. Jeffrey Rondeau, twenty-nine, a native of Keene, New Hampshire. Rondeau had departed Germany in the mid-1980s and was serving as an army recruiter in Bangor, Maine. Next on the Gator's target list would be SSgt. Jeff Gregory, thirty-one, an airborne infantryman who had recently been transferred from Fort Benning in Georgia to a unit in Alaska.

Gator's job was daunting. The persistent Joe Navarro had managed to land Ramsay, but it had taken almost two years of a patient, father-confessor approach to wear down Conrad's star protégé and obtain a confession. Rod Ramsay's admission that Rondeau and Gregory had assisted him was insufficient to justify arrest and prosecution of the two sergeants. If they were to be indicted, Gator would have to somehow elicit damaging admissions from each man.

For three months in mid-1992, Gator and FBI colleague Jim Blackburn haunted SSgt. Jeffrey Rondeau. Seemingly oblivious to the danger that the price of talking could be a jail sentence, the married father strove to be cooperative, no doubt hoping against hope that his cooperation might somehow prove his innocence. Before every interview, the Gator read Rondeau his Miranda rights, yet the New Hampshire native did not choose to hide behind an attorney. Like many spies, the suspect tried to talk his way out of trouble.

The Gator engaged the sergeant is innocuous conversations about his family upbringing and army career. Best to circle the target and take the measure of the man first, thought the Gator. Like Rod Ramsay, Rondeau was a bright, bespectacled, almost scholarly fellow. Raised in a religious household, he impressed Gator as an essentially decent person who was deeply burdened by his mistakes.

Still, Rondeau knew what he had done, and he must have sensed that his army and FBI visitors knew as well. Gator stuck to his low-key approach, knowing that the one thing that could torpedo the investigation would be a decision by Rondeau to retain an attorney.

By June 1992, the determined FCA investigator had interviewed the soft-spoken staff sergeant three times. Each interview lasted three days. The unspoken message was, this will not go away. Better to unburden yourself now and get it over with.

Rondeau surrendered. The Gator recalls the moment:

> We'd reached a point of emotional climax. Rondeau was weary. Up to that point, I had never mentioned Rod Ramsay, but I did have an ace-in-the-hole. Ramsay had given us one half of a torn dollar bill—the other half of which he had given to Jeff Rondeau as a recognition signal. I put the torn bill on the table, fixed him with a stare, and asked gently, "Can you tell me what this is, where it came from, and why it's torn like this?"

Rondeau was shattered. For almost a five full minutes, he sat in numb silence, shifting his weight, grooming himself, looking at the floor, and averting eye contact with his interrogator. Then the deeply shaken noncom turned his back on his tormentors, stared at the far wall, and began to weep.

Turning slowly to face Gator, Rondeau sobbed, "Where did you get that?"

The Gator shook his head slowly, arched his eyebrows, and responded with a question of his own. "It doesn't matter, does it?"

Rondeau hung his head and began to talk about his relationship with Roderick Ramsay, unburdening himself cautiously. By October 1992, the New Hampshire native's confession was complete. Rod Ramsay had enticed him into what he called "the business." Rondeau had clearly understood that the enterprise was run by Clyde Conrad, who was marketing military secrets to the Hungarians. He had assisted Rod in copying classified documents and removing them from the division headquarters. For this contribution, Ramsay had paid him with cocaine, hashish, and other recreational drugs, as well as several hundred dollars to repair his car.

Within two weeks of these admissions, the devastated sergeant was arrested by the FBI. Another member of the ring had talked himself into jail.

Next on the Gator's list was the infantryman from Arizona SSgt. Jeff Gregory. Clyde Conrad's covey of enlisted protégés had consisted largely of high-IQ soldiers. Rod Ramsay and Jeffrey Rondeau fit this profile. Jeff Gregory was something quite different.

Bob Gaiter recalls the initial encounters with Gregory.

> Gary [Pepper] made the first contact with the guy at Ft. Benning. Later it fell to me to follow up on Rod Ramsay's admissions and roll him up as we had done with Rondeau. But unlike Ramsay or Rondeau, this guy was a criminal type with a criminal mind. A real dirtbag—crude, not too bright, and given to throwing a big word into the conversation to show how smart he was, except that he invariably used the wrong word. It would have been laughable, but for the fact that it was such serious business. We knew from Ramsay that Gregory had "done the deed," but this one was going to be tough going. He was a real thug.

The Gator pursued the belligerent infantryman in the spring of 1993 with his characteristic pit bull approach. Each time the two met, Gator "Mirandized" Gregory. Like Rondeau, Gregory did not request an attorney, apparently thinking that he was clever enough to verbally tap-dance his way out of trouble. The staff sergeant with the blond crew cut was defiant. Investigators reminded him of the many contradictions surrounding his conduct: Ramsay's allegations, the inconsistencies in his story, and his failure to pass a polygraph. Confronted with this litany, the stubborn infantryman would hang his head, wring his hands, and hunker down in his chair. Each time the Gator thought he was about to unburden himself, Gregory would raise his head and murmur, "I just don't remember doing what you say I did."

When Gregory transferred to an airborne outfit in Alaska's Fort Richardson, agents followed him to Anchorage. Hoping to identify an exploitable weakness, Gator and FBI agent Lisa Skinner obtained a psychological profile of Gregory from the FBI's famed Behavioral Science Unit at Quantico, Virginia. The profile was not encouraging. Bureau experts determined that the dull-witted, stubborn man showed signs of having been abused as a child. Like many who have endured deprived childhoods, Gregory may have developed the capability to lock away unpleasant experiences as if they had never happened. Subjects such as Gregory—wounded birds with few if any values—were invariably the most difficult for an interrogator to overcome.

Gator pushed the staff sergeant harder, employing the time-tested "the truth will set you free" approach. Federal Bureau of Investigation agent Skinner, a dark-tressed Alabama native with formidable acting talents, provided the counterpoint to the Gator's unrelenting pressure. Donning the mask of the kind, understanding female, the quick-witted FBI agent deftly nudged Gregory in the direction of the truth.

Gregory endured the assault in silence. Rod Ramsay was facing a possible life sentence. He had gotten Gregory into this mess, and now he was down there in Florida spilling his guts to feather his own nest. The staff sergeant listened sullenly, eyes downcast. Eventually, like many guilty suspects, he asked the question, "What's going to happen to me if I cooperate?"

The Gator was ready for this one. Giving Gregory his most sincere look, he answered in a soft voice. "We don't know. My job is to do the interview, write the report, and send it up to my superiors. What happens up there is not my job. But one thing I do know. This is your chance to state your side of what happened—to explain any mitigating circumstances. So if you're truthful, that can only help. But if you lie, that can only hurt. You got talked into this thing by Ramsay, who's put who-knows-what spin on the whole affair. This is your chance to give us your side of the story, without which we have no choice but to assume the worst and sign up to whatever it is that Rod related."

Gregory nodded. It must have seemed that the Gator was somehow on his side. The Gator pushed, ever so gently. Cooperation was the only smart course of action, he told Gregory. The more you retreat into denial, the worse you'll feel about yourself. Think of your family, consider the agony you are subjecting them to by dragging this out. Anyone can make a mistake and start over, but the process must begin with a clean sheet of music.

In April 1993, the dour Arizonan caved in and executed a sworn statement. He had been enticed by Ramsay to serve as a lookout during the theft of the infamous "mother lode" of documents from the division headquarters. Rod had promised great riches, but in the end, Jeff Gregory's espionage career had netted him small amounts of marijuana and hashish and a couple of hundred dollars at most.

The FBI arrested Gregory. At FCA's Fort Meade headquarters, Bob Gaiter's exploits were becoming legendary. Agents marveled at the parade of jailbirds in the Gator's wake. Didn't these people understand that all they had to do was hire an attorney and zip their lips?

On March 28, 1994, the two sergeants stood before U.S. District Judge Ralph W. Nimmons in Tampa, Florida, and pleaded guilty to multiple counts of espionage. Ultimately, each received a sentence of eighteen years in federal prison. Sixteen years had elapsed since the initial CIA tip-off about an espionage ring in Germany. Clyde Conrad had already been in prison for six years.

By the time Rondeau and Gregory were turned over to the Bureau of Prisons, FCA agent Gary Pepper had been working the Canasta Player investigation without respite for nine years. The unchallenged expert in the complex case, Pepper was certain that the Szabo-Conrad ring had not yet been completely unmasked. The veteran agent was joined in this conviction by his FBI partner of five years, Joe Navarro.

There were several additional suspects still at large, but the one who interested Navarro and Pepper was a former female soldier, Kelly Church Warren.

Private First Class Kelly Church had worked as a clerk in the division G-3 section from December 1986 until her separation from active duty in the spring of 1988. One of her duties was processing classified documents. This made her of interest to investigators, even though her service in Bad Kreuznach began after Clyde Conrad's

1985 retirement from active duty. Clyde, agents knew, had continued to haunt the headquarters after retirement. With access to classified documents, Church would have been a logical target for him.

But more than logic caused investigators to suspect Church. In mid-March 1988, FCA surveillance agents had observed Clyde Conrad meeting in a Bad Kreuznach bowling alley with a young soldier they identified as Amos Church, Kelly Church's husband. No great leap of faith was required to see the possibilities in this relationship. Had Conrad recruited Church and her husband to provide classified documents that he could no longer directly obtain in retirement? Agents thought it possible. The couple's names were added to the growing list of those who would be interviewed immediately after Conrad's arrest.

Soon after the German BKA arrested Conrad, investigators interviewed the couple. Both denied that they had any relationship with Clyde Conrad, contending that they barely knew who he was. Agents were certain that the Churches were lying, but absent any other evidence to the contrary, there was little use in pursuing the matter. Bigger fish—Ramsay, Szabo, and others—were awaiting their turn in the frying pan. The Kelly Church lead was shelved but not forgotten.

With the Gregory and Rondeau cases completed, Gary Pepper and Joe Navarro turned their attention back to Kelly Church. By the summer of 1994, she had divorced husband Amos and remarried. Now known as Kelly Warren, the twenty-eight year old had resettled in Warner Robins, Georgia, where she lived in a trailer on the property of an RV sales and parts business.

Pepper and Navarro had long since mastered a disarming technique of dialogue with people such as Warren. "No one will confess to someone they dislike or mistrust," Pepper was fond of saying. There was no magic formula for such interviews, but the FBI-FCA partners shared the conviction that it was important to be as cordial, nonthreatening, and up-front as possible from the outset.

Pepper and Navarro first visited Kelly Warren at her trailer in May 1994. Before the interview, both agents did their homework, paying particular attention to Warren's contention in 1988 that she barely knew the popular Conrad.

The subject was Clyde Conrad, Pepper and Navarro informed Warren cordially. "We need some help and think you might be able to assist."

Warren was friendly, animated, and cooperative. Having obviously forgotten what she had said six years earlier, her response was, "Oh, yeah, I remember Clyde."

The meeting inaugurated a two-year relationship with the former soldier. Because Warren was a civilian, the FBI's Joe Navarro took the lead role for the government. Each time Pepper and Navarro visited Warren, she provided additional glimpses into her relationship with Conrad, ultimately admitting that she had taken documents, which had been passed to Clyde. But the real spy, she insisted, was her former husband, Amos. Amos, she whined, had forced her to steal classified documents, which he would then screen to determine which would be of interest to the retired Conrad.

Confronted with these allegations, Amos Church insisted that his ex-wife was lying. The former soldier made a persuasive case for his innocence. He was illiterate, a fact to which many family members and friends could attest. How could he have read and understood the complicated war plans produced by the division G-3 section, as his ex-wife contended? Amos Church volunteered to take a polygraph examination, which he easily passed.

Joe Navarro challenged Kelly Warren, who shrugged and retracted the accusations against her ex-husband. Subsequently, during more than twenty interviews between mid-1994 and 1997, the former clerk-typist made a series of admissions that, taken together, were sufficient to obtain an indictment for espionage from the Tampa grand jury.

Warren admitted that Clyde Conrad had recruited her in 1987 to provide classified documents that he could no longer obtain from the division headquarters due to his retired status. She also acknowledged that the glib retired sergeant had told her that the reason he needed access to the documents was that he was selling them to a foreign government. She said that Conrad would sometimes visit her in her Rose Barracks office, during which she would permit him to read and copy classified documents, including the 8th Infantry Division's counterattack plan. On other occasions, she had ren-

dezvoused with Clyde at various locations on the base to pass classified information and receive payment for her efforts in cash and
gifts.

In November 1998, Kelly Warren pleaded guilty to providing classified defense information to Clyde Conrad. As part of her plea bargain, she can be sentenced to no longer than twenty-five years. Sentencing was scheduled by the court for February 1999. Based upon
the sentences meted out thus far, a term of twenty years would not
be surprising.

# Epilogue

## Canasta Player

The 1997 arrest of Kelly Church Warren did not mark the end of the Canasta Player investigation. The FBI and FCA investigators remain confident that other conspirators from Conrad's inner circle in Bad Kreuznach remain to be rolled up. At Fort Meade and at FBI headquarters, the case file remains open.

As of 1998, ten years after Conrad's arrest, eleven persons have been unmasked as a result of the CIA's 1978 tip-off. Nine of them were members of the U.S. Army. The other two were the naturalized Swedish citizens Imre and Sandor Kercsik.

The members of the Budapest network fathered by the bold and enterprising Zoltan Szabo got away with the theft of our most sensitive defense secrets in Europe for seventeen years.

By the time Clyde Conrad stared into the muzzle of Holger Klein's pistol and the door slammed shut on the Szabo espionage ring, the horses were in the barnyard. Because of Szabo and Conrad's treason, throughout the tense decades of the 1970s and 1980s the Soviets were reading our military playbook in Europe. As Gen. Glenn Otis stated in a deposition to the court in Tampa, the consequences of this, had a war broken out, would have been calamitous and measured in the blood of American soldiers and their allies.

Once the Canasta Player case landed on the desk of the FCA director, it developed into a textbook example of close cooperation between the military, the CIA, and the FBI. It also provided all concerned agencies with opportunities to work in a fraternal manner with the services of Italy, Austria, Sweden, and Germany. To this day, our colleagues from the German side of the Conrad investigation speak wistfully of that halcyon time when army counterintelligence and German agencies pulled off the espionage case of the century. Norman Runk, Gary Pepper, Dave Guethlein, and Mike McAdoo will always have friends in Germany.

In June 1989, CIA director William Webster presented the men and women of the Foreign Counterintelligence Activity the CIA's coveted Agency Seal Medallion. The citation on the award reads:

> To Colonel Stuart A. Herrington and the men and women of the Department of the Army's Foreign Counterintelligence Activity.
>
> In appreciation and admiration for the outstanding professionalism and extraordinary dedication displayed in your successful resolution of two complex counterintelligence cases of major significance to our national security.
>
> It was a privilege to be associated with you.
>
> From your colleagues in the Central Intelligence Agency.
>
> 1989

Standing at my side to receive the medal and represent the hundreds of army counterintelligence agents who were responsible for the Conrad and Hall cases were Norman Runk, Al Puromaki, Gary Pepper, Bob Watson, Bob Thayer, Bob Bell, Jim Whittle, and Lt. Col. Dave Owen. All of us have a copy of the historic photo taken that day as a reminder of what army counterintelligence agents accomplished when confronted with the most challenging cases of the Cold War.

German authorities sent Clyde Lee Conrad to Dietz Prison. On January 7, 1998, the fifty-year-old convicted spy died in his cell of a heart attack without ever having spoken of his espionage to investigators of any nationality. Because of a quirk in the law, to the day he breathed his last, Conrad continued to collect his U.S. Army pension. Had he been found guilty in an American court, the U.S. government could have cut off this entitlement.

Shortly after Conrad's June 1990 sentencing, our German partners reminded us that "In Germany, life in prison means life in prison." They were correct.

German investigators were never able to track down Conrad's ill-gotten gains. After the sentencing, Manfred Rutkowski's BKA investigators noted that Annja Conrad had resumed work as a cleaning lady, which they dismissed as a transparent attempt to mislead them. All who worked the investigation are convinced that, somehow, Annja Conrad has access to her husband's espionage nest egg.

Zoltan Szabo served a brief portion of his ten-month sentence and lives in Austria with Ilona. The founder of the most damaging ring of army spies in history is now sixty years old. The former Hungarian agent continues to collect his military retirement pay from the Department of Defense. Because of this anomaly, new legislation has since been passed by Congress. Future military spies convicted in a foreign court can now be deprived of their retirement pay, assuming that the justice system of the foreign country meets certain standards—a necessary proviso to protect American citizens from consequences at the hands of arbitrary overseas justice.

Szabo will not travel to Germany or the United States—a wise decision on his part. In 1994, agents noted that he was driving a taxi in Vienna. By 1995, the former spy was exploring a new enterprise, in which antiquities obtained in Hungary could be marketed for profit in Austria. Those who had been in contact with Szabo in 1997 reported that he was refurbishing a rundown house in Hungary, close to the Austrian border. Still unwelcome in the West, the international pariah would like to make a deal with the United States to alleviate his circumstances. To date, federal authorities have refused to entertain any concessions.

A Swedish judge suspended nine months of the eighteen-month sentences of the Kercsik brothers. The Hungarian-born physicians remain in their adopted country. During the investigation of Rod Ramsay, the brothers accepted an invitation by the Department of Justice to appear before the grand jury in Tampa. One of the lures to bring the pair to Florida was the promise of a trip to Disney World.

Thanks to his cooperation with Italian authorities, Thomas Mortati's twenty-month sentence was suspended. Mortati thus served only a brief time in investigative custody. He is a lucky man. Had he been court-martialed or tried in a U.S. court, he would have received a well-earned twenty-year sentence.

Rod Ramsay is serving his thirty-six-year sentence in a federal penitentiary near Tallahassee, Florida. He still sends Christmas cards to
FBI agent Joe Navarro, who put him there—a genuine tribute to
Navarro's professionalism. The court estimated that Ramsay would
likely serve twenty-four years of his sentence. If this occurs, he will
be released at age fifty-six.

Former sergeant Jeffrey Rondeau is serving the sixth year of his
eighteen-year sentence at a medium-security federal penitentiary in
Allenwood, Pennsylvania. In 1997, he was considered for parole but
not selected. His next scheduled parole hearing is in the year 2000.
Federal authorities in Tampa may well support parole at that time.
When Rondeau walks through the prison gates to freedom, he will
be thirty-six years old. His wife has remained faithful to him.

Former sergeant Jeff Gregory is serving his sentence at a federal
prison in Arizona. He is now thirty-six years old. His wife divorced
him.

Special agent Al Puromaki retired soon after Conrad's conviction.
For his brilliant investigative work, culminating in the identification
of Clyde Lee Conrad, special agent Puromaki was honored in 1989
as the Department of Defense Investigator of the Year.

Having achieved his goal of seeing Clyde Conrad behind bars, special agent Al Eways departed FCA for one final tour of duty in the
human intelligence field before retiring in the early 1990s after more
than forty years as an intelligence officer. Settled near Fort Meade,
he can be found puttering in the post craft shop. The veteran
agent's memory for the details of the complicated case remains astounding.

In tribute to his key role in the Gregory and Rondeau cases, special agent Bob Gaiter was honored as the Department of Defense's
Investigator of the Year in 1993.

The ebullient Norman Runk was rapidly promoted to senior rank
and continues to terrorize the intelligence services of our adversaries wherever he goes. Among our many German friends, Norman
is regarded the way Conrad was hailed in Budapest—"legendary."
Displayed in a frame on the wall of his office in the National Counterintelligence Center hangs the original napkin on which I scrib-

bled his Canasta Player marching orders in a German beer cellar ten years ago.

Special agent Gary Pepper, who left the 766th MI Detachment as a buck sergeant in 1985 to work on Canasta Player, is now in his fourteenth year on the investigation. Among our German comrades, Gary Pepper continues to be remembered with near reverence for his poised and damaging testimony in the landmark trial of Clyde Conrad. His marathon service on the Canasta Player investigation made counterespionage history. Someday he will be nominated for the Military Intelligence Hall of Fame.

Federal Bureau of Investigation agent Joe Navarro, whose energy and cunning were vital to the roll-up of Conrad's network, continues his successful career. In 1998, Navarro received orders to report to the U.S. embassy in Brasilia, Brazil, for duty as the legal attaché.

In the wake of the Conrad and Hall cases, special agent Dave Guethlein was assigned as the army representative in the CIA's Counterintelligence Center, where for six years he was heavily involved in the exploitation of information obtained in the wake of the collapse of East Germany's communist government. Guethlein completed his twenty-year military career in 1992, earned a master's degree in administration, and resumed his career as a spy catcher in the Foreign Counterintelligence Activity.

Special agent Joe Herda, who lived for almost eighteen months in a Wiesbaden hotel room and worked closely with the charismatic Sgt. Maj. Mike Barnes, continues to serve as an army special agent. With three years remaining in his army career, the thirty-five-year-old Herda will retire as a master sergeant and return to his native Alaska.

Special agent Mike McAdoo spent seven more years in Europe, primarily as a special investigator juggling a crushing load of cases in the wake of the collapse of East Germany. For most of 1997, McAdoo served in Bosnia as the task force's counterterrorism adviser. In 1996, for actions unrelated to the Conrad case, he was honored as the Department of Defense's Case Officer of the Year.

The resourceful and courageous Danny Wilson, who initially would not believe that his role model Clyde Conrad could betray the United States, was awarded the Legion of Merit for his key role in the investigation and was promoted to sergeant major, the highest noncommissioned officer rank in the army. Wilson retired from the army and devoted two years to studying for the ministry. He and his wife, Shirley, are retired in Arizona.

Sergeant Major Mike Barnes, whose trial testimony remains the single most dramatic moment of Clyde Conrad's six-month trial, retired and settled in Fishbach, Germany. He now runs a professional football team, manned by a mixture of American and German players. Foxy, politically incorrect cheerleaders grace the sidelines.

Gus Hathaway, whose strong will and leadership made the identification and arrest of Clyde Conrad possible, retired from the CIA shortly after Conrad's demise and lives quietly in his native Virginia, eschewing interviews with the parade of authors who would like to quote him concerning the rash of damaging espionage cases that have been revealed since the end of the Cold War. He remains one of the CIA's most respected Cold Warriors.

Lieutenant General William E. Odom, without whom there would have been no Canasta Player investigation, retired from active duty in 1988 and continued his distinguished career as a national security strategist. As director of national security studies of the Hudson Institute in Washington, D.C., General Odom was the coauthor of a 1997 study that recommended a long-overdue modernization of the intelligence community. Like Gus Hathaway, if he were to attend an FCA reunion, his drinks would be on the house.

Kriminaldirektor Manfred Rutkowski has been twice decorated by the U.S. Army for his contributions as the leader of the elite ST-13 section of the Bundeskriminalamt. Rutkowski has since been promoted and currently serves as a deputy in the BKA, with responsibility for combating all forms of left extremism in reunited Germany.

German investigator Holger Klein, who arrested Clyde Lee Conrad and interrogated Zoltan Szabo in Vienna, was decorated by the U.S. Army for his distinguished service during the Canasta Player investigation. Today, Hauptkommissar Klein works with Manfred Rutkowski in investigating left extremism in Germany.

Dr. Peter Frisch, whose decision to bring the BfV in on the side of the Americans in Canasta Player marked a major turning point in the intractable case, is now the president of the Federal Office for the Protection of the Constitution. Dirk Doerrenberg and Werner Goll continue to play major roles in the hard-pressed organization. Doerrenberg has been elevated to the position of Abteilungsleiter of the BfV's Department IV, Counterintelligence and Security, where he and Herr Goll work together as in the past.

Prosecutor Volkhard Wache continues his brilliant career in the Generalbundesanwalt, which was overloaded with espionage cases in the wake of German reunification. His colleague, Friederich Hecking, has moved on to a well-earned retirement.

The FBI opened an investigation to identify the source of the leak to the *New York Times*. Like most leak investigations, it went nowhere. Journalist Gerth, in the tradition of his trade, will not betray his source. In the unique world occupied by our media colleagues, trusted government civil servants who betray sensitive information are First Amendment heroes. It is a concept that eludes me, but then I still believe that children should be born in wedlock and raised in a two-parent home.

In Moscow, several years before the collapse of the Soviet Union, all three CIA sources who provided the clues that led to Clyde Conrad's arrest were identified and executed. One of them was GRU officer Vladimir Vasilev. Vasilev, who had grown to hate what Soviet communism was doing to his country, had been a CIA mole for years. It was he who provided a significant number of the critical clues that ultimately enabled FCA to identify Clyde Conrad. The heroic GRU officer was one of a score of agency penetrators betrayed by KGB mole Aldrich Ames, the disaffected CIA officer who volunteered his services to the Soviets in 1985. In accordance with the KGB's custom, Vasilev was led into a cellar room of a special prison and ordered to kneel. A KGB executioner, wearing gloves and a rubber apron to protect his clothing, shot Vasilev in the back of the head with a Makarov automatic. His body was buried in an unmarked grave. To his former KGB colleagues, he is a traitor. To others in Russia and the West, Vladimir Vasilev is a fallen hero of the Cold War who fought against the well-documented evils of Soviet communism.

The United States Army Foreign Counterintelligence Activity received the Department of the Army's Superior Unit Award for its handling of the investigation, the same honor bestowed on the 766th Military Intelligence Detachment for Operation Lake Terrace.

Most press accounts of the Canasta Player investigation gave well-earned credit to the Germans or the FBI. Nowhere did the Foreign Counterintelligence Activity's name appear. A single journalistic account of the case correctly identified the investigation as an army counterintelligence success—an *Army Times* interview with Lt. Gen. (ret.) William E. Odom, who had directed Bob Lunt in 1985 to tackle the case. The investigation, Odom revealed, was a joint endeavor among the army, the CIA, and the FBI, but was actually "95% Army."

Foreign Counterintelligence Activity's professionals were grateful for Odom's loyalty and proud that their elite unit had stayed the course and shut down Zoltan Szabo's organization. Yet all knew that the history-making case would not have happened without the original tip from the CIA. As for the gratifying outcome, it could not have occurred without assistance from the CIA, the FBI, and, above all, the superlative clutch performance of our German allies.

## The Hall Investigation

James Hall remained locked up at Fort Meade for months while he was debriefed by FCA and NSA investigators. At times, James seemed genuinely remorseful for what he had done; at other times, his actions conveyed the sense that his major regret was his own stupidity and the fact that he had been caught.

Hall, now forty-one years old, is still incarcerated in Leavenworth, Kansas. He and Heidi are divorced. Heidi has remarried and settled in the United States. Daughters Jessica and Amanda are sixteen and nine years old, respectively.

Captain Bob Watson received the Legion of Merit for his brilliant performance in Savannah. Watson continued to serve with FCA for several years, during which he received a coveted "below the zone" promotion to major. Major Watson did his time in the Pentagon trenches as a counterintelligence staff officer, then moved overseas to carry out his trade.

Bob Thayer was promoted to GS-15 and served four years as the deputy commander of FCA before moving to Heidelberg, Germany, to become the senior civilian counterintelligence officer in Europe. He and his wife, Jodene, of Operation Lake Terrace fame, own a home in Sebring, Florida, where they may one day settle down in time for their daughter Elanna to attend the university.

Foreign Counterintelligence Activity deputy director Bob Bell retired in 1994 and resettled to his beloved central Pennsylvania. Tragically, Bob passed away shortly thereafter, a victim of lung cancer. A Cold War soldier who excelled in every challenge, Bob at least had the satisfaction of witnessing the collapse of communism in Europe—a victory for the United States and her allies that his forty years of service helped to secure. Robert L. Bell rests in the Fort Indiantown Gap National Cemetery, mourned by his family and the legion of army intelligence professionals whose lives he touched during his long career.

For his contributions to the arrest of James Hall, above all for hatching the concept of the memorable sting in the Savannah Days Inn, CWO Jim Whittle was decorated with the Legion of Merit. Jim continues to serve in FCA, where he is entrusted with one of the unit's most sacred missions: graduate-level training of handpicked counterintelligence agents.

Special agent Roger Clifford, who handled Canna Clay in West Berlin, is retired in Sierra Vista, Arizona. His comrades who have visited him report that he divides his time between his Corvette and his pickup truck. Clifford's partner Pete Kelly, after an extended tour teaching advanced counterintelligence skills at the FCA school, is once again deployed overseas, embroiled in the Silent Wars of the post–Cold War era.

Sergeant Major Nick Pokrovsky joined me in the quest for information about American prisoners of war who were captured or kidnapped by the Soviet Intelligence Services during the long Cold War and taken to the former Soviet Union. Pokrovsky retired from active duty in 1998 after a twenty-two-year career. Upon retirement, the talented Cold Warrior decided to leave the intelligence field and devote his talents to the development of a positive relationship between the United States and Russia.

After the James Hall court-martial, Maj. Gen. Pete Taylor, commanding general, 24th Infantry Division, sent the following letter to Maj. Gen. Stan Hyman, commanding general of the army's Intelligence and Security Command. Its text is a fitting postscript to this account of the role played by the Foreign Counterintelligence Activity during the Silent War.

VICTORY DIVISION
April 14, 1989

Dear Stan,

I'd like to take this opportunity to express my thanks for the superb work done by members of the Foreign Counterintelligence Activity (FCA) during the Warrant Officer Hall investigation. Throughout this long and complex operation the professionalism, dedication, and competence of the men and women of FCA were clearly evident. I particularly appreciated being brought into the case from the outset. This ensured that I was able to provide the necessary guidance and allowed me to effectively handle post-arrest publicity.

The briefings provided by Colonel Herrington, Mr. Bob Thayer, and Captain Bob Watson were invariably outstanding. The numerous individuals who provided the surveillance and technical coverage performed with the same exceptional level of dedication and commitment. To have such a sizeable element involved over an extended period of time without a single problem is truly remarkable.

Lastly, I would like to point out that the leadership of FCA showed significant concern and understanding with regard to Mrs. Hall and her two children. In an investigation like this, such compassion is the mark of true professionals.

Again, my thanks to the professionals of the Foreign Counterintelligence Activity and my congratulations on a highly successful and significant operation.
Sincerely,
H. G. Taylor Major General
U.S. Army Commanding

As he signed the letter, General Taylor penned this postscript: "A tremendous job by as professional a group of soldiers as I have had the pleasure to know. You should be proud of them."

• • •

Coming from an infantry division commander, no words can convey higher praise. The original of General Taylor's generous letter hangs on the Wall of Fame at the Foreign Counterintelligence Activity. Directly across from it, in a place of dishonor on the Wall of Shame, is a picture of James Hall in handcuffs. Hall's image is flanked by those of Clyde Lee Conrad, Zoltan Szabo, Roderick Ramsay, and others who were convicted of being traitors among us during the Cold War.

In November 1998, Kelly Warren pleaded guilty to providing classified defense information to Clyde Lee Conrad. Three months later, in February 1999, Warren was sentenced to twenty-five years in a federal penitentiary. At the time of the sentencing, prosecutors reminded the judge that Warren had passed war plans for the use of nuclear weapons in such a contingency. Reviewing these documents, former U.S. Army Europe Commander-in-Chief Glen T. Otis responded with a written statement to the Court. "The compromise of this classified material was devastating to our national security," Otis said. Armed with this information, the four-star added, "the enemy probably could have defeated a conventional counterattack."